Why Do You Need This New Edition?

If you're wondering why you should buy this new edition of *Active Reading Skills: Reading and Critical Thinking in College*, here are 6 good reasons!

1. **Learn to think critically as you read with new *Thinking Critically About . . .* sections.** Each chapter in Part I includes a new *Thinking Critically About . . .* section linking the reading skills covered in the chapter with related critical reading and thinking skills.
2. **Challenge yourself to adapt your reading skills to different contexts with our new *Textbook Challenge* and *Critical Thinking Challenge* sections.** Chapters 1–8 contain *Textbook Challenge* sections that use textbook excerpts from a wide range of disciplines to guide you through the process of applying textbook reading skills. In Chapters 9–12, *Critical Thinking Challenges* focus on the application of critical thinking skills to selections from newspapers, magazines, and blogs.
3. **Prepare for exams with the new Student Resource Guide: Test Taking, Exit Exams, and Competency Tests.** Many colleges require students to pass an exam at the end of their reading course to move forward; the Resource Guide provides test-taking strategies and sample practice test sections for this type of test.
4. **Identify what you need to learn with new Learning Goals at the beginning of each chapter.** Listed at the beginning of each chapter, the learning goals correspond to the major headings in the chapter to help you recognize the topics and skills you need to master. At the end of each chapter, **new Self-Test Summaries** provide you with an opportunity to test your mastery of these learning goals.
5. **Explore lively, up-to-date, and thought-provoking topics in our many new readings.** In addition to new longer readings in most Mastery Test 3s, over 25% of the brief reading selections and accompanying pedagogy throughout the text have been revised.
6. **Get extra practice when you need it with MyReadingLab.** New icons in the margins provide easy-to-follow click paths to areas in MyReadingLab that relate to the content being discussed.

PEARSON

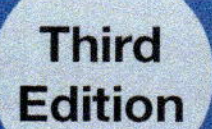

Active Reading Skills

Reading and Critical Thinking in College

Kathleen T. McWhorter

Niagara County Community College

Brette McWhorter Sember

Longman

Boston Columbus Indianapolis New York San Francisco Upper Saddle River Amsterdam
Cape Town Dubai London Madrid Milan Munich Paris Montreal Toronto Delhi
Mexico City São Paulo Sydney Hong Kong Seoul Singapore Taipei Tokyo

Editor-in-Chief: Eric Stano
Development Editor: Erin Reilly
Senior Supplements Editor: Donna Campion
Senior Media Producer: Stefanie Liebman
Marketing Manager: Thomas DeMarco
Production Manager: Ellen MacElree
Project Coordination, Text Design, and Electronic Page Makeup:
PreMediaGlobal
Cover Design Manager: John Callahan
Cover Designer: Kay Petronio
Cover Image: Commercial Eye/© Getty Images
Photo Researcher: Jody Potter
Senior Manufacturing Buyer: Dennis J. Para
Printer and Binder: RR Donnelley/Crawfordsville
Cover Printer: RR Donnelley/Crawfordsville

For permission to use copyrighted material, grateful acknowledgment is made to the copyright holders on pp. 517–521, which are hereby made part of this copyright page.

Copyright © 2012, 2008, 2005 by Pearson Education, Inc.

All rights reserved. No part of this publication may be reproduced, stored in a retrieval system, or transmitted, in any form or by any means, electronic, mechanical, photocopying, recording, or otherwise, without the prior written permission of the publisher. Printed in the United States. To obtain permission to use material from this work, please submit a written request to Pearson Education, Inc., Permissions Department, 1900 E. Lake Ave., Glenview, IL 60025 or fax to (847) 486-3938 or e-mail *glenview.permissions@pearsoned.com*. For information regarding permissions, call (847) 486-2635.

12 16

Longman
is an imprint of

www.pearsonhighered.com

Student Edition ISBN-13: 978-0-205-02843-6
Student Edition ISBN-10: 0-205-02843-8

Annotated Instructor's Edition ISBN-13: 978-0-205-02845-0
Annotated Instructor's Edition ISBN-10: 0-205-02845-4

BRIEF CONTENTS

Copyright © 2012 by Pearson Education

DETAILED CONTENTS

Copyright © 2012 by Pearson Education

Copyright © 2012 by Pearson Education

Copyright © 2012 by Pearson Education

PREFACE

The Second in a Two-Book Series

Active Reading Skills: Reading and Critical Thinking in College is the second in a two-book series that emphasizes skill development, concise instruction, extensive guided practice, and college reading.

Essential Reading Skills: Preparing for College Reading is the first book in the series. It is ideal for use in a basic reading course to introduce students to textbook learning aids and the foundations of college reading. It is well suited for instructors whose students come from a variety of educational backgrounds, as well as instructors whose students demonstrate widely different levels of preparedness for college reading.

Active Reading Skills: Reading and Critical Thinking in College is the second book in the series. Designed for the second reading course, it offers skills review with an emphasis on critical reading and thinking. It is ideal for instructors who want to teach critical thinking skills early and throughout the course. It also offers a review of active reading, vocabulary development, literal comprehension, and organizing information.

Changes to the Third Edition

The third edition of *Active Reading Skills* brings a new critical thinking emphasis to the text. The book builds college textbook reading skills in Part One, but also considers critical reading skills appropriate to chapter topics. Part Two offers an in-depth focus on critical thinking skills. The new critical thinking emphasis includes the following features.

- **Revised Chapter 1: Reading College Textbooks: An Active Approach.** Chapter 1 now includes an introduction to critical reading that sets the scene for its expanded coverage throughout the book. Coverage of SQ3R, textbook learning aids, and recall and retention strategies has also been added.
- **New "Thinking Critically About . . ." Sections.** Each chapter in Part One includes a new section linking the chapter reading skills with related critical reading and thinking skills. For example, in the Vocabulary chapter, "Thinking Critically about Vocabulary" discusses denotative and connotative meanings.

Copyright © 2012 by Pearson Education

- **New Textbook Challenge Sections in Part One.** Chapters 1–8 contain a two-part feature designed to guide students in applying chapter content to textbooks. Using longer textbook excerpts representative of a wide range of disciplines, this section guides students in integrating and applying textbook reading skills. Each Textbook Challenge opens with a box offering tips for reading in the specific academic discipline. In Part A students preview the excerpt, apply SQ3R, examine both general and specialized vocabulary, evaluate textbook learning features, write an essay exam answer, and answer critical thinking questions. Students also apply chapter-specific content. For example, in Chapter 3, on main ideas, students practice highlighting topic sentences. In Part B, students are directed to apply chapter skills to their own college textbooks.
- **New Critical Thinking Challenge in Part Two.** Similar to the Textbook Challenge in Part One, this feature also includes longer reading selections; it focuses on the application of critical thinking skills. Each Critical Thinking Challenge opens with a box that describes how to approach the types of readings it contains. The types represented are newspapers, magazines, blogs, and editorials. Students first read, highlight, annotate, and summarize the reading and then answer critical thinking questions focusing on the critical thinking skills taught in Chapters 1–8, as well as those in the current chapter. Students link their reading and writing skills by responding to the reading in paragraph form.
- **New Student Resource Guide: Test Taking, Exit Exams, and Competency Tests.** This new section on test taking, exit exams, and competency tests includes test taking strategies and sample practice test sections.
- **New Learning Goals.** These objectives listed at the beginning of each chapter appear as a numbered list (Goal 1, Goal 2, . . .) and correspond to the major headings in the chapter. At the end of each chapter, **new Self-Test Summaries** provide students with an opportunity to test themselves for mastery of these learning goals.
- **New Readings.** In addition to new longer readings in most Mastery Test 3s, over 25 percent of the brief reading selections and accompanying pedagogy throughout the text have been revised, giving students new reading material that is lively, up-to-date, and thought-provoking.
- **New Connections to MyReadingLab.** New icons in the margins point out easy-to-follow click paths to areas in MyReadingLab that relate to the content being discussed.

Chapter Format

Each chapter follows a regular format and sequence, giving students the benefit of a predictable, consistent structure.

Thinking About

Each chapter opener consists of an eye-catching visual (a photograph, cartoon, or drawing) and thought-provoking text to elicit student response. This section immediately engages the students, sparks their interest, demonstrates the relevance of chapter content, and motivates them to progress through the chapter.

Concise Skill Instruction

Chapter skills are presented briefly and concisely, using frequent examples. This section tells students what they need to know in the simplest terms possible.

Practice Exercises

Interspersed within the concise skill instruction section are numerous exercises that provide students with ample opportunity to develop and apply skills. The exercises usually involve small steps, leading students through skills gradually and sequentially.

Challenge Sections

Chapters 1–8 contain a Textbook Challenge feature that uses longer textbook excerpts from a wide range of disciplines to guide students in integrating and applying textbook reading skills. In Chapters 9–12, Critical Thinking Challenges focus on the application of critical thinking skills to longer selections from newspapers, magazines, and blogs.

Self-Test Summary

Each chapter includes a Self-Test Summary that provides a review of chapter content organized by learning goals. Presented in a two-column question/answer format, this summary enables students to test themselves and check their responses at a glance.

Practice Tests

Two review tests at the end of every chapter encourage students to synthesize the skills they have learned. Often, these tests are based on slightly longer material.

Mastery Tests

Three mastery tests conclude each chapter. They may be used by students as additional practice or by the instructor as evaluative instruments. The first two tests require students to apply and integrate chapter-specific reading skills to paragraphs and short passages. The third mastery test, based on a full-length reading selection, includes general comprehension questions as well as questions on the specific skills taught within the chapter.

Copyright © 2012 by Pearson Education

Special Features

The following features enhance the text's effectiveness and directly contribute to student success:

- **Emphasis on essential reading comprehension skills.** A chapter on main ideas, a chapter on supporting details, a chapter on implied main ideas, and two chapters on patterns of organization offer the student reader the basic building blocks for reading success.
- **Emphasis on critical reading skills.** Students need extensive instruction and practice to develop critical reading skills. Three chapters are devoted to critical reading skills and another to reading and evaluating arguments. Topics include inference, author's purpose, fact and opinion, tone, and bias.
- **Full chapter on argument.** Unlike many other texts, this book offers complete coverage of reading arguments. It includes recognizing the parts of an argument, evaluating arguments, and recognizing errors in logical reasoning.
- **Visual elements.** Increasingly, college students have become visual learners as visual literacy has become critical to success in today's world. This four-color book uses visual material to teach key concepts. Photographs, diagrams, and charts are used to clarify relationships, depict sequences, and demonstrate paragraph organization.
- **Extensive practice.** Numerous exercises enable students to successfully apply their learning. The chapter tests provide students with observable, measurable evidence that they are learning and improving their skills. Students may use these exercises as practice tests—as the "test before the test."
- **Full-length reading selections.** Students are given ample opportunity to apply their skills to full-length reading selections. Each chapter concludes with a full-length reading as part of Mastery Test 3. Topics include choosing a major, male friendship, global warming, and terrorism.
- **Writing component after each Mastery Test 3.** Following the objective apparatus in each Mastery Test 3, Writing Activities allow students to address issues suggested in the reading and develop their expressive skills.

Text-Specific Supplements

Annotated Instructor's Edition

This is an exact replica of the student text, with answers provided on the write-on lines in the text. (ISBN 0-205-028454)

Instructor's Manual and Test Bank

This manual includes an answer key and describes in detail the basic features of the text. This manual also offers suggestions for structuring the course, teaching non-traditional students, and approaching each chapter of the text. (ISBN 0-205-028446)

Vocabulary Supplement

Instructors may choose to shrink-wrap *Active Reading Skills* with a copy of *Vocabulary Simplified*. Written by Kathleen T. McWhorter, this book works well as a supplemental text, providing additional instruction and practice in vocabulary. Students can work through the text independently, or units may be incorporated into weekly lesson plans. Topics covered include methods of vocabulary learning, contextual aids, word parts, connotative meanings, idioms, euphemisms, and many more interesting and fun topics. The book concludes with vocabulary lists and exercises representative of 11 academic disciplines. To preview this book, contact your Pearson representative for an exam copy.

The Pearson Longman Developmental Reading Package

Pearson Longman is pleased to offer a variety of support materials to help make teaching developmental reading easier for teachers and to help students excel in their course work. Visit www.pearsonhighered.com or contact your local Pearson sales representative for a detailed listing of our supplements package or for more information on pricing and how to create a package.

Acknowledgements

I wish to express my gratitude to reviewers of this text for their excellent ideas, suggestions, and advice on the preparation and revision of this text:

Karin Alderfer, Miami Dade College; Brenda Essig, Reading Area Community College; Danette Walls Foster, Central Carolina Community College; Richard Gair, Valencia Community College; Sarah Garman, Miami Dade College; Rebecca Ingraham, St. Charles Community College; Sheila P. Kerr, Florida Community College at Jacksonville; Amber Kinonen, Bay de Noc Community College; Kristin Lewis, Fresno City College; Deborah Maness, Wake Technical College; Jane Nickerson, Gallaudet University; Adalia Reyna, South Texas College; Jennifer Roos, North Dakota State College of Science; Dr. Lijun Shen, Highline Community College; Sharette Simpkins, Florida Community College at Jacksonville; Marisol Varela, Miami Dade College; Robert Vettese, Southern

Copyright © 2012 by Pearson Education

Maine Community College; and Carol Wray, Northeast Alabama Community College.

I am particularly indebted to Erin Reilly, development editor, for overseeing this project and attending to the many details to ready the book for production and to Eric Stano, editor-in-chief, for his support and assistance in planning the revision of this book.

Finally, I would like to introduce my co-author who has been working on my books throughout much of her life. At age 12, long before computers, she helped me number manuscript pages. While in high school, being a top-notch student newspaper editor, she proofread my final drafts. As a college student and English major, she was an excellent source of topics for new readings and a serious critic, as well. While in law school, she began drafting apparatus to accompany new readings. As author of more than 15 law-related books, she has significant writing experience as well as expertise in all the technical details of publishing, including design, page layout, and indexing. Please welcome my daughter—Brette McWhorter Sember. You may visit her Web site at http://BretteSember.com.

Kathleen T. McWhorter

PART

I

College Reading Skills

Copyright © 2012 by Pearson Education

THINKING ABOUT

Active Reading

This photograph shows fans attending a sporting event. Can you sense their excitement and team spirit? The fans demonstrate *active* involvement with the team and the game. The fans in the photograph are responding and reacting to a play on the field. Fans often direct plays, criticize calls, encourage the players, and reprimand the coaches. They become part of the game, and the team is their team.

In a similar way, *active* readers get involved with the material they read. They think, question, challenge, and criticize the author's ideas. They try to make the material *their* material. This chapter will give you some strategies for becoming an active, successful reader.

CHAPTER 1

Reading College Textbooks: An Active Approach

Keys to Academic Success

GOAL 1
Discover the keys to academic success

What does it take to do well in psychology? In history? In your writing class? In business? Many students will answer by saying such things as

- "Hard work!"
- "Knowledge about the subject."
- "A good instructor!"
- "You have to like the course."

Students seldom mention reading as a key to academic success. When you think of college, you think of attending classes and labs, completing assignments, studying for and taking exams, and writing papers. A closer look at these activities, however, reveals that reading is an important part of each one. Reading is not an obvious key to success because it is not evaluated directly. Grades are based on how well you express your ideas in papers and how well you do on exams. Yet reading is the primary means by which you acquire your ideas and gather information. Here are a few tips to get you started using reading to build academic success.

LEARNING GOALS

GOAL 1
Discover the keys to academic success

GOAL 2
Read and learn actively

GOAL 3
Preview before you read

GOAL 4
Use guide questions

GOAL 5
Develop skills to learn from textbooks

GOAL 6
Focus on critical thinking

- **Approach an assignment positively and confidently.** Send yourself positive messages. Tell yourself that the assignment is manageable and that you can

Copyright © 2012 by Pearson Education

learn from it. Avoid negative thoughts such as, "This looks boring" or "I don't know if I'll ever get through this." A negative mind-set almost guarantees poor comprehension and concentration. To overcome this, find some way to become interested in the subject. Question or challenge the authors as you read, or try to develop questions about the material.

- **Plan on spending time.** Assignments are not something you can rush through. The time you invest will pay off later in reduced study time and higher grades.
- **Define the task.** Before you begin, decide what you need to learn, how much detail is needed, and what is the best way to approach the task. For example, will you highlight as you read, take notes, outline, or write a summary (These techniques are discussed in Chapter 6.)
- **Set goals for yourself.** Don't just start an assignment and plan to work on it as long as you can. Instead, decide how much is reasonable to cover in one session and set a time by which you expect to finish.
- **Search for ideas.** Think of reading as a way of sifting and sorting out what you need to learn from less important information.
- **Stick with an assignment.** If an assignment is troublesome, experiment with different methods of completing it. Try reading difficult sections aloud, for example, or express what you are reading in your own words.

myreadinglab

To practice controlling external distractions, go to

> Study Plan
> Reading Skills
> Memorization and Concentration

Control External Distractions

A phone ringing, a dog barking, friends arguing, or parents reminding you about errands can break your concentration and cost you valuable time. Each time you are interrupted, you have to find where you left off and refocus your attention.

Although you cannot eliminate all distractions, you can control many of them by choosing wisely when and where you study. For a week or so, analyze the times and places you study. Try to notice situations in which you accomplished a great deal as well as those in which you accomplished very little. At the end of the week, look for a pattern. Where and when did you find it was easy to concentrate? Where and when was it most difficult? Use the information from your analysis along with the following suggestions to choose a regular time and place for study.

- **Choose a place to study that is relatively free of interruptions and distractions.** Consider studying at the campus or neighborhood library. Do not study where you are too comfortable.
- **Choose a time of day when you are mentally alert.** Establish a fixed time for reading or studying. Studying at the same time and place each day will help you get into the habit of studying more easily. For example, if you establish, as part of a schedule, that you will study in the library right after dinner, soon it will become almost automatic.

Increase Your Attention Span

Most people can keep their minds focused on one task for only a limited period of time. This period of time represents their *attention span*. You can increase your attention span by using the following techniques:

- **Read with a purpose.** If you are looking for specific information as you read, it will be easier to keep your attention focused on the material.
- **Keep a distractions list.** As you are reading, often you will think of something you should remember to do. Keep a piece of paper nearby, and whenever something distracts you or you are reminded of something, jot it down on the paper.
- **Vary your reading.** Work on several assignments in an evening rather than finishing one assignment completely. The variety in subject matter will provide a needed change and maintain your interest.
- **Combine physical and mental activities.** Activities such as highlighting, underlining, making marginal notes, or writing summary outlines provide an outlet for physical energy and supply useful study aids (see Chapter 6).
- **Take frequent breaks.** They will refresh your mind.
- **Establish goals and time limits for each assignment.** Deadlines will keep you motivated and create a sense of urgency that will make you less likely to daydream or become distracted.

EXERCISE 1-1 Building Academic Success

Directions: *Rate each of the following items as either helpful (H) or not helpful (NH) in building academic success. Then discuss how each of the statements marked NH could be changed to be more helpful.*

_______ 1. Checking with a classmate when you find an assignment difficult or confusing

_______ 2. Studying late at night after going out with friends

_______ 3. Blaming your instructor when you get a low grade on an exam

_______ 4. Thinking you've never been very good with numbers, and expecting not to do well in a math course

_______ 5. Deciding what kinds of information you need to learn before beginning to study for a biology test

Copyright © 2012 by Pearson Education

Read and Learn Actively

GOAL 2

Read and learn actively

myreadinglab

To practice reading and learning actively, go to

> Study Plan
> Reading Skills
> Active Reading Strategies

Have you ever gone to a ball game and watched the fans? Most do not sit and watch passively. Instead, they direct the plays, criticize the calls, encourage the players, and reprimand the coach. They care enough to become actively engaged with the game. Just like interested fans, active readers get involved. They question, challenge, and criticize, as well as understand. Table 1-1 contrasts the active strategies of successful readers with the passive ones of less successful readers.

Throughout the remainder of this chapter, you will discover specific strategies for becoming a more active learner. Not all strategies will work for everyone. Experiment to discover those that work for you.

TABLE 1-1 Active versus Passive Reading

Active Readers . . .	Passive Readers . . .
Tailor their reading to suit each assignment.	Read all assignments the same way.
Analyze the purpose of an assignment.	Read an assignment *because* it was assignment.
Adjust their speed to suit their purpose.	Read everything at the same speed.
Question ideas in the assignment.	Accept whatever is in print as true.
Compare and connect textbook material with lecture content.	Study lecture notes and textbook separately.
Skim headings to find out what an assignment is about before beginning to read.	Check the length of an assignment and then begin reading.
Make sure they understand what they are reading as they go along.	Read until the assignment is completed.
Read with pencil in hand, highlighting, jotting down notes, and marking key vocabulary.	Simply read.
Develop personalized strategies that are particularly effective.	Follow routine, standard methods.

EXERCISE 1-2 Becoming an Active Reader

Directions: *Choose one of the courses that you are taking this semester. List at least four strategies you will use to become a more active reader.*

Course: ______________________________

Strategies:

1. ______________________________
2. ______________________________
3. ______________________________
4. ______________________________

Preview Before Reading

Preview before you read

You probably would not jump into a pool without checking its depth. You would not buy clothes without trying them on. You would not purchase a CD if you knew nothing about the artist.

Similarly, you should not begin reading a textbook chapter without knowing what it is about and how it is organized. **Previewing** is a way of quickly familiarizing yourself with the organization and content of a chapter or article *before* beginning to read it. Once you try previewing, you will discover that it makes a dramatic difference in how effectively you read and how much you can remember.

How to Preview

Think of previewing as getting a sneak peek at what a chapter will be about.

Previewing Textbook Chapters

1. **Read the title and subtitle.** The title provides the overall topic of the chapter. The subtitle suggests the specific focus, aspect, or approach toward the overall topic.
2. **Read the introduction or the first paragraph.** The introduction or first paragraph serves as a lead-in to the chapter, establishing the overall subject and suggesting how it will be developed.
3. **Read each boldfaced (dark print) heading.** Headings label the contents of each section, announcing the major topic of the section.
4. **Read the first sentence under each heading.** The first sentence often states the central thought of the section. If the first sentence seems introductory, read the last sentence; often this sentence states or restates the central thought.
5. **Note any typographical aids.** Italics emphasize important terminology and definitions by using slanted *(italic)* type to distinguish them from the rest of the passage. Notice any material that is numbered 1, 2, 3; lettered a, b, c; or presented in list form.
6. **Note any graphic aids.** Graphs, charts, photographs, and tables often suggest what is important in the chapter. Be sure to read the captions for photographs and the legends on graphs, charts, or tables.
7. **Read the last paragraph or summary.** This provides a condensed view of the chapter, often outlining the chapter's key points.
8. **Read quickly any end-of-chapter material.** This might include references, study questions, discussion questions, chapter outlines, or vocabulary lists. If there are study questions, read them through quickly since they will indicate what is important to remember in the chapter. If a vocabulary list is included, skim through it to identify terms that you will need to learn as you read.

Copyright © 2012 by Pearson Education

Demonstration of Previewing

The following selection is a section from a business textbook. The parts of the text that should be read during previewing are highlighted.

ALTERNATIVE SCHEDULING ARRANGEMENTS

An increasing number of employees are finding that managing the demands of work and personal life results in doing neither well. The added stresses that face employees today from child care, elder care, commuting, and other work/life conflicts have led to a decrease in productivity and an increase in employee absenteeism and tardiness. As a result, more and more employers are offering alternatives to the traditional 9 AM to 5 PM, Monday to Friday workweek. In fact, according to the U.S. Bureau of Labor and Statistics, over one-quarter of U.S. employees take advantage of some from of flexible work arrangement. The most popular flexible work arrangements include the following:

Alternative Scheduling Plans (Flextime)

In *alternative scheduling plans* or **flextime**, management defines a total number of required hours as a core workday and is flexible with starting and ending times. Managers must rise to the challenge of ensuring that required hours are met and monitoring employee performance. However, overall, flexible arrangements allow for increased productivity due to reductions in absenteeism and tardiness.

Permanent Part-Time

Permanent part-time employees are hired on a permanent basis to work a part-time week. Unlike temporary part-time workers who are employed to fill short-term needs, permanent part-time employees enjoy the same benefits that full-time employees receive.

Job Sharing

Job sharing is an arrangement in which two employees work part-time sharing one full-time job. Those who share a job have been found to be very motivated to make this flexible situation work, so productivity and employee satisfaction increase. On the other hand, conflicts may arise if the job sharers don't have a clear understanding of who is in charge of what or if there is confusion from other employees about whom to contact and when. Therefore, job sharers must carefully coordinate and communicate both with one another and their employer to ensure that all responsibilities are met.

Compressed Workweek

A **compressed workweek** allows employees to work four 10-hour days instead of five 8-hour days or nine days (not ten) in a two-week schedule for 80 hours. Such arrangements can reduce worker overtime, make more efficient use of facilities, and provide employees with longer blocks of personal time and less commuting time. The disadvantages are a potential increase in employee fatigue and conflicts with state labor laws that cite over time requirements for hours worked in excess of eight a day.

Telecommuting

Telecommuting allows employees to work in the office part-time and work from home part-time, or to work completely from home, making only occasional visits to the office. Telecommuting reduces commuting costs and allows employees to take care of home needs while also fulfilling work responsibilities. Telecommuting arrangements are also necessary for those employees dealing with clients, colleagues, or suppliers who are on the other side of the globe. Taking calls at 2 AM is much easier at home than at the office. The disadvantages of telecommuting include monitoring employees' performance at a distance, servicing equipment for off-site employees, and communication issues. Additionally, employees who telecommute may become isolated from other employees.

Despite the costs associated with designing and implementing flexible working arrangements, employers can expect positive bottom-line results due to increases in employee satisfaction, decreases in absenteeism, and increases in worker productivity. Similarly, reductions in employee turnover lead to a decrease in time and costs associated with employee recruiting and replacement training.

—Solomon et al., *Better Business*, pp. 264–265

EXERCISE 1-3 Evaluating Your Previewing

Directions: *Indicate whether each of the following statements is true (T) or false (F) based on what you learned by previewing the selection above.*

_______ 1. A decrease in worker productivity is tied to work/life conflicts.

_______ 2. Most U.S. employees take advantage of some sort of flexible work arrangement.

_______ 3. Flextime means that workers can choose how many hours they want to work.

_______ 4. Compressed workweeks allow employees to fit a full workweek into fewer days.

_______ 5. Alternative scheduling has not been shown to improve employee absenteeism.

This exercise tested your recall of some of the important ideas in the article. Check your answers by referring back to the article. Did you get most or all of

Copyright © 2012 by Pearson Education

the items correct? This exercise demonstrates, then, that previewing helps you learn the key ideas in a selection before actually reading it.

Making Predictions

While previewing a reading assignment, you can make predictions about its content and organization. Specifically, you can anticipate what topics will be covered and how they will be presented. Ask the following questions to sharpen your previewing skills and strengthen your recall of what you read:

- How difficult is the material?
- How is it organized?
- What is the overall subject and how is it approached?
- What type of material is it (for example, practical, theoretical, historical background, or a case study)?
- Where are the logical breaking points where you might divide the assignment into portions, perhaps reserving a portion for a later study session?
- At what points should you stop and review?
- Why was this material assigned?

EXERCISE 1-4 Practicing Previewing

Directions: *Preview Chapter 6 in this book. After you have previewed it, complete the items below.*

1. What is the subject of Chapter 6?

   ____

2. List the five major topics Chapter 6 covers.

   a. ______________________________

   b. ______________________________

   c. ______________________________

   d. ______________________________

   e. ______________________________

EXERCISE 1-5 Practicing Previewing

Directions: *Preview a chapter from one of your other textbooks. After you have previewed it, without referring to the chapter write a list of topics it covers.*

Use Guide Questions

Use guide questions

Did you ever read an entire page or more and not remember anything you read? Have you found yourself going from paragraph to paragraph without really thinking about what the writer is saying? Guide questions can help you overcome these problems. **Guide questions** are questions you expect to be able to answer while or after you read. Most students form them mentally, but you can jot them in the margin if you prefer.

The following tips can help you form questions to guide your reading. It is best to develop guide questions *after* you preview but *before* you read.

- **Turn each major heading into a series of questions.** The questions should ask something that you feel is important to know.
- **As you read a section, look for the answers to your questions.** Highlight the answers as you find them.
- **When you finish reading a section, stop and check to see whether you can recall the answers.** Place check marks by those you cannot recall. Then reread.
- **Avoid asking questions that have one-word answers, like *yes* or *no*.** Questions that begin with *what*, *why*, or *how* are more useful.

Here are a few textbook headings and some examples of questions you might ask:

Heading	Questions
Reducing Prejudice	How can prejudice be reduced? What type of prejudice is discussed?
The Deepening Recession	What is a recession? Why is it deepening?
Newton's First Law of Motion	Who was Newton? What is his First Law of Motion?

EXERCISE 1-6 Writing Guide Questions

Directions: *Write at least one guide question for each of the following headings.*

Heading	Questions
1. World War II and Black Protest	1. ______________________________
2. Foreign Policy Under Obama	2. ______________________________
3. The Increase of Single-Parent Families	3. ______________________________
4. Changes in Optical Telescopes	4. ______________________________
5. Causes of Violent Behavior	5. ______________________________

Copyright © 2012 by Pearson Education

EXERCISE 1-7 Writing Guide Questions

Directions: *Preview Chapter 6 of this book. Then write a question for each major heading.*

1. ______
2. ______
3. ______
4. ______
5. ______

EXERCISE 1-8 Writing Guide Questions

Directions: *For the chapter you choose for Exercise 1-5, write a list of guide questions.*

______

______

______

______

Learn from Textbooks

GOAL 5

Develop skills to learn from textbooks

myreadinglab

To practice learning, from textbooks, go to

> Study Plan
> Reading Skills
> Reading Textbooks

Each semester you will spend many hours reading, reviewing, and studying textbooks. This section presents many useful strategies for reading and learning from textbooks.

Textbook Learning Aids

Most textbooks are written by college professors who are experienced teachers. They know their subject matter and they also know their students. They know what topics you may have difficulty with and know the best way to explain them. Because textbooks are written by teachers, they contain numerous features to help you learn. Table 1-2 summarizes these features and explains how to use each.

TABLE 1-2 Textbook Aids to Learning

Feature	How to Use It
Preface or "To the Student"	■ Read it to find out how the book is organized, what topics it covers, and what learning features it contains.
Chapter Opener (may include chapter objectives, photographs, and chapter outlines)	■ Read it to find out what the chapter is about. ■ Use it to test yourself later to see if you can recall the main points.
Marginal Vocabulary Definitions	■ Learn the definition of each term. ■ Create a vocabulary log (in a notebook or computer file) and enter words you need to learn.
Photographs and Graphics	■ Determine their purpose: what important information do they illustrate? ■ For diagrams, charts, and tables, note the process or trend they illustrate. Make marginal notes. ■ Practice redrawing diagrams without referring to the originals.
Test Yourself Questions (after sections within the chapter)	■ Always check to see if you can answer them before going on to the next section. ■ Use them to check your recall of chapter content when studying for an exam.
Special Interest Inserts (can include profiles of people, coverage of related issues, critical thinking topics, etc.)	■ Discover how the inserts are related to the chapter content: what key concepts do they illustrate?
Review Questions/ Problems/Discussion Questions	■ Read them once *before* you read the chapter to discover what you are expected to learn. ■ Use them after you have read the chapter to test your recall.
Chapter Summary	■ Test yourself by converting summary statements into questions using the words *Who? Why? When? How?* and *So What?*
Chapter Review Quiz	■ Use this to prepare for an exam. Pay extra attention to items you get wrong.

EXERCISE 1-9 Evaluating Textbook Learning Aids

Directions: *Using this textbook or a textbook from one of your other courses, use Table 1-2 to analyze the features the author includes to guide your learning. Identify particularly useful features and decide how you will use each when you study.*

The SQ3R Reading/Study Method

SQ3R is an established method of actively learning while you read. Instead of reading now and studying later when an exam is scheduled, the SQ3R method enables you to integrate reading and learning by using the five steps listed

Copyright © 2012 by Pearson Education

below. By using SQ3R, you will strengthen your comprehension, remember more of what you read, and need less time to prepare for an exam. Don't get discouraged if you don't see dramatic results the first time you use it. It may take a few practice sessions to get used to the system.

Feel free to adapt the SQ3R method to suit how you learn and the type of material you are studying. For example, if writing helps you recall information, you might add an *Outline* step and make the *Review* step a *Review of Outline* step. Or if you are studying a course in which terminology is especially important, such as biology, then add a *Vocabulary Check* step.

Steps in the SQ3R System

Survey Become familiar with the overall content and organization of the material using the steps for previewing in the box on page 7.

Question Ask questions about the material that you expect to be able to answer as you read. As you read each successive heading, turn it into a question.

Read As you read each section, actively search for the answers to your guide questions. When you find the answers, underline or mark the portions of the text that concisely state the information.

Recite Probably the most important part of the system, "recite" means that after each section or after each major heading you should stop, look away from the page, and try to remember the answer to your question. If you are unable to remember, look back at the page and reread the material. Then test yourself again by looking away from the page and "reciting" the answer to your question.

Review Immediately after you have finished reading, go back through the material again, reading headings and summaries. As you read each heading, recall your question and test yourself to see whether you can still remember the answer. If you cannot, reread that section. Once you are satisfied that you have understood and recalled key information, move toward the higher-level thinking skills. Ask application, analysis, evaluation, and creation questions. Some students like to add a fourth "R" step—for "React."

EXERCISE 1-10 Using SQ3R

Directions: Apply the SQ3R system to a section of a chapter in one of your textbooks. List your questions in the margin or on a separate sheet of paper, and highlight the answers in your textbook. After you have finished the section, evaluate how well SQ3R worked.

myreadinglab

To practice learning and recall strategies, go to
- > Study Plan
- > Reading Skills
- > Memorization and Concentration

Learning and Recall Strategies

Some students think that as long as they spend time studying they will get good grades. However, spending time is not enough. You have to plan when to study and use the right techniques to get the most out of the time you spend. Use the following strategies.

Immediate Review Forgetting occurs most rapidly right after learning. **Immediate review** means reviewing new information as soon as possible after you hear or read it. Think of immediate review as a way of fixing in your mind what you have just learned. Here are some ways to use immediate review:

- **Review your lecture notes as soon as possible after taking them.** This review will help the ideas stick in your mind.
- **Review a textbook chapter as soon as you finish reading it.** Do this by rereading each chapter heading and then rereading the summary.
- **Review all new course materials again at the end of each day of classes.** This review will help you pull together information and make it more meaningful.

Periodic Review To keep from forgetting what you have learned, you will need to review it several times throughout the semester. **Periodic review,** then, means returning to and quickly reviewing previously learned material on a regular basis. Suppose you learned the material in the first three chapters of your criminology text during the first two weeks of the course. Unless you review that material regularly, you are likely to forget it and have to relearn it by the time your final exam is given. Therefore, you should establish a periodic review schedule in which you quickly review these chapters every three weeks or so.

Final Review **Final review** means making a last check of material before a test or exam. This should not be a lengthy session; instead, it should be a quick once-over of everything you have learned. A final review is helpful because it fixes in your mind what you have learned. Be sure to schedule your final review as close as possible to the exam in which you will need to recall the material.

Building an Intent to Remember Very few people remember things that they do not intend to remember. Before you begin to read an assignment, define as

Copyright © 2012 by Pearson Education

clearly as possible what you need to remember. Your decision will depend on the type of material, why you are reading it, and how familiar you are with the topic. For instance, if you are reading an essay assigned in preparation for a class discussion, plan to remember not only key ideas but also points of controversy, applications, and opinions with which you disagree. Your intent might be quite different in reviewing a chapter for an essay exam. Here you would be looking for important ideas, trends, and significance of events.

As you read a text assignment, sort important information from that which is less important. Ask and continually answer questions such as:

1. **How important is this information?**
2. **Will I need to know this for the exam?**
3. **Is this a key idea or is it an explanation of a key idea?**
4. **Why did the writer include this?**

Organizing and Categorizing Information that is organized, or that has a pattern or structure, is easier to remember than material that is randomly arranged. One effective way to organize information is to *categorize* it, to arrange it in groups according to similar characteristics. Suppose, for example, that you had to remember the following list of items to buy for a picnic: cooler, candy, 7-Up, Pepsi, napkins, potato chips, lemonade, peanuts, paper plates. The easiest way to remember this list would be to divide it in groups. You might arrange it as follows:

Drinks	Snacks	Picnic Supplies
7-Up	peanuts	cooler
Pepsi	candy	paper plates
lemonade	potato chips	napkins

By grouping the items into categories, you are putting similar items together. Then, rather than learning one long list of unorganized items, you are learning three shorter, organized lists.

Now imagine you are reading an essay on discipline in public high schools. Instead of learning one long list of reasons for disruptive student behavior, you might divide the reasons into groups such as peer conflicts, teacher-student conflicts, and so forth.

Associating Ideas Association involves connecting new information with previously acquired knowledge. For instance, if you are reading about divorce in a sociology class and are trying to remember a list of common causes, you might try to associate each cause with a person you know who exhibits that problem. Suppose one cause of divorce is lack of communication between the partners.

You might remember this by thinking of a couple you know whose lack of communication has caused relationship difficulties.

Using a Variety of Sensory Modes Your senses of sight, hearing, and touch can all help you remember what you read. Most of the time, most of us use just one sense—sight—as we read. However, if you are able to use more than one sense, you will find that recall is easier. Activities such as highlighting, note-taking, and outlining involve your sense of touch and reinforce your learning. Or, if you are having particular difficulty remembering something, try to use your auditory sense as well. You might try repeating the information out loud or listening to someone else repeat it.

Visualizing Visualizing, or creating a mental picture of what you have read, often aids recall. In reading about events, people, processes, or procedures, visualization is relatively simple. However, visualization of abstract ideas, theories, philosophies, and concepts may not be possible. Instead, you may be able to create a visual picture of the relationship of ideas in your mind or on paper. For example, suppose you are reading about the invasion of privacy and learn that there are arguments for and against the storage of personal data about each citizen in large computer banks. You might create a visual image of two lists of information—advantages and disadvantages.

Using *Mnemonic* Devices Memory tricks and devices, often called mnemonics, are useful in helping you recall lists of factual information. You might use a rhyme, such as the one used for remembering the number of days in each month: "Thirty days hath September, April, June, and November. . . ." Another device involves making up a word or phrase in which each letter represents an item you are trying to remember. If you remember the name Roy G. Biv, for example, you will be able to recall the colors in the light spectrum: **r**ed, **o**range, **y**ellow, **g**reen, **b**lue, **i**ndigo, **v**iolet.

EXERCISE 1-11 Using Recall Strategies

Directions: *Five study-learning situations follow. Indicate which of the strategies described in this section—organization/categorization, association, sensory modes, visualization, and mnemonic devices—might be most useful in each situation.*

1. In a sociology course, you are assigned to read about and remember the causes of child abuse. How might you remember them easily?

____

Copyright © 2012 by Pearson Education

2. You are studying astronomy and you have to remember the names of the eight planets: Mercury, Venus, Earth, Mars, Jupiter, Saturn, Uranus, and Neptune. What retention aid(s) could help you remember them?

____

3. You are taking a course in anatomy and physiology and must learn the name and location of each bone in the human skull. How could you learn them easily?

____

4. You have an entire chapter to review for a history course, and your instructor has told you that your exam will include 30 true/false questions on Civil War battles. What could you do as you review to help yourself remember the details of various battles?

____

5. You are taking a course in twentieth-century history and are studying the causes of the Vietnam War in preparation for an essay exam. You find that there are many causes, some immediate, others long-term. Some have to do with international politics; others, with internal problems in North and South Vietnam. How could you organize your study for this exam?

____

Thinking Critically: An Introduction

Focus on critical thinking

The biggest difference between high school and college is the difference in your instructors' expectations of how you should *think*. High school classes focus on developing a basic foundation of knowledge, often built through memorization. In college, however, you are expected not only to learn and memorize new information, but also to *analyze* what you are learning. In other words, your college instructors expect you to be a **critical thinker**.

"Critical" does not mean "negative." Critical thinking means evaluating and reacting to what you read, rather than accepting everything as "the truth." Thinking critically sometimes requires you to consult multiple sources of information to develop perspective on the topic. For example, when writing an essay on how post-traumatic stress disorder affects returning veterans, you might read several accounts written by vets and consult several research studies, gleaning ideas from each.

The Benefits of Critical Thinking

The ability to think critically offers many benefits. In your college courses, critical thinking allows you to

- Do well on essay exams, particularly those that ask for analysis.
- Write effective essays and term papers.
- Distinguish good information from incomplete, inaccurate, or misleading information.

In everyday life and in the workplace, a good set of critical thinking skills will help you

- Make informed, reasonable decisions.
- Spend money wisely and make good financial choices.
- Understand issues in the news, including business and political issues.
- Expand your interests beyond "passive entertainment" (such as watching TV or movies) to active entertainment that engages your mind and creativity.

Critical Thinking Is Active Thinking

Critical reading and thinking are essential parts of reading. For example,

- When reading a college textbook, you might ask yourself if the author is trying to influence your opinions.
- When reading a newspaper, you might ask yourself if the article is telling the full story or if the journalist is leaving something out.
- When reading an advertisement, you might ask yourself what message the ad is sending to get you to buy the product.

To help you strengthen your critical reading skills, Chapters 1–8 of this textbook feature a section devoted to critical thinking skills. Chapters 9–12 are devoted entirely to critical thinking.

EXERCISE 1-12 Understanding Critical Thinking

Directions: *Indicate whether each of the following statements is true (T) or false (F) based on your understanding of critical thinking.*

_______ 1. Thinking critically about a reading selection means finding ways to criticize it and show all the ways it is wrong.

_______ 2. Critical reading is not necessary unless the instructor specifically assigns some sort of "critical thinking" exercise to go along with the reading.

Copyright © 2012 by Pearson Education

_______ 3. While textbooks offer good opportunities for critical reading, so do other reading materials, such as magazines and Web sites.

_______ 4. Critical thinking skills are important in college but do not have much relevance in the "real world."

_______ 5. Engaging in critical thinking sometimes requires you to consult additional sources of information beyond what you are currently reading.

EXERCISE 1-13 Thinking Critically

***Directions:** Read the paragraph and answer the questions that follow.*

In survey after survey, 60 to 80 percent of food shoppers say they read food labels before selecting products; they consume more vegetables, fruits, and lower-fat foods; and they are cutting down on portion sizes and total calories. Diet-book sales are at an all-time high as millions of people make the leap toward what they think is healthy eating. But we still have a long way to go. In fact, although reports indicate that increasing numbers of us read labels and are trying to eat more healthfully, nearly 78% of all adults indicate that they are not eating the recommended servings of fruits and vegetables and that they are still eating too many refined carbohydrates and high-fat foods.

—Donatelle, *Health: The Basics*, p. 255

(Hint: Think analytically and critically to answer the following questions.)

1. The passage talks about *surveys*, which is another word for *questionnaires*. Why might the survey results not truly reflect reality?

____

____

____

2. Does the fact that diet-book sales are at an all-time high mean that more people are going on diets and/or eating more healthfully? Why or why not?

____

____

____

3. Based on this passage, what do you think the author sees as the most important parts of a healthy diet?

____

____

4. What phrase does the author use to imply that people may have good intentions but don't necessarily understand how to eat more healthfully?

____

____

TEXTBOOK CHALLENGE

TIPS for Reading in Communication/Speech

When reading communication/speech textbooks, pay attention to

- **Terminology.** Often authors will introduce you to new words and phrases used within this discipline that have to do with important concepts.
- **Principles.** Communication and speech textbooks often include rules that explain how human communication works.
- **Processes.** Speech and communication are complicated processes, and courses frequently address the parts of those processes.

Copyright © 2012 by Pearson Education

Part A: Analyzing a Textbook Excerpt

This excerpt was taken from a communications textbook chapter about creating messages. Read the following excerpt using the steps listed on p. 14.

Kinesics

1 **Kinesics**, or the category of body movement and position, includes gestures, body orientation and posture, touch, and facial expressions and eye behavior.

2 **Gestures** **Gestures** are movements of the body used to communicate thoughts, feelings, and/or intentions. Gestures appear to naturally accompany speech, and people need not learn hand gestures by watching and modeling others' behavior. Researchers have discovered that children and adolescents who are blind from birth gesture as often and in the same manner as sighted people. Therefore, people don't need to see gestures prior to gesturing on their own.

3 Recent research suggests that people not only gesture to communicate information to others and to acknowledge interaction partners but also to help retrieve language. For example, stroke patients gesture more when they attempt to name or label objects, and people who don't even realize they gesture in fact do so when asked to come up with words that match particular definitions. In general, people gesture more when they refer to words and concepts with spatial connotations such as "under" and "adjacent" than when they refer to abstract concepts such as "thought" or "evil." One interesting study demonstrated that people have difficulty finding words when they can't gesture freely. Gestures precede spoken words by as much as three seconds, and it may be that gestures aid in accessing words. Just as memories are retrieved when the senses are activated, words may be retrieved with gestures.

4 **Body Orientation and Posture** In addition to gestures, **body orientation and posture** can communicate meaning. Body orientation involves the extent to which we face or lean toward or away from others. Both body orientation and posture can indicate whether we are open to interaction. For example, the positioning of the arms and legs while standing can indicate that we are available to talk with some people but not others, and the positioning of the arms, legs, and torso while seated can inhibit other people from entering into our conversations.

5 **Haptics** **Haptics**, or touch, is related to the development of emotional and mental adjustment. Touch provides infants with comfort and protection and helps young children develop their identities. Adults also need touching and may turn to licensed touchers such as massage therapists to fulfill the need for touch. The meanings that are associated with touching behavior depend on what body part is touched, the

KNOWLEDGE power • "My Hands Are Tied."

Do you gesture when you speak primarily to complement your verbal communication or to help you retrieve language while labeling objects and while referring to words with spatial connotations? Engage in a conversation with others in which you firmly clasp your hands in front of you or behind your back. Communicate for at least five minutes without allowing yourself to gesture. Did you find it difficult to communicate without gesturing? Why or why not?

How we position our bodies can indicate whether we want to communicate to others.

intensity of the touch, the duration of the touch, the method of the touch (such as closed or open fist), and the frequency of the touch. The meaning of touch is also dependent on the physical context (such as the home, the university setting, an airport) and the age, sex, and relationship between the person who is touched and the person who does the touching.

6 **Facial Expression and Eye Behavior** **Facial expression and eye behavior** are difficult to describe and measure because there are so many configurations and types of face and eye behavior. However, the face and eyes are an extremely potent source of nonverbal communication in that they are involved in opening, closing, and regulating the channels of interaction, and they function as the prime communicator of emotion.

7 Facial expression and eye behavior are related to **interaction management**, or the regulation of communication. For example, we open our mouths and simultaneously inhale as a sign of our readiness to speak. Making eye contact with someone also indicates that communication channels are open, whereas avoiding eye contact suggests that communication channels are closed. Eye contact also regulates the flow of communication with turn-taking signals. Glancing at grammatical breaks and the end of thought units enables us to obtain feedback about how we are being received, to see if our conversation partner will allow us to continue, and to signal to our partner that we are ready to switch to the role of the listener. When the speaking and listening roles change, the speaker will gaze at the listener as the utterance comes to a close. The listener will maintain the gaze until he or she assumes the speaking role, at which time the new speaker will look away.

8 In addition to regulating interaction, the face is the clearest indicator of what someone is feeling. Paul Ekman's research has established that seven emotions have a universal facial expression: sadness, surprise, disgust, happiness, anger, fear, and contempt.

—Lane, *Interpersonal Communication*, pp. 154–156

Copyright © 2012 by Pearson Education

1. **Preview.** Preview the reading using the guidelines on p. 7 and then answer the following questions.
   a. What is kinesics?
   b. How are gestures used in communication?
   c. If you wanted to get the clearest impression of how a person is feeling, what part of the body should you look at?
2. **SQ3R.** Write at least three questions for the Q step of SQ3R. Answer them after completing the reading.
3. **Textbook Features.** Try the experiment in the "Knowledge Power" box on p. 22 and report your results. What do you think is going on in the photo on p. 23?
4. **Vocabulary.**
   a. Identify the important new terms that are introduced in the reading.
   b. Define each of the following words and phrases as used in the reading: *interaction partners* (par. 3), *connotations* (par. 3), *inhibit* (par. 4), *intensity* (par. 5), *configurations* (par. 6)
5. **Applying Chapter Skills.** Describe how you could use visualization to remember the types of kinesics. What other learning strategies might be useful?
6. **Essay Question.** Write an answer to the following essay question. To test your memory, write it without referring to the excerpt.
   Kinesics is an important part of how people share information with each other. Write an essay in which you describe kinesics, how it is used, and examples of it.
7. **Thinking Critically.** Use your critical thinking skills to answer each of the following questions.
   a. What common gestures do you find yourself using? How do you think they add to or enhance the words you are saying?
   b. Describe a situation in which the meaning of what a person is saying is unclear unless kinesics is also considered.
   c. If kinesics plays such an important role in how people communicate, what implication does that have for telephone, Internet, and text communications?

Part B: Your College Textbook

Choose a chapter that you have been assigned to read in a textbook for one of your other courses. Use SQ3R strategies when reading the chapter and write an evaluation of how well it worked.

SELF-TEST SUMMARY

To test yourself, cover up the Answer column with a sheet of paper and answer each question listed in the left column. Evaluate each of your answers as you work by sliding the paper down and comparing your answer with what is printed in the Answer column.

	Question	Answer
GOAL 1	What are the keys to academic success?	Keys include approaching the assignment with the right mind-set, controlling distractions, and increasing your attention span.
GOAL 2	What do active readers and learners do?	Active readers and learners interact with the material by tailoring their reading and learning to suit the assignment, checking their understanding, questioning, and analyzing.
GOAL 3	Why is previewing important?	Previewing helps you become familiar with the chapter's content and organization and enables you to make predictions.
GOAL 4	What are guide questions?	Based on headings, guide questions are questions you expect to be able to answer while or after reading.
GOAL 5	How can you improve your skills in learning from textbooks?	Improve textbook reading skills by using textbook learning aids, the SQ3R method, and effective learning/recall strategies.
GOAL 6	What is critical thinking?	Critical thinking means evaluating and reacting to what you read, rather than accepting everything as "the truth."

Copyright © 2012 by Pearson Education

PRACTICE TEST 1-1

NAME ______________________ SECTION ______________________
DATE ______________________ SCORE ______________________

Active Reading

Directions: *Assume you have read the following headings while previewing a section of a sociology textbook chapter on substance abuse. Select the choice that best completes each of the statements that follow.*

Section Title: **THE SCOPE OF THE DRUG PROBLEM**

Headings:

(1) What Are Drugs?

(2) Americans' Pro-Drug Attitude

(3) The Social Function of Drugs

(4) Social Acceptability of Alcohol

(5) Nicotine: The Deadly Drug

(6) What Is Addiction?

(7) Craving and Withdrawal

(8) Illegal Drugs

(9) Are There Special Cases for Drug Use?

_______ 1. A preview of these headings suggests that the section will focus on
- a. combatting drug misuse.
- b. alcohol withdrawal.
- c. drug usage and effects.
- d. legalization of drugs.

_______ 2. The best guide question for the heading "Americans' Pro-Drug Attitude" would be
- a. How are Americans pro-drug?
- b. What drugs do Americans use?
- c. Are Americans pro-drug?
- d. Why are Americans using drugs?

_______ 3. The first sentence of the section "Social Acceptability of Alcohol" might be
- a. Alcohol is created by fermenting a type of grain.
- b. Alcohol is the most socially accepted drug in America.
- c. Teen drinking is one of the biggest problems facing society.
- d. When something is socially accepted, it is not questioned by the majority of people in a society.

_______ 4. The best guide question for the heading "Nicotine: The Deadly Drug" is
- a. When was nicotine first used by humans?
- b. How do people become addicted to nicotine?
- c. Why is nicotine a deadly drug?
- d. Is nicotine a deadly drug?

_______ 5. Under which of the following headings would you expect cocaine to be discussed?

a. What Are Drugs?
b. Illegal Drugs
c. The Social Function of Drugs
d. What Is Addiction?

_______ 6. Under which of the following headings would you expect the topic of alcoholism to be addressed?

a. Are There Special Cases for Drug Use?
b. Illegal Drugs
c. Nicotine: The Deadly Drug
d. Craving and Withdrawal

_______ 7. This textbook selection will probably *not* discuss

a. criminal penalties for drinking and driving.
b. drug addiction.
c. chewing tobacco.
d. rehabilitation programs.

_______ 8. Under which heading would you expect to find definitions?

a. The Social Function of Drugs
b. Americans' Pro-Drug Attitude
c. What Are Drugs?
d. Social Acceptability of Alcohol

_______ 9. Under which heading are you likely to find mention of the use of marijuana to treat medical conditions?

a. Craving and Withdrawal
b. Are There Special Cases for Drug Use?
c. What Is Addiction?
d. Illegal Drugs

_______ 10. Under which heading are you likely to find a discussion of the use of alcohol at functions such as weddings, parties, and sporting events?

a. Are There Special Cases for Drug Use?
b. Social Acceptability of Alcohol
c. What Are Drugs?
d. Illegal Drugs

Copyright © 2012 by Pearson Education

PRACTICE TEST 1-2

NAME ______________________ SECTION ______________________

DATE ______________________ SCORE ______________________

Active Reading

Directions: *The following excerpt is from a health textbook. Preview by reading* **only** *the highlighted sections of the reading, and then select the choice that best completes each of the statements that follow. Do* **not** *read the section completely.*

Psychosocial Sources of Stress

Psychosocial stress refers to the factors in our daily lives that cause stress. Interactions with others, the subtle and not-so-subtle expectations we and others have of ourselves, and the social conditions we live in force us to readjust continually. Sources of psychosocial stress include change, hassles, pressure, inconsistent goals and behaviors, and conflict.

Change

Any time change occurs in your normal daily routine, whether good or bad, you will experience stress. The more changes you experience and the more adjustments you must make, the greater the stress effects may be.

Hassles

Psychologists such as Richard Lazarus have focused on petty annoyances and frustrations, collectively referred to as hassles. Minor hassles—losing your keys, slipping and falling in front of everyone as you walk to your seat in a new class, finding that you went through a whole afternoon with a big chunk of spinach stuck in your front teeth—seem unimportant, but their cumulative effects may be harmful in the long run.

Pressure

Pressure occurs when we feel forced to speed up, intensify, or shift the direction of our behavior to meet a higher standard of performance. Pressures can be based on our personal goals and expectations, on concern about what others think, or on outside influences. Among the most significant outside influences are society's demands that we compete and be all that we can be.

Inconsistency between Goals and Behaviors

For many of us, the negative effects of stress are magnified when there is a disparity between our goals (what we value or hope to obtain in life) and our behaviors (actions that may or may not lead to these goals). For instance, you may want good grades, and your family may expect them. But if you party and procrastinate throughout the term, your behaviors are inconsistent with your goals, and significant stress in the form of guilt, last-minute frenzy before exams, and disappointing grades may result. By contrast, if you dig in and work and remain committed to getting good grades, this may eliminate much of your negative stress. Thwarted goals can lead to frustration, and frustration has been shown to be a significant disrupter of homeostasis. Determining whether behaviors are consistent with goals is an essential component of maintaining balance in life.

Conflict

Conflict occurs when we are forced to make difficult decisions concerning two or more competing motives, behaviors, or impulses or when we are forced to face incompatible demands, opportunities, needs or goals. What if your best friends all choose to smoke marijuana and you don't want to smoke but fear rejection? Conflict often occurs as our values are tested. College students who are away from home for the first time often face conflict between parental values and their own set of developing beliefs.

—Elise, *Health,* 1994

_______ 1. The title suggests that the reading's general topic will be
   a. health problems caused by stress.
   b. the negative and positive effects of stress.
   c. social and psychological factors that cause stress.
   d. how the environment affects our health.

_______ 2. All of the following previewing aids are found in this selection *except*
   a. a title.
   b. a subtitle.
   c. an introductory paragraph.
   d. section headings.

_______ 3. Having read the introductory paragraph as part of your preview, you would expect the reading to focus on
   a. how people react physically to stress.
   b. what types of people experience the most stress.
   c. how stress is measured.
   d. what causes stress in our daily lives.

Copyright © 2012 by Pearson Education

_______ 4. Change leads to stress when the change

a. is positive only.

b. is negative only.

c. is unexpected.

d. disrupts your normal daily routine.

_______ 5. The "hassles" discussed in this selection refer to

a. major disagreements with family members.

b. petty annoyances and frustrations.

c. harassment and discrimination in the workplace.

d. financial problems.

_______ 6. The most helpful guide question to ask for the heading "Pressure" is

a. Is pressure related to stress?

b. Are most people under pressure?

c. How is pressure related to stress?

d. Does pressure cause an increase or a decrease in stress?

_______ 7. The sentence that follows the heading "Pressure" describes when pressure occurs. In this section you would also expect to read about

a. factors that create pressure.

b. health problems related to stress.

c. being prepared for change.

d. learning to cope with minor hassles.

_______ 8. The most helpful guide question to ask for the heading "Inconsistency between Goals and Behaviors" is

a. What is inconsistency?

b. Are goals the same as behaviors?

c. Is it possible to have inconsistencies between goals and behaviors?

d. How does inconsistency between our goals and our behaviors lead to stress?

_______ 9. Because the last heading is titled "Conflict," you know that

a. conflict is another psychosocial source of stress.

b. conflict is a physical source of stress.

c. stress is considered a source of conflict.

d. there are conflicting theories about stress.

_______ 10. Conflict occurs when we must

a. make hard decisions about competing motives, behaviors, or impulses.

b. confront incompatible demands, opportunities, needs, or goals.

c. both a and b

d. neither a nor b

Copyright © 2012 by Pearson Education

MASTERY TEST 1-1

NAME ______________________ SECTION ______________________

DATE ______________________ SCORE ______________________

Practicing Active Reading

***Directions:** Preview the following selection, which is from a sociology text. So that your instructor can see the parts you read, highlight each part you looked at. (Normally, it is too time-consuming to highlight while previewing.)*

Who Lives in the City?

1 Whether you find alienation or community in the city depends on many factors, but consider the five types of urban dwellers that Gans (1962, 1968, 1991a) identified. Which type are you? How does this affect your chances of finding alienation or community?

The first three types live in the city by choice; they find a sense of community.

The Cosmopolites

2 The cosmopolites are the city's students, intellectuals, professionals, musicians, artists, and entertainers. They have been drawn to the city because of its conveniences and cultural benefits.

The Singles

3 Young, unmarried people come to the city seeking jobs and entertainment. Business and services such as singles bars, singles apartment complexes, and computer dating companies cater to their needs. Their stay in the city is often temporary, for most move to the suburbs after they marry and have children.

The Ethnic Villagers

4 United by race–ethnicity and social class, these people live in tightly knit neighborhoods that resemble villages and small towns. Moving within a close circle of family and friends, the ethnic villagers try to isolate themselves from what they view as the harmful effects of city life.

5 The next two groups, the deprived and the trapped, have little choice about where they live. As alienated outcasts of industrial society, they are always skirting the edge of disaster.

The Deprived

6 The deprived live in blighted neighborhoods that are more like urban jungles than urban villages. Consisting of the very poor and the emotionally disturbed, the deprived represent the bottom of society in terms of income, education, social status, and work skills. Some of them stalk their jungle in search of prey, their victims usually deprived people like themselves. Their future holds little chance for anything better in life.

The Trapped

7 The trapped can find no escape either. Some could not afford to move when their neighborhood was "invaded" by another ethnic group. Others in this group are the elderly who are not wanted elsewhere, alcoholics and other drug addicts, and the downwardly mobile. Like the deprived, the trapped also suffer high rates of assault, mugging, robbery, and rape.

—Henslin, *Sociology,* pp. 623–624

Directions: *Match each type of urban dweller listed in column A with the correct description in column B.*

	Column A	Column B
______	1. the cosmopolites	a. people united by race–ethnicity and social class
______	2. the singles	b. people who can find no escape
______	3. the ethnic villagers	c. students, intellectuals, professionals, musicians, artists, and entertainers
______	4. the deprived	d. young, unmarried people seeking jobs and entertainment
______	5. the trapped	e. people who live in blighted neighborhoods that are like urban jungles

Copyright © 2012 by Pearson Education

MASTERY TEST 1-2

NAME ______________________ SECTION ______________________

DATE ______________________ SCORE ______________________

Practicing Active Reading

A. Directions: *Preview the following selection, which is from a sociology text. So that your instructor can see the parts you read, highlight each part you looked at. (Normally, it is too time-consuming to highlight while previewing.)*

The Mass Media

The mass media help to shape gender roles. The media give messages to children—and to the rest of us—that certain behaviors are considered "right" for boys and other behaviors "right" for girls. They also give messages about the "proper" relationships between men and women. To get some insight into how this occurs, we will look first at children's books, then at television, music, video games, and advertising.

Children's Books

Children's picture books have been a major focus of sociologists. It is easy to see that illustrated books for children are more than just entertainment; little children learn about the world from the pictures they see and the stories read to them. What the pictures show girls and boys doing becomes part of their view of what is "right."

When sociologists first examined children's picture books in the 1970s, they found that it was unusual for a girl to be the main character. Almost all the books featured boys, men, and even male animals. The girls, when pictured at all, were passive and doll-like, whereas the boys were active and adventuresome. While the boys did things that required independence and self-confidence, most girls were shown trying to help their brothers and fathers. Feminists protested these stereotypes and even formed their own companies to publish books that showed girls as leaders, as active and independent.

The result of these efforts, as well as that of the changed role of women in society, is that children's books now have about an equal number of boy and girl characters. Girls are also now depicted in a variety of nontraditional activities. Researchers find, however, that males are seldom depicted as caring for the children or doing grocery shopping, and they never are seen doing housework. As gender roles continue to change, I assume that this, too, will change.

More powerful than picture books is television, both because of its moving images and the number of hours that children watch television. In the cartoons that so fascinate young children, males outnumber females, giving the message that boys are more important than girls. A children's TV show that ran from 1987 to 1996, *Teenage Mutant Ninja Turtles,* captures the situation. The original turtles were Michelangelo, Leonardo, Raphael, and Donatello—named after men artists whose accomplishments have been admired for centuries. A female turtle was added. Her name? Venus de Milo. The female turtle was named not for a person, but for a statue that is world famous for its curvaceous and ample breasts. She never did anything. And, how could she—she has no head or arms.

Adult television reinforces stereotypes of gender, age, and sexuality. On prime time, male characters outnumber female characters, and men are more likely to be portrayed in higher-status positions. Starting at age 30, fewer and fewer women are shown, and about 9 out of 10 women on prime time are below the age of 46. Older women practically disappear from television. Women are depicted as losing their sexual attractiveness earlier than men. Men are portrayed as aging more gracefully, with their sexual attractiveness lasting longer.

Music

There are so many kinds (genres) of music that it is difficult to summarize their content accurately. In many songs for teens and preteens, the listeners learn that boys should dominate male–female relationships. A common message for girls is that they should be sexy, passive, and dependent—and that they can control boys by manipulating the boys' sexual impulses. In music videos, females are most often only background ornaments for the dominant males. Some rap groups glorify male sexual aggression and revel in humiliating women. In Country-Western songs, which have become so popular, the common message is that men are aggressive and dominant, whereas women are passive and dependent. These men do have a tender side, however: They cry into their beers after their cheating women have left them. But, never mind, some honkey-tonk woman is waiting to revel in her dominant man.

Video Games

More than any other medium, video games give the message that women are not important: Male characters outnumber female characters seven to one. Matching the depictions of sex roles in the other media, video women show more skin than do video men.

Advertising

> Advertising is an insidious propaganda machine for a male supremacist society. It spews out images of women as sex mates, housekeepers, mothers, and menial workers—images that perhaps reflect the true status of most women in society, but which also make it increasingly difficult for women to break out of the sexist stereotypes that imprison them.

This observation from the 1970s reminds us that little has changed in advertising. Although fewer women are now depicted as "housekeepers, mothers,

Copyright © 2012 by Pearson Education

and menial workers," television advertising continues to reinforce stereotypical gender roles. Commercials aimed at children are more likely to show girls as cooperative and boys as aggressive. They are also more likely to show girls at home and boys at other locations. Men are portrayed in higher status positions. Women make most purchases, they are underrepresented as primary characters, and they are shown primarily as supportive counterparts to men.

Fighting Back

The use of the female body—especially exposed breasts—to sell products also continues. Feminists have fought back. In one campaign, they spray-painted their own lines to billboards. One billboard featured a Fiat with a woman reclining on its roof saying, "It's so practical, Darling." Feminists added the spray-painted line, "When I'm not lying on cars, I'm a brain surgeon."

Such resistance, as you know from the average 1,600 ads that pummel you each day, has had little impact. The major change with how bodies are depicted in advertising is that the male body has become more prominent. More than ever, parts of the male body are also selected for exposure and for irrelevant associations with products.

In Sum

The essential point is that the mass media—children's books, television, music video games, and advertising—influence us. They shape the images that we hold in the way people "ought" to be, and we tend to see one another as men and women through those images. Mostly subtle and beneath our level of awareness, these images channel our behavior, becoming part of the means by which men maintain their dominance in social life. This includes politics, to which we now turn.

—Henslin, *Social Problems,* 7/e, pp. 293–296

B. Directions: *The following guide questions are based on the headings in the selection. Read the entire selection, and then select the choice that best answers each of the following questions.*

_______ 1. How do children's books transmit stereotypes?

a. They do not; they are simply entertainment.

b. They present positive images of both males and females.

c. Females in award-winning books are portrayed as more action-oriented than males.

d. Male characters greatly outnumber females, and portrayals of both males and females are sexist.

_______ 2. What message is sent by television?

a. Females outnumber males.

b. Role models are usually based on famous historical figures.

c. Men are more likely to have higher-status positions than women.

d. Accomplishment is not based on gender.

_______ 3. How are male-female relationships portrayed through music and video games?

a. Males are dominant and females are passive and dependent.

b. Males and females are equal partners in relationships.

c. Females control relationships.

d. Both males and females are capable of "rescuing" others in peril.

_______ 4. How does advertising reinforce stereotypes?

a. by using feminists to create advertising campaigns

b. by using more males than females in advertisements

c. by promoting a positive image of male-female relationships

d. by depicting women (and men) as objects for selling products

_______ 5. The summary of this selection indicates that

a. television and video games are more influential than children's literature.

b. we should not be concerned about the influence of the mass media on our lives.

c. the mass media shape our behavior by influencing our perceptions.

d. most men support the images portrayed by the mass media.

Copyright © 2012 by Pearson Education

MASTERY TEST 1-3

NAME ____________________ SECTION ____________________

DATE ____________________ SCORE ____________________

READING SELECTION

Diversity in U.S. Families

James M. Henslin

This reading selection, taken from a sociology textbook, explores the family structure of several racial–ethnic groups. Read the selection to discover the family characteristics of each group. Which one is most similar to your family structure?

Vocabulary Preview

These are some of the difficult words in this essay. The definitions here will help you if you can't figure out the meanings from the sentence context or word parts.

diversity (par. 1) the condition of being made up of different characteristics, qualities, or elements

preservation (par. 2) the act of maintaining or keeping

merger (par. 2) combination or union

cultural (par. 4) relating to the behavior patterns, beliefs, and institutions of a particular population

machismo (par. 7) an emphasis on male strength and dominance

emigrated (par. 9) moved away from one country or place to another

assimilate (par. 12) to become part of

permissive (par. 13) tolerant or lenient

1 As we review some of the vast diversity of U.S. families, it is important to note that we are not comparing any of them to *the* American family. There is no such thing. Rather, family life varies widely throughout the United States. We have already seen in several contexts how significant social class is in our lives. Its significance will continue to be evident as we examine diversity in U.S. families.

African American Families

2 Note that the heading reads African American *families,* not *the* African American family. There is no such thing as *the* African American family any more than there is *the* white family or *the* Latino family. The primary distinction is not between African Americans and other groups, but between social classes. Because African Americans who are members of the upper class follow the class interests reviewed in Chapter 10—preservation of privilege and

There is no such thing as *the* African American family, any more than there is *the* Native American, Asian American, Latino, or Irish American family. Rather, each racial–ethnic group has different types of families, with the primary determinant being social class.

family fortune—they are especially concerned about the family background of those whom their children marry. To them, marriage is viewed as a merger of family lines. Children of this class marry later than children of other classes.

3 Middle-class African American families focus on achievement and respectability. Both husband and wife are likely to work outside the home. A central concern is that their children go to college, get good jobs, and marry well—that is, marry people like themselves, respectable and hardworking, who want to get ahead in school and pursue a successful career.

4 African American families in poverty face all the problems that cluster around poverty. Because the men are likely to have few skills and to be unemployed, it is difficult for them to fulfill the cultural roles of husband and father. Consequently, these families are likely to be headed by a woman and to have a high rate of births to single women. Divorce and desertion are also more common than among other classes. Sharing scarce resources and "stretching kinship" are primary survival mechanisms. People who have helped out in hard times are considered brothers, sisters, or cousins to whom one owes obligations as though they were blood relatives; and men who are not the biological fathers of their children are given fatherhood status. Sociologists use the term *fictive kin* to refer to this stretching of kinship.

5 From Figure A (p. 40) you can see that, compared with other groups, African American families are the least likely to be headed by married couples and the most likely to be headed by women. Because African American women tend to go farther in school than African American men, they are more likely than women in other racial–ethnic groups to marry men who are less educated than themselves (2008).

Copyright © 2012 by Pearson Education

FIGURE A Family Structure: U.S. Families with Children Under Age 18 Headed by Mothers, Fathers, and Both Parents

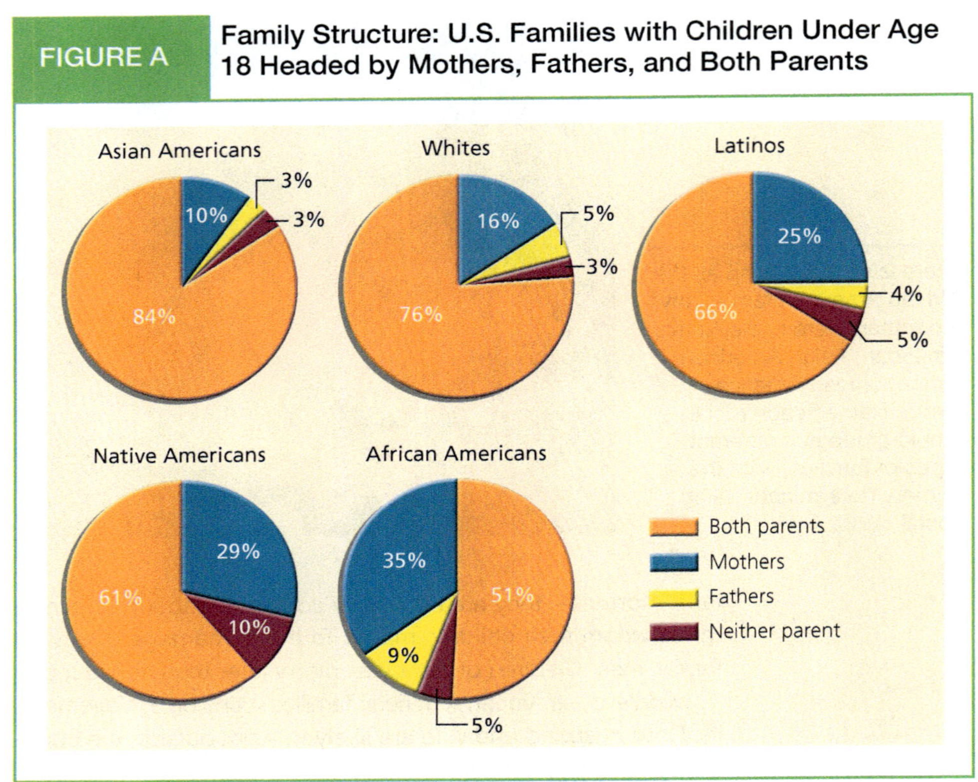

Latino Families

6 As Figure A shows, the proportion of Latino families headed by married couples and women falls in between that of whites and Native Americans. The effects of social class on families, which I just sketched, also apply to Latinos. In addition, families differ by country of origin. Families from Mexico, for example, are more likely to be headed by a married couple than are families from Puerto Rico. The longer that Latinos have lived in the United States, the more their families resemble those of middle-class Americans.

7 With such wide variety, experts disagree on what is distinctive about Latino families. Some researchers have found that Latino husbands-fathers play a stronger role than husbands-fathers in white and African American families. Others point to the Spanish language, the Roman Catholic religion, and a strong family orientation coupled with a disapproval of divorce, but there are Latino families who are Protestants, don't speak Spanish, and so on. Still others emphasize loyalty to the extended family, with an obligation to support the extended family in times of need, but this, too, is hardly unique to Latino families.

Descriptions of Latino families used to include **machismo**—an emphasis on male strength, sexual vigor, and dominance—but *machismo* decreases with each generation in the United States and is certainly not limited to Latinos. Compared to their husbands, Latina wives-mothers tend to be more family-centered and display more warmth and affection for their children, but this is probably true of all racial-ethnic groups.

8 With such diversity among Latino families, you can see how difficult it is to draw generalizations. The sociological point that runs through all studies of Latino families, however, is this: Social class is more important in determining family life than is either being Latino or a family's country of origin.

Asian American Families

9 As you can see from Figure A on the previous page, Asian American children are more likely than children in other racial–ethnic groups to grow up with both parents. As with the other groups, family life also reflects social class. In addition, because Asian Americans emigrated from many different countries, their family life reflects those many cultures. As with Latino families, the more recent their immigration, the more closely their family life reflects the patterns in their country of origin.

10 Despite such differences, sociologist Bob Suzuki, who studied Chinese American and Japanese American families, identified several distinctive characteristics of Asian American families. Although Asian Americans have adopted the nuclear family structure, they tend to retain Confucian values that provide a framework for family life: humanism, collectivity, self-discipline, hierarchy, respect for the elderly, moderation, and obligation. Obligation means that each member of a family owes respect to other family members and has a responsibility never to bring shame on the family. Conversely, a child's success brings honor to the family. To control their children, Asian American parents are more likely to use shame and guilt than physical punishment.

11 Seldom does the ideal translate into the real, and so it is here. The children born to Asian immigrants confront a bewildering world of incompatible expectations—those of the new culture and those of their parents. As a result, they experience more family conflict and mental problems than do children of Asian Americans who are not immigrants.

Native American Families

12 Perhaps the single most significant issue that Native American families face is whether to follow traditional values or to assimilate into the dominant culture. This primary distinction creates vast differences among families. The traditionals speak native languages and emphasize distinctive Native American values and beliefs. Those who have assimilated into the broader culture do not.

Copyright © 2012 by Pearson Education

13 Figure A on page 40 depicts the structure of Native American families. You can see how close it is to that of Latinos. In general, Native American parents are permissive with their children and avoid physical punishment. Elders play a much more active role in their children's families than they do in most U.S. families: Elders, especially grandparents, not only provide child care but also teach and discipline children. Like others, Native American families differ by social class.

14 **In Sum:** From this brief review, you can see that race—ethnicity signifies little for understanding family life. Rather, social class and culture hold the keys. The more resources a family has, the more it assumes the characteristics of a middle-class nuclear family. Compared with the poor, middle-class families have fewer children and fewer unmarried mothers. They also place greater emphasis on educational achievement and deferred gratification.

Directions: *Select the choice that best completes each of the following statements.*

CHECKING YOUR COMPREHENSION

_______ 1. The purpose of this selection is to

a. describe the typical American family.

b. summarize the achievements of successful American families.

c. describe the characteristics of families in various racial–ethnic groups in America.

d. list statistics about marriage and divorce among racial–ethnic groups in America.

_______ 2. The selection discusses all of the following racial–ethnic groups *except*

a. African Americans.

b. Arab Americans.

c. Asian Americans.

d. Native Americans.

_______ 3. According to the selection, the primary interest of the upper class is

a. preservation of privilege and family fortune.

b. acquisition of real estate and material possessions.

c. strengthening of extended family relationships.

d. assimilation into the dominant culture.

_______ 4. In African American families, the term *fictive kin* refers to

a. your spouse's relatives.

b. people who have helped you and to whom you owe obligations.

c. people from your childhood neighborhood.

d. friends who have sworn a blood vow.

_______ 5. All of the following characteristics are linked to the culture of Latino families *except*

a. the Spanish language.

b. the Roman Catholic religion.

c. an emphasis on strict discipline.

d. a strong family orientation.

_______ 6. In Asian American families, "obligation" specifically means that

a. Asian Americans must marry other Asian Americans only.

b. Asian American children are responsible for taking care of their elderly relatives.

c. each family is obligated to maintain the traditions of its country of origin.

d. each individual owes respect to other family members and must never bring shame on the family.

_______ 7. According to the selection, a significant issue that Native American families face is whether to

a. be strict or permissive with their children.

b. follow traditional values or assimilate into the broader culture.

c. allow elders to play a more active role in their children's families.

d. adopt the nuclear family structure or emphasize loyalty to the community.

Copyright © 2012 by Pearson Education

USING WHAT YOU KNOW ABOUT COLLEGE TEXTBOOK READING

_______ 8. The most useful guide question for this selection would be

a. Is there a typical American family?

b. How are families in America diverse?

c. Which racial–ethnic groups have been studied?

d. What percentage of U.S. households are part of a racial–ethnic group?

_______ 9. Figure A indicates that the group most likely to have families headed by women is

a. African Americans.

b. Native Americans.

c. Asian Americans.

d. white (non-Latino) Americans.

_______ 10. According to Figure A, the group of children most likely to grow up with both parents is

a. African Americans.

b. Native Americans.

c. Asian Americans.

d. white (non-Latino) Americans.

_______ 11. In his summary, the author emphasizes that the primary determinant of different types of families in the United States is

a. race.

b. ethnicity.

c. social class.

d. geographic origin.

_______ 12. All of the following previewing aids are found in this selection *except*

a. section headings.

b. an introduction.

c. italics.

d. a subtitle.

REVIEWING DIFFICULT VOCABULARY

Directions: *Complete each of the following sentences by inserting a word from the Vocabulary Preview on page 38 in the space provided. Use each word only once.*

13. After the ____________ was approved by the board of directors, they decided on a name for the newly formed company.
14. The actor's reputation for ____________ seemed to conflict with his hobbies of knitting, calligraphy, and yoga.
15. Many immigrants have difficulty trying to ____________ into a new country, especially if they do not speak the language.
16. The school was known for its ____________; at least twelve different countries were represented among the student body.
17. Many people who live in North America have ancestors who at one time ____________ from their native countries.
18. Perhaps because his parents had been so strict with him, Gabriel took a more ____________ approach with his own children.
19. The group's mission statement declared that it was dedicated to the ____________ of historical buildings and landmarks.
20. Before conducting business in other countries, executives often receive training in local customs and other important ____________ differences.

THINKING CRITICALLY

1. What is your impression of the photograph that accompanies this selection? What key point(s) does the caption emphasize?
2. How did the graphics in Figure A help you understand the family structures discussed in the selection?
3. Do you think the author is trying to influence your opinions in this selection? Why or why not?

Copyright © 2012 by Pearson Education

QUESTIONS FOR DISCUSSION

1. Consider your own family and your racial–ethnic group, as well as other groups with which you are familiar. Discuss whether the information in this reading selection accurately reflects your experience.
2. Do you perceive social class as being a more important factor than racial–ethnic identity?
3. Would this reading selection help you to understand someone from a racial–ethnic group different from your own, or has it already?

WRITING ACTIVITIES

1. Write a paragraph describing a person who does or does not fit the characteristics of his or her racial–ethnic profile described in the reading.
2. This reading presents a profile of four racial–ethnic groups. Write a short essay exploring the dangers of such profiling.
3. Visit the Presence of the Past Web site at: http://chnm.gmu.edu/survey/1_1gnrlact.html. Study the information in this table from a study about the relevance of the past to different racial–ethnic groups. Write a paragraph explaining why you think each group responded the way it did.

CHAPTER 1

Reading College Textbooks: An Active Approach

RECORDING YOUR PROGRESS

Test	Number Right		Score
Practice Test 1-1	_______	× 10 =	_______%
Practice Test 1-2	_______	× 10 =	_______%
Mastery Test 1-1	_______	× 20 =	_______%
Mastery Test 1-2	_______	× 20 =	_______%
Mastery Test 1-3	_______	× 5 =	_______%

GETTING MORE PRACTICE myreadinglab

To get more practice with Active Reading, go to http://www.myreadinglab.com and click on

> Study Plan
> Reading Skills
> Active Reading
  and Reading Textbooks
  and Memorization and Concentration

EVALUATING YOUR PROGRESS myreadinglab

To measure your progress after reading and viewing the information in the Review Materials section, complete the Practices and Tests in the Activities section. You can check your scores by clicking on the Gradebook tab.

Then, based on your performance in this chapter and/or on the MyReadingLab Practices and Tests, write your own evaluation.

YOUR EVALUATION: ____

____

____

____

Copyright © 2012 by Pearson Education

THINKING ABOUT

Vocabulary

A portion of this photograph is blocked out. Can you figure out what is missing? Draw a quick sketch of it. How did you know what to sketch? You probably used clues from the visible portions of the photograph to figure out what is missing. The image of the performer and the shape of the block out suggests he is playing a guitar. When reading a sentence or paragraph, if you find a word is missing from your vocabulary, you can figure out its meaning by studying the rest of the sentence or paragraph in which it appears. The words surrounding an unknown word provide clues to its meaning, just as the details in the photograph provide clues about what is missing.

Now read the following brief paragraph. Several words are missing. Try to figure out the missing words and write them in the blanks.

The ideal time to __________ a tree is in the fall. The warm days and cool __________ of autumn allow a tree's root system to develop and become established. The young tree will mature further during the spring season before facing the heat of __________.

CHAPTER 2

Strengthening Your Vocabulary

What Is Context?

GOAL 1
Understand context

To practice using context clues, go to
- Study Plan
- Reading Skills
- Vocabulary

Did you insert the word *plant* or *transplant* in the first blank, *nights* in the second blank, and *summer* in the third blank? Most likely, you correctly identified all three missing words. You could tell from the sentence which word to put in. The words around the missing words—the sentence context—gave you clues as to which word would fit and make sense. Such clues are called **context clues.**

While you probably won't find missing words on a printed page, you will often find words that you do not know. Context clues can help you to figure out the meanings of unfamiliar words.

LEARNING GOALS

GOAL 1 Understand context

GOAL 2 Learn the types of context clues

GOAL 3 Use word parts

GOAL 4 Think critically about vocabulary

Example

During his lecture, the **ornithologist** described his research on western spotted owls as well as many other species of birds.

From the sentence, you can tell that *ornithologist* means "a person who studies birds."

Here's another example:

Example

We were so **enervated** by the heat that we decided to go back to our air-conditioned hotel room for a nap before dinner.

You can figure out that *enervated* means "weakened or worn out" by the heat.

Copyright © 2012 by Pearson Education

Types of Context Clues

Learn the types of context clues

There are five types of context clues to look for: (1) definition, (2) synonym, (3) example, (4) contrast, and (5) inference.

Definition Clues

Many times a writer defines a word immediately following its use. The writer may directly define a word by giving a brief definition of the unknown word. Such words and phrases as *means, is, refers to,* and *can be defined as* are often used. Here are some examples:

Examples

Induction refers to *the process of reasoning from the known to the unknown.*

A **prosthesis** is *an artificial replacement for a missing body part, such as an eye, a limb, or a heart valve.*

Punctuation is often used to signal that a definition clue to a word's meaning is to follow. Punctuation also separates the meaning clue from the rest of the sentence. Three types of punctuation are used in this way. In the examples below, notice that the meaning clue is separated from the rest of the sentence by punctuation.

Examples

1. Commas

   Hypochondria, *excessive worry over one's health,* afflicts many Americans over forty.

   Glen was especially interested in **nephology,** *the branch of meteorology that deals with clouds.*

2. Parentheses

   Deciduous trees *(trees bearing leaves that are shed annually)* respond differently to heat and cold than **coniferous trees** *(trees bearing cones).*

   Middle age *(35 years to 65 years)* is a time for strengthening and maintaining life goals.

3. Dashes

   Most societies are **patriarchal**—*males exert dominant power and authority.*

   The **rapier**—*a light sword with a narrow, pointed blade*—was traditionally used for thrusting rather than cutting.

EXERCISE 2-1 Understanding Definition Context Clues

Directions: *Using the definition clues in each sentence, select the choice that best defines each boldfaced word.*

_______ 1. There was a **consensus,** or unified opinion, among the students that the exam was difficult.

a. dispute
b. unified opinion
c. change
d. question

_______ 2. The continents and ocean basins of the Earth's crust are separated from the Earth's liquid core by the **mantle**—1,800 miles of a solid layer of rock.

a. crust
b. liquid core
c. ocean basins
d. solid layer of rock

_______ 3. Jane Goodall has spent many years of her life observing the behavior of animals in their natural settings, a field of study known as **ethology.**

a. the behavior of animals
b. the study of animals in their natural environment
c. the study of the environment
d. the observation of behavior

_______ 4. The play **satirized** several famous political figures, using wit and sarcasm to expose their folly.

a. admired
b. ignored
c. defeated
d. ridiculed

_______ 5. Philippe was upset that he had lost the folder containing his **dossier,** which included his college transcripts, résumé, and letters of recommendation.

a. wallet
b. bank statement
c. license
d. collection of papers

_______ 6. In 1898, the Spanish **ceded,** or surrendered possession of, both Guam and Puerto Rico to the United States.

a. maintained
b. purchased
c. gave up
d. battled

_______ 7. The professor often used **paradigms,** or models, to illustrate difficult concepts.

a. typical examples
b. mastery tests
c. brief reviews
d. illustrated reports

_______ 8. People who practice **totemism**—the worship of plants, animals, or objects as gods—usually select for worship objects that are important to the community.

a. the worship of community
b. the worship of gods
c. the worship of plants, animals, or objects
d. the worship of no gods

Copyright © 2012 by Pearson Education

_______ 9. In police investigations, **interrogation** (examination by questioning) is vital, but it can be psychologically and emotionally draining to the person being questioned.

a. writing answers
b. asking questions
c. interfering
d. complaining

_______ 10. The **mean**—the mathematical average of a set of numbers—will determine whether grades will be based on a curve.

a. the highest number in a set
b. the lowest number in a set
c. the average of a set of numbers
d. the total of a set of numbers

Synonym Clues

At other times, rather than formally define the word, a writer may provide a synonym—a word or brief phrase that is close in meaning. The synonym may appear in the same sentence as the unknown word.

Example

The author purposely left the ending of his novel **ambiguous,** or *unclear,* so readers would have to decide for themselves what happened.

Other times, it may appear anywhere in the passage, in an earlier or later sentence.

Example

After the soccer match, a **melee** broke out in the parking lot. Three people were injured in the *brawl,* and several others were arrested.

EXERCISE 2-2 Understanding Synonym Context Clues

Directions: *Using the synonym clues in each sentence, select the choice that best defines each boldfaced word.*

_______ 1. The mayor's assistant was accused of **malfeasance,** although he denied any wrongdoing.

a. denial
b. misconduct
c. motivation
d. authority

_______ 2. The words of the president seemed to **galvanize** the American troops, who cheered enthusiastically throughout the speech.

a. excite
b. anger
c. announce
d. discourage

_______ 3. Mia Hamm's superior ability and **prowess** on the soccer field have inspired many girls to become athletes.

a. meekness
b. training
c. exceptional skill
d. sound advice

_______ 4. Many gardeners improve the quality of their soil by **amending** it with organic compost.

a. turning
b. spoiling
c. removing
d. enriching

_______ 5. Eliminating salt from the diet is a **prudent,** sensible decision for people with high blood pressure.

a. thoughtless
b. advisable
c. unnecessary
d. economical

_______ 6. The **cadence,** or rhythm, of the Dixieland band had many people tapping their feet along with the music.

a. appearance of the band
b. melody
c. beat of the music
d. noise

_______ 7. Edgar Allan Poe is best known for his **macabre** short stories and poems. His eerie tale, "The Fall of the House of Usher," was made into a horror movie starring Vincent Price.

a. humorous
b. magical
c. entertaining
d. frightening

_______ 8. While she was out of the country, Greta authorized me to act as her **proxy,** or agent, in matters having to do with her business and her personal bank accounts.

a. representative
b. adviser
c. partner
d. accountant

_______ 9. The **arsenal** of a baseball pitcher ideally includes several different kinds of pitches. From this supply of pitches, he or she needs to have at least one that can fool the batter.

a. collection
b. performance
c. attitude
d. profession

_______ 10. A **coalition** of neighborhood representatives formed to fight a proposed highway through the area. The group also had the support of several local businesses.

a. report or summary
b. business or enterprise
c. alliance or partnership
d. part or category

Copyright © 2012 by Pearson Education

Example Clues

Writers often include examples that help to explain or clarify a word. Words and phrases used to introduce examples include *to illustrate, for instance, for example, such as,* and *including.* Suppose you do not know the meaning of the word *pathogens,* and you find it used in the following sentence:

Example

Microscopic **pathogens,** such as *viruses, bacteria, and fungi,* constantly threaten our health as we go about our daily lives.

This sentence gives three examples of pathogens. From the examples given, which are known to cause disease or sickness, and from the clue about health, you could conclude that *pathogens* means "disease-causing agents."

Examples

Collecting **demographic** data on potential consumers, *including age, marital status, and income,* is an essential part of market research.

Students in the introductory literature course were required to read several selections in each **genre**—*drama, fiction, and poetry.*

Orthopterans *such as crickets, grasshoppers, and cockroaches* thrive in damp conditions.

The symptoms of Erin's **malady** *included a high fever, a headache, and an itchy rash.*

EXERCISE 2-3 Understanding Example Context Clues

Directions: *Using the example clues in each sentence, select the choice that best defines each boldfaced word.*

_______ 1. Some **debilities** of old age, including loss of hearing, poor eyesight, and diseases such as arthritis, can be treated medically.

a. deafness
b. medical treatments
c. weaknesses
d. notices

_______ 2. The actor has a wide **repertoire,** including Shakespearean drama, Broadway plays, and classical theater.

a. budget for artistic performances
b. stock of material that can be performed
c. requirements that must be fulfilled
d. ability to both sing and dance

_______ 3. Many people have turned to herbal **remedies,** such as flaxseed, yarrow, and St. John's wort, to treat a variety of health conditions.

a. foods
b. payments
c. challenges
d. medicines

_______ 4. Children between the ages of three and six occasionally experience some form of **parasomnia**—sleepwalking, night terrors, or bed-wetting.

a. sleep disorder
b. excitement
c. anger
d. daydreaming

_______ 5. Certain environmental hazards—including asbestos, arsenic, and tar—are considered **carcinogens;** people exposed to these materials are at risk for cancer.

a. unknown benefits
b. possible pollutants
c. cancer-causing substances
d. illegal substances

_______ 6. The stray dog was **submissive**—crouching, flattening its ears, and avoiding eye contact.

a. wild and excitable
b. yielding and meek
c. angry and aggressive
d. active and alert

_______ 7. To **substantiate** his theory, Watson offered experimental evidence, case study reports, testimony of patients, and a log of observational notes.

a. revise
b. uncover
c. withdraw
d. prove

_______ 8. Companies often use **nonmonetary** rewards to motivate their employees. For example, new job titles, compensatory time, privileges, and awards can be effective motivational tools.

a. private
b. not involving money
c. not required
d. natural and realistic

_______ 9. Many wills include at least one **codicil,** which is appended to the original will, such as an instruction about the disbursement of assets to stepchildren.

a. additional part
b. error
c. fee
d. request

_______ 10. **Unconditioned responses,** including heartbeat, blinking, and breathing, occur naturally in all humans.

a. traumas
b. medical terms
c. involuntary actions
d. learned skills

Copyright © 2012 by Pearson Education

Contrast Clues

It is sometimes possible to determine the meaning of an unknown word from a word or phrase in the context that has an opposite meaning. Notice, in the following sentence, how a word opposite in meaning to the boldfaced word provides a clue to its meaning:

Example

At the wedding reception, the parents of the bride seemed to *welcome* all the attention, whereas the groom's parents **eschewed** it by staying at their table.

Although you may not know the meaning of *eschewed,* you know that the parents who eschewed the attention were different from the ones who welcomed it. The word *whereas* suggests this. Since one couple enjoyed the attention, you can tell that the other did not; in fact, they avoided it. Thus, *eschew* means the opposite of *welcome;* that is, to avoid.

Words and phrases that suggest a contrasting word or phrase include *on the one hand, on the other hand, however, in contrast, unlike, but, despite, yet, rather,* and *nevertheless.*

Examples

Polytheism, the worship of more than one god, is common throughout India; however, **monotheism** is the most familiar religion to Americans.

Although the cottage appeared **derelict,** we discovered that an elderly man had been *living* in a portion of it.

My friend is quite **gregarious** at parties, whereas her husband is *extremely shy.*

The old man lived a **frugal** life, but he left a *generous inheritance* for his grandchildren.

EXERCISE 2-4 Understanding Contrast Context Clues

Directions: Using the contrast clues in each sentence, select the choice that best defines each boldfaced word.

_______ 1. Most members of Western society marry only one person at a time, but in other cultures **polygamy** is common and acceptable.

a. marriage to one person at a time
b. marriage to more than one person at a time
c. living together without marriage
d. divorce

_______ 2. During a drought, plants that are **indigenous** to the area typically do better than non-native plants.

a. native
c. dry
b. imported
d. growing

_______ 3. The turkey was overcooked and extremely dry, so we added gravy to make it more **palatable.**

a. cooked
b. edible
c. spicy
d. unpleasant

_______ 4. Although every effort was made to ensure that the test was fair, several students complained that the questions were **skewed.**

a. equal
b. too easy
c. biased
d. repeated

_______ 5. Everyone on the jury was persuaded of the defendant's innocence except for one juror, who remained **dubious.**

a. doubtful
b. convinced
c. curious
d. trusting

_______ 6. Despite the **secular** nature of public schools, many teachers begin each day by leading their students in a short prayer.

a. spiritual
b. educational
c. private
d. nonreligious

_______ 7. The author seemed **taciturn** during his television interview, but when I met him in person, he was quite sociable.

a. loud and talkative
b. anxious and upset
c. quiet and reserved
d. unhappy and distraught

_______ 8. While several aspects of the zoo's mission were still open to discussion, its commitment to preserving endangered species was **immutable.**

a. not decided
b. not subject to change
c. too expensive
d. ideal

_______ 9. Most humans are **omnivores,** in contrast to herbivores such as cattle and deer, which are more selective in their diets and feed mainly on plants.

a. those who eat plants only
b. those who eat meat only
c. those who eat plants and meat
d. those who are selective about what they eat

_______ 10. One of the school board candidates was **vehement** about the new truancy policy; his opponent, on the other hand, expressed her views calmly and quietly.

a. forceful
b. polite
c. confused
d. mistaken

Copyright © 2012 by Pearson Education

Inference Clues

Many times you can figure out the meaning of an unknown word by using logic and reasoning skills. For instance, look at the following sentence:

Example

Langston Hughes was a **protean** writer; although he is known mainly for his poetry, he also wrote plays, novels, short stories, children's books, songs, and essays.

You can see that Hughes wrote many different kinds of literature, and you could reason that *protean* means "producing a variety of work."

Examples

The editor would not allow the paper to go to press until certain passages were **expunged** from an article naming individuals involved in a political scandal.

The differences between the two photo processing centers were **negligible,** so we chose to go to the one closer to our house.

Since the hammering next door had been going on for days, we had become somewhat **inured** to it.

EXERCISE 2-5 Understanding Inference Context Clues

Directions: *Using logic and reasoning skills, select the choice that best defines each boldfaced word.*

_______ 1. Although my grandmother is 82, she is far from **infirm;** she is active, ambitious, and healthy.

a. weak
b. youthful
c. retired
d. capable

_______ 2. After leaving Manila, we flew over the Philippine **archipelago,** admiring the islands from our airplane window.

a. airport
b. government
c. group of islands
d. population

_______ 3. The senator has served eight **contiguous** six-year terms in office.

a. intensive
b. uninterrupted
c. unintended
d. disconnected

_______ 4. One **fallacy** about smokeless tobacco is that it is less harmful than smoking. In fact, smokeless tobacco contains ten times the amount of cancer-producing substances found in cigarettes.

a. truth
b. false belief
c. advertisement
d. advantage

_______ 5. The massive **influx** of refugees put such a severe strain on the country's economy that many of the refugees had to be relocated to other countries.

a. exit
b. arrival
c. money
d. assistance

_______ 6. After he was caught cheating, the student suffered the **ignominy** of being expelled from the school.

a. frequency
b. agreement
c. disgrace
d. attitude

_______ 7. By studying their genealogy, many people hope to **glean** knowledge about their family history and their ancestors.

a. change
b. gather
c. authorize
d. hide

_______ 8. Maria was able to **parlay** her computer skills into a successful career as a Web page designer.

a. use to her advantage
b. reduce job stress
c. talk about her talents
d. question her career choice

_______ 9. In her victory speech, the newly elected state representative thanked her supporters and pledged to be responsive to her **constituency.**

a. the residents of an electoral district
b. government officials
c. state representatives
d. personal interests

_______ 10. After tasting and eating most of seven different desserts, my appetite was completely **satiated.**

a. satisfied
b. unfulfilled
c. tempted
d. created

What Are Word Parts?

Use word parts

Although many people build their vocabulary word by word, studying word parts is a better and faster way to do it. For example, if you learn that *pre-* means "before," then you can begin to figure out hundreds of words that begin with *pre* (premarital, premix, prepay).

Copyright © 2012 by Pearson Education

myreadinglab

To practice using word parts, go to

> Study Plan
> Reading Skills
> Vocabulary

Suppose you came across the following sentence in a child psychology text:

Example

The parents thought their child was **unteachable.**

If you did not know the meaning of *unteachable,* how could you figure it out? Since there are no clues in the sentence context, you might decide to look up the word in a dictionary. An easier way, though, is to break the word into parts. Many words in the English language are made up of word parts called *prefixes, roots,* and *suffixes.* A **prefix** comes at the beginning of a word, and a **suffix** comes at the end of a word. The **root**—which contains a word's basic meaning—forms the middle.

Let's look at the word *unteachable* again and divide it into three parts: its prefix, root, and suffix.

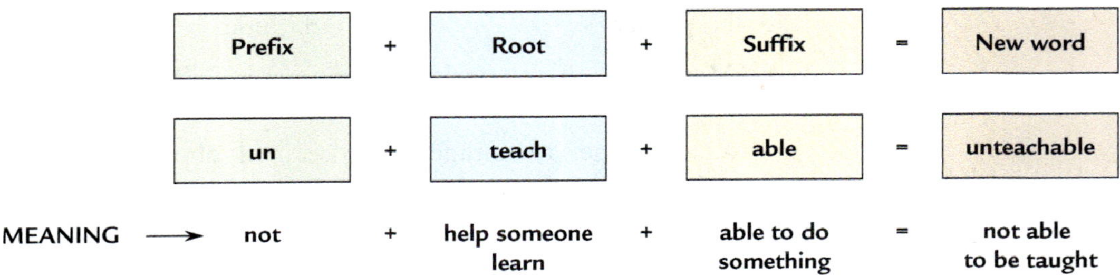

By using word parts, you can see that *unteachable* means "not able to be taught."

Example

My friend Josh is a **nonconformist.**

non- = not

conform = go along with others

-ist = one who does something

nonconformist = someone who does not go along with others

To use word parts effectively, you should learn some of the most common ones. The prefixes and roots listed in Tables 2-1 and 2-2 are a good place to start. By knowing just *some* of these prefixes and roots, you can figure out the meanings of thousands of words without looking them up in a dictionary. For instance, more than 10,000 words can begin with the prefix *non-*. Another common prefix, *pseudo-* (which means "false") is used in more than 400 words. As you can see, by learning only a few word parts, you can add many new words to your vocabulary.

Prefixes

Though some English words do not have a prefix, many of them do. Commonly used prefixes are listed in Table 2-1. Prefixes appear at the *beginnings* of words

TABLE 2-1 Common Prefixes

Prefix	Meaning	Sample Word
Prefixes Referring to Amount or Number		
mono/uni	one	monocle/unicycle
bi/di/du	two	bimonthly/divorce/duet
tri	three	triangle
quad	four	quadrant
quint/pent	five	quintet/pentagon
deci	ten	decimal
centi	hundred	centigrade
milli	thousand	milligram
micro	small	microscope
multi/poly	many	multipurpose/polygon
semi	half	semicircle
equi	equal	equidistant
Prefixes Meaning "Not" (Negative)		
a	not	asymmetrical
anti	against	antiwar
contra	against, opposite	contradict
dis	apart, away, not	disagree
in/il/ir/im	not	incorrect/illogical/ irreversible/impossible
mis	wrongly	misunderstand
non	not	nonfiction
un	not	unpopular
pseudo	false	pseudoscientific
Prefixes Giving Direction, Location, or Placement		
ab	away	absent
ad	toward	adhesive
ante/pre	before	antecedent/premarital
circum/peri	around	circumference/perimeter
com/col/con	with, together	compile/collide/convene
de	away, from	depart
dia	through	diameter
en/em	into, within	encase/embargo
ex/extra	from, out of, former	ex-wife/extramarital
hyper	over, excessive	hyperactive
inter	between	interpersonal
intro/intra	within, into, in	introduction
post	after	posttest
re	back, again	review
retro	backward	retrospect
sub	under, below	submarine
super	above, extra	supercharge
tele	far	telescope
thermo	heat	thermometer
trans	across, over	transcontinental

Copyright © 2012 by Pearson Education

and change the meaning of the root to which they are connected. For example, if you add the prefix *re-* to the word *read,* the word *reread* is formed, meaning "to read again." If *dis-* is added to the word *respect,* the word *disrespect* is formed, meaning "lack of respect."

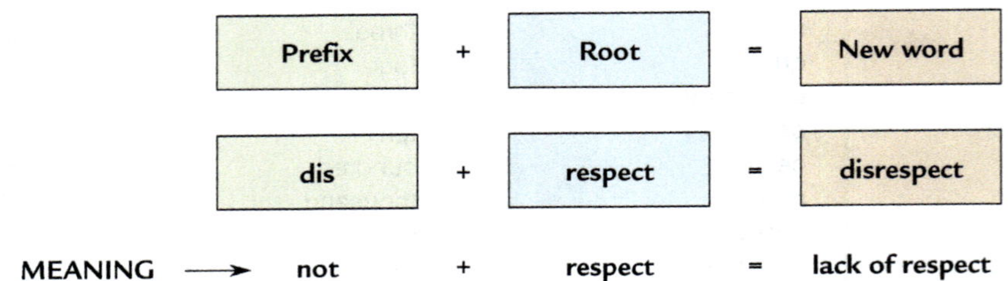

EXERCISE 2-6 Using Prefixes

Directions: *Using the list of common prefixes in Table 2-1, match each word in column A with its meaning in column B.*

	Column A	Column B
_______	1. inedible	a. using many tonalities in a musical composition
_______	2. bifocal	b. plan or arrange ahead of time
_______	3. premeditate	c. occurring after a glacial period
_______	4. antibacterial	d. not fit to be eaten
_______	5. hypertensive	e. to act against
_______	6. polytonality	f. having all sides or faces equal
_______	7. postglacial	g. having two focal lengths
_______	8. contravene	h. to cross beyond the limits
_______	9. transcend	i. having high blood pressure
_______	10. equilateral	j. destroying or inhibiting the growth of bacteria

EXERCISE 2-7 Understanding Prefixes

Directions: *Select a prefix from the box below to complete the word indicated in each of the following sentences.*

bi	ir	sub	circum	multi
tele	deca	post	dis	pseudo

1. We ________vented the problem by calculating in metrics.
2. Because of its ________standard performance on safety tests, the release of the new model car was delayed.
3. The new ________purpose building contained conference rooms, a dining area, and a gym.
4. The damaging effects of long-term exposure to the sun are ________reversible.
5. After surgery, patients should discuss their ________operative care with their physician.
6. A ________nary star system contains two stars.
7. In a ________thlon, each athlete competes in ten track and field events.
8. Samuel Langhorne Clemens is better known by his ________nym, Mark Twain.
9. Production of the camera was ________continued because of declining sales.
10. Amateur astronomers use a ________scope to view the sky.

Roots

Think of roots as being at the core of a word's meaning. You already know many roots—like *bio* in *biology* and *sen* in *insensitive*—because they are used in everyday speech. Thirty-one of the most common and useful roots are listed in Table 2-2. Learning the meanings of these roots will help you unlock the meanings of many words. For example, if you knew that the root *dic/dict* means "tell or say," then you would have a clue to the meanings of such words as *dictate* (to speak for someone to write down) or *dictionary* (a book that "tells" what words mean).

Copyright © 2012 by Pearson Education

TABLE 2-2 Common Roots

Root	Meaning	Sample Word
aud/audit	hear	audible/auditory
aster/astro	star	asteroid/astronaut
bene	good, well	benefit
bio	life	biology
cap	take, seize	captive
chron(o)	time	chronology
corp	body	corpse
cred	believe	incredible
dict/dic	tell, say	dictate/predict
duc/duct	lead	introduce/conduct
fact/fac	make, do	factory/factor
graph	write	telegraph
geo	earth	geophysics
log/logo/logy	study, thought	logic/psychology
mit/miss	send	permit/dismiss
mort/mor	die, death	immortal/mortician
path	feeling	sympathy
phono	sound, voice	telephone
photo	light	photosensitive
port	carry	transport
scop	seeing	microscope
scrib/script	write	scribe/inscription
sen/sent	feel	sensitive/sentiment
spec/spic/spect	look, see	retrospect/spectacle
tend/tent/tens	stretch or strain	tendon/tension
terr/terre	land, earth	terrain/territory
theo	god	theology
ven/vent	come	convention/venture
vert/vers	turn	invert/inverse
vis/vid	see	invisible/video
voc	call	vocation

When you see a word you don't know and you can't figure it out from the sentence context, follow these tips:

1. **Look for the root first.**
2. **Keep in mind that the spelling of a root may change a bit if it is combined with a suffix.**

   (Table 2-2 includes some examples of spelling changes.)

EXERCISE 2-8 Using Roots

Directions: *Using the list of common roots in Table 2-2, match each word in column A with its meaning in column B. To help you, the root in each word in column A is in italics.*

	Column A	Column B
_______	1. *spect*ator	a. happening at the same time
_______	2. *mort*ality	b. a scholarly piece of writing on a single subject
_______	3. syn*chron*ous	c. a device for looking at objects below the surface of water
_______	4. *aud*ial	d. the quality of being subject to death
_______	5. *dic*tion	e. related to the sense of hearing
_______	6. mono*graph*	f. a person who looks on at an event
_______	7. sub*terr*anean	g. centering on God
_______	8. hydro*scope*	h. beneath the earth's surface; underground
_______	9. *theo*centric	i. to call on for help or support
_______	10. in*voke*	j. choice and use of words in speech and writing

EXERCISE 2-9 Understanding Roots

Directions: *Select the word from the box below that best completes each of the following sentences. Refer to the list of roots in Table 2-2 if you need help.*

asters	benefactor	capacity	chronology	exportation
graphology	pathos	phototropic	sensor	transmit

1. The witness carefully described the _______________ of events to the detective.
2. Certain countries forbid the _______________ of endangered animals.
3. We planted _______________ because we loved their star-shaped flowers.

Copyright © 2012 by Pearson Education

4. Mosquitoes ______________ the West Nile virus from infected birds to humans.
5. Our skin serves as a ______________ for heat, cold, pressure, touch, and pain.
6. An anonymous ______________ donated $10,000 worth of books to the school library.
7. The final scene of the play was one of ______________ and sorrow.
8. The study of handwriting is known as ______________.
9. On the night of the debate, the town hall was filled to ______________.
10. Most plants are ______________; that is, they grow in the direction of their light source.

Suffixes

Suffixes are word *endings*. Think of them as add-ons that make a word fit grammatically into a sentence. For example, adding the suffix *y* to the noun *cloud* forms the adjective *cloudy*. The words *cloud* and *cloudy* are used in different ways:

Examples

The rain **cloud** above me looked threatening.

It was a **cloudy,** rainy weekend.

You can often form several different words from a single root by adding different suffixes.

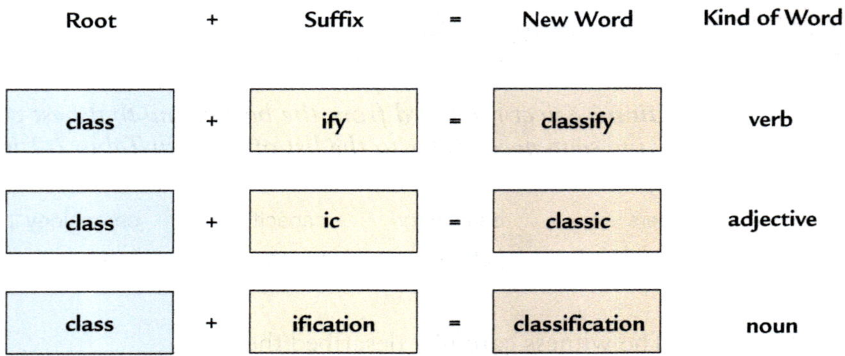

Root	+	Suffix	=	New Word	Kind of Word
class	+	ify	=	classify	verb
class	+	ic	=	classic	adjective
class	+	ification	=	classification	noun

As you know, when you find a word that you do not know, you should look for the root first. Then try to figure out what the word means with the suffix added. A list of common suffixes and their meanings appears in Table 2-3.

TABLE 2-3 Common Suffixes

Suffix	Sample Word	Suffix	Sample Word
Suffixes Referring to a State, Condition, or Quality			
able	touchable	ive	permissive
ance	assistance	like	childlike
ation	confrontation	ment	amazement
ence	reference	ness	kindness
ful	playful	ous	jealous
ible	tangible	ty	loyalty
ion	discussion	y	creamy
ity	superiority		
Suffixes Meaning "One Who"			
an	Italian	ent	resident
ant	participant	er	teacher
ee	referee	ist	activist
eer	engineer	or	advisor
Suffixes Meaning "Pertaining to or Referring to"			
al	autumnal	hood	brotherhood
ship	friendship	ward	homeward

Sometimes you may find that the spelling of the root word changes because of the suffix. For instance, a final *e* may be dropped, a final consonant may be doubled, or a final *y* may be changed to *i*. Keep these possibilities in mind when you're trying to identify a root word.

Examples

David's article was a **compilation** of facts.

Root: *compil(e)*

Suffix: *-ation*

New word: *compilation* (something that has been compiled, or put together, in an orderly way)

We were concerned with the **legality** of our decision about our taxes.

Root: *legal*

Suffix: *-ity*

New word: *legality* (involving legal matters)

Our college is one of the most **prestigious** in the state.

Root: *prestig(e)*

Suffix: *-ious*

New word: *prestigious* (having prestige or distinction)

Copyright © 2012 by Pearson Education

EXERCISE 2-10 Using Suffixes

***Directions:** From each list of four words, select the choice that best completes the sentence that follows. Write your answer in the space provided.*

1. *uniforms, uniformity, uniformed, uniforming*

   The ______________ of a law requires that it be applied to all relevant groups without bias.

2. *competed, competitor, competition, competitive*

   When food sources are not large enough to support all the organisms in a habitat, environmental ______________ occurs.

3. *effective, effected, effectively, effectiveness*

   When evaluating a piece of art, consider its ______________—how well the artist's message has been conveyed to the audience.

4. *instruction, instructor, instructive, instructs*

   The lecture on Islamic traditions was ______________.

5. *attendees, attendance, attends, attending*

   All ______________ at the conference received a complimentary tote bag.

6. *inherit, inheritable, inherited, inheritance*

   The university was stunned by the size of its ______________ from one of its former students.

7. *driven, driver, drivable, drivability*

   After the accident, our car was not ______________ so we called a tow truck.

8. *participate, participation, participant, participative*

   Students in the workshop were graded partly on their ______________ in class discussions.

9. *identify, identifier, identifiable, identification*

   Taxonomy is the branch of science concerned with the ______________ and classification of species.

10. *internship, internist, interned, interning*

During my senior year in college, I accepted an ________________ at the local newspaper.

Thinking Critically About Vocabulary

Think critically about vocabulary

Words have incredible power. On the positive side, words can inspire, comfort, and educate. At the other end of the spectrum, words can inflame, annoy, or deceive.

Professional writers understand that word choices greatly influence the reader, and they choose the words that will help them achieve their goals. Critical thinkers understand the nuances of words and how they affect the reader.

To understand the nuances (shades of meaning) of words, it is important to understand the difference between denotation and connotation.

Denotation and Connotation

A word's **denotation** is its literal meaning or definition. Even the simplest of words has a denotation. For example, the denotation of *frugal* is "thrifty." Many words have more than one denotation; for example the denotation of *bat* could mean a "winged nocturnal mammal" or a "rounded stick used to hit baseballs."

A word's **connotation** is the set of additional associations that it takes on. Often, connotations have strong emotions connected to them. For example, the word *frugal* almost always has a positive connotation. Who wouldn't want to be described as *frugal*? But saying that someone is *cheap* can carry quite a negative connotation, as few people would want to be described as *cheap*.

Connotations can help a writer paint a picture to influence the reader's opinion. Thus a writer who wishes to be kind to an overweight politician might describe him as "pleasingly plump" (which carries an almost pleasant connotation) or even "quite overweight" (which is a statement of fact that remains mostly neutral). However, a writer who wishes to be negative about the same politician might describe him as "morbidly obese."

The point is: as a reader, you are likely to be influenced by the author's word choice, so always pay attention to words and their connotations. Ask yourself: What descriptive words does the writer use, and how do they affect me?

Copyright © 2012 by Pearson Education

EXERCISE 2-11 Understanding Connotations

Directions: *Practice understanding connotations by answering the following questions.*

_______ 1. One of your friends owns a rusty old car that you think should be brought to the junkyard. Which word or phrase would you use to describe it?

a. a hot rod   b. a sweet ride   c. a clunker

_______ 2. Another friend owns a 1970 Mustang convertible that's in perfect condition. Which word would you use to describe the Mustang?

a. classic   b. old   c. nostalgic

_______ 3. The Rolex company wants to use a word with positive connotations to advertise its expensive watches. Which word would you advise Rolex to use?

a. wristwatch   b. clock   c. timepiece

EXERCISE 2-12 Analyzing Connotative Meanings

Directions: *Read the following excerpt from a college textbook and answer the questions that follow.*

> Whenever society changes, so do our lives. Consider the information explosion. When you graduate from college, you will most likely do some form of "knowledge work." Instead of working in a factory, you will manage information or design, sell, or service products. The type of work you do has profound implications for your life. It produces social networks, nurtures attitudes, and even affects how you view yourself and the world.
>
> —Henslin, *Sociology: A Down-to-Earth Approach,* p. 399

1. Why does the author use the word *explosion* to describe the information society? What are the word's denotation and connotation?

____

____

2. The author uses the words *profound* and *nurture*. What are the connotations of these words? How do they make you feel as you read the paragraph?

____

____

____

TEXTBOOK CHALLENGE

TIPS for Reading in the Sciences

When reading science textbooks, pay attention to

- **Scientific terminology**. Learning subject-specific vocabulary will allow you to read, speak, and write in the language of the discipline.
- **Cause and effect**. Your science textbook and course will focus on examining how and why events happen.
- **Scientific method**. Throughout the class, your instructor will expect you to observe and question what you are learning so you can analyze problems, propose solutions, and provide explanations.

Part A: Analyzing a Textbook Excerpt

This excerpt was taken from a biology textbook. Read the excerpt and follow the directions on p. 73.

14.7 What Causes Extinction?

Every living organism must eventually die, and the same is true of species. Just like individuals, species are "born" (through the process of speciation), persist for some period of time, and then perish. The ultimate fate of any species is **extinction,** the death of the last of its members. In fact, at least 99.9% of all the species that have ever existed are now extinct. The natural course of evolution, as revealed by fossils, is continual turnover of species as new ones arise and old ones become extinct.

The immediate cause of extinction is probably always environmental change, in either the living or the nonliving parts of the environment. Two major environmental factors that may drive a species to extinction are competition among species and habitat destruction.

Endangered by habitat destruction and loss of genetic diversity Only a few hundred Sumatran rhinoceroses remain.

Interactions with Other Species May Drive a Species to Extinction

Interactions such as competition and predation serve as agents of natural selection. In some cases, these same interactions can lead to extinction rather than to adaptation.

Organisms compete for limited resources in all environments. If a species' competitors evolve superior adaptations and the species doesn't evolve fast enough to keep up, it may become extinct. A particularly striking example of extinction through competition occurred in South America, beginning about 2.5 million years ago. At that time, the isthmus of Panama rose above sea level and formed a land bridge between North America and South America. After the previously separated continents were connected, the mammal species that had evolved in isolation on each continent were able to mix. Many species did indeed expand their ranges, as North American mammals moved southward and South American mammals moved northward. As they moved, each species encountered resident species that occupied the same kinds of habitats and exploited the same kinds of resources. The ultimate result of the ensuing competition was that the North American species diversified and underwent an adaptive radiation that displaced the vast majority of the South American species, many of which went extinct. Clearly, evolution had bestowed on the North American species a set of adaptations that enabled their descendants to exploit resources more efficiently and effectively than their South American counterparts could.

Habitat Change and Destruction Are the Leading Causes of Extinction

Habitat change, both contemporary and prehistoric, is the single greatest cause of extinctions. Present-day habitat destruction due to human activities is proceeding at a rapid pace. Many biologists believe that we are presently in the midst of the fastest-paced and most widespread episode of species extinction in the history of life on Earth. Loss of tropical forests is especially devastating to species diversity. As many as half the species presently on Earth may be lost during the next 50 years as the tropical forests that contain them are cut for timber and to clear land for cattle and crops.

—Audesirk, Audesirk, and Byers, *Biology: Life on Earth,* pp. 249–251

1. **Preview.** Preview the reading using the guidelines on p. 7 and then answer the following questions.
   a. What is extinction?
   b. What are two causes of extinction?
2. **SQ3R.** Write at least three questions for the Q step of SQ3R. Answer them after completing the reading.
3. **Textbook Features.** Study the photo on p. 72. What does this photograph add to the reading?
4. **Vocabulary.**
   Identify the important new terms that are introduced in the reading.
5. **Applying Chapter Skills.**
   a. Define each of the following words and phrases as used in the reading based on context and/or using a dictionary.
   persist (par. 1), *perish* (par. 1), *isthmus* (par. 4), *diversity* (par. 5), *adaptive radiation* (par. 4)
   b. Define each of the following words as used in the reading using word parts and/or a dictionary.
   speciation (par. 1), *interactions* (par. 3), *predation* (par. 3), *diversified* (par. 4), *displaced* (par. 4)
6. **Essay Question.** Write an answer to the following essay question. To test your memory, write it without referring to the excerpt.
   Explain how extinction occurs, offering two causes with details.
7. **Thinking Critically.** Use your critical thinking skills to answer each of the following questions.
   a. What connotative meaning for the word *extinction* did you have before you read this selection? Was it positive or negative? What connotation do the authors give to it? Do they regard it as positive or negative?
   b. If extinction is a process that has happened for millions of years, why should there be concern about extinction that may be under way in our current time period?
   c. Draw an analogy to extinction caused by competition by writing about something you are interested in, such as competition in the music business, in sports, or in fashion. Explain how competition functions in that environment and how the process plays out. How is it similar to or different from species extinction by competition?
   d. According to this selection, 99.9 percent of all species that have ever existed are now extinct. What does this say about survival of humans? Can we beat the odds? If so, what do you think we need to do?

Part B: Your College Textbook

Choose a chapter that you have been assigned to read in a textbook for one of your other courses. Choose one page and circle new vocabulary and underline the clues to meaning.

Copyright © 2012 by Pearson Education

SELF-TEST SUMMARY

To test yourself, cover up the Answer column with a sheet of paper and answer each question listed in the left column. Evaluate each of your answers as you work by sliding the paper down and comparing your answer with what is printed in the Answer column.

	Question	Answer
GOAL 1	What is context?	Taken together, all of the words in a reading provide context. Surrounding words help you understand the meaning of individual words.
GOAL 2	What are the types of context clues?	Context clues include definition, synonym, example, contrast, and inference clues.
GOAL 3	Why are word parts important?	Learning basic roots, prefixes, and suffixes allows you to determine the meaning of words you might not otherwise know.
GOAL 4	What is the difference between denotation and connotation?	Denotation refers to a word's basic definition. Connotation refers to emotional meaning a word takes on in certain contexts.

NAME ________________ SECTION ________________

DATE ________________ SCORE ________________

PRACTICE TEST 2-1

Context and Word Parts

Directions: *Using context clues and/or word parts, select the choice that best defines the boldfaced word in each sentence.*

_____ 1. It is more efficient to take lecture notes in your own words than to try to record the lecture **verbatim.**

a. word for word
b. using abbreviations
c. using verbs
d. using an outline

_____ 2. In some societies, young children are on the **periphery** instead of in the center of family life.

a. focus
b. inside
c. edge
d. middle

_____ 3. Amelia enjoys all **equestrian** sports, including jumping, riding, and racing horses.

a. group
b. indoor
c. organized
d. horseback

_____ 4. Despite his love of the country, he **renounced** his citizenship when war broke out.

a. kept
b. publicized
c. gave up
d. applied for

_____ 5. After we bought a grill on the Internet, we were **inundated** with e-mail offers for related items.

a. sold
b. flooded
c. convinced
d. investigated

_____ 6. To treat the inflammation, the patient must receive shots **intramuscularly.**

a. within the muscle
b. next to the muscle
c. between muscles
d. away from the muscle

_____ 7. The students reacted to the extra assignment with **incredulity.**

a. relief
b. indifference
c. excitement
d. disbelief

Copyright © 2012 by Pearson Education

_____ 8. The poll was conducted by a **nonpartisan** group based in Maryland.

a. associated with several political parties

b. not associated with a political party

c. locally funded

d. volunteer

_____ 9. A key part of the experiment involved **photosensitive** cells.

a. responsive to light

b. responsive to heat

c. responsive to sound

d. responsive to color

_____ 10. The surface of the moon appears to be **abiotic.**

a. without heat

b. without life

c. producing heat

d. producing life

NAME ______________ SECTION ______________

DATE ______________ SCORE ______________

PRACTICE TEST 2-2

Context and Word Parts

Directions: *Using context clues and/or word parts, select the choice that best defines each boldfaced word in the following paragraphs.*

If you have ever tried to perform heavy manual labor on a hot summer day, you may have become weak and dizzy as a result. If your **exertions** were severe, you may have even collapsed and lost **consciousness** momentarily. If this has happened to you, then you have experienced *heat exhaustion.* Heat exhaustion is a **consequence** of the body's effort to regulate its temperature—in particular, its efforts to get rid of **excess** heat. When the body must get rid of a large quantity of heat, **massive** quantities of sweat can be produced, leading to a significant **reduction** in blood volume. In addition, blood flow to the skin increases markedly, which **diverts** blood from other areas of the body. Together, these changes produce a reduction in blood pressure, which reduces blood flow to the brain and **precipitates** the symptoms just described.

A far more serious condition is *heat stroke,* in which the body's temperature rises out of control due to failure of the **thermoregulatory** system. The skin of individuals experiencing heat stroke has a flushed appearance but will also be dry, in contrast to the **profuse** sweating of heat exhaustion. If someone is experiencing heat stroke, immediate medical attention is of the utmost importance.

—adapted from Germann and Stanfield, *Principles of Human Physiology,* p. 9

______ 1. exertions
- a. temperature
- b. conditions
- c. breaks
- d. efforts

______ 2. consciousness
- a. sense of right and wrong
- b. carefulness
- c. state of awareness
- d. insensitivity

______ 3. consequence
- a. cause
- b. result
- c. difference
- d. complication

______ 4. excess
- a. quality
- b. normal
- c. scarce
- d. extra

______ 5. massive
- a. huge
- b. harmless
- c. minor
- d. immediate

Copyright © 2012 by Pearson Education

______ 6. reduction

a. increase
b. decrease
c. strengthening
d. improvement

______ 7. diverts

a. redirects
b. forms
c. continues
d. conceals

______ 8. precipitates

a. prevents
b. follows
c. brings on
d. alters

______ 9. thermoregulatory

a. controlling hearing
b. controlling vision
c. controlling feeling
d. controlling heat

______ 10. profuse

a. dry
b. scarce
c. extensive
d. healthy

NAME ______________________ SECTION ______________

DATE ______________________ SCORE ______________

MASTERY TEST 2-1

Context and Word Parts

Directions: *Using context clues and/or word parts, select the word from the box on the next page that best defines each of the boldfaced words in the following paragraphs. Not all of the words in the box will be used.*

Probiotics: What Are They, Can They Improve Gastrointestinal Health, and Should You Eat Them?

1 The last time you ate a cup of creamy, fruity yogurt, did you think about the fact that you were also eating *bacteria?* Don't worry—these microorganisms won't harm you; they'll help your body to function. They are one of a group of substances called ***probiotics:*** live microorganisms found in, or added to, fermented foods that optimize the bacterial environment of the large intestine.

2 In the United States foods that contain probiotics include fortified milk, yogurt, and a creamy beverage called *kefir* that is made from fermented milk. Probiotics are also sold in supplement form.

3 When a person consumes a product containing probiotics, the bacteria **adhere** to the intestinal wall for a few days, exerting their beneficial actions. Because their activity is **short-lived,** they probably need to be consumed on a daily basis to be most effective. The exact means by which probiotics benefit human health is currently being researched. One theory is that they increase the number and activity of **immune cells** that help us fight infections. However, although they appear to improve immune function, there is still limited research on how this occurs.

4 Although the research supporting the potential of probiotics to successfully treat these conditions is promising, more research is needed before we can identify with certainty the **circumstances** under which probiotics **enhance** human health.

5 Bacteria only live for a short time. This means that foods and supplements containing probiotics have a limited shelf life and must be properly stored and **consumed** within a relatively brief period of time to confer **maximal** benefit. In general, refrigerated foods containing probiotics have a **shelf-life** of 3 to 6 weeks, whereas the shelf life for supplements containing probiotics is about 12 months. However, because the probiotic content in refrigerated foods is much more stable than that in supplements, the more **perishable** forms may be a better health bet.

—Thompson et al., *Nutrition* p. 54

Copyright © 2012 by Pearson Education

eaten	destroyed	brief
live microorganisms in fermented foods	alternate days	improve
bacteria found only in supplements	situations	useful period
destroyed	able to decay	cells that fight infection
heaviest	highest	stick

1. probiotics (par. 1) ______________________
2. adhere (par. 3) ______________________
3. short-lived (par. 3) ______________________
4. immune cells (par. 3) ______________________
5. circumstances (par. 4) ______________________
6. enhance (par. 4) ______________________
7. consumed (par. 5) ______________________
8. maximal (par. 5) ______________________
9. shelf-life (par. 5) ______________________
10. perishable (par. 5) ______________________

NAME ______________________ SECTION ______________________

DATE ______________________ SCORE ______________________

MASTERY TEST 2-2

Context and Word Parts

Directions: *Using context clues and/or word parts, select the word from the box below that best defines each of the boldfaced words in the following paragraph. Not all of the words in the box will be used.*

Thomas Jefferson had no desire to surround himself with pomp and ceremony; the excessive formality and punctilio of the Washington and Adams administrations had been **distasteful** to him. From the moment of his election, he played down the **ceremonial** aspects of the presidency. In the White House he often wore a **frayed** coat and carpet slippers, even to receive the representatives of foreign powers when they arrived, **resplendent** with silk ribbons and a sense of their own importance, to present their **credentials.** At social affairs he paid little **heed** to the status and **seniority** of his guests. The guests, carefully chosen to make **congenial** groups, were seated at a round table to encourage general conversation, and the food and wine were first-class. These were **ostensibly** social occasions—shop talk was avoided—yet they paid large political **dividends.**

—adapted from Carnes and Garraty, *The American Nation,* pp. 175–176

qualifications	dazzlingly impressive	related to formal occasions
worn out	unpleasant	rank based on length of service
seemingly	agreeable	benefits
attention	drawbacks	up-to-date

1. distasteful ______________________
2. ceremonial ______________________
3. frayed ______________________
4. resplendent ______________________
5. credentials ______________________
6. heed ______________________
7. seniority ______________________
8. congenial ______________________
9. ostensibly ______________________
10. dividends ______________________

Copyright © 2012 by Pearson Education

MASTERY TEST 2-3

NAME ______________________ SECTION ______________________

DATE ______________________ SCORE ______________________

READING SELECTION

Unfair Advantage

Teresa Audesirk, Gerald Audesirk, and Bruce E. Byers

This essay describes the illegal use of blood doping by some athletes attempting to gain a competitive edge in bicycle racing. Read it to find out what blood doping is, how it works, and the issues surrounding its use.

Vocabulary Preview

These are some of the difficult words in this essay. The definitions here will help you if you can't figure out the meanings from the sentence context or word parts.

arcane (par. 2) known or understood by only a few people; mysterious

molecules (par. 5) the smallest particles of an element or compound that have all the properties of that substance

glucose (par. 6) a monosaccharide sugar occurring in most plant and animal tissue; an important source of cellular energy

fiasco (par. 8) a complete failure

metabolism (par. 8) the total of all chemical reactions that occur in the body

1 On a sunny July morning in 1998, the members of the Festina bicycle racing team, the top-rated team in the world, sat in a French café. Nearby, dozens of other professional bicyclists made their final preparations for the impending start of the day's segment of the grueling Tour de France race. The Festina riders, however, would not be joining the race. Hours earlier, the entire team had been expelled from the Tour de France for the offense of blood doping.

2 The dramatic expulsion of top athletes from the world's premier bicycle race focused attention on the arcane practice of blood doping. By using blood-doping techniques, some athletes try to gain a competitive edge. But what is blood doping, and how does it enhance athletic performance?

3 Blood doping increases a person's physical endurance by increasing the capacity of the blood to carry oxygen. One crude method for accomplishing this goal is to simply inject extra red blood cells into the bloodstream. Red blood cells transport oxygen to the body's tissues, so simply adding more of them is a straightforward way of increasing the amount of oxygen that reaches the tissues. In recent years, however, blood-doping athletes have increasingly turned to injections of erythropoietin (Epo) as a more effective approach to increasing blood oxygen.

4 Epo is a protein molecule that is present in a normal human body, where it functions as a chemical messenger that stimulates bone marrow to produce more red blood cells. Under normal circumstances, the body produces just enough Epo to ensure that red blood cells are replaced as they age and die. An injection of extra Epo, however, can stimulate the production of a huge number of extra red blood cells. The extra cells greatly increase the oxygen-carrying capacity of the blood. Unfortunately, the excess blood cells also thicken the blood and make it harder to move through blood vessels, so those who inject Epo suffer increased risk of heart failure.

5 Why would professional athletes take such a risk to get more oxygen molecules into their bloodstreams? How does extra oxygen increase endurance? The answers to those questions lie in the role of oxygen in supplying energy to muscle cells.

6 Human cells most efficiently extract energy from glucose when an ample supply of oxygen is available to them. The aim of blood-doping cyclists, then, is to extend as long as possible the period in which their muscle cells have access to oxygen. During a difficult hill-climb, a cyclist who has doped his blood with erythropoietin may be able to pedal efficiently, his muscle cells using the Krebs cycle to turn out abundant ATP. At the same time, his "clean" competitor may labor painfully, leg muscles laden with lactate from fermentation.

7 The extra endurance that Epo supplies can tempt elite athletes to risk their health for an extra edge, despite the penalties that await those who are caught using a banned substance. The temptation may be especially large in the case of Epo. Because this substance forms naturally in the human body, its abuse is hard to detect; standard drug-screening procedures cannot distinguish between natural Epo and that injected in blood doping. In fact, the Festina team that was banned from the Tour de France was caught not by any blood or urine test, but only because a large supply of Epo was found in the team's car at a border crossing.

Copyright © 2012 by Pearson Education

8 Since the Festina fiasco, however, researchers have worked hard at developing better tests for blood doping with Epo. A new urine test for Epo was introduced for the summer Olympics. This test detects a subtle chemical difference between the breakdown products of natural Epo and those of the manufactured version that is used in doping injections. Olympic officials, however, are not totally confident in the accuracy of the new urine test, and they use it only in conjunction with blood tests that screen for unusually high density of blood cells. Only athletes who fail both tests are disqualified. Meanwhile, researchers continue to explore the chemistry of Epo metabolism in hope of discovering a definitive test for blood doping.

Directions: *Select the choice that best completes each of the following statements.*

CHECKING YOUR COMPREHENSION

_______ 1. The main point of the reading is that

a. bicyclists in the Tour de France have been caught using illegal drugs.

b. the drug Epo is a naturally occurring substance that should not be banned in athletic competitions.

c. researchers are attempting to create a safe and legal form of Epo.

d. athletes risk penalties and their health by using Epo to enhance their performance in races.

_______ 2. The main idea of paragraph 3 is that

a. red blood cells transport oxygen to the body's tissues.

b. blood doping enhances physical endurance by increasing blood oxygen.

c. blood-doping techniques are complicated and ineffective.

d. the drug Epo stimulates the production of red blood cells.

_______ 3. The Festina bicycling team was banned from the 1998 Tour de France because

a. a blood test revealed that members of the team had used steroids.

b. a urine test revealed that members of the team had used Epo.

c. a member of the team was caught injecting Epo.

d. the team's car was found to contain Epo.

_______ 4. Athletes use Epo (or blood doping) in order to

a. extend the period in which their muscle cells have access to oxygen.
b. decrease the amount of oxygen that reaches their tissues.
c. reduce their risk of heart failure during a strenuous race.
d. decrease the period in which their muscle cells require oxygen.

_______ 5. Before a race, athletes introduce Epo into their bodies typically by

a. injecting a manufactured version of Epo.
b. swallowing a protein supplement that contains Epo.
c. rubbing an ointment containing Epo on their legs.
d. working out to increase the quantities of naturally occurring Epo in their bodies.

USING CONTEXT CLUES AND WORD PARTS

_______ 6. In paragraph 1, **impending** means

a. historic.
b. about to happen.
c. dangerous.
d. unofficial.

_______ 7. In paragraph 1, **grueling** means

a. shocking.
b. pleasant.
c. exhausting.
d. training.

_______ 8. In paragraph 2, **expulsion** means

a. elimination.
b. attendance.
c. participation.
d. reception.

Copyright © 2012 by Pearson Education

______ 9. In paragraph 3, **capacity** means
a. decrease.
b. production.
c. changeable.
d. ability.

______ 10. In paragraph 6, **laden** means
a. heavy or filled.
b. necessary.
c. strong and forceful.
d. missing.

______ 11. In paragraph 7, **elite** means
a. amateur.
b. educated.
c. top quality.
d. worst.

______ 12. In paragraph 7, **banned** means
a. unnatural.
b. large quantity.
c. forbidden.
d. inefficient.

______ 13. In paragraph 8, **subtle** means
a. strange.
b. hardly noticeable.
c. physical.
d. obvious.

______ 14. In paragraph 8, **density** means
a. concentration.
b. quality.
c. variation.
d. similarity.

_______ 15. In paragraph 8, **disqualified** means
   a. allowed.
   b. examined.
   c. competed.
   d. denied participation.

REVIEWING DIFFICULT VOCABULARY

Directions: *Complete each of the following sentences by inserting a word from the Vocabulary Preview on page 82 in the space provided. Use each word only once.*

16. The most common monosaccharides, or simple sugars, include __________________, fructose, and galactose.
17. The dinner party was a __________________: the guests were late, the food was overcooked, and the ceiling began to leak halfway through dinner.
18. After describing several __________________ economic theories, the professor moved on to the more familiar and well-known Keynesian theories.
19. When an animal hibernates, its __________________ slows down and its temperature drops.
20. In the process of diffusion, __________________ of a substance spread evenly through a gas, liquid, or solid.

THINKING CRITICALLY

1. How might this essay be different if the authors included quotes from athletes? What information or positions might the athletes offer?
2. What conclusions can you draw about competition in the world of professional sports based on this essay?
3. Explain the tone and message of the photograph.

Copyright © 2012 by Pearson Education

QUESTIONS FOR DISCUSSION

1. In what other sports is the use of drugs to enhance performance an issue?
2. Do you think all athletes should be screened for drug use before each performance? Discuss the advantages and disadvantages of such a policy.
3. Why do athletes resort to the use of drugs to enhance their performance? Discuss whether athletics have become too competitive.

WRITING ACTIVITIES

1. Brainstorm a list of characteristics of professional athletes. Consider whether these characteristics are appropriate for national heroes or for role models of aspiring athletes. Write a paragraph summarizing your findings.
2. In a letter to the captain of the Festina bicycle racing team, explain your reactions to his team's use of blood doping.
3. Each sport, special interest, or hobby has its own special language. Visit the White House's Web page on drugs and sports http://www.whitehousedrugpolicy.gov/prevent/sports/doping.html.

   Write a paragraph that summarizes the information, including a definition of doping and examples of illegal substances and their effects.

CHAPTER 2

Strengthening Your Vocabulary

RECORDING YOUR PROGRESS

Test	Number Right		Score
Practice Test 2-1	______	× 10 =	______%
Practice Test 2-2	______	× 10 =	______%
Mastery Test 2-1	______	× 10 =	______%
Mastery Test 2-2	______	× 10 =	______%
Mastery Test 2-3	______	× 5 =	______%

GETTING MORE PRACTICE myreadinglab

To get more practice with Active Reading, go to http://www.myreadinglab.com and click on

- Study Plan
- Reading Skills
- Vocabulary

EVALUATING YOUR PROGRESS myreadinglab

To measure your progress after reading and viewing the information in the Review Materials section, complete the Practices and Tests in the Activities section. You can check your scores by clicking on the Gradebook tab.

Then, based on your performance in this chapter and/or on the MyReadingLab Practices and Tests, write your own evaluation.

YOUR EVALUATION: ______________________________

____

____

____

____

Copyright © 2012 by Pearson Education

THINKING ABOUT

Main Ideas

Look at the photograph on this page. Write a sentence describing what is happening in the photograph.

The sentence you have written states the main idea—or main point—the photo conveys. However, unless you interviewed the persons shown in the photograph, you would not know the details of the situation: why the man was being arrested, why the FBI was involved, or where the arrest took place.

CHAPTER 3

Identifying and Analyzing Main Ideas

Why Are Main Ideas Important?

GOAL 1
Understand main ideas

To practice identifying and analyzing main ideas, go to
> Study Plan
> Reading Skills
> Main Idea

The way we organize and present ideas in writing is similar to the way we present them when speaking. When we speak, we speak in groups of sentences. Seldom does our conversation consist of single, isolated sentences. For example, you probably would *not* simply say to a friend "I think you are making a mistake if you rent that apartment you just looked at." Instead, you would support your statement by offering reasons why the apartment is undesirable or describing what is wrong with it—poor location, high price, and so forth. Similarly, in writing, we groups ideas into paragraphs. A **paragraph** is a group of sentences that explain or develop one idea.

The one general subject a whole paragraph is about is called the **topic.** The most important point a whole paragraph makes is called the **main idea.** For example, read the following paragraph:

> Today, super-sized meals are the norm at many restaurants. Biscuits and gravy, huge steaks, and plate-filling meals are popular fare. Consider the 25-ounce prime rib dinner served at a local steak chain. At nearly 3,000 calories and 150 grams of fat for the meat alone, this meal both slams shut arteries and adds on pounds. Add a baked potato with sour cream and/or butter, a salad loaded with creamy salad dressing, and fresh bread with real butter, and

LEARNING GOALS

GOAL 1
Understand main ideas

GOAL 2
Grasp the difference between general and specific ideas

GOAL 3
Identify the topic of a paragraph

GOAL 4
Locate main ideas

GOAL 5
Understand central thoughts

GOAL 6
Think critically about main ideas

Copyright © 2012 by Pearson Education

the meal may surpass the 5,000-calorie mark and ring in at close to 300 grams of fat. In other words, it exceeds what most adults should eat in two days!

—Snow, *Akron Beacon Journal*, 2000.

In this paragraph, the topic is "super-sized meals," and the main idea is that "super-sized meals have become common in many restaurants." Here the main point of the paragraph is stated in the first sentence. The rest of the sentences then support or back up the main idea. As you will see later, however, the main idea doesn't always come first.

Distinguishing Between General and Specific Ideas

GOAL 2
Grasp the difference between general and specific ideas

To identify topics and main ideas in paragraphs, it helps to understand the difference between general and specific. A *general* idea applies to a large number of individual items. The term *television programs* is general because it refers to a large collection of shows—soap operas, sports specials, sitcoms, and so on. A *specific* idea or term is more detailed or particular. It refers to an individual item. The term *reality TV,* for example, is more specific than the word *program.* The title *Survivor* is even more specific.

Examples	*General*:	Cakes	*General*:	Vegetables
	Specific:	chocolate	*Specific*:	carrots
		spice		corn
		angel food		peas
	General:	Continents	*General*:	Parts of Speech
	Specific:	Asia	*Specific*:	noun
		Africa		verb
		Australia		adjective

EXERCISE 3-1 Using General Terms

Directions: Select the choice that represents the most general term in each group of words.

_______ 1. a. American literature c. anthropology
b. college courses d. biochemistry

_______ 2. a. horror films b. westerns c. movies d. comedies

_______ 3. a. computers b. laptops c. notebooks d. mainframes

_______ 4. a. parkas b. windbreakers c. coats d. raincoats

_______ 5. a. station wagons b. vehicles c. SUVs d. minivans

_______ 6. a. volleyball b. soccer c. football d. sports

_______ 7. a. hardbacks b. e-books c. books d. paperbacks

_______ 8. a. brothers b. grandmothers c. relatives d. cousins

_______ 9. a. math b. geometry c. algebra d. calculus

_______ 10. a. pines b. trees c. maples d. oaks

EXERCISE 3-2 Using General and Specific Terms

Directions: *For each list of items, select the choice that best describes that grouping.*

_______ 1. dodo bird, Tyrannosaurus rex, woolly mammoth, stegosaurus

a. extinct animals c. endangered animals
b. animals d. zoo animals

_______ 2. single-parent, divorced, two-career, married

a. children c. families
b. incomes d. societies

_______ 3. for money, for experience, to meet people

a. reasons to attend a party
b. reasons to get a part-time job
c. reasons to apply for loans
d. reasons to date

_______ 4. U.S. Constitution, Bill of Rights, Federalist Papers, Twenty-fifth Amendment

a. policies c. historical documents
b. historical events d. party politics

_______ 5. Mars, Saturn, Jupiter, Mercury

a. asteroids c. galaxies
b. solar systems d. planets

Now that you are familiar with the difference between general and specific, you will be able to use these concepts in the rest of the chapter.

Copyright © 2012 by Pearson Education

Locating the Topic

Identify the topic of a paragraph

You already know that the topic is the general subject of an entire paragraph. Every sentence in a paragraph in some way discusses or explains this topic. To find the topic of a paragraph, ask yourself: What is the one idea the author is discussing throughout the paragraph? Read the following paragraph with that question in mind:

> The major motive for excuse making seems to be to maintain our self-esteem, to project a positive image to ourselves and to others. Excuses are also offered to reduce stress that may be created by a bad performance. We feel that if we can offer an excuse—especially a good one that is accepted by those around us—it will lessen the negative reaction and the subsequent stress that accompanies poor performance.
>
> —DeVito, *Human Communication: The Basic Course,* p. 178

In this example, the author is discussing one topic—making excuses—throughout the paragraph. Notice that the word *excuse* is used several times. As you can see, the repeated use of a word often serves as a clue to the topic.

EXERCISE 3-3 Locating Topics

Directions: *After reading each of the following paragraphs, select the choice that best represents the topic of the paragraph.*

_______ 1. You've probably heard that older men die before older women virtually everywhere in the world. In the United States, women are expected to live an average of 80.4 years, while men live only 75.2 years. Sociologists attribute many factors to this trend. For example, men have higher testosterone levels than women, which may make men more likely to abuse alcohol and tobacco, drive aggressively, and engage in other life-threatening behaviors. Men also choose riskier types of work and become involved in wartime aggression, which are connected to men's decreased life expectancy. Studies also show that women are less likely to experience life-threatening illnesses and health problems than men are.

—Carl, *Think Sociology,* p. 211

a. women's health
b. men and risky behaviors
c. testosterone and age
d. men's life expectancy

_______ 2. Many people look back to the 1950s as the golden age of the traditional family, but was it really? Teenage pregnancy rates were higher in the 1950s than they are today, although a higher proportion of teenage mothers were married (primarily due to "shotgun weddings," a colloquialism that developed from the idea that many fathers of pregnant girls had to force, possibly with a weapon, a man to marry his daughter once she became pregnant). Many families were unable to survive the traumas of war and its aftermath, and the divorce rate rose from one in six in 1940 to one in four marriages in 1946. Although many families prospered in the years following World War II, many others suffered from economic hardship. In 1948, *Newsweek* reported that most of the 27 million schoolchildren in the United States were badly in need of medical or dental care, while more than 900 thousand children were malnourished.

—Kunz, *Think Marriages & Families,* p. 8

a. teenage pregnancy rates
b. the effect of war on divorce
c. family problems in the 1950s
d. golden age

_______ 3. In the past few years, social networking sites such as MySpace, Facebook, and Twitter have become hugely popular across all ages. Despite the opinions of some that young people are in danger of turning into crouching androids glued to their computers, research shows that the majority of friendships are still maintained offline. Offline friendships are characterized by more interdependence, depth, understanding, and commitment, but online friendships can gain some of these qualities with time. Most online friends tend to be rather cautious about disclosing personal information. However, this does not apply to people with a negative view of themselves and others; they instead seem to share more information, possibly in an attempt to become more self-confident in their interactions. Interestingly, even in online friendships people seem to gain more satisfaction when befriending people of a similar age and place of residence.

—Kunz, *Think Marriages & Families,* p. 82

a. offline vs. online friendships
b. technology and self-image
c. personal information sharing online
d. satisfaction in online friendships

Copyright © 2012 by Pearson Education

_______ 4. A century ago politicians used to say, "Vote early and often." Cases such as West Virginia's 159,000 votes being cast by 147,000 eligible voters in 1888 were not that unusual. Largely to prevent corruption associated with stuffing ballot boxes, states adopted voter registration laws around the turn of the century, which require individuals to first place their name on an electoral roll in order to be allowed to vote. Although these laws have made it more difficult to vote more than once, they have also discouraged some people from voting at all. Voter registration requirements in the United States are, in part, to blame for why Americans are significantly less likely to go to the polls than citizens of other democratic nations.

—Edwards, *Government in America*, p. 313

a. voter turnout
b. voter registration
c. voter eligibility
d. voter fraud

_______ 5. Compared with the technical resources of a theater of today, those of a London public theater in the time of Queen Elizabeth I seem hopelessly limited. Plays had to be performed by daylight, and scenery had to be kept simple: a table, a chair, a throne, perhaps an artificial tree or two to suggest a forest. But these limitations were, in a sense, advantages. What the theater of today can spell out for us realistically, with massive scenery and electric lighting, Elizabethan playgoers had to imagine and the playwright had to make vivid for them by means of language. Not having a lighting technician to work a panel, Shakespeare had to indicate the dawn by having Horatio, in *Hamlet*, say in a speech rich in metaphor and descriptive detail:

> But look, the morn in russet mantle clad
> Walks o'er the dew of yon high eastward hill.

—Kennedy, *Literature*, p. 1243

a. impact of technological limitations on Elizabethan theater
b. benefits of modern technology in theater performances
c. effects of Shakespeare's writing style
d. the use of language to make ideas vivid

Locating the Main Idea

Locate main ideas

You learned earlier that the **main idea** of a paragraph is its most important point. The main idea is also the most *general* statement the writer makes about the topic. Pick out the most general statement among the following sentences.

1. Animals differ according to when they sleep.
2. Some animals sleep during daylight while others sleep during darkness.
3. Animals' sleeping habits differ in a number of ways.
4. Hibernation is another kind of sleep for some animals.

Did you choose sentence 3 as the most general statement? Now we will change this list into a paragraph by rearranging the sentences and adding a few facts.

> Animals' sleeping habits differ in a number of ways. They differ according to what time of day they sleep. Some animals sleep during daylight hours while others sleep during darkness. They also differ in the length of time they sleep. Other animals sleep for weeks or months at a time when they hibernate.

In this brief paragraph, the main idea is expressed in the first sentence. This sentence, known as the **topic sentence**, is the most general statement in the paragraph. All the other sentences are specific details that explain this main idea.

Tips for Finding the Main Idea

Here are some tips that will help you find the main idea.

1. **Identify the topic.** As you did earlier, figure out the general subject of the entire paragraph. In the preceding sample paragraph, "animals' sleeping habits" is the topic.
2. **Locate the most general sentence (the topic sentence).** This sentence must be broad enough to include all of the other ideas in the paragraph. The topic sentence in the sample paragraph ("Animals' sleeping habits differ in a number of ways") covers all of the other details in that paragraph. The tips in the next section will help you locate topic sentences.
3. **Study the rest of the paragraph.** The main idea must make the rest of the paragraph meaningful. It is the one idea that ties all of the other details together. In the sample paragraph, sentences 2, 3, 4, and 5 all give specific details about how animals' sleeping habits differ.

Copyright © 2012 by Pearson Education

Tips for Locating the Topic Sentence

Although a topic sentence can be located anywhere in a paragraph, it is usually *first* or *last*.

Topic Sentence First In most paragraphs, the topic sentence comes first. The author states his or her main point and then explains it.

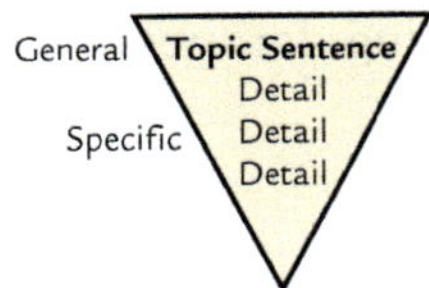

A **focus group** is a small group, usually consisting of about seven to ten people who are brought together to discuss a subject of interest to the researcher. Focus groups are commonly used today in business and politics; that flashy slogan you heard for a political campaign or a new toothpaste was almost certainly tested in a focus group to gauge people's reactions. Social researchers may use a focus group to help design questions or instruments for quantitative research or to study the interactions among group members on a particular subject. In most cases, researchers ask predetermined questions, but the discussion is unstructured. Focus groups are a relatively cheap method of research and can be completed quickly. They also allow for the flexible discussions and answers that are desirable in qualitative research. However, they definitely require a skilled leader to avoid leading participants in a predetermined direction, to establish an atmosphere in which all participants feel comfortable speaking, and to allow discussion of uncomfortable or challenging topics. It is also possible for two different researchers to analyze the discussion in different ways.

—Kunz, *Think Marriages & Families*, p. 36

Here, the writer first defines a focus group. The rest of the paragraph provides more details about focus groups.

Topic Sentence Last The second most likely place for a topic sentence to appear is last in a paragraph. When using this arrangement, a writer leads up to the main point and then states it at the end.

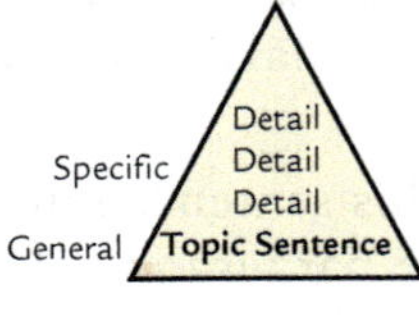

In the developing world 1.1 billion people still lack access to safe drinking water, 2.6 billion do not have access to adequate sanitation services, and more than 1.6 million deaths each year are traced to waterborne diseases (mostly in children under five). All too often in developing countries, water is costly or inaccessible to the poorest in society, while the wealthy have it piped into their homes. In addition, because of the infrastructure that is used to control water, whole seas are being lost, rivers are running dry, millions of people have been displaced to make room for reservoirs, groundwater aquifers are being pumped down, and disputes over water have raised tensions from local to international levels. Fresh water is a limiting resource in many parts of the world and is certain to become even more so as the 21st century unfolds.

—Wright, Environmental Science, p. 247

In this paragraph, the author discusses water as a limiting resource and concludes that water will become more limited throughout the 21st century.

Topic Sentence in the Middle If a topic sentence is placed neither first nor last, then it may appear somewhere in the middle of a paragraph. In this arrangement, the sentences before the topic sentence lead up to or introduce the main idea. Those that follow the main idea explain or describe it.

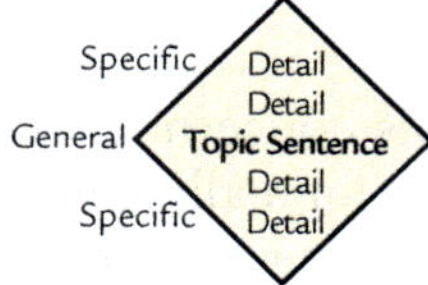

In colonial days, huge flocks of snowy egrets inhabited the coastal wetlands and marshes of the southeastern United States. In the 1800s, when fashion dictated fancy hats adorned with feathers, egrets and other birds were hunted for their plumage. By the late 1800s, egrets were almost extinct. In 1886, the newly formed National Audubon Society began a press campaign to shame "feather wearers" and end the practice. The campaign caught on, and gradually, attitudes changed; new laws followed. Government policies that protect animal from overharvesting are essential to keep species from the brink of extinction. Even when cultural standards changes due to the efforts of individual groups (such as the National Audubon Society), laws and policy measures must follow to ensure that endangered populations remain protected. Since the 1800s, several important laws have been passed to protect a wide variety of species.

—Wright and Boorse, *Environmental Science: Toward a Sustainable Future*, p. 150

In this paragraph, the author discusses how one species nearly became extinct and concludes that government regulations are necessary to prevent this from happening again.

Topic Sentence First and Last Occasionally writers put the main idea at the beginning of a paragraph and again at the end. Writers may do this to emphasize the main point or to clarify it.

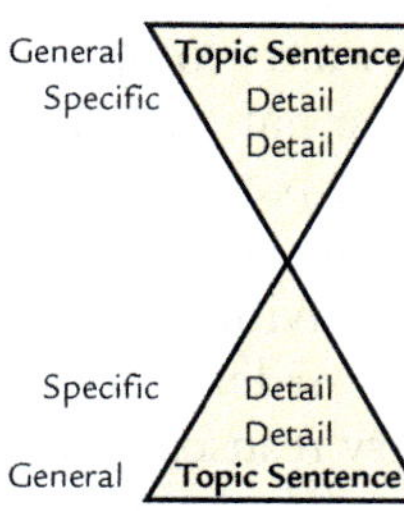

The National Cancer Institute (NCI) has taken a brute-force approach screening species for cancer-suppressing chemicals. NCI scientists receive frozen samples of organisms from around the world, chop them up, and separate them into a number of extracts, each probably containing hundreds of components. These extracts are tested against up to 60 different types of cancer cells for their efficacy in stopping or slowing growth of the cancer. Promising extracts are then further analyzed to determine their chemical nature, and chemicals in the extract are tested singly to find the effective compound. This approach is often referred to as the "grind 'em and find 'em" strategy.

—Belk, *Biology*, p. 334

The first and last sentences together explain that the NCI takes an aggressive strategy to finding and testing samples for cancer-suppression.

Copyright © 2012 by Pearson Education

EXERCISE 3-4 Locating Topic Sentences

***Directions:** Underline the topic sentence in each of the following paragraphs.*

1. Crime is a major concern in the United States. The possibility of becoming a victim of crime, particulary of a violent assault, is the number one fear of millions of Americans. This concern is well founded, as 5.3 million people over the age of 12 annually will be victimized by violent crimes. That nearly 14 million serious crimes are reported yearly to the police indicates only part of the situation. An annual study by the Bureau of Justice Statistics surveys American households to determine the extent of serious crime not being reported to law-enforment authorities. Initiated in 1973, the National Crime Survey measures the number of crimes unreported to the police as opposed to reported crime, which is documented annually by the FBI's *Uniform Crime Reports Bulletin.* The result of the National Crime Survey are disturbing to the entire criminal justice system, indicating that people and households in the United States face 49 million crime attempts a year when unreported and reported crime occurences are combined.

   —Gilbert et al., *Criminal Investigation,* p. 33

2. A living will is a legal document prepared by a patient. This document gives instructions about the health care to be provided if the patient becomes terminally ill or falls into a permanent coma or presistent vegetative state. A living will is a way for the patient to make health care decisions before experiencing a health-care emergency. A living will specifies whether the patient wants to be kept on life-support machines. It specifies whether the patient wants tube feedings or artificial (IV) hydration when the patient is in a coma or persistent vegetative state. It may also contain other instructions related to health care. For example, the living will may contain a Do Not Resuscitate (DNR) order. This order instructs any health care worker not to use cardiopulmonary resuscitation if the comatose or terminally ill patient experiences a life threatening event, such as heart attack or stroke.

   —adapted from Badasch, *Health Science Fundamentals,* p. 88

3. The United States has a severe fire problem that if not addressed, will continue to worsen drastically. Fire statistics show that our nation, one of the richest and most technologically sophisticated countries in the world, lags behind its peer nations in fire security. Nationally, there are millions of fires, thousands of deaths, tens of thousands of injuries, and billions of dollars lost each year—figures which far exceed comparable statistics for other industrialized countries. In 2001, for example, the direct value of property

destroyed in fires was $11 billion ($44 billion if the World Trade Center loss is included). More recently in 2004, direct property losses from fires were estimated at over $9.8 billion.

—Loyd and Richardson, *Fundamentals of Fire and Emergency Services,* p. 12

4. Vitamin B12 (cyanocobalamin) is found in mollusks, clams, beef liver, rainbow trout, and fortified cereals. Vitamin B12 is needed for healthy nerve cells, to make DNA, and for the formation of red blood cells. Vitamin B12 is bound to the protein in food, and hydrochloric acid in the stomach releases B12 from the protein during digestion. Once released, B12 combines with a substance called intrinsic factor (IF) before it is absorbed into the bloodstream. Deficiency is a very serious problem, ultimately leading to irreversible nerve damage signified by numbness and tingling in the hands and feet. Signs and symptoms include fatigue, weakness, nausea, constipation, flatulence, loss of appetite, weight loss, difficulty in maintaining balance, depression, confusion, poor memory, and soreness of the mouth or tongue. The RDI is 2.4 mg/day for both males and females.

—Johnson, *Pharmacy Technician,* p. 455

5. The star system has been the backbone of the American film industry since the mid 1910s. Stars are the creation of the public, its reigning favorities. Their influence in the fields of fashion, values, and public behavior has been enormous. "The social history of a nation can be written in terms of its film stars," Raymond Durgnat has observed. Stars confer instant consequence to any film they appear in. Their fees have staggered the public. In the 1920s, Mary Pickford and Charles Chaplin were the two highest paid employees in the world. Contemporary stars such as Julia Roberts and Tom Cruise command salaries of many millions per film, so popular are these box-office giants. Some stars had careers that spanned five decades: Bette Davis and John Wayne, to name just two.

—Giannetti, *Understanding Movies,* p. 251

6. For decades, we have looked at our steadily increasing life expectancy rates and proudly proclaimed that Americans health has never been better. Recently, however, health organizations and international groups have attempted to quantify the number of years a person lives with a disability or illness, compared with the number of healthy years. The World Health Organization summarizes this concept as **healthy life expectancy**. Simply stated, *healthy life expectancy* refers to the number of years a newborn can expect to live in full health, based on current rates of illness and mortality and also on the quality of their lives. For example, if we could delay the onset of diabetes so that a person didn't

Copyright © 2012 by Pearson Education

develop the disease until he or she was 60 years old, rather than developing it at 30, there would be a dramatic increase in this individual's healthy life expectancy.

— Donatelle, *Health: The Basics,* p. 6

7. The functions of desktop publishing software are similar to those of word processing programs, except that some capabilities are more sophisticated. A user can enter text using the desktop publishing program in the same way that he or she can enter text with a word processing program. In addition, the user can retrieve text from a file created by another program. For example, the user may enter, edit, and save text using a word processing program and then retrieve the saved text using the desktop publishing program.

—Nickerson, *Business and Information Systems,* p. 249

8. Are you "twittered out"? Is all that texting causing your thumbs to seize up in protest? If so, you're not alone. Like millions of others, you may find that all of the pressure for contact is more than enough stress for you! Known as *technostress,* the bombardment is defined as stress created by a dependence on technology and the constant state of being plugged in or wirelessly connected, which can include a perceived obligation to respond, chat, or tweet.

—Donatelle, *Health: The Basics,* p. 66

9. In the past, exposure to liability made many doctors, nurses, and other medical professionals reluctant to stop and render aid to victims in emergency situations, such as highway accidents. Almost all states have enacted a **Good Samaritan law** that relieves medical professionals from liability for injury caused by their ordinary negligence in each circumstances. Good Samaritan laws protect medical professionals only from liability for their *ordinary negligence,* not for injuries caused by their gross negligence or reckless or intentional conduct. Most Good Samaritan laws protect licensed doctors and nurses and laypersons who have been certified in CPR. Good Samaritan statutes generally do not protect laypersons who are not trained in CPR—that is, they are liable for injuries caused by their ordinary negligence in rendering aid.

—Goldman, *Paralegal Professional,* p. 459

10. At some time or another, many close relationships go through a conflict phase. "We're always fighting," complains a newlywed. But if she were to analyze these fights, she would discover important differences among them. According to communication researchers Miller and Steinberg, most conflicts fit into three different categories. There is (1) pseudoconflict—triggered by a lack of understanding. There is (2) simple conflict—stemming from

different ideas, definitions, perceptions, or goals. Finally there is (3) ego conflict—which occurs when conflict gets personal.

—adapted from Beebe, Beebe, and Redmond, *Interpersonal Communication*, pp. 243, 248

Locating the Central Thought

Understand central thoughts

Just as a paragraph has a main idea, so articles, essays, and sections of textbook chapters have a main point. The main point of a group of paragraphs appearing together as a unit is called the **central thought.** You may also hear it called a thesis statement, especially in your writing classes. A central thought states what the entire piece of writing is about. It is often stated in a single sentence. The central thought often appears in the first or second paragraph of a piece of writing, although it may appear anywhere in the selection.

To find the central thought, ask yourself, "What big, general idea is discussed throughout the selection?" Now, use this question to find the central thought of the following brief article.

TWITTERING IN THE DIGITAL AGE

1 Why would anyone want to Twitter? Do you really want to know the up-to-the-minute and by-the-minute blow-by-blow detailed activities and thoughts of your friends? All those instantaneous, brief messages (up to 140 characters, like a mobile phone text) recounting feelings ("I'm so down today"), work problems ("boss is mad at me again"), and activities ("making a sandwich—ham, cheese, egg, and ketchup—yummy").

2 So, who cares?

3 This doesn't make sense—until you try it.

4 Ben Haley thought that such streaming trivia ("tweets") was absurd, but for the fun of it, he and his friends signed on to Twitter. Each day, he was greeted with a page of one- or two-line notes. At first the stream of trivia made no sense. But then he found himself caught up in his friends' lives as never before. Starting to sense the rhythm of their lives, he found himself checking and rechecking his account several times a day, sometimes several times an hour.

5 When a friend came down with a virus, Haley could tell from the updates that she was getting worse, and he became aware when she was turning the corner. He followed his friends' emotions as they went through their days—from scoring successes to finding themselves in hell. Even the daily sandwich-making started to make sense, part of the rhythm of that person's life.

6 When Haley and his friends get together (physically), they don't have to ask, "What have you been up to?" They already know—and in more detail than practically any friends have had in history. Instead, their topics begin from threads of the updates, as though they are picking up a conversation in the middle.

7 *Ambient awareness* is the name social scientists have given to this not-being-there-and yet-being-there. The term *digital co-presence* or even *twittering* might be better, but whatever you call it, the computer, with all its

Copyright © 2012 by Pearson Education

related gizmos, is changing social life. As this more recent one unfolds, other changes will be in hot pursuit—each nudging adjustments in our lives.

8 Technology often has uses and implications for social life that go far beyond the expectations and even imaginations of its developers. So it is with Twitter. Without warning, this electronic toy that helped people keep up with one another was turned into a political weapon. As Iranians protested election fraud in 2009, they used Twitter to bypass censors so they could organize mass protests. Then they used Twitter to transmit up-to-the-minute information on their demonstrations to friends—and to the world.

—Henslin, *Sociology: A Down-to-Earth Approach*, p. 664

In this selection from a sociology book, the central thought is that Twitter and new technologies are changing social life. Ben Haley's experience is described to show how the technology has had an impact on friendships. The central thought is stated in the second sentence of paragraph 7.

EXERCISE 3-5 Locating Central Thoughts

Directions: *In each of the following groups of sentences, three of the sentences are topic sentences in an article. The fourth is the central thought of the entire article. Select the central thought in each group of sentences.*

_______ 1. a. Monotheism is a belief in one supreme being.
b. Polytheism is a belief in more than one supreme being.
c. Theisms are religions that worship a god or gods.
d. Monotheistic religions include Christianity, Judaism, and Islam.

_______ 2. a. Vincent Van Gogh is an internationally known and respected artist.
b. Van Gogh's art displays an approach to color that was revolutionary.
c. Van Gogh created seventy paintings in the last two months of his life.
d. Van Gogh's art is respected for its attention to detail.

_______ 3. a. The Individuals with Disability Education Act offers guidelines for inclusive education.
b. The inclusive theory of education says that children with special needs should be placed in regular classrooms and have services brought to them.
c. The first movement toward inclusion was mainstreaming—a plan in which children with special needs were placed in regular classrooms for a portion of the day and sent to other classrooms for special services.

d. Families play an important role in making inclusive education policies work.

_______ 4. a. Stress can have a negative effect on friendships and marital relationships.

b. Stress can affect job performance.

c. Stress is a pervasive problem in our culture.

d. Some health problems appear to be stress related.

Thinking Critically About Main Ideas

Think critically about main ideas

A main idea is the most general statement a writer makes about a topic. Often, main ideas are simple statements of fact that cannot be disputed. However, not all main ideas and topic sentences are completely factual. Sometimes a main idea presents an opinion about a topic, and that statement may not offer all sides of the story. (To learn more about distinguishing fact and opinion, refer to Chapter 10.) Look at the following passage:

> No doubt about it, lobbying is a growth industry. Every state has hundreds of public relations practitioners whose specialty is representing their clients to legislative bodies and government agencies. In North Dakota, hardly a populous state, more than 300 people are registered as lobbyists in the capital city of Bismarck. The number of registered lobbyists in Washington, D.C., exceeds 10,000 today. In addition, there are an estimated 20,000 other people who have slipped through registration requirements but who nonetheless ply the halls of government to plead their clients' interests.
>
> In one sense, lobbyists are expediters. They know local traditions and customs, and they know who is in a position to affect policy. Lobbyists advise their clients, which include trade associations, corporations, public interest groups and regulated utilities and industries, on how to achieve their goals by working with legislators and government regulators. Many lobbyists call themselves "government relations specialists."
>
> —Vivian, *The Media of Mass Communication*, pp. 278–279

The main idea of the first paragraph is a statement of fact; the author can prove without a doubt that "lobbying is a growth industry." The main idea of the second paragraph is: "Lobbyists are expediters." That is, lobbyists help their clients influence the government in their favor. But this main idea presents *only "one sense"* of the topic. What is the other sense or view? Lobbying is actually a controversial activity, and many people believe that lobbyists spend large amounts of money influencing government employees in unethical or illegal ways. However, that belief is not reflected in the main idea of this passage.

Copyright © 2012 by Pearson Education

EXERCISE 3-6 Identifying Topics

Directions: *For each of the following sets of topic sentences, specify the topic that is being discussed. Note that each topic sentence presents a different facet of (or opinion about) the topic.*

1. - "The continued flow of immigrants into the United States has created a rich, diverse society that has been beneficial to the country."
   - "The presence of guest workers from South America in states like Arizona and California has a positive effect on the U.S. economy."
   - "Because the country is suffering from high unemployment, we must reduce the number of people who come here looking for jobs."

   Topic: ______________________________

2. - "Most scientists agree that temperatures now are warmer than they were 20 years ago."
   - "It is hard to draw any definite conclusions from the hundreds of studies that have considered whether climate change is occurring or not."
   - "People who claim that the Earth is now hotter miss the point that the Earth has been getting warmer over the last several thousand years, not just the last 50 years."

   Topic: ______________________________

EXERCISE 3-7 Writing Topic Sentences

Directions: *For each of the following topic sentences, write another topic sentence that expresses a different opinion or point of view.*

1. It is better to live in a city than in the country because the city offers many more activities and opportunities to its residents.

   ____

   ____

2. Because tobacco products harm people's health, all tobacco products should be banned.

   ____

   ____

3. Social networking sites like Facebook and MySpace create communities of close-knit friends.

____

____

4. *Dancing with the Stars* entertains us by allowing famous celebrities to exhibit their unknown dance talents.

____

____

TEXTBOOK CHALLENGE

TIPS for Reading in Business

When reading in business textbooks, pay attention to

- **Processes and procedures.** Courses in business often focus on how things work and how things get done.
- **Examples.** Many authors illustrate their main points by giving examples of businesses and corporations.
- **Graphics.** Business texts include plenty of illustrations and diagrams. Be sure you know why each is included and what it adds to the print text.

Copyright © 2012 by Pearson Education

Part A: Analyzing a Textbook Excerpt

This excerpt was taken from a business advertising chapter on alternative marketing. Read the excerpt and follow the directions listed on pp. 109–110.

Guerrilla Marketing

1 Historically, one of the most successful alternative media marketing programs is guerrilla marketing, as first developed by marketing guru Jay Conrad Levinson. **Guerrilla marketing** programs are designed to obtain instant results while using limited resources. The tactics rely on creativity, quality relationships, and the willingness to try unusual approaches. These programs were originally aimed at small businesses; however, now guerrilla marketing tactics are found in wide array of firms. Guerrilla marketing emphasizes a combination of media, advertising, public relations, and surprise tactics to reach consumers.

FIGURE A Traditional vs. Guerrilla Marketing

Traditional Marketing	Guerrilla Marketing
• Requires money	• Requires energy and imagination
• Geared to large businesses with big budgets	• Geared to small businesses and big dreams
• Results measured by sales	• Results measured by profits
• Based on experience and guesswork	• Based on psychology and human behavior
• Increases production and diversity	• Grows through existing customers and referrals
• Grows by adding customers	• Cooperates with other businesses
• Obliterates the competition	• Aims messages at individuals and small groups
• Aims messages at large groups	• Uses marketing to gain customer consent
• Uses marketing to generate sales	• "You Marketing" that looks at how can we help "You"
• "Me Marketing" that looks at "My" company	

2 Figure A compares guerrilla marketing to traditional marketing. Guerrilla marketing tends to focus on specific regions or areas. It is not a national or international campaign, and instead features personal communication. The idea is to create excitement that will spread to others by word-of-mouth. Guerrilla marketing often involves interacting with consumers, not just sending out a message. The idea is to build relationships with customers. By getting consumers to react or to do something, the program enhances the chance that the message will hit home. Advertisements are made accessible to consumers, where they live, play, and work in a way that it is noticed. The eventual relationships that evolve help create brand loyalty and positive recommendations to other consumers.

3 A notable example of guerrilla marketing was used by the Harley-Davidson franchise in Gloversville, New York. The company advertised a "cat shoot", to be held at the store. Local police, the Humane Society, the mayor, and the Society for Prevention of Cruelty to Animals all inquired, and the event generated front-page stories for 3 straight days in local papers. The event was actually a three-for-a-dollar paintball shoot at a 6-foot-high cartoon cat, with proceeds benefiting the local Humane Society. It was tremendously successful in helping customers find their way to the store. Although bizarre, the approach used by Van's Harley-Davidson illustrates the concept of guerrilla marketing.

4 Guerrilla marketing should be an aggressive, grassroots approach to marketing. It promotes a one-to-one relationship with consumers through innovative, alternative means of branding. Touchmedia CEO Mickey Fung used guerrilla marketing tactics by placing more than 3,000 interactive PDA-type screens on the back of taxi cabs headrests in Shanghai, China. The touch screens play ads and

videos, but passengers in the taxi can also choose the content they want to view through multiple icons on the screen. Follow-up research on the program indicated that 89 percent of the passengers accessed the screen in some way.

5 The location of the touch screens is ideal for companies attempting to reach wealthy Chinese consumers. Only the top 10 percent of Chinese citizens in Shanghai can afford to ride in a taxi. The passengers are mostly 21 to 49 years of age, white collar workers, and 45 percent have managerial-level jobs. Brands such as Heineken, Chivas, Virgin, Nokia and companies like Estee Lauder, Procter & Gamble, KFC, and Volkswagen have advertised on the taxi screens. More than 4 million people watched an ad while in the taxi promoting a Christina Aguilera concert in Shanghai. Of those who purchased tickets, 49 percent were reserved by individuals who used the hot line listed on the taxi touch screens. The touch screens are not only an alternative media, but they are also touching consumers with an innovative approach that allows the consumer to interact and choose what they want to watch.

6 Guerrilla marketing not only utilizes alternative media tactics and venues; the program focuses on finding creative ways of doing things. The objective is to change the thinking process in the marketing department itself. The first step is to discover "touch points" with customers. In other words, where do the customers eat, drink, shop, hang out, and sleep? This makes it possible to reach customers at the points the product interconnects with their lives in creative and imaginative ways. Figure B identifies six reasons to use guerrilla marketing.

- To find a new way to communicate with consumers
- To interact with consumers
- To make advertising accessible to consumers
- To impact a spot market
- To create buzz
- To build relationships with consumers

FIGURE B
Reasons for Using Guerrilla Marketing

—Clow and Baack, *Integrated Advertising, Promotion, and Marketing Communications*, pp. 274–276

1. **Preview.** Preview the reading using the guidelines on p. 7, and then answer the following questions.
   a. What is guerrilla marketing?
   b. To what other type of marketing is it compared?
2. **SQ3R.** Write at least three questions for the Q step of SQ3R. Answer them after completing the reading.
3. **Textbook Features.** Explain the purpose of Figures A and B. Why did the author present this information in tabular rather than paragraph form? What strategies could you use to learn this information for an exam?
4. **Vocabulary.**
   a. Identify the important new terms that are introduced in the reading.
   b. Define each of the following words as used in the reading.
   array (par. 1), *bizarre* (par. 3), *aggressive* (par. 4), *grassroots* (par. 4), *venues* (par. 6)

Copyright © 2012 by Pearson Education

5. **Applying Chapter Skills.** Highlight the topic sentence of each paragraph.
6. **Essay Question.** Write an answer to the following essay question. To test your memory, write it without referring to the excerpt.

   Guerrilla marketing is growing in popularity. Write an essay explaining what it is, how it is used, and how it compares to more traditional forms of advertising.
7. **Thinking Critically.** Use your critical thinking skills to answer each of the following questions.
   a. Give an example of guerrilla advertising that you have seen or heard.
   b. Choose a product and create a guerrilla advertising plan for it.
   c. The main ideas in this excerpt suggest that the writers regard guerrilla advertising positively. What could be some drawbacks or negative aspects/outcomes of guerrilla marketing?

Part B: Your College Textbook

Choose a chapter that you have been assigned to read in a textbook for one of your other courses. Highlight the topic sentence of each paragraph in the first five pages.

SELF-TEST SUMMARY

To test yourself, cover up the Answer column with a sheet of paper and answer each question listed in the left column. Evaluate each of your answers as you work by sliding the paper down and comparing your answer with what is printed in the Answer column.

	Question	Answer
GOAL 1	What is a main idea?	A main idea is the one important point that a paragraph makes.
GOAL 2	What are general and specific ideas?	A general idea is broad and can apply to many things. A specific idea is detailed and refers to a much smaller group, or to an individual item.
GOAL 3	How do you identify the topic of a paragraph?	Look for the one idea the author is discussing throughout the paragraph.
GOAL 4	How do you locate the main idea of a paragraph?	Find the topic and then locate the sentence in the paragraph that is the most general. Check to be sure this one sentence brings all other details together under one common concept.
GOAL 5	What is the function of the central thought of a passage?	The central thought states what the entire piece of writing is about.
GOAL 6	How can you think critically about main ideas?	Ask if there are other views that can be held about the topic.

Copyright © 2012 by Pearson Education

PRACTICE TEST 3-1

NAME ______________________ SECTION ______________________
DATE ______________________ SCORE ______________________

Finding Main Ideas

Directions: *For each of the following paragraphs, (1) select the choice that best represents the topic of the paragraph, and (2) underline the topic sentence.*

_______ 1. Contrary to popular assumption, slavery was not usually based on racism, but on one of three other factors. The first was debt. In some cultures, an individual who could not pay a debt could be enslaved by the creditor. The second was crime. Instead of being killed, a murderer or thief might be enslaved by the family of the victim as compensation for their loss. The third was war and conquest. When one group of people conquered another, they often enslaved some of the vanquished. Historian Gerda Lerner notes that the first people enslaved through warfare were women. When premodern men raided a village or camp, they killed the men, raped the women, and then brought the women back as slaves. The women were valued for sexual purposes, for reproduction, and for their labor.

—Henslin, *Sociology: A Down-to-Earth Approach*, p. 246

a. war and conquest
b. debt and slavery
c. causes of slavery
d. warfare among women

_______ 2. At Steelcase Inc., the country's largest maker of office furnishings, two very talented women in the marketing division both wanted to work only part-time. The solution: They now share a single full-time job. With each working 2.5 days a week, both got their wish and the job gets done—and done well. In another situation, one person might work mornings and the other afternoons. The practice, known as work sharing (or job sharing) has "brought sanity back to our lives," according to at least one Steelcase employee.

—Ebert and Griffin, *Business Essentials*, p. 208

a. creative solutions
b. dissatisfied employees
c. women in the workforce
d. job sharing

_______ 3. Suppose a friend holds up her hand, palm flattened to signal "stop" to someone standing across the room from you. A basketball coach may motion "time out" with his hands to communicate to a player on the court that the player should signal the referee to stop play so that the team can discuss a new strategy. Both of these situations demonstrate the use of emblems—body motions that take the place of words. In order for emblems to be an effective form of nonverbal communication, both parties must readily understand the motions being used. A spectator unfamiliar with sports might not understand the "time out" motion used by those involved in the game and therefore might question why the referee officially signaled time out. Emblems can also be used effectively when there are obstacles to verbal communication. The example of the basketball game applies here as well; the coach may signal to a player to call for time out because the crowd is generating too much noise for the coach to be heard by the player.

—adapted from Dunn and Goodnight, *Communication: Embracing the Difference,* p. 92

a. speech
b. nonverbal communication
c. hand signals
d. emblems

______ 4. Piracy is the illegal theft of intellectual property, and there are no reasons to excuse it. It has reached a point where it is significantly affecting the very existence of small game developers and is devastating to the game industry. When the initial sales are over, the developer has almost no means to make more money. If half the people who play pirated versions of a game paid for it instead, smaller developers would be getting a significant increase in royalties and might actually make a profit instead of barely surviving on advances against royalties. As development costs continue to rise, the survival of many small developers is in doubt, and piracy is a leading reason why many small companies have to shut their doors. Every user who offhandedly makes a copy of a game for a friend contributes to the piracy problem and threatens the continuing existence of the game industry.

—Moore, *Game Design and Development,* p. 681

a. poor payout to game developers
b. immorality of piracy
c. economic impact of game piracy
d. small game developers limited chances of success

Copyright © 2012 by Pearson Education

_______ 5. For years, the loyal Dalmatian has been the trusted companion of firefighters. Few realize that this breed was originally chosen because of the strong bonds that the dogs formed with fire horses, protecting them and keeping them company at the station. The dogs were also expected to rouse the horses at the sound of the alarm bell, then run out and bark a warning at anyone who might be obstructing the firehouse exit. The dogs would then chase the fire apparatus all the way to the scene, sometimes barking the whole way. They served the same function, essentially, as the emergency traffic signals located outside many fire stations today and the sirens on fire trucks. When horses were replaced by steam- or gasoline-driven fire engines, many departments opted to keep their beloved mascots. It is not unusual even today to see a proud Dalmatian riding on a fire engine as it races to the scene of an emergency.

—Loyd and Richardson, *Fundamentals of Fire and Emergency Services*, p. 12

a. fire apparatus-chasing dogs
b. the history of Dalmatians at firehouses
c. human–Dalmatian bonding
d. uses of dogs and horses

NAME ____________ SECTION ____________
DATE ____________ SCORE ____________

PRACTICE TEST 3-2

Topics, Main Ideas, and Central Thoughts

***Directions:** After reading the following passage, select the choice that best completes each of the statements that follow.*

Sports Beverages: Help or Hype?

1 Once considered specialty drinks used exclusively by elite athletes, sports beverages have become popular everyday choices for both active and nonactive people. The market for these drinks has become so lucrative that many of the large soft drink companies now produce them. This surge in popularity leads us to ask three important questions:

- Do sports beverages benefit athletes?
- Do sports beverages benefit recreationally active people?
- Do nonactive people benefit from consuming sports beverages?

2 The first question is relatively easy to answer. Sports beverages were originally developed to meet the unique fluid, electrolyte, and carbohydrate needs of competitive athletes. Highly active people need to replenish both fluids and electrolytes to avoid both dehydration and hyponatremia (low blood sodium). Sports beverages can especially benefit athletes who exercise in the heat and are thus at an even greater risk for loss of water and electrolytes through respiration and sweat. The carbohydrates in sports beverages provide critical fuel during relatively intense (more than 60% of maximal effort) exercise bouts lasting more than 1 hour. Thus, competitive athletes are able to exercise longer, maintain a higher intensity, and improve performance times when they drink a sports beverage during exercise.

3 In addition, sports beverages may help athletes consume more energy than they could by eating solid foods and water alone. Some competitive athletes train or compete for 6 to 8 hours each day on a regular basis. It is virtually impossible for these athletes to consume enough solid foods to support this intense level of exercise.

4 Do recreationally active or working people benefit from consuming sports beverages? The answer depends on the duration and intensity of exercise, the environmental conditions, and the characteristics of the individual.

5 Recently, sports beverages have become very popular with people who do little or no regular exercise or manual labor. However, there's no evidence that people who don't exercise derive any benefits from consuming sports beverages. Even if they live in a hot climate, they should be able to replenish the fluid and electrolytes they lose during sweating by drinking water and other beverages and eating a normal diet.

Copyright © 2012 by Pearson Education

6 The primary negative consequence of drinking sports beverages without exercising is weight gain. Sports beverages contain not only fluid and electrolytes, but also energy. Drinking 12 fl. oz (1.5 cups) of Gatorade adds 90 kcal to a person's daily energy intake. Many inactive people consume two to three times this amount each day, adding 180 to 270 kcal of energy to their diet. With obesity rates at an all-time high, it is important that we attempt to consume only the foods and beverages necessary to support our health. Sports beverages are not designed to be consumed by inactive people, and they do not contribute to their health.

—Thompson, *Nutrition,* p. 242

_____ 1. The central thought of the passage is
   a. most people can benefit from drinking sports drinks.
   b. the calorie content of sports drinks makes them unhealthy.
   c. sports drinks are an excellent replacement for water.
   d. sports drinks have benefits and drawbacks, depending on who uses them.

_____ 2. The topic of paragraph 1 is
   a. questions to ask about sports drinks.
   b. the benefits of sports drinks.
   c. reasons to use sports drinks.
   d. the cost of sports drinks.

_____ 3. Sports drinks can help athletes avoid
   a. hypoglycemia.
   b. weight gain.
   c. hyponatremia.
   d. electrolysis.

_____ 4. Paragraph 2 primarily concerns the
   a. ways sports drinks can replace important bodily needs.
   b. effects of intensive exercise.
   c. ways to cope with long periods of exercise.
   d. development of sports drinks.

_____ 5. The topic sentence of paragraph 3 appears in
   a. the third sentence.
   b. the first and third sentences.
   c. the second sentence.
   d. the first sentence.

_______ 6. The topic of paragraph 5 is
a. hot climates and exercise.
b. sports drinks and nonactive people.
c. replenishment of fluids.
d. the popularity of sports drinks.

_______ 7. The main idea of paragraph 5 is that
a. sports drinks are gaining in popularity among non-athletes.
b. fluid loss from heat can be replaced with other beverages.
c. sports drinks do not benefit people who do not exercise often.
d. sports drinks can have benefits even if you don't exercise.

_______ 8. The topic of paragraph 6 is
a. daily calorie consumption.
b. national obesity rates.
c. weight gain from sports drinks.
d. the purpose of sports drinks.

_______ 9. How many calories do 12 ounces of Gatorade add to a person's daily energy intake?
a. 180 kcal
b. 90 kcal
c. 270 kcal
d. 1.5 cups

_______ 10. The topic sentence of paragraph 6 is found in the
a. first sentence.
b. last sentence.
c. second sentence.
d. first and last sentences.

Copyright © 2012 by Pearson Education

MASTERY TEST 3-1

NAME ______________________ SECTION ______________________

DATE ______________________ SCORE ______________________

Finding Main Ideas

Directions: *After reading the following passage, select the choice that best completes each of the statements that follow.*

Chronemics

Chronemics, the study of how we use our time, reveals several important uses of time. In our culture, time is viewed as a commodity or thing we can trade or buy. Think about the words we use to describe time: We *save* time by taking a short cut; we *budget* our time by working longer hours on Thursday so we can leave early on Friday; our group *invested* so much time in this project in order to get our grade up; and we *waste* time by watching television. As Anderson says, "Psychologically and rhetorically, most Americans treat time like their most prized possession or like money itself: something to be earned, saved, spent, and treasured."

We send messages by our use of time. What does being prompt or on time mean? What about being late? If you are consistently late for class, how might the instructor think about you and your attitude toward the course? Probably not very positively. We value promptness because it communicates professionalism, caring and respect. Spending a lot of time with someone is also considered a sign of caring and respect. In one study, the amount of time spent with someone was the leading predictor of relational satisfaction and understanding.

Time can communicate status. Think about the people who can keep you waiting. We often wait thirty minutes to an hour to see a physician. We accept that our supervisor, instructor, or other authority figure can and will make us wait because their time is perceived as more valuable.

—adapted from Dunn and Goodnight, *Communication: Embracing Difference,* p. 103

______ 1. The central thought of the selection is
   a. time is important to everyone.
   b. time reveals attitudes and feelings.
   c. chronemics has limited usefulness.
   d. chronemics demonstrates several uses of time.

______ 2. The topic of the first paragraph is
   a. trading time.
   b. loss of time.
   c. the value of time.
   d. wasting time.

______ 3. In paragraph 1, the word **chronemics** means
   a. the study of the use of time.
   b. the study of time.

c. cultural views about time.
d. time is prized.

_______ 4. In paragraph 1, the word **commodity** means
a. something fleeting.
b. something saved.
c. something bought or traded.
d. an item measured by time.

_______ 5. In paragraph 2, the word **predictor** means
a. effect.
b. indicator.
c. distress.
d. device.

_______ 6. The topic of the second paragraph is the
a. importance of being on time.
b. messages people send by their use of time.
c. importance of measuring the amount of time you spend with people.
d. importance of spending time on relationships.

_______ 7. In the second paragraph, the topic sentence begins with the words
a. "Spending a lot of time."
b. "We value promptness."
c. "What does being."
d. "We send messages."

_______ 8. According to the selection, which of the following is *not* correct?
a. Time is not highly valued in our society.
b. Spending a lot of time with someone is a sign of caring.
c. Time is often viewed as a commodity.
d. Time is often treated like a prized possession.

_______ 9. According to the selection, one way that we demonstrate the value of time is
a. by hurrying.
b. through the use of language.
c. by checking our watches often.
d. through setting alarms.

_______ 10. The paragraphs in this reading support the idea that a topic sentence often comes
a. in the middle.
b. first.
c. last.
d. first and last.

Copyright © 2012 by Pearson Education

MASTERY TEST 3-2

NAME ______________________ SECTION ______________________

DATE ______________________ SCORE ______________________

Finding Main Ideas

Directions: *After reading the following passage, select the choice that best completes each of the statements that follow.*

Picking Partners

Just as males and females may find different ways to express emotions themselves, the process of partner selection also shows distinctly different patterns. For both males and females, more than just chemical and psychological processes influence the choice of partners. One of these factors is *proximity,* or being in the same place at the same time. The more you see a person in your hometown, at social gatherings, or at work, the more likely that an interaction will occur. Thus, if you live in New York, you'll probably end up with another New Yorker. If you live in northern Wisconsin, you'll probably end up with another Wisconsinite.

The old adage that "opposites attract" usually isn't true. You also pick a partner based on *similarities* (attitudes, values, intellect, interests). If your potential partner expresses interest or liking, you may react with mutual regard known as *reciprocity.* The more you express interest, the safer it is for someone else to return the regard, and the cycle spirals onward.

Another factor that apparently plays a significant role in selecting a partner is *physical attraction.* Whether such attraction is caused by a chemical reaction or a socially learned behavior, males and females appear to have different attraction criteria. Men tend to select their mates primarily on the basis of youth and physical attractiveness. Although physical attractiveness is an important criterion for women in mate selection, they tend to place higher emphasis on partners who are somewhat older, have good financial prospects, and are dependable and industrious.

—Donatelle, *Health: The Basics,* p. 105

______ 1. The central thought of the entire selection is

a. several factors influence choice of partners.

b. physical attraction is more important to men than to women.

c. proximity is the key to mate selection.

d. opposites attract.

______ 2. The topic sentence of the first paragraph begins with the words

a. "For both."

b. "One of these."

c. "The more."

d. "Just as."

_______ 3. In paragraph 1, the word **proximity** means

a. interaction based on attraction.

b. being in the same place at the same time.

c. state-by-state attraction.

d. partner selection.

_______ 4. The easiest way to figure out the meaning of the word **reciprocity** in the second paragraph is to

a. use word parts.

b. use a dictionary.

c. use sentence context.

d. reread the entire paragraph.

_______ 5. The topic of the second paragraph is

a. physical attraction.

b. interaction.

c. the old adage.

d. similarities.

_______ 6. In the second paragraph, the topic sentence begins with the words

a. "You also pick."

b. "The more you express."

c. "If your potential."

d. "The old adage."

_______ 7. In paragraph 2, the word **adage** means

a. saying.

b. information.

c. fact.

d. joke.

_______ 8. The topic of the third paragraph is

a. differences between men and women.

b. physical attraction.

c. chemical reactions.

d. behavioral characteristics.

_______ 9. In paragraph 3, the word **criteria** means

a. standards.

b. faults.

c. criticisms.

d. charms.

_______ 10. According to the selection,

a. men are never attracted to women who are not physically attractive.

b. physical location is the most important partner selection criterion.

c. women are more attracted to men they are different from.

d. men and women have different attraction criteria.

Copyright © 2012 by Pearson Education

MASTERY TEST 3-3

NAME ______________________ SECTION ______________________

DATE ______________________ SCORE ______________________

READING SELECTION

Stop Asking Me My Major

Scott Keyes

This essay, which originally appeared in *The Chronicle of Higher Education*, was written by a recent college graduate. Read the selection to find out what he believes is most important for college students to focus on when choosing a major.

Vocabulary Preview

These are some of the difficult words in this essay. The definitions here will help you if you can't figure out the meanings from the sentence context or word parts.

render (par. 4) cause to be

hindering (par. 7) interfering with

perpetuates (par. 8) continues

realm (par. 9) area

prominent (par. 9) important or well-known

Scott Keyes, a recent college graduate, advises against gearing one's study concentration to fickle job prospects. Instead, he says, follow your intellectual passion.

1 One of my best friends from high school, Andrew, changed majors during his first semester at college. He and I had been fascinated by politics for years, sharing every news story we could find and participating in the Internet activism that was exploding into a new political force. Even though he was still passionate about politics, that was no longer enough. "I have to get practical," he messaged me one day, "think about getting a job after graduation. I mean, it's like my mom keeps asking me: What can you do with a degree in political science anyway?"

2 I heard the same question from my friend Jesse when students across campus were agonizing about which major was right for them. He wasn't quite sure what he wanted to study, but every time a field sparked his interest, his father would pepper him with questions about what jobs were available for people in that discipline. Before long, Jesse's dad had convinced him that the only way he could get a job and be successful after college was to major in pre-med.

3 My friends' experiences were not atypical.

4 Choosing a major is one of the most difficult things students face in college. There are two main factors that most students consider when making

this decision. First is their desire to study what interests them. Second is the fear that a particular major will render them penniless after graduation and result in that dreaded postcollege possibility: moving back in with their parents.

5 All too often, the concern about a major's practical prospects are pushed upon students by well-intentioned parents. If our goal is to cultivate students who are happy and successful, both in college as well as in the job market, I have this piece of advice for parents: Stop asking, "What can you do with a degree in (fill in the blank)?" You're doing your children no favors by asking them to focus on the job prospects of different academic disciplines, rather than studying what interests them.

6 It is my experience, both through picking a major myself and witnessing many others endure the process, that there are three reasons why parents (and everyone else) should be encouraging students to focus on what they enjoy studying most, rather than questioning what jobs are supposedly available for different academic concentrations.

7 The first is psychological. For his first two years of college, Jesse followed his dad's wishes and remained a pre-med student. The only problem was that he hated it. With no passion for the subject, his grades slipped, hindering his chances of getting into medical school. As a result his employability, the supposed reason he was studying medicine in the first place, suffered.

8 The second reason to stop asking students what they can do with a major is that it perpetuates the false notion that certain majors don't prepare students for the workplace. The belief that technical majors such as computer science are more likely to lead to a job than a major such as sociology or English is certainly understandable. It's also questionable. "The problem," as my friend Jose explained to me, "is that even as a computer-science major, what I learned in the classroom was outdated by the time I hit the job market." He thought instead that the main benefit of his education, rather than learning specific skills, was gaining a better way of thinking about the challenges he faced. "What's more," he told me, "no amount of education could match the specific on-the-job training I've received working different positions."

9 Finally it is counterproductive to demand that students justify their choice of study with potential job prospects because that ignores the lesson we were all taught in kindergarten (and shouldn't ignore the closer we get to employment): You can grow up to be whatever you want to be. The jobs people work at often fall within the realm of their studies, but they don't have to. One need look no further than some of the most prominent figures in our society to see illustrations. The TV chef Julia Child studied English in college. Author Michael Lewis, whose best sellers focus on sports and the financial industry,

Copyright © 2012 by Pearson Education

majored in art history. Matt Groening, creator of *The Simpsons*, got his degree in philosophy, as did the former Hewlett Packard chief executive Carly Fiorina. Jeff Immelt, chief executive of General Electric, focused on mathematics. Indeed, with the Department of Labor estimating that on average people switch careers (not just jobs) two or three times in their lives, relying on a college major as career preparation is misguided.

10 I'm not saying any applicant can get any job. Job seekers still need marketable skills if they hope to be hired. However, in a rapidly changing economy, which majors lead to what jobs is not so clear cut. Many employers look for applicants from a diverse background—including my friend who has a degree in biochemistry but was just hired at an investment consulting firm.

11 That doesn't mean that majors no longer matter. It is still an important decision, and students are right to seek outside counsel when figuring out what they want to study. But questioning how a particular major will affect their employability is not necessarily the best approach. Although parents' intentions may be pure—after all, who doesn't want to see their children succeed after graduation?—that question can hold tremendous power over impressionable freshmen. Far too many of my classmates let it steer them away from what they enjoyed studying to a major they believed would help them get a job after graduation.

12 One of those friends was Andrew. He opted against pursuing a degree in political science, choosing instead to study finance because "that's where the jobs are." Following graduation, Andrew landed at a consulting firm. I recently learned with little surprise that he hates his job and has no passion for the work.

13 Jesse, on the other hand, realized that if he stayed on the premed track, he would burn out before ever getting his degree. During his junior year he changed tracks and began to study engineering. Not only did Jesse's grades improve markedly, but his enthusiasm for the subject recently earned him a lucrative job offer and admission to a top engineering master's program.

14 Andrew and Jesse both got jobs. But who do you think feels more successful?

Scott Keyes is a 2009 graduate of Stanford University, where he majored in political science.

Directions: *Select the choice that best completes each of the following statements.*

CHECKING YOUR COMPREHENSION

_____ 1. The central thought of this selection is that

a. on-the-job training is more valuable than studying a particular major.

b. college students should choose a major based on its job potential.

c. parents should question how a particular major will lead to employment.

d. college students should choose a major based on what interests them.

_____ 2. According to the author, people should stop asking students about the job prospects of different majors because

a. it creates psychological consequences for the student.

b. it promotes the mistaken belief that certain majors do not prepare students for the workplace.

c. it ignores the fact that people often work in jobs outside the realm of their studies.

d. all of the above.

_____ 3. The author's friend Jose believes that the main benefit of his education was gaining

a. specific, technical skills for the workplace.

b. information about what jobs were available in his discipline.

c. a better way of thinking about the challenges he faced.

d. training for a variety of different types of jobs.

_____ 4. According to the author, the kindergarten lesson that should not be ignored is:

a. Hard work pays off.

b. You can grow up to be whatever you want to be.

c. Never stop learning.

d. Be willing to try new things.

Copyright © 2012 by Pearson Education

______ 5. All of the following people were named in the article as examples of prominent figures with jobs outside the realm of their studies *except*

a. Julia Child.
b. Matt Groening.
c. Bill Gates.
d. Carly Fiorina.

USING WHAT YOU KNOW ABOUT MAIN IDEAS

______ 6. The main idea of paragraph 4 is that

a. most parents are well intentioned.
b. choosing a major is a difficult decision.
c. most students are focused on job prospects.
d. students often dread moving back in with their parents.

______ 7. The topic sentence of paragraph 5 begins with the words

a. "All too often."
b. "If our goal."
c. "Stop asking."
d. "You're doing."

______ 8. The topic sentence of paragraph 8 begins with the words

a. "The second reason."
b. "The belief that."
c. "It's also."
d. "He thought instead."

______ 9. The topic of paragraph 9 is

a. famous people.
b. the Department of Labor.
c. students.
d. careers.

______ 10. The main idea of paragraph 11 is that

a. majors no longer matter.
b. students should not seek outside advice when choosing a major.
c. job seekers need marketable skills to be hired.
d. questioning the job prospects of a particular major is not helpful.

USING CONTEXT CLUES AND WORD PARTS

_______ 11. In paragraph 3, the word **atypical** means
a. uncommon.
b. advisable.
c. normal.
d. uncomfortable.

_______ 12. In paragraph 5, the word **cultivate** means
a. plant.
b. distract.
c. develop.
d. change.

_______ 13. In paragraph 9, the word **counterproductive** means
a. against one's purpose.
b. worthwhile.
c. extremely useful.
d. practical.

_______ 14. In paragraph 9, the word **misguided** means
a. unprepared.
b. encouraged.
c. allowed.
d. mistaken.

_______ 15. In paragraph 13, the word **lucrative** means
a. unsuccessful.
b. profitable.
c. insignificant.
d. inexpensive.

REVIEWING DIFFICULT VOCABULARY

Directions: *Complete each of the following sentences by inserting a word from the Vocabulary Preview on page 122 in the space provided. Use each word only once.*

16. College is an ideal time for students to explore subjects outside their usual ____________ of interest.

17. The guest list for the fund-raiser included the mayor and several other ____________ members of the community.

18. Allie found that working the late shift was ____________ her ability to earn good grades.

19. The shock of a surprise party can sometimes ____________ the guest of honor speechless.

20. Despite criticism, the fashion industry ____________ the idea that thin is beautiful.

Copyright © 2012 by Pearson Education

THINKING CRITICALLY

1. How does the author try to influence your opinions in this selection? Is he successful in convincing you to agree with his point of view?
2. What arguments could you make *against* the author's central thought?
3. What ideas does the image of the graduates suggest? How does it put forth the reading's central point?

QUESTIONS FOR DISCUSSION

1. How did you decide what your major would be? Discuss the factors that influenced your decision, including your family, your intellectual interests, and the job potential of your chosen major.
2. How important do you think the "practical prospects" of a college major should be when choosing a major?
3. Discuss what you think will be the main benefit of your education. Will it be the specific skills you learn, the ability to think differently about challenges, or some other benefit?

WRITING ACTIVITIES

1. Imagine that you have been asked to advise a younger friend or relative about choosing a major. Write a letter to that person expressing your opinion about how to decide on a major.
2. Write a paragraph describing your ideal job. How will the classes you take now prepare you for this job?
3. Think about someone you know who you consider successful. If possible, interview the person to discover what factors were key in his or her success; then write a paragraph describing what you found out.
4. Read these myths about choosing a college major: http://www.york.cuny.edu/academics/advisement/choosing-a-college-major/five-myths-about-college-majors

   Write a personal reflection essay that describes your experience with choosing a major and facing some of these myths. Look on the lefthand side of the Web page for more help in choosing a major if you need it.

CHAPTER 3

Identifying and Analyzing Main Ideas

RECORDING YOUR PROGRESS

Test	Number Right		Score
Practice Test 3-1	______	× 20 =	______%
Practice Test 3-2	______	× 10 =	______%
Mastery Test 3-1	______	× 10 =	______%
Mastery Test 3-2	______	× 10 =	______%
Mastery Test 3-3	______	× 5 =	______%

GETTING MORE PRACTICE PEARSON myreadinglab

To get more practice with Active Reading, go to http://www.myreadinglab.com and click on

> Study Plan
> Reading Skills
> Main Idea

EVALUATING YOUR PROGRESS PEARSON myreadinglab

To measure your progress after reading and viewing the information in the Review Materials section, complete the Practices and Tests in the Activities section. You can check your scores by clicking on the Gradebook tab.

Then, based on your performance in this chapter and/or on the MyReadingLab Practices and Tests, write your own evaluation.

YOUR EVALUATION: ______________________________

____

____

____

____

Copyright © 2012 by Pearson Education

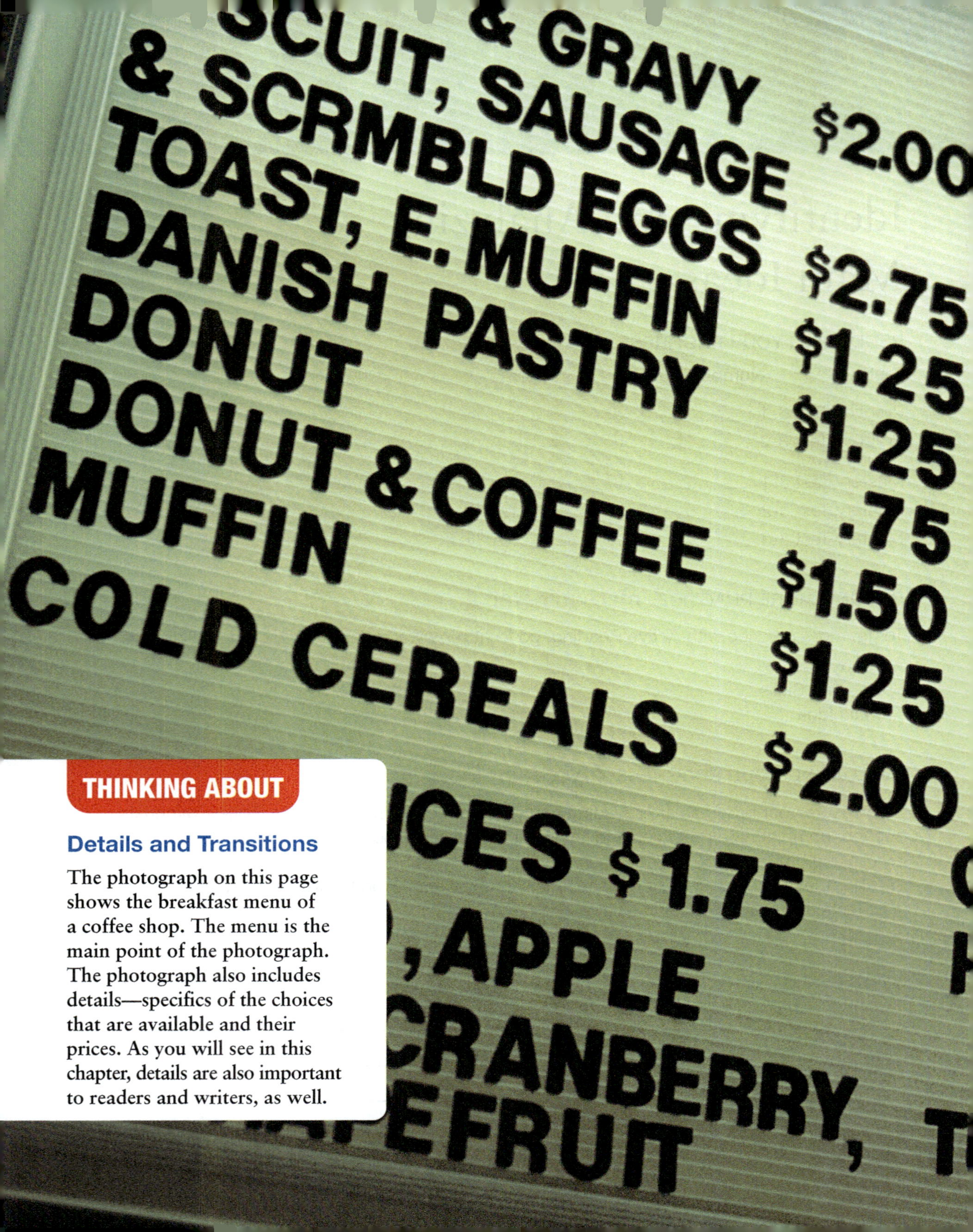

THINKING ABOUT

Details and Transitions

The photograph on this page shows the breakfast menu of a coffee shop. The menu is the main point of the photograph. The photograph also includes details—specifics of the choices that are available and their prices. As you will see in this chapter, details are also important to readers and writers, as well.

CHAPTER 4

Examining Details and Transitions

Why Are Supporting Details Important?

GOAL 1
Identify supporting details

To practice examining supporting details, go to
> Study Plan
> Reading Skills
> Supporting Details

Just as the menu offers choices that help you decide what to order, writers use details in a paragraph to help them explain fully the point they want to make. **Supporting details** are those facts and ideas that prove or explain the main idea of a paragraph. As you read, you will notice that some details are more important than others. Pay particular attention to the **major details**—the most important details that directly explain the main idea. You should also note **minor details**—details that may provide additional information, offer an example, or further explain one of the major details.

LEARNING GOALS

GOAL 1 Identify supporting details

GOAL 2 Identify transitional words and phrases

GOAL 3 Think critically about details

Figure 4-1 on page 132 shows how details relate to the main idea. As you recall from Chapter 3, the main idea is usually stated in a topic sentence.

Read the following paragraph and then study the diagram in Figure 4-2 (p. 132).

> The Abkhasians (an agricultural people who live in a mountainous region of Georgia, a republic of the former Soviet Union) may be the longest-lived people on earth. Many claim to live past 100—some beyond 120 and even 130. Although it is difficult to document the accuracy of these claims, government records indicate that an extraordinary number of Abkhasians do live to a very old age. Three main factors appear to account for their long lives. The first is their diet, which consists of little meat, much fresh fruit, vegetables, garlic, goat cheese, cornmeal, buttermilk and wine. The second is

Copyright © 2012 by Pearson Education

FIGURE 4-1

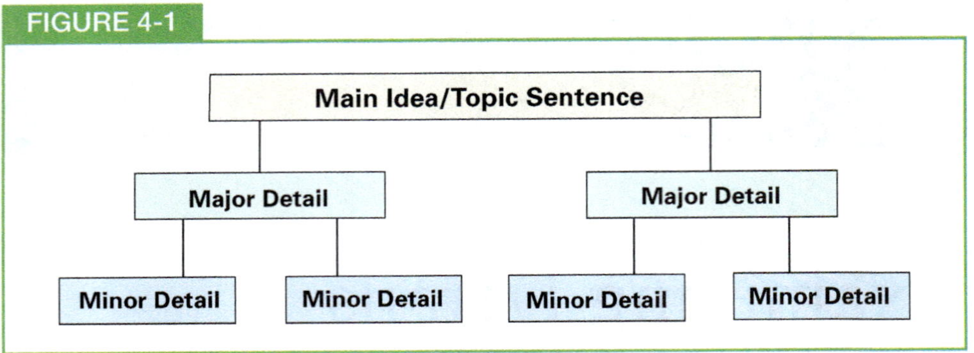

FIGURE 4-2

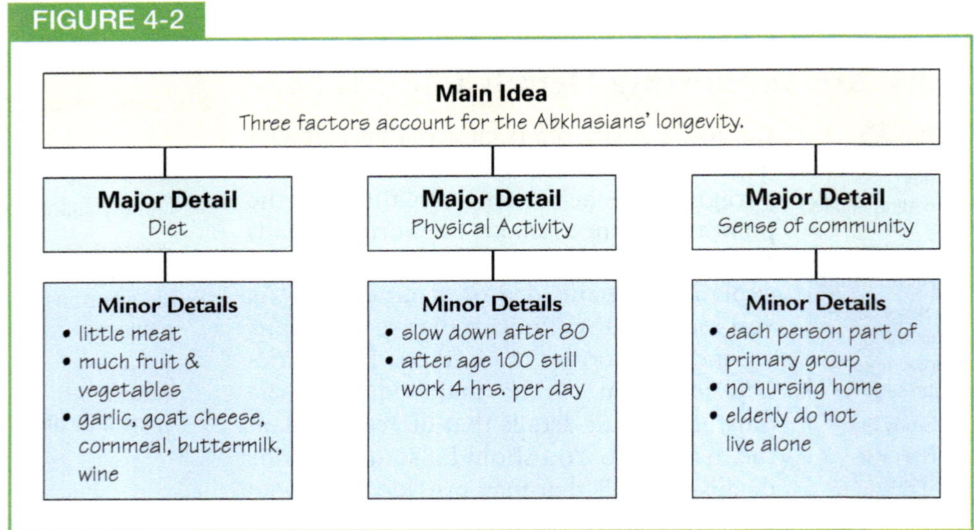

their lifelong physical activity. They do slow down after age 80, but even after the age of 100 they still work about four hours a day. The third factor—a highly developed sense of community—goes to the very heart of the Abkhasian culture. From childhood, each individual is integrated into a primary group, and remains so throughout life. There is no such thing as a nursing home, nor do the elderly live alone.

—adapted from Henslin, *Sociology: A Down-to-Earth Approach*, pp. 380–381

From Figure 4-2 you can see the three main reasons why Abkhasians live long lives. These are the major details. The minor details are less important than the major details. Minor details may provide additional information, offer an example, or further explain one of the major details. In the paragraph above, the example about Abkhasians' primary group structure provides further information and is a minor detail. The minor details are the sentences that explain other, less important details.

Look at the paragraph again, and notice how the author has used **transitions**—words that lead you from one major detail to the next. The words *first, second,* and *third* are a few of the transitions that can help you find the major details in a paragraph. Be on the lookout for transitions as you read; they are discussed more fully later in this chapter.

EXERCISE 4-1 Understanding Supporting Details

A. Directions: *Read the following paragraph and then complete the diagram that follows. Some of the items have been filled in for you.*

Small group discussions progress through four phases. The first is orientation, when the members become comfortable with each other. Second is the conflict phase. Disagreements and tensions become evident. The amount of conflict varies with each group. The third phase is known as emergence. The members begin to try to reach a decision. The members who created conflict begin to move toward a middle road. The final phase is the reinforcement phase when the decision is reached. The members of the group offer positive reinforcement toward each other and the decision.

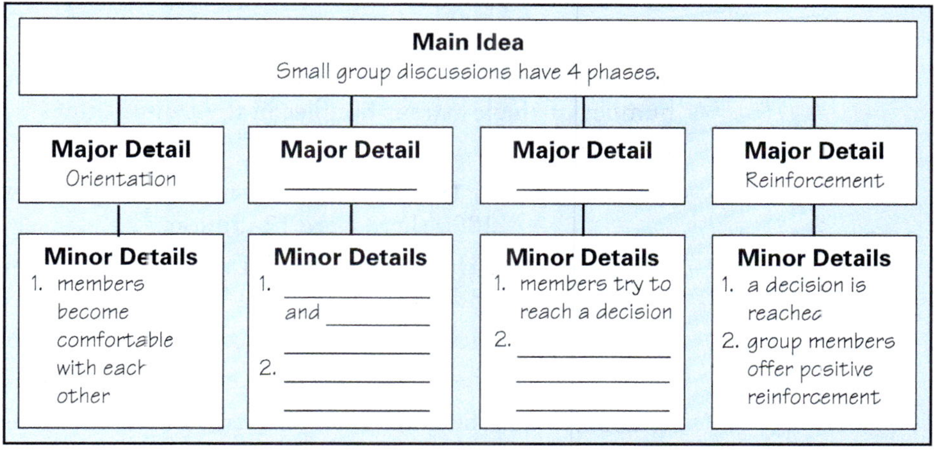

B. Directions: *Read the paragraph again and list the four transitions the writer uses to help you find the four major details.*

1. ____________ 2. ____________ 3. ____________ 4. ____________

The diagram you completed in the exercise above is a **map**—a visual way of organizing information. By filling in—or drawing—maps you can "see" how ideas in a paragraph or essay are related. Chapter 6 gives you more information about mapping (see page 212) and about other ways of organizing information.

Copyright © 2012 by Pearson Education

EXERCISE 4-2 Using Major Details

Directions: *Each of the following topic sentences states the main idea of a paragraph. After each topic sentence are sentences containing details that may or may not support the topic sentence. Read each sentence and write an "M" beside those that contain major details that support the topic sentence.*

1. *Topic sentence:* Most Mexican Americans are in the United States as a result of immigration that has taken place since 1900.

   Details:

   _______ a. Puerto Rico was added as a territory of the United States in 1898.

   _______ b. Emigration is the process of permanently leaving one's country, while immigration is the process of entering a foreign country to become a citizen.

   _______ c. Mexico's economic problems prompted many people to emigrate.

   _______ d. Hispanic Americans are often called Latinos.

   _______ e. Many Mexican immigrants came to California in order to work in agriculture.

2. *Topic sentence:* Divorce and out of wedlock births have led to a rise in the number of single-parent families in the United States.

   Details:

   _______ a. In 1970 there were 3 million single-parent families, while in 2000 there were 12 million.

   _______ b. Partners who cohabitate usually do so on a temporary basis and eventually marry.

   _______ c. Most single-parent families are headed by females.

   _______ d. Blended families make up one-third of all U.S. families.

   _______ e. There has been an increase in the number of couples attending marriage counseling since 1980.

3. *Topic sentence:* The Internet has allowed people to become more socially connected and engage in more communication with greater numbers of people.

   Details:

   _______ a. Technology has made contact with others easier and less expensive than it used to be.

   _______ b. The Internet allows people to choose friends based on interest rather than geography.

_______ c. The Internet allows people to work from home and decreases their one-on-one exposure to other people.

_______ d. The Internet allows people to make contact with others while still maintaining anonymity, making it easier to take personal risks in relationships.

_______ e. E-mail and chat rooms allow for communication at any time of the day, making interpersonal communication more accessible.

EXERCISE 4-3 Recognizing Details

Directions: *Read the paragraph and answer the questions that follow.*

A person's personality type can determine how he or she creates and reacts to self-imposed stress. The first kind of personality type is known as Type A. Type A personalities work hard, are anxious, competitive, and driven and often create high expectations for themselves. Type As are more likely than others to have heart attacks. Type B is the second personality type. Type Bs tend to be relaxed, laid-back, and noncompetitive. A third personality type is Type C. Type Cs are Type A's who thrive under stress, achieve things, and experience little or no stress-related health problems. Most people can't be categorized as one personality type and display characteristics of different types at different times.

1. Does the topic sentence occur first, last, or in the middle of the paragraph?

   ____

2. List the paragraph's three major details:

   ____

   ____

   ____

3. What transition words does the writer use to take the reader from one major detail to the next? _______________

4. In the third sentence, what does the word *expectations* mean?

   ____

   ____

5. Is the last sentence the main idea of the paragraph, a major detail, or a minor detail? _______________

Copyright © 2012 by Pearson Education

Using Transitions

GOAL 2 Identify transitional words and phrases

As you know, **transitions** are linking words or phrases that lead the reader from one idea to another. If you get into the habit of recognizing transitions, you will see that they often help you read a paragraph more easily.

In the following paragraph, notice how the underlined transitions lead you from one detail to the next.

> When Marcita takes an exam, she follows a certain procedure. <u>First of all</u>, she tries to find a seat in the room away from others. She might sit at the back of the room, <u>for example</u>, or sit in the front row so no one is in front of her. <u>Next</u>, she gets her supplies ready, <u>such as</u> pencils, pens, and paper. Sometimes, <u>however</u>, she brings things like a calculator or textbook if the instructor permits them. <u>Finally</u>, she sits quietly for a moment before the test begins. She does this because it usually helps her relax and clear her mind.

Not all paragraphs contain such obvious transitions, and not all transitions serve as such clear markers of details. As you can see, transitions may be used for a variety of reasons. They may alert you to what will come next in the paragraph, they may tell you that an example will follow, or they may predict that a different, opposing idea is coming. Table 4-1 lists some of the most common transitions and indicates what they tell you.

TABLE 4-1 Common Transitions

Type of Transition	Example	What They Tell the Reader
Time sequence	first, later, next, finally	The author is arranging ideas in the order in which they happened.
Example	for example, for instance, to illustrate, such as	An example will follow.
Enumeration	first, second, third, last, another, next	The author is marking or identifying each major point. (Sometimes these may be used to suggest order of importance.)
Continuation	also, in addition, and, further, another	The author is continuing with the same idea and is going to provide additional information.
Contrast	on the other hand, in contrast, however	The author is switching to a different, opposite, or contrasting idea than previously discussed.
Comparison	like, likewise, similarly	The writer will show how the preceding idea is similar to what follows.
Cause/effect	because, thus, therefore	The writer will show a connection between two or more things, how one thing caused another, or how something happened as a result of something else.

EXERCISE 4-4 Using Transitions

Directions: *Select the transitional word or phrase from the box below that best completes each of the following sentences. Some of the transitions in the box may be used more than once.*

on the other hand	for example	because
in addition	similarly	after
next	however	also

1. Typically, those suffering from post-traumatic stress disorder are soldiers after combat. Likewise, civilians who have experienced events such as the World Trade Center destruction can ____________________ experience this syndrome.
2. Columbus was determined to find an oceanic passage to China ____________________ finding a direct route would mean increased trading and huge profits.
3. In the event of a heart attack, it is important to first identify the symptoms. ____________________, call 911 or drive the victim to the nearest hospital.
4. In the 1920s, courtship between men and women changed dramatically. ____________________, instead of paying calls at the woman's home with her parents there, men now invited women out on dates.
5. Direct exposure to sunlight is dangerous because the ultraviolet rays can lead to skin cancer. ____________________, tanning booths also emit ultra violet rays and are as dangerous as, if not more dangerous than, exposure to sunlight.
6. Lie detector tests are often used by law enforcement to help determine guilt or innocence. ____________________, since these tests often have an accuracy rate of only between 60 and 80 percent, the results are not admissible in court.
7. The temporal lobes of the brain process sound and comprehend language. ____________________, this area of the brain is responsible for storing visual memories.

Copyright © 2012 by Pearson Education

8. The theory of multiple intelligences holds that there are many different kinds of intelligence, or abilities. ____________________, musical ability, control of bodily movements (athletics), spatial understanding, and observational abilities are all classified as different types of intelligence.

9. During World War II, Japanese Americans were held in relocation camps. ____________________ the war was over, the United States paid reparations and issued an apology to those who were wrongfully detained.

10. Support continues to grow for the legalization of marijuana. ____________________, legalization has not yet been passed in any state and it is unlikely this will happen anytime soon.

EXERCISE 4-5 Understanding Transitions

Directions: *Many transitions have similar meanings and can sometimes be used interchangeably. Match each transition in column A with a similar transition in column B.*

	Column A	Column B
_______	1. because	a. therefore
_______	2. in contrast	b. also
_______	3. for instance	c. likewise
_______	4. thus	d. after that
_______	5. first	e. since
_______	6. one way	f. finally
_______	7. similarly	g. on the other hand
_______	8. next	h. one approach
_______	9. in addition	i. in the beginning
_______	10. to sum up	j. for example

Thinking Critically About Details

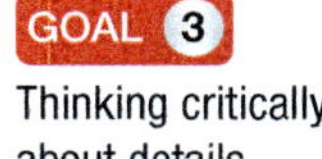

Thinking critically about details

Writers choose the details they provide to support a main idea. They rarely have the time, or the space, to list every available supporting detail. Consider the following paragraph:

> Cross-sex friendships [that is, friendships between a man and a woman] have many benefits. Befriending a person of the opposite sex can give one a unique perspective on the other sex, and gender roles become mitigated. Cross-sex friendships are even associated with higher self-esteem and self-confidence.
>
> —Kunz, *Think Marriages & Families*, p. 83

The author provides two details to support the topic sentence "Cross-sex friendships have many benefits." These are: (1) having a friend of the opposite sex can help you better understand the opposite sex, and (2) friends of the opposite sex can make you feel better about yourself. But the author could also have chosen other details. For example, some people believe that men become better listeners when they have female friends.

As you read, be aware of the details that the writer has chosen to include. Has the writer omitted any important details to make a stronger case? Has he or she used any specific words to influence you? For example, suppose you are looking to rent an apartment, and you see an ad that reads as follows:

> 1 bedroom, 1 bath apartment. Cozy and cute, very conveniently located. Monthly rent includes water and gas. Most appliances also included. On-street parking is available.

This apartment may seem appealing, but look carefully at the details. What exactly does "cozy" mean? Often, the word *cozy* really means "small." And "conveniently located" might mean the apartment is located at a busy intersection (which might be very noisy). The rent includes water and gas . . . but what about electricity? "Most" appliances are included—which ones aren't? (Maybe you'd have to buy a stove or a refrigerator.) And the fact that on-street parking is "available" doesn't guarantee that you'll always get a parking spot in front of the building.

Copyright © 2012 by Pearson Education

EXERCISE 4-6 Thinking Critically About Details

Directions: Read the paragraphs and answer the questions that follow.

A lot of people are looking for a "magic pill" that will help them maintain weight loss, reduce their risk of diseases, make them feel better, and improve their quality of sleep. Although many people are not aware of it, regular physical activity is this "magic pill." That's because it promotes physical fitness: the ability to carry out daily tasks with vigor and alertness, without undue fatigue, and with ample energy to enjoy leisure-time pursuits and meet unforeseen emergencies.

—Thompson and Manore, *Nutrition for Life*, p. 302

1. What essential ingredient of good health/physical fitness is missing from this paragraph? ____________________

The world's most livable cities are not those with "perfect" auto access between all points. Instead, they are cities that have taken measures to reduce outward sprawl, diminish automobile traffic, and improve access by foot and bicycle in conjunction with mass transit. For example, Geneva, Switzerland, prohibits automobile parking at workplaces in the city's center, forcing commuters to use the excellent public transportation system. Copenhagen bans all on-street parking in the downtown core. Paris has removed 200,000 parking places in the downtown area. Curitiba, Brazil, is cited as the most livable city in all of Latin America. The achievement of Curitiba is due almost entirely to the efforts of Jaime Lerner, who, serving as mayor for many decades, guided development with an emphasis on mass transit rather than cars. The space saved by not building highways and parking lots has been put into parks and shady walkways, causing the amount of green area per inhabitant to increase from 4.5 square feet in 1970 to 450 square feet today.

—Wright and Boorse, *Environmental Science: Toward a Sustainable Future*, p. 604

2. What is main idea of the paragraph?

____

____

3. Which four cities are offered as examples (supporting details) of livable cities?

____

4. By not listing any U.S. examples of "livable cities," what might the author be implying (but not stating directly)?

____

____

5. What other cities might have been mentioned as having good systems of mass transit? (Hint: Think of U.S. cities that have reliable train and bus service.)

____

____

TEXTBOOK CHALLENGE

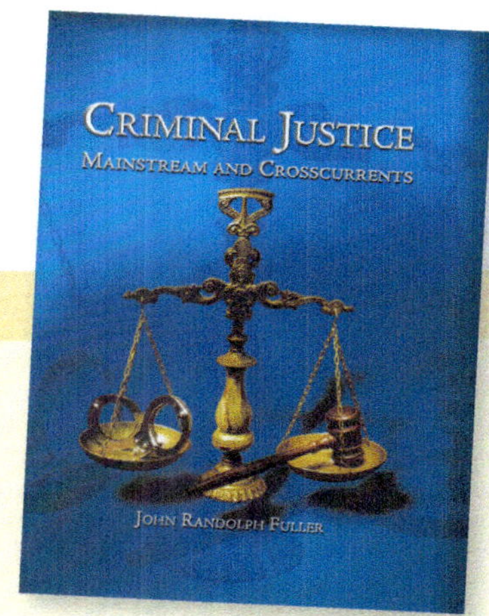

TIPS for Reading in Career Fields

When reading career textbooks, pay attention to

- **Practical explanations.** Career textbooks prepare you for a specific job and offer information that can be directly applied once you are working.
- **Trends and projections.** Courses in career fields emphasize current information and changes in direction that you will need to rely on in the workplace.
- **Professional language.** Learn to communicate effectively and understand what you're reading.

Copyright © 2012 by Pearson Education

Part A: Analyzing a Textbook Excerpt

This excerpt was taken from a criminal justice textbook chapter about crime. Read the excerpt and follow the directions on pp. 143–144.

Fear of Crime

1 Only the direct consumers of crime statistics are affected by the limitations of crime-measuring efforts. Government funding agencies, law enforcement departments, and the media are concerned with discovering the overall crime picture so they can decide where to allocate resources or how to enlighten the public. However, most of us know little about these elaborate and expensive ways to measure crime and make our daily decisions to prevent, avoid, or respond to crime based on our perceptions of danger and assumed likelihood of victimization. Despite our relative lack of knowledge of the actual level and seriousness of crime in our communities, we have a healthy respect for the potential effect of crime on our lives, and we take measures to reduce the chances of becoming crime victims. In this way, a realistic fear of crime is useful. The questions to be addressed here concern where our fear of crime comes from and whether that fear is justified.

2 For many people, the fear of crime is a constant feature that dictates how they conduct their daily lives. While waxing poetically about the "good old days" when they could leave their homes for an afternoon of shopping and not bother to lock their doors, they spend considerable amounts of money on deadbolt locks, security systems, cameras, and noise machines that sound like big, barking dogs. More generally, they isolate themselves in gated communities, are suspicious of delivery people, and to a large degree, surrender public spaces to street people at night. The fear of crime, although healthy to some degree, has also diminished our sense of community and has developed into a self-fulfilling prophecy that stimulates crime by reducing the interconnectedness of people. How justified is this fear?

3 In his book *Random Violence*, sociologist Joel Best addressed the perception of many people that crime is a significant problem that will soon affect their lives unless they take steps to avoid it. Best contended that perceptions of violence are constructed not by official measures of crime, but by the media, which can distort and sensationalize particular incidents. Isolated violent events can appear to be a threat to everyone. One of the first issues that Best confronted was the notion of random violence, pointing out problems with three popular conceptions that compose the idea of random violence.

The news media can inflame the public's fear of crime, especially after particularly shocking incidents.

Source: Joel Gordon/Joel Gordon Photography

66 PART I Crime: Problems, Measurement, Theories, and Law

4 **1. Patternlessness.** The term *random violence* implies that anyone could be a victim at any time. In fact, crime is highly patterned. That is, certain people are more likely to be victims than are other people. When we examine homicide rates (for which we have the most reliable statistics), we see that age, race, and gender clearly affect the probability of victimization. For example, Best argued that homicide rates for white males peak for those between ages 20 and 24, then gradually decline as the men grow older. Crime can be examined for patterns, and according to Best, the patterns are so clear and distinct that the term *random violence* is inaccurate.

5 **2. Pointlessness.** Sensational incidents of crime can appear to be pointless. When the car driven by Susan Smith in South Carolina was allegedly carjacked and found at the bottom of a lake with her two small children still strapped into their car seats, people were at a loss to explain such a senseless and pointless act of cruelty. It was later discovered that Smith drowned her children because she had had an affair with a man who did not want a long-term relationship with her because of her children. Smith then killed her children to get them out of the way of her quest to maintain her relationship with her boyfriend. Most criminal offenses have a motive. Violence can be instrumental, but even when it seems random, on further examination it is often found to have a purpose.

6 **3. Deterioration of society.** When the media report a number of sensational offenses, random violence appears to be epidemic. Because of the national and international scope of the media, all news can be perceived as local news. Widely scattered occurrences of firearm violence in schools can appear to constitute a wave of school shootings that makes all teenagers seem violent.

7 Violent crime is usually not random. Crime has clear patterns, and it almost always has a purpose despite initial appearances. Unrelated offenses distributed over large geographic areas do not constitute an epidemic and do not signal the deterioration of the social order and a rapid descent into chaos. Yet the public's fear of crime suggests that crime is such a serious problem that society has lost its cohesion and that the old processes of social control are no longer effective.

—Fuller, *Criminal Justice*, pp. 65–67

1. **Preview.** Preview the reading using the guidelines on p. 7 and then answer the following questions.
   a. What aspects of crime does this excerpt address?
   b. How are sensational crimes often perceived?
   c. Is crime random or purposeful?
2. **SQ3R.** Write at least three questions for the Q step of SQ3R. Answer them after completing the reading.
3. **Textbook Features.** What key point in the excerpt does the image illustrate? How did you react to it?

Copyright © 2012 by Pearson Education

4. **Vocabulary.**
   a. Identify the important new terms that are introduced in the reading.
   b. Define each of the following words and phrases as used in the reading.
   allocate (par. 1), *waxing poetically* (par. 2), *distort* (par. 3), *motive* (par. 5), *cohesion* (par. 7)
5. **Applying Chapter Skills.** Complete the diagram based on information in the selection.

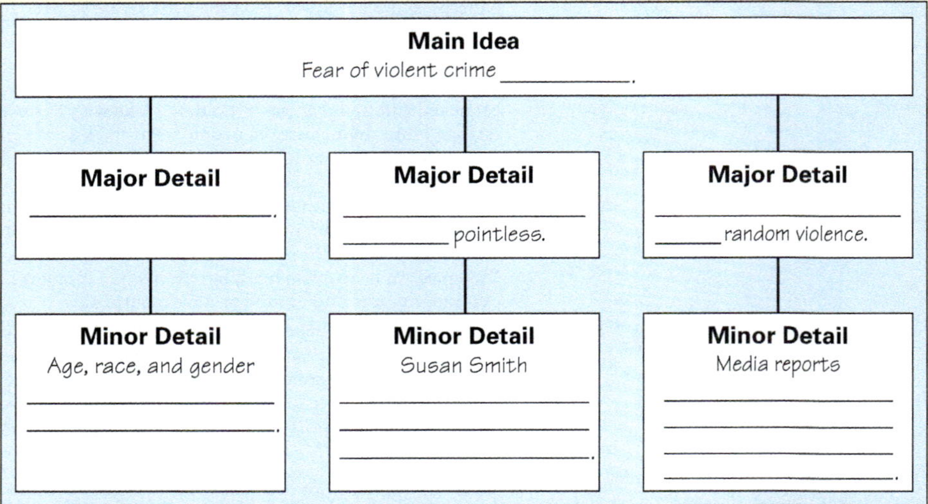

6. **Essay Question.** Write an answer to the following essay question. To test your memory, write it without referring to the excerpt.
   Write an essay discussing the fear of crime. Explain why people fear crime and what popular misconceptions they hold.
7. **Thinking Critically.** Use your critical thinking skills to answer each of the following questions.
   a. If you wanted to reassure someone about his or her safety, what details from this selection would you offer?
   b. What kinds of supporting details would you include in this selection to give credence to people's fears about crime?
   c. Based on the tone of this selection, do you think the author or his family members have ever been affected by crime? Why or why not?

Part B: Your College Textbook

Choose a chapter that you have been assigned to read in a textbook for one of your other courses. Create a chart outlining the main idea, major details, and minor details for a selection of your choice of one to two pages within the chapter.

SELF-TEST SUMMARY

To test yourself, cover up the Answer column with a sheet of paper and answer each question listed in the left column. Evaluate each of your answers as you work by sliding the paper down and comparing your answer with what is printed in the Answer column.

	Question	Answer
GOAL 1	What are supporting details?	Supporting details explain or add support to the paragraph's main idea.
GOAL 2	How can you recognize a transition in a paragraph?	A transition is a word or phrase that links one idea to the next in the paragraph.
GOAL 3	How can you think critically about details?	Analyze the details the writer has chosen; determine whether the writer has omitted details or has selectively chosen details to influence you.

Copyright © 2012 by Pearson Education

PRACTICE TEST 4-1

NAME ______________________ SECTION ______________________

DATE ______________________ SCORE ______________________

Identifying Details

Directions: *Read the paragraph and then complete the diagram below. Some of the items have been filled in for you.*

What can you do if you have trouble sleeping? Four techniques may help. *Restrict your sleeping hours to the same nightly pattern.* Keep regular sleeping hours. Avoid sleeping late in the morning, napping longer than an hour, or going to bed earlier than usual, all of which will throw you off schedule, creating even more sleep difficulties. And try to get up at the same time every day, even on weekends or days off. *Control bedtime stimuli* so that things normally associated with sleep are associated only with sleep. Use your bed only for sleep (don't read or watch tv in bed). *Avoid ingesting substances with stimulant properties.* Don't smoke cigarettes or drink beverages with alcohol or caffeine in the evening. Alcohol may cause initial drowsiness, but it has a "rebound effect" that leaves many people wide awake in the middle of the night. Don't drink water close to bedtime; getting up to use the bathroom can lead to poor sleep. *Consider meditation or progressive muscle relaxation.* Either technique can be helpful, if used regularly.

—adapted from Kosslyn and Rosenberg, *Fundamentals of Psychology,* pp. 368–369

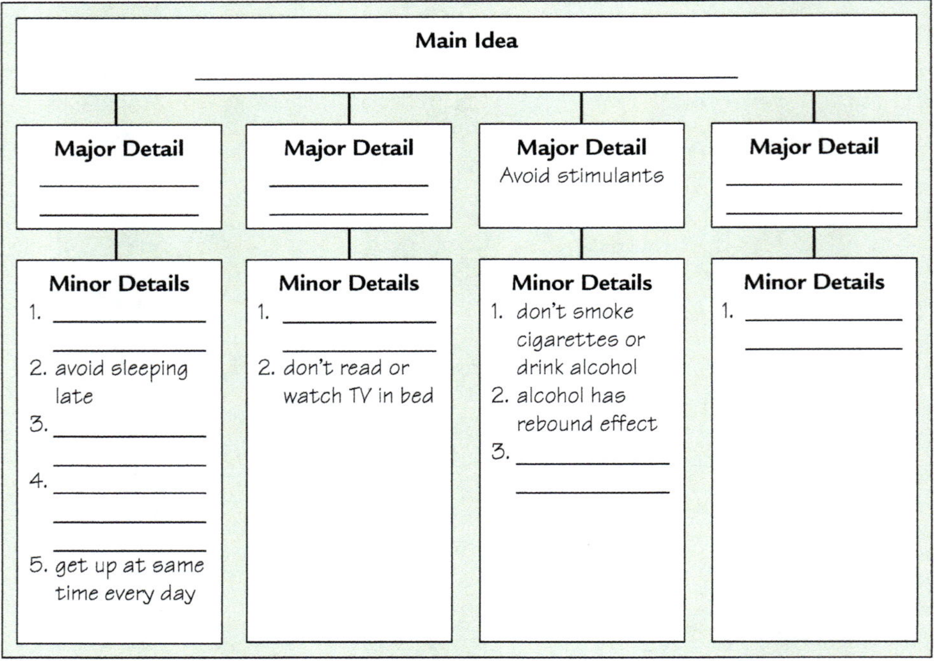

NAME ______________ SECTION ______________
DATE ______________ SCORE ______________

PRACTICE TEST 4-2

Understanding Paragraph Structure

***Directions:** After reading each paragraph, select the choice that best completes each of the statements that follow.*

Paragraph A

Two general types of meaning are essential to identify: denotation and connotation. The term *denotation* refers to the meaning you'd find in a dictionary; it's the meaning that members of the culture assign to a word. *Connotation* is the emotional meaning that specific listeners give to a word. Take as an example the word *death.* To a doctor this word might mean (denote) the time when the heart stops. This is an objective description of a particular event. On the other hand, to a mother who is informed of her son's death, the word means (connotes) much more. It recalls her son's youth, ambitions, family, illness, and so on. To her, *death* is a highly emotional, subjective, and personal word. These emotional, subjective, or personal associations are the word's connotative meaning. The denotation of a word is its objective definition. The connotation of a word is its subjective or emotional meaning.

—DeVito, *Messages: Building Interpersonal Communication Skills,* p. 121

_______ 1. The main idea of the paragraph is that
- a. the word *death* has several meanings.
- b. denotation refers to dictionary meanings.
- c. words have emotional meanings.
- d. there are two types of meaning for many words.

_______ 2. The phrase *on the other hand* suggests that
- a. a reason is to follow.
- b. a contrasting idea will follow.
- c. a list will follow.
- d. more detailed information will follow.

_______ 3. The fifth sentence, which begins with "To a doctor," is
- a. a transition.
- b. a major detail.
- c. the topic sentence.
- d. a minor detail.

Copyright © 2012 by Pearson Education

_______ 4. The second sentence of the paragraph, which begins with "The term *denotation*," is

a. the topic sentence.

b. a major detail.

c. a transitional statement.

d. a minor detail.

_______ 5. According to the paragraph,

a. doctors do not use emotional language.

b. connotative meanings are the same for everyone in a culture.

c. connotative meanings vary from person to person.

d. descriptions can never be truly objective.

Paragraph B

Communicating your emotions and responding appropriately can be difficult, but it is helpful to view the process as involving a number of specific tasks. Your first task is to understand the emotions you're feeling. For example, consider how you would feel if your best friend just got the promotion you wanted or if your brother, a police officer, was shot while breaking up a street riot. Try to answer the question, "Why am I feeling this way?" or "What happened to lead me to feel as I do?" Your second task is to decide, if, in fact, you want to express your emotions. In circumstances in which you have time to think before you react, ask yourself whether you wish to communicate your emotions. Remember, it is not always wise to give vent to every feeling you have. If you do decide to express your emotions, the third task is to evaluate your communication options in terms of both effectiveness and ethics (what is right or morally justified). When thinking in terms of effectiveness, consider, for example, the time and setting, the persons you want to reveal these feelings to, and the available methods of communication. When thinking in terms of ethics, consider the legitimacy of appeals based on emotions.

—adapted from DeVito, *Messages: Building Interpersonal Communication Skills,* pp. 197–198

_______ 6. The main idea of the paragraph is expressed in

a. the first sentence.

b. the second sentence.

c. the fifth sentence.

d. the last sentence.

_______ 7. The second sentence, which begins with "Your first task," is

a. the main idea.

b. a transitional sentence.

c. a minor detail.

d. a major detail.

_______ 8. Which of the following is a transitional word or phrase?

a. Remember

b. Your second task

c. Try to answer

d. When thinking in

_______ 9. The third sentence, which begins with "For example, consider," is

a. the topic sentence.

b. a transitional sentence.

c. a minor detail.

d. a major detail.

_______ 10. According to the passage,

a. emotions do not always need to be expressed.

b. it is never morally justified to withhold your feelings.

c. you never have time to think before you react emotionally.

d. you can never express emotions effectively; they just happen.

Copyright © 2012 by Pearson Education

MASTERY TEST 4-1

NAME ______________________ SECTION ______________________

DATE ______________________ SCORE ______________________

Recognizing Details

Directions: *After reading the passage, select the choice that best completes each of the statements that follow.*

Physical Appearance and Clothing

In our Western culture, appearance matters. People's perceptions of our outward appearance make a big difference in our opportunities to establish relationships, find jobs, and succeed in school. Studies have shown that we care about appearance, and attractive people, overall, find it easier to make friends, gain employment, and earn good grades. What messages are you sending by wearing several earrings or piercing your nose or belly button? In some social groups, this is a sign of being cool or stylish. How might a future employer at a bank, for example, perceive the body piercings? Our physical appearance matters, and we need to be aware that others may view us differently because of it.

The way we dress becomes part of the message we send to others, whether we intend it to or not. Our clothes and style of dress contribute to the way we see ourselves and the way others perceive us. Our style of clothing also reflects our ability or willingness to adjust to a variety of social situations. In other words, what we choose to wear can reflect our desire to gain acceptance within a given social situation. For instance, if we wanted to "fit in" among the other guests at a formal dinner party, we would wear a tuxedo or an appropriate evening dress. Moreover, our choice of dress reveals information about ourselves and affects our impact in both interpersonal and public communication settings.

What specifically does our clothing communicate? One thing it can indicate is our age or an age we wish to project. If, for example, we want to appear youthful, we would dress according to the latest styles or trends. Beware, however, that we can inadvertently give away our age by wearing clothes considered to be out of date.

Certain types of dress identify individuals as members of particular groups or professions. When we see someone dressed in a blue uniform, we presume (usually correctly) that he or she is a member of a police department. Other examples include black collars worn by priests, military uniforms worn by men and women in the armed forces, uniforms representing different sports, leather jackets worn by members of motorcycle gangs, and native dress representing foreign nations (sarongs worn by Indian women, for example).

—Dunn and Goodnight, *Communication: Embracing Difference,* pp. 100–101

______ 1. The central thought of the entire selection is
   a. body piercings may send the wrong message.
   b. the way we dress identifies us as a group member.
   c. clothing helps you to fit into social situations.
   d. physical appearance, as evidenced by what we wear, matters.

______ 2. The topic of paragraph 1 is
   a. dressing for careers.
   b. group membership.
   c. styles of clothing.
   d. physical appearance.

______ 3. In paragraph 1, which of the following is a minor detail?
   a. Appearance affects the establishment of relationships.
   b. People may view us differently because of our physical appearance.
   c. Attractive people find it easier to build friendships, find jobs, and get good grades.
   d. Body piercing may be a sign of being cool.

______ 4. The topic sentence of paragraph 2 begins with the words
   a. "For instance, if."
   b. "The way we dress."
   c. "Moreover, our choice."
   d. "In other words."

______ 5. In paragraph 2, all the following are major supporting details *except*
   a. Clothing and style of dressing contribute to our self-image.
   b. Our style of clothing reflects our willingness to fit into a social situation.
   c. A tuxedo or evening dress is appropriate formal attire.
   d. Choice of clothing affects both interpersonal and public communication.

Copyright © 2012 by Pearson Education

_____ 6. In paragraph 2, the transitional word *moreover* signals
a. the topic.
b. another example.
c. a major detail.
d. a minor detail.

_____ 7. The second sentence of paragraph 3, which begins with the words "One thing," is
a. a minor detail.
b. a major detail.
c. a transition.
d. the paragraph's main idea.

_____ 8. The transitional phrase "other examples" in paragraph 4 indicates that the writers will
a. put ideas in order.
b. offer examples.
c. switch to an opposite idea.
d. show how one thing caused another.

_____ 9. In paragraph 4, which of the following is *not* a minor detail?
a. Priests wear collars.
b. Motorcycle gang members wear leather jackets.
c. Dress can identify people as members of groups.
d. Members of the armed forces wear uniforms.

_____ 10. According to the selection,
a. people are judged only by appearance.
b. appearance has an important impact on how we are perceived.
c. clothing only sends messages when we intend it to.
d. we should change how we dress to gain acceptance.

NAME ______________________ SECTION ______________

DATE ______________________ SCORE ______________

MASTERY TEST 4-2

Recognizing Details

Directions: *After reading the passage, select the choice that best completes each of the statements that follow.*

Advantages and Disadvantages of Modified Schedules and Alternative Workplaces

Flextime [a system that allows employees to set their own daily work schedules] gives employees more freedom in their professional and personal lives. It allows workers to plan around the work schedules of spouses and the school schedules of young children. Studies show that the increased sense of freedom and control reduces stress and thus improves individual productivity.

Companies also benefit in other ways. In urban areas, for example, such programs can reduce traffic congestion and similar problems that contribute to stress and lost work time. Furthermore, employers benefit from higher levels of commitment and job satisfaction. John Hancock Insurance http://www.jhancock.com, Atlantic Richfield http://www.arco.com, and Metropolitan Life http://www.metlife.com are among the major American corporations that have successfully adopted some form of flextime.

Conversely, flextime sometimes complicates coordination because people are working different schedules. For example, Sue may need some important information from Joe at 4:30 PM, but because Joe is working an earlier schedule, he leaves for the day at 3:00. In addition, if workers are paid by the hour, flextime may make it difficult for employers to keep accurate records of when employees are actually working.

As for telecommuting and virtual offices, although they may be the wave of the future, they may not be for everyone. For example, consultant Gil Gordon points out that telecommuters are attracted to the ideas of "not having to shave and put on makeup or go through traffic, and sitting in their blue jeans all day." However, he suggests that would-be telecommuters ask themselves several other questions: "Can I manage deadlines? What will it be like to be away from the social context of the office five days a week? Can I renegotiate the rules of the family, so my spouse doesn't come home every night expecting me to have a four-course meal on the table?" One study has shown that even though telecommuters may be producing results, those with strong advancement ambitions may miss networking and rubbing elbows with management on a day-to-day basis.

—Griffin and Ebert, *Business Essentials,* pp. 210–211

Copyright © 2012 by Pearson Education

_____ 1. The central thought of the entire selection is that

a. there are both advantages and disadvantages to flextime and to working at home.

b. telecommuting creates problems for workers who are not self-directed.

c. flextime benefits employers as well as employees.

d. flextime increases workers' sense of freedom and reduces stress.

_____ 2. In paragraph 1, the word **productivity** means

a. ability to get work done.

b. expenses created by a worker.

c. quality of work done.

d. training needed by a worker.

_____ 3. In paragraph 1, the major details explain

a. the advantages and disadvantages of flextime.

b. how flextime creates stress.

c. that flextime has a negative impact on productivity.

d. how flextime benefits employees.

_____ 4. In paragraph 2, the sentence that begins with the words "Furthermore, employees benefit," is

a. the paragraph's main idea.

b. a minor detail.

c. a major detail.

d. an example.

_____ 5. The last sentence of paragraph 2 is

a. a minor detail.

b. a transition.

c. a major detail.

d. the main idea.

_____ 6. In paragraph 2, the topic sentence is expressed in the

a. first sentence.

b. second sentence.

c. third sentence.

d. last sentence.

_____ 7. When the writers move from discussing the benefits of flextime to the discussion in paragraph 3 of its problems, they use the transition

a. *for example.*

b. *conversely.*

c. *in contrast.*

d. *on the other hand.*

_____ 8. In paragraph 3, the word **coordination** means

a. simplifying complex things.

b. flexibility.

c. scheduling.

d. working together.

_____ 9. The major supporting details of paragraph 4 explain

a. the advantages and disadvantages of telecommuting.

b. why virtual offices and telecommuting are not for everyone.

c. how to renegotiate family rules.

d. why telecommuters like to wear blue jeans.

_____ 10. According to the selection,

a. flextime is the best option for workers.

b. companies as well as employees benefit from flextime.

c. flextime costs companies a lot of money.

d. telecommuting usually has a negative impact on home life.

Copyright © 2012 by Pearson Education

NAME ______________________ SECTION ______________________

DATE ______________________ SCORE ______________________

READING SELECTION

Talking a Stranger Through the Night

Sherry Amatenstein

This reading first appeared in *Newsweek*. Read it to find out how one woman connected with another person in an impersonal city and saved a life.

Vocabulary Preview

These are some of the difficult words in this essay. The definitions here will help you if you can't figure out the meanings from the sentence context or word parts.

Holocaust (par. 1) extermination of Jewish people during World War II

empathetic (par. 2) understanding others' emotions and feelings

idealism (par. 3) naïve belief in the good aspects of something

succession (par. 3) series occurring one after another, in an orderly line

untethered (par. 4) alone and not connected to anyone

rationale (par. 4) line of reasoning

imminent (par. 5) immediate, happening soon

dictum (par. 7) pronouncement, rule

1 The call came 60 minutes into my third shift as a volunteer at the crisis hot line. As the child of Holocaust survivors, I grew up wanting to ease other people's pain. But it wasn't until after September 11 that I contacted Help Line, the nonprofit telephone service headquartered in New York. The instructor of the nine-week training course taught us how to handle a variety of callers, from depressed seniors to "repeats" (those who checked in numerous times a day).

2 We spent two sessions on suicide calls but I prayed I wouldn't get one until I felt comfortable on the line. Drummed over and over into the 30 trainees' heads was that our role wasn't to give advice. Rather, we were to act as empathetic sounding boards and encourage callers to figure out how to take action.

3 My idealism about the hot line's value faded that first night, as in quick succession I heard from men who wanted to masturbate while I listened, repeats who told me again and again about their horrific childhoods, know-nothing shrinks and luckless lives, and three separate callers who railed about the low intellect of everyone living in Queens (my borough!). Sprinkled into the mix were people who turned abusive when I refused to tell them how to solve their problems.

4 I tried to remain sympathetic. If I, who had it together (an exciting career, great friends and family) found New York isolating, I could imagine how frightening it was for people so untethered they needed a hot line for company. That rationale didn't help. After only 10 hours, I no longer cringed each time the phone rang, terrified it signified a problem I wasn't equipped to handle. Instead I wondered what fresh torture this caller had up his unstable sleeve.

Touching others through a hot line

5 Then Sandy's (not her real name) quavering voice nipped into my ear: "I want to kill myself." I snapped to attention, remembering my training. Did she have an imminent plan to do herself in? Luckily, no. Sandy knew a man who'd attempted suicide via pills, threw them up and lived. She was afraid of botching a similar attempt. Since she was handicapped, she couldn't even walk to her window to jump out.

6 Sandy's life was certainly Help Line material. Her parents had disowned her 40 years before. She'd worked as a secretary until a bone-crushing fall put her out of commission. Years later she was working again and had a boyfriend who stuck with her even after a cab struck Sandy and put her back on the disabled list. They became engaged, and then, soap-opera like, tragedy struck again. Sandy's boyfriend was diagnosed with cancer and passed away last year. Now she was in constant pain, confined to a dark apartment, her only companion a nurse's aide. "There's nothing left," she cried. "Give me a reason to live."

7 Her plea drove home the wisdom of the "no advice" dictum. How could I summon the words to give someone else's life meaning? The best I could do was to help Sandy fan the spark that had led her to reach out. I tossed life-affirming statements at her like paint on a canvas; hoping some would stick. I ended with "Sandy, I won't whitewash your problems. You've had more than your share of sorrow. But surely there are some things that have given you pleasure."

8 She thought hard and remembered an interest in books on spirituality. The downside followed immediately. Sandy's limited eyesight made it difficult for her to read. She rasped, "My throat hurts from crying, but I'm afraid if I get off the phone I'll want to kill myself again."

9 I said, "I'm here as long as you need me."

Copyright © 2012 by Pearson Education

10 We spoke another two hours. She recalled long-ago incidents—most depressing, a few semi-joyful. There were some things she still enjoyed: peanuts, "Oprah," the smell of autumn. I again broached the topic of spirituality. My supervisor, whom I'd long ago motioned to listen in on another phone, handed me a prayer book. I read, and Sandy listened. After "amen," she said, "I think I'll be all right for the night."

11 Naturally, she couldn't promise to feel better tomorrow. For all of us, life is one day, sometimes even one minute, at a time. She asked, "When are you on again?"

12 I said, "My schedule is irregular, but we're all here for you, anytime you want. Thanks so much for calling."

13 As I hung up, I realized the call had meant as much to me as to Sandy, if not more. Despite having people in my life, lately I'd felt achingly lonely. I hadn't called a hot line, but I'd manned one, and this night had been my best in a long time. Instead of having dinner at an overpriced restaurant or watching HBO, I'd connected with another troubled soul in New York City.

Directions: *Select the choice that best completes each of the following statements.*

CHECKING YOUR COMPREHENSION

______ 1. The main point of the selection can be stated as follows:
   a. A woman helped herself by reaching out to others.
   b. Hotlines receive a variety of calls, and not all are what you would expect.
   c. Hot line operators are not permitted to offer advice to callers.
   d. New York City is a lonely place where many people contemplate suicide.

______ 2. Which statement best summarizes Sandy's state of mind at the end of the hotline call?
   a. Sandy was comforted and hoped to talk to the author again.
   b. Sandy will not consider suicide again.
   c. Sandy is more depressed than before the hotline call.
   d. Sandy lost her idealistic view of a hotline.

_______ 3. After a few hours of calls, the author

a. believed there were more calls for help than could be handled.

b. felt afraid that each call might be a person threatening suicide.

c. wanted to go home.

d. believed that most of the calls were not really people seeking help.

_______ 4. According to paragraph 2, a hotline operator should

a. pray with callers.

b. listen and help the callers decide what to do.

c. give advice to callers.

d. suggest callers see a therapist.

_______ 5. How did Sandy's call change the author's attitude about the hotline?

a. The call made her realize she needed a supervisor's help with the challenging calls.

b. The call depressed her because she realized she couldn't really solve the callers' problems.

c. The call showed her that dealing with serious emotional problems is something you need training for.

d. The call helped her to realize that she could connect with people in need and make a difference in their lives.

USING WHAT YOU KNOW ABOUT SUPPORTING DETAILS AND TRANSITIONS

_______ 6. In paragraph 2, the transition *but* tells the reader that

a. an example will follow.

b. the author will show how one thing caused another.

c. the author will switch to a contrasting idea.

d. the author will identify each major point.

_______ 7. In paragraph 6, the sentence that begins with the words "Sandy's life" is a

a. minor detail.

b. transition.

c. major detail.

d. main idea.

Copyright © 2012 by Pearson Education

_____ 8. The details in paragraph 6

a. suggest that Sandy is a hypochondriac.
b. provide background about Sandy's predicament.
c. offer reasons why Sandy should not commit suicide.
d. point to Sandy's spirituality.

_____ 9. In paragraph 7, where does the topic sentence occur?

a. first sentence
b. second sentence
c. fourth sentence
d. last sentence

_____ 10. In paragraph 10, which of the following is a minor detail?

a. The author read from a prayer book.
b. Sandy recalled events from the past.
c. The supervisor handed the author a prayer book.
d. Sandy still enjoys peanuts.

USING CONTEXT CLUES AND WORD PARTS

_____ 11. In paragraph 3, the word **horrific** means

a. terrible.
b. exciting.
c. poor.
d. short-lasting.

_____ 12. In paragraph 3, the word **abusive** means

a. gentle and calm.
b. bored and indifferent.
c. slow and careful.
d. insulting and harmful.

_____ 13. In paragraph 4, the word **signified** means

a. wrote.
b. meant.
c. acted out.
d. demanded.

_______ 14. In paragraph 7, the word **dictum** means

a. hurdle.
b. crisis.
c. department.
d. rule.

_______ 15. In paragraph 7, the word **summon** means

a. pronounce.
b. enjoy.
c. strengthen and intensify.
d. gather together.

REVIEWING DIFFICULT VOCABULARY

Directions: *Complete each of the following sentences by inserting a word from the Vocabulary Preview on page 156 in the space provided. Use each word only once.*

16. The British history class studied the ____________ of English monarchs.
17. I explained my ____________ for selling my car to my father.
18. Sara looked up at the dark sky and knew that rain was ____________.
19. Mark's high standards and ____________ made if difficult for him to accept the compromise offer.
20. As Alfredo explained his problem, I tried to be ____________ and understand what was bothering him.

THINKING CRITICALLY

1. What does the first paragraph tell you about the author and her reasons for volunteering at a crisis hotline? What feelings are you left with at the end of the article?
2. Describe your reaction to the illustration that accompanies this passage. How do the details in the illustration correspond to the author's story?
3. Evaluate the effectiveness of the title, "Talking a Stranger Through the Night." Can you think of another title that would work for this material?

Copyright © 2012 by Pearson Education

QUESTIONS FOR DISCUSSION

1. Discuss why it is the hotline's policy not to offer advice.
2. If you worked at a hotline, what would be your reaction to frequent callers who take advantage of the service? How would you react?
3. Evaluate the level of training and supervision this hotline offered its volunteers.

WRITING ACTIVITIES

1. Brainstorm a list of volunteer options available in your community. Write a paragraph explaining where you could make the best possible contribution and why. Explain the tasks involved and the talents you bring to the task.
2. Have you ever found it necessary to be a good listener to a friend with a problem? Write a paragraph describing your feelings. Was it difficult not to offer advice? What did your friend expect or not expect of you?
3. Many Americans spend time each year volunteering. Look over the report from the U.S. Bureau of Labor Statistics at http://www.bls.gov/news.release/volun.nr0.htm. Write a paragraph that analyzes a part of the report that interests or surprises you.

CHAPTER 4

Examining Details and Transitions

RECORDING YOUR PROGRESS

Test	Number Right		Score
Practice Test 4-1	______	× 10 =	______%
Practice Test 4-2	______	× 10 =	______%
Mastery Test 4-1	______	× 10 =	______%
Mastery Test 4-2	______	× 10 =	______%
Mastery Test 4-3	______	× 5 =	______%

GETTING MORE PRACTICE PEARSON myreadinglab

To get more practice with Active Reading, go to http://www.myreadinglab.com and click on

- Study Plan
- Reading Skills
- Supporting Details

EVALUATING YOUR PROGRESS PEARSON myreadinglab

To measure your progress after reading and viewing the information in the Review Materials section, complete the Practices and Tests in the Activities section. You can check your scores by clicking on the Gradebook tab.

Then, based on your performance in this chapter and/or on the MyReadingLab Practices and Tests, write your own evaluation.

YOUR EVALUATION: ______________________________

____

____

____

____

Copyright © 2012 by Pearson Education

THINKING ABOUT

Implied Main Ideas

Study the cartoon on this page. The point the cartoonist is making is clear—some companies claim they are environmentally friendly, but in reality, do so only superficially. To get the cartoonist's point, you had to study the details in the cartoon and then figure out what the cartoonist is trying to communicate.

When you read a paragraph that lacks a topic sentence, you need to use the same reasoning process. You have to study all of the details and figure out the writer's main point. This chapter will show you how to figure out implied main ideas.

CHAPTER 5

Working with Implied Main Ideas

LEARNING GOALS

GOAL 1 Understand implied meaning

GOAL 2 Use general versus specific meanings

GOAL 3 Find implied main ideas in paragraphs

GOAL 4 Find implied main ideas in visuals

GOAL 5 Think critically about visuals and implied meaning

What Does Implied Mean?

Understand implied meaning

myreadinglab
To practice working with implied main ideas, go to
> Study Plan
> Reading Skills
> Main Idea

Just as you figured out the cartoonist's main point, you often have to figure out the implied main ideas of speakers and writers. When an idea is **implied,** it is suggested but not stated outright. Suppose you discover that the gas gauge in your car is on empty and you remember that your sister recently borrowed your car. Thus you say to her, "If I run out of gas on the way to the station, I'll be sure to call you." This statement does not directly accuse your sister of failing to refill the tank, but your message is clear—Don't leave the gas tank empty!

Speakers and writers often imply ideas rather than state them directly. Here is another statement. What is the writer implying?

Example

You couldn't pay me to eat in that restaurant.

You can figure out that the writer does not want to eat in the restaurant under any circumstances, even though this is not stated directly.

Copyright © 2012 by Pearson Education

EXERCISE 5-1 Understanding Implied Meaning

Directions: *For each of the following statements, select the choice that best explains what the writer is implying or suggesting.*

_______ 1. The lead singer in Henry's band sounded like an injured moose.

a. The singer was hurt.
b. The singer had a terrible voice.
c. The singer was imitating an animal.
d. Henry's band needed practice.

_______ 2. We were on the edge of our seats during the entire movie.

a. Our seats were uncomfortable.
b. We wanted to leave.
c. We were deeply engrossed in the movie.
d. Our seats were broken.

_______ 3. The airplane was crowded and hot, the flight was bumpy, we missed our connecting flight, and the airline lost our luggage. We'll be driving next time.

a. We enjoyed our travel experience.
b. We had an exciting trip.
c. The airline handled our difficulties well.
d. We had an unpleasant travel experience.

_______ 4. During the lecture, Alex could barely keep his eyes open.

a. The lecture was scary.
b. The lecture was boring.
c. The room was too bright.
d. Alex's eyes were dry.

_______ 5. The paint on the house was faded and peeling; the shutters dangled to one side and the front windows were boarded shut; the yard was full of weeds and pieces of rusted metal.

a. There had just been a storm.
b. The house was for sale.
c. The house was abandoned.
d. The homeowners were on vacation.

Distinguishing Between General and Specific Ideas

Use general versus specific meanings

When trying to figure out the implied main idea of a paragraph, it is important to remember the distinction between general and specific. In Chapter 3 you learned that a *general* idea applies to many items or ideas, whereas a *specific* idea refers to a particular item. The word *color,* for instance, is general because it refers to many other specific colors—purple, yellow, red, and so forth. The word *jewelry* is general because it can apply to many types of body adornment, such as rings, bracelets, earrings, and necklaces. (For more information on general and specific ideas, see Chapter 3, p. 92.)

EXERCISE 5-2 Reviewing General and Specific Ideas

Directions: *For each set of specific items or ideas, select the choice that best applies to them. When choosing a general idea, be careful that it is not too general or too narrow.*

_____ 1. Martha Washington, Jacqueline Kennedy, Rosalynn Carter, Laura Bush

a. famous twentieth-century women
b. famous American parents
c. wives of American presidents
d. famous women

_____ 2. mosquito, wasp, gnat, butterfly

a. garden pests
b. harmful insects
c. living creatures
d. insects

_____ 3. watching videos, reading travel magazines, vacationing in new cities, talking with international students

a. ways to spend your vacation
b. ways to spend an evening
c. ways to meet new people
d. ways to learn about other places

_____ 4. landscaping your yard, painting your house, adding a deck, remodeling the kitchen

a. inexpensive activities
b. outdoor activities
c. home improvements
d. daily chores

Copyright © 2012 by Pearson Education

_______ 5. to support your community, to help others in need, to feel good about yourself, to meet people

a. reasons to give money to charity

b. reasons to become a volunteer

c. reasons to go to a movie

d. reasons to start a business

You also know from Chapter 3 that the main idea of a paragraph is not only its most important point but also its most *general* idea. *Specific* details back up or support the main idea. In the paragraphs you studied in Chapters 3 and 4, the main idea was always stated in a topic sentence. In this chapter, however, because main ideas are implied, you have to look at the specific details to figure out the main idea. Like main ideas that are stated directly, implied main ideas are usually larger, more important, and more general than the details.

What larger, more general idea do the following specific details and the accompanying photograph point to?

- The wind began to howl at over 90 mph.
- A dark gray funnel cloud was visible in the sky.
- Severe storms had been predicted by the weather service.

Together these three details and the photograph suggest that a tornado devastated the area.

What general idea do the following specific sentences suggest?

- The doctor kept patients waiting hours for an appointment.
- The doctor was hasty and abrupt when talking with patients.
- The doctor took days to return phone calls from patients.

You probably determined that the doctor was inconsiderate and managed her practice poorly.

EXERCISE 5-3 Identifying General Ideas

Directions: *Read the specific details in each item, and then select the word or phrase from the box below that best completes the general idea in the sentence that follows. Make sure that each general idea fits all of its specific details. Not all words or phrases in the box will be used.*

different factors	genetic	contributes	nonverbal messages
store's image	advertisers	characteristics	
process	problems	dangerous effects	

1. a. Major life catastrophes, such as natural disasters, can cause stress.
   b. Significant life changes, such as the death of a loved one, elevate one's level of stress.
   c. Daily hassles, such as long lines at the drugstore, take their toll on a person's well-being.
   General idea: A number of ____________________ contribute to stress.
2. a. Humorous commercials catch consumers' attention.
   b. Fear emphasizes negative consequences unless a particular product or service is purchased.
   c. "Sex sells" is a common motto among those who write commercials.
   General idea: ____________________ use a variety of appeals to sell products.
3. a. Acid rain may aggravate respiratory problems.
   b. Each year millions of trees are destroyed by acid rain.
   c. Acid rain may be hazardous to a pregnant woman's unborn child.
   General idea: Acid rain has ____________________.
4. a. Facial expressions reveal emotions.
   b. Hand gestures have meanings.
   c. Posture can reveal how a person feels.
   General idea: The body communicates ____________________.
5. a. The smell of a store can be appealing to shoppers.
   b. Colors can create tension or help shoppers relax.
   c. The type of background music playing in a store creates a distinct impression.
   General idea: Retailers create a ____________________ to appeal to consumers.

Copyright © 2012 by Pearson Education

6. a. Creative people are risk takers.
   b. Creative people recognize patterns and make connections easily.
   c. Creative people are self-motivated.

   General idea: A number of different ____________________ contribute to creativity.

EXERCISE 5-4 Understanding Visuals

Directions: *Study the photo shown here and then answer each of the following questions.*

1. What do you think is happening in the photograph?

____

____

____

____

2. What general idea is the photographer trying to express through the photograph?

____

____

____

____

Identifying Implied Main Ideas in Paragraphs

Find implied main ideas in paragraphs

As you know, when a writer leaves his or her main idea unstated, it is up to you, the reader, to look at the details in the paragraph and figure out the writer's main point.

The details, when taken together, will all point to a general and more important idea. You might want to think of such a paragraph as the pieces of a puzzle.

You must put together the pieces or details to determine the meaning of the paragraph as a whole. Use the following steps as a guide to find implied main ideas.

1. **Find the topic.** As you know from earlier chapters, the *topic* is the general subject of the entire paragraph. Ask yourself: "What is the one thing the author is discussing throughout the paragraph?"
2. **Figure out what is the most important idea the writer wants you to know about that topic.** Look at each detail and decide what larger idea is being explained.
3. **Express this main idea in your own words.** Make sure that the main idea is a reasonable one. Ask yourself: "Does it apply to all of the details in the paragraph?"

Example

Men's friendships are often built around shared activities—attending a ball game, playing cards, working on a project at the office. Women's friendships, on the other hand, are built more around a sharing of feelings, support, and "personalism." One study found that similarity in status, in willingness to protect one's friend in uncomfortable situations, in academic major, and even in proficiency in playing Password were significantly related to the relationship closeness of male-male friends but not of female-female or female-male friends.

—DeVito, *Messages: Building Interpersonal Communication Skills,* p. 290

The general topic of this paragraph is friendships. More specifically, the paragraph is about the differences between male and female friendships. Three details are given: (1) men's friendships are based on shared activities, (2) women's friendships are based on shared feelings, and (3) similarity is important in men's friendships but not in women's. Each of the three details is a difference between male and female friendships. The main point the writer is trying to make, then, is that men and women have different criteria for building friendships. You can figure out this writer's main idea even though no single sentence states this directly. You might visualize this paragraph as follows:

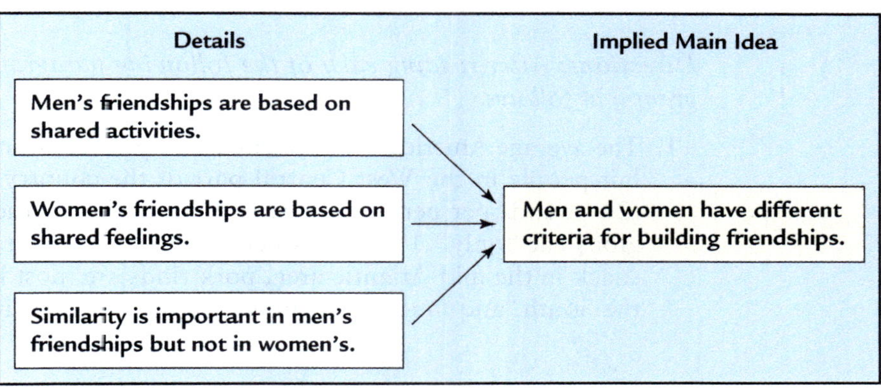

Copyright © 2012 by Pearson Education

Here is another paragraph. Read it and then fill in the diagram that follows:

Example

By now most people know that the herb echinacea may help conquer the common cold. Herbal remedies that are less well known include flaxseed, for treating constipation, and fennel, for soothing an upset stomach. In addition, the herb chamomile may be brewed into a hot cup of tea for a good night's sleep.

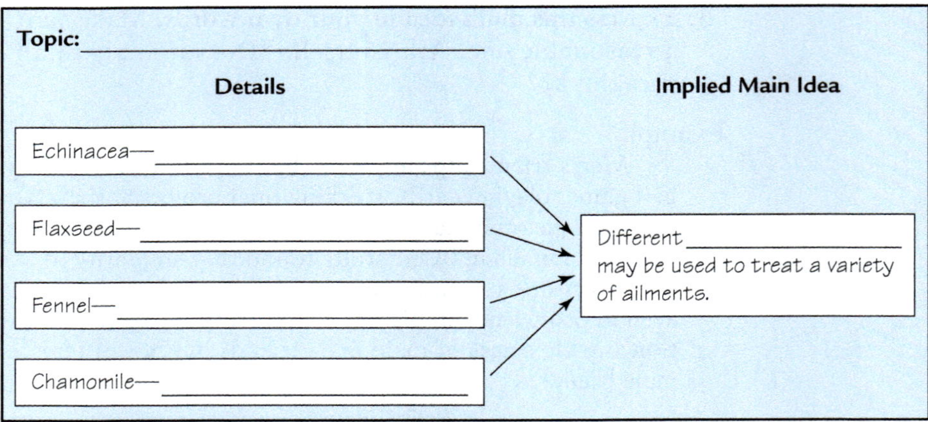

After you come up with a main idea, make sure it is broad enough. Every sentence in the paragraph should support the idea you have chosen. Work through the paragraph sentence by sentence. Check to see if each sentence explains or gives more information about the main idea. If some sentences do not explain your chosen idea, it probably is not broad enough. You may need to expand your idea and make it more general.

EXERCISE 5-5 Understanding Implied Meaning

Directions: *After reading each of the following paragraphs, complete the diagram that follows.*

1. The average American consumer eats 21 pounds of snack foods in a year, but people in the West Central part of the country consume the most (24 pounds per person) whereas those in the Pacific and Southeast regions eat "only" 19 pounds per person. Pretzels are the most popular snack in the mid-Atlantic area, pork rinds are most likely to be eaten in the South, and multigrain chips turn up as a favorite in the West. Not

surprisingly, the Hispanic influence in the Southwest has influenced snacking preferences—consumers in that part of the United States eat about 50 percent more tortilla chips than do people elsewhere.

—adapted from Solomon, *Consumer Behavior*, p. 184

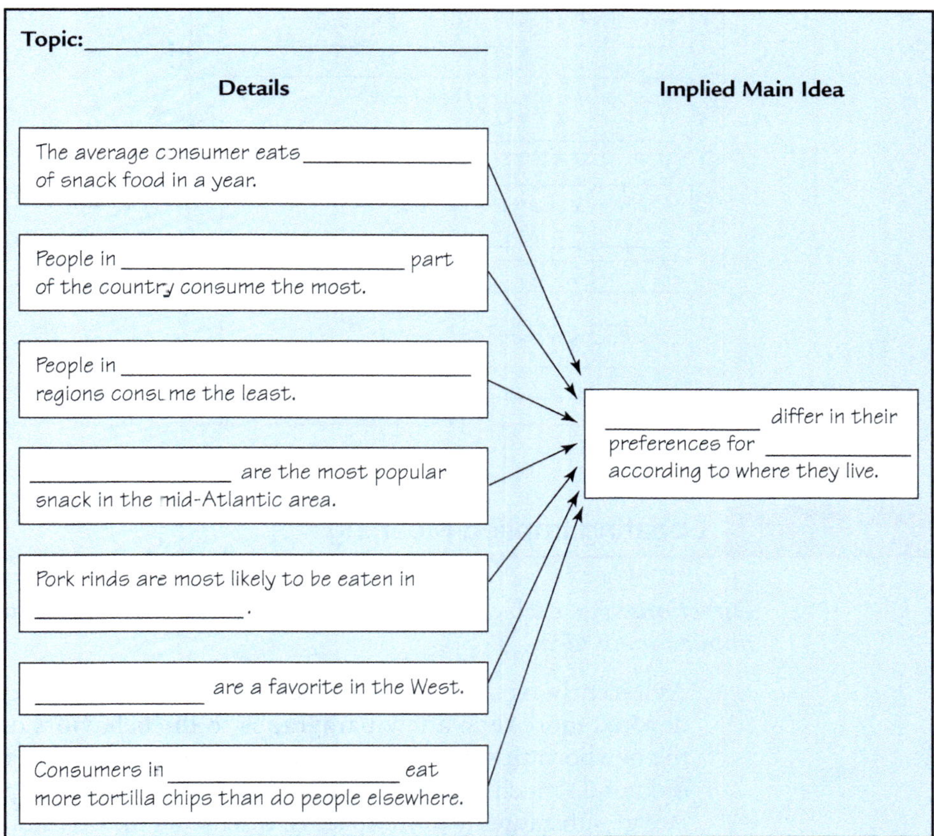

2. A dozen years ago, Starbucks had just 1,015 stores, total—that's about 1,550 fewer than opened last year alone. Starbucks's strategy has been to put stores *everywhere*. One three-block stretch in Chicago contains six of the trendy coffee bars. In New York City, there are two Starbucks in one Macy's store. In fact, cramming so many stores close together caused one satirical publication to run this headline: "A New Starbucks Opens in the Restroom of Existing Starbucks."

— Kotler, *Principles of Marketing*, p. 44

Copyright © 2012 by Pearson Education

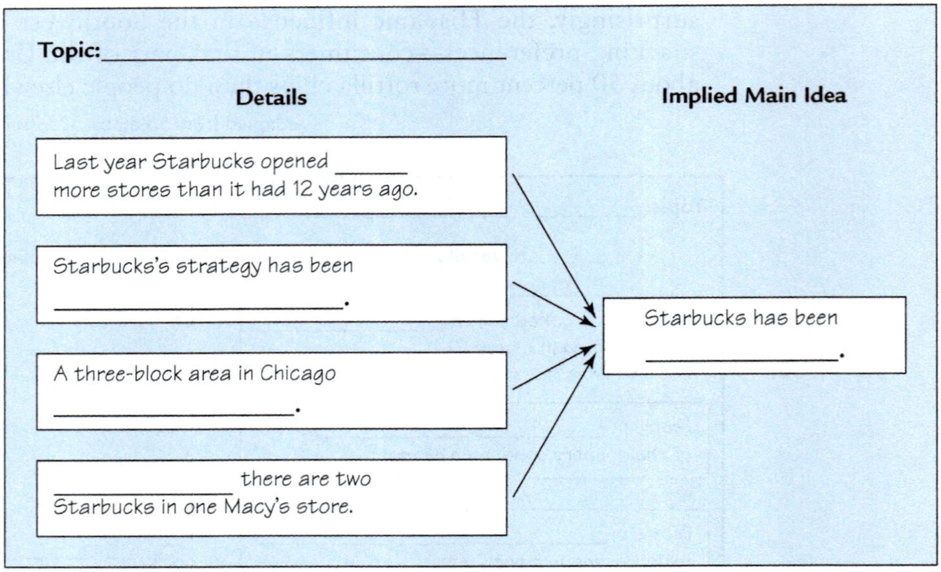

Topic: ______________________________

Details

Last year Starbucks opened ______ more stores than it had 12 years ago.

Starbucks's strategy has been ______________________.

A three-block area in Chicago ____________________.

______________ there are two Starbucks in one Macy's store.

Implied Main Idea

Starbucks has been ____________________.

EXERCISE 5-6 Locating Implied Meaning

Directions: *For each of the following paragraphs, write a sentence that states its implied main idea.*

1. As recently as 20 years ago, textbooks on child psychology seldom devoted more than a few paragraphs to the behaviors of the neonate—the newborn through the first 2 weeks of life. It seemed as if the neonate did not do much worth writing about. Today, most child psychology texts devote substantially more space to discussing the abilities of newborns. It is unlikely that over the past 20 years neonates have gotten smarter or more able. Rather, psychologists have. They have devised new and clever ways of measuring the abilities and capacities of neonates.

   —Gerow, *Psychology: An Introduction*, p. 319

   Implied main idea: ____

   ____

2. Severe punishment may generate such anxiety in children that they do not learn the lesson the punishment was designed to teach. Moreover, as a reaction to punishment that they regard as unfair, children may avoid punitive parents, who therefore will have fewer opportunities to teach and guide the child. In addition, parents who use physical punishment provide aggressive models. A child who is regularly slapped,

spanked, shaken, or shouted at may learn to use these forms of aggression in interactions with peers.

—Newcombe, *Child Development*, p. 354

Implied main idea: ______________________________

____

3. Legal research may involve federal, state, or local law. Some quetions point to a certain jurisdiction—for example, "What is the age of majority in Florida?" Others are not as clear, "What law controls the situation of an unruly passenger on a flight from Los Angeles to Philadelphia?" Here the paralegal must consider jurisdictional issues related to California, Pennsylvania, and federal statutes. Or consider the case of the driver from Georgia who is driving a truck belonging to a South Carolina company and has an accident in Alabama. The legal team working on that case might want to know the law in each jurisdiction before deciding where to file suit.

—Goldman, *The Paralegal Professional*, p. 372

Implied main idea: ______________________________

____

Finding Implied Main Ideas in Visuals

Find implied main ideas in visuals

Photographs, images, and graphics are visual ways of communicating information. Usually visuals are included in a textbook chapter to clarify or emphasize an important concept. Most photographs, images, and graphics, however, do not directly state their main point in words. Instead, the main point is implied through the visual, detailed in content and form.

Interpreting Graphics

Use the following suggestions to help you interpret graphics.

How to Read Graphics

1. **Read the title or caption and legend.** The title tells you what situation or relationship is being described. The legend is the explanatory caption that may accompany the graphic. The legend may also function as a key, indicating what particular colors, lines, or pictures mean.
2. **Determine how the graphic is organized.** If you are working with a table, note the column headings. For a graph, notice what is marked on the vertical and horizontal axes (top to bottom and left to right lines).

3. **Determine what variables the graphic is concerned with.** Identify the pieces of information that are being compared or the relationship that is being shown. Note any symbols and abbreviations used.
4. **Determine the scale or unit of measurement.** Note how the variables are measured. For example, does a graph show expenditures in dollars, thousands of dollars, or millions or dollars?
5. **Identify the trend(s), pattern(s), or relationships the graphic is intended to show.** The following sections discuss this step in greater detail.
6. **Read any footnotes and identify the source.** Footnotes, printed at the bottom of a graph or chart, indicate how the data were collected, explain what certain numbers or headings mean, and describe the statistical procedures used. Identifying the sources is helpful in assessing the reliability of the data.
7. **Make a brief summary note.** In the margin, jot a brief note about the trend or pattern the graphic emphasizes. Writing will crystallize the idea in your mind, and your note will be useful when you review.

Study the graphic below, taken from a sociology textbook. What trend or pattern does it show? The bar graph demonstrates a steady decrease in the white non-Hispanic population and a steady increase in Asian/Pacific Islanders and in Hispanic groups. Little change is evident in American Indian, Eskimo, and Aleut groups.

DIVERSITY: RACE

Percent of the Population, by Race and Hispanic Origin: 1990, 2000, 2025, and 2050

(Middle-series projections)

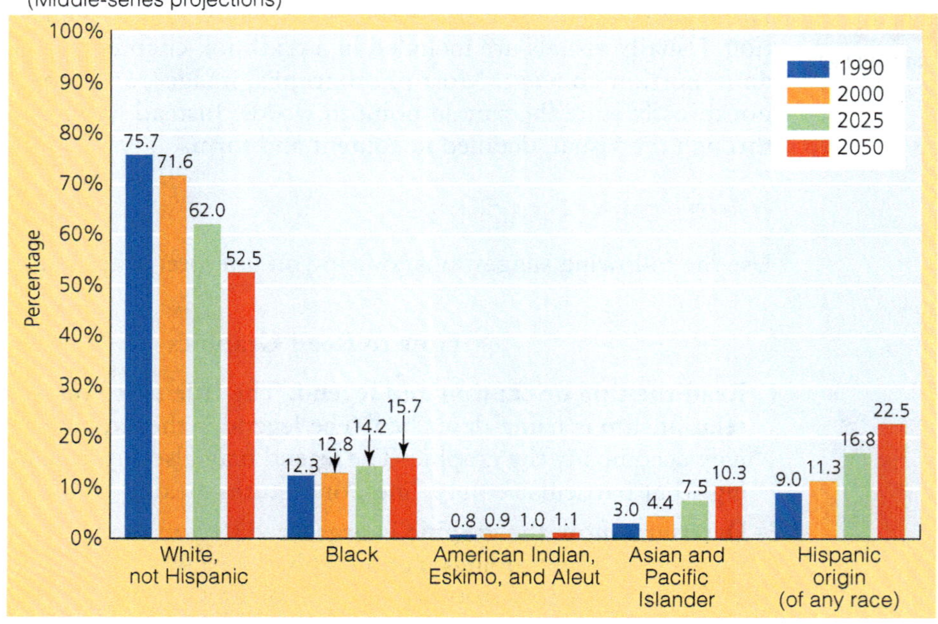

—Zinn and Eitzen, *Diversity in Families*, Fourth Edition.

Interpreting Images and Photographs

To interpret images and photographs, begin by determining what the photograph or image is intended to illustrate. Photographs and images usually convey details that add up to a single impression. That impression is often the implied main idea. Study the photograph to the right, taken from a criminal justice chapter titled "Death Investigations." What point does it make about weapons used as evidence in a homicide? The Evidence tag shown in the photograph suggests an implied single impression: Evidence is carefully documented and detailed records of its chain of possession are kept.

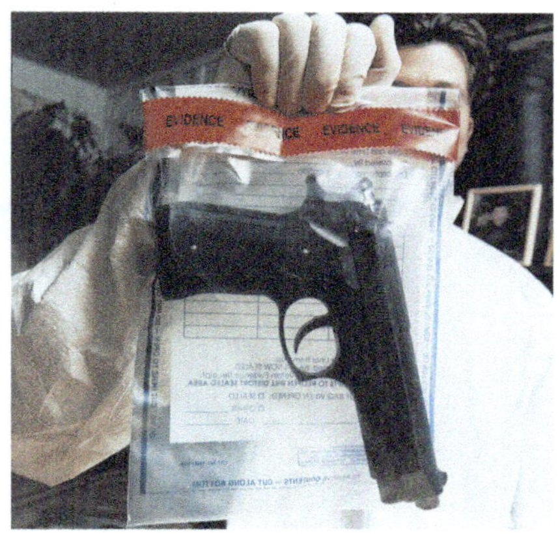

A shotgun used in a homicide is being tagged as evidence.
(Courtesy of Mike Himmel)
—Lyman, *Criminal Investigation*, p. 306

EXERCISE 5-7 Finding Implied Main Ideas in Images and Graphics

Directions: *For each of the following, identify the implied main idea.*

1.

Muslim girls at an elementary school in Dearborn, Michigan.
—Henslin, *Sociology*, p. 345

Implied main idea: ______________________________

Copyright © 2012 by Pearson Education

2.

THE REVOLUTIONARY CHANGE IN THE U.S. WORK FORCE

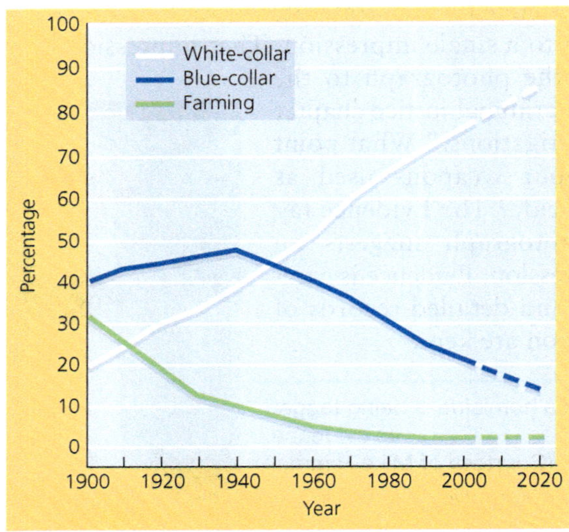

Note: From 1900 to 1940, "workers" refers to people age 14 and over; from 1970, to people age 16 and over. Broken lines are the author's projections. The totals shown here are broadly accurate only, as there is disagreement on on how to classify some jobs. Agriculture, for example, includes forestry, fishing, and hunting.

Source: James M. Henslin, *Essentials of Sociology: A Down-to-Earth Approach*, Seventh Edition, Figure 11–3, p. 308, © 2007 Pearson Education, Inc. Reproduced by permission of Pearson Education, Inc. Figure by Henslin based on *Statistical Abstract*, various years, and 2005: Tables 597, 1354.

Implied main idea: ____

Thinking Critically About Visuals and Implied Main Ideas

Think critically about visuals and implied meaning

You certainly noticed the various photos and graphics in this chapter. Visual aids like these are very common in textbooks and provide excellent opportunities for critical thinking. Because the writers *choose* the visual aids to accompany the text, they can select photos that reflect their opinions or beliefs. Consider the following excerpt and the photo that accompanies it.

> Alcohol is *the* standard recreational drug of Americans. The *average* adult American drinks 25 gallons of alcoholic beverages per year—about 21 gallons of beer, 2 gallons of wine, and almost 2 gallons of whiskey, vodka, and other distilled spirits. Beer is so popular that Americans drink more of it than they do tea and fruit juices combined.
>
> Is alcohol bad for health? This beverage cuts both ways. One to two drinks a day for men and one drink for women reduces the risk of heart attacks, strokes, gallstones, and diabetes. Beyond these amounts, however, alcohol scars the liver, damages the heart, and increases the risk of breast cancer. It also increases the likelihood of birth defects. One-third of the 43,000 Americans who die each year in vehicle accidents are drunk. Each year, 700,000 Americans seek treatment for alcohol problems.

Everyone knows that drinking and driving don't mix. Here's what's left of a Ferrari in Newport Beach, California. The driver of the other car was arrested for drunk driving and vehicular manslaughter.

—adapted from Henslin, *Sociology: A Down-to-Earth Approach*, pp. 580–581

Note that the passage is very matter-of-fact. It talks about alcohol consumption in the United States, then summarizes the benefits and drawbacks of alcohol. But also note how intense the photo is. Just looking it at, you know that a horrible accident has occurred and someone has died. Thus the photo makes the author's message about the drawbacks of alcohol much stronger than his message about the benefits of alcohol. If the author had wanted to emphasize the benefits of alcohol, he would have perhaps included a photo showing friends enjoying a drink together with a caption emphasizing its positive effects when people drink it in moderation.

EXERCISE 5-8 Evaluating Images

Directions: *Read the passage and then choose the image and caption that best support it.*

> Despite all of the research and the emergence of some promising possibilities, the best prevention method known for common colds is still the old standby—keep your hands clean. Numerous studies have indicated that rates of common cold infection are 20% to 30% lower in populations who employ effective hand-washing procedures. Cold viruses can survive on surfaces for many hours; if you pick them up on your hands from a surface and transfer them to your mouth, eyes, or nose, you may inoculate yourself with a 7-day sniffle.
>
> —Belk and Maier, *Biology: Science for Life with Physiology*, pp. 22–23

Which of the following photos/captions would best support the authors' beliefs? Why?

____

____

Copyright © 2012 by Pearson Education

a.

Some studies have shown that tea made from *Echinacea purpurea*, the American coneflower, can help to prevent colds.

b.

The best defense against the common cold is effective hand washing. Lather with a liquid soap for 20 seconds, then rinse under running water for 10 seconds.

TEXTBOOK CHALLENGE

TIPS for Reading in the Social Sciences

When reading social science textbooks, pay attention to

- **Explanations and theories.** Social science textbooks often focus on human behavior and reasons for it.
- **Supporting evidence.** Authors frequently include statistics, research evidence, and examples to help convey information.
- **Practical applications.** The information you learn in social science courses generally is useful in real-life situations.

Part A: Analyzing a Textbook Excerpt

This excerpt was taken from a social sciences textbook chapter about health. Read the excerpt and follow the directions on pp. 181–182.

Who Should Live, and Who Should Die? The Dilemma of Rationing Medical Care

1 A 75-year old woman enters the emergency room, screaming and in tears from severe pain. She is suffering from metastatic cancer (cancer that has spread through her body). She has only weeks to live, and she needs immediate admittance to the intensive care unit.

2 At this same time, a 20-year old woman, severely injured in a car wreck, is wheeled into the emergency room. To survive, she must be admitted to the intensive care unit.

3 As you probably guessed, there is only one unoccupied bed left in intensive care. What do the doctors do?

4 This story, not as far-fetched as you might think, distills a pressing situation that faces U.S. medical health care. Even though a particular treatment is essential to care for a medical problem, there isn't enough of it to go around to everyone who needs it. Other treatments are so costly that they could bankrupt society if they were made available to everyone who had a particular medical problem. Who, then, should receive the benefits of our new medical technology?

5 In the situation above, medical care would be rationed. The young woman would be admitted to intensive care, and the elderly person would be directed into some ward in the hospital. But what if the elderly woman had already been admitted to intensive care? Would physicians pull her out? That is not as easily done, but probably.

6 Consider the much less dramatic, more routine case of dialysis, the use of machines to cleanse the blood of people who are suffering from kidney disease. Dialysis is currently available to anyone who needs it, and the cost runs several billion dollars a year. Many wonder how the nation can afford to continue to pay this medical bill. Physicians in Great Britain act much like doctors would in our opening example. They ration dialysis informally, making bedside assessments of patients' chances of survival and excluding most older patients from this treatment.

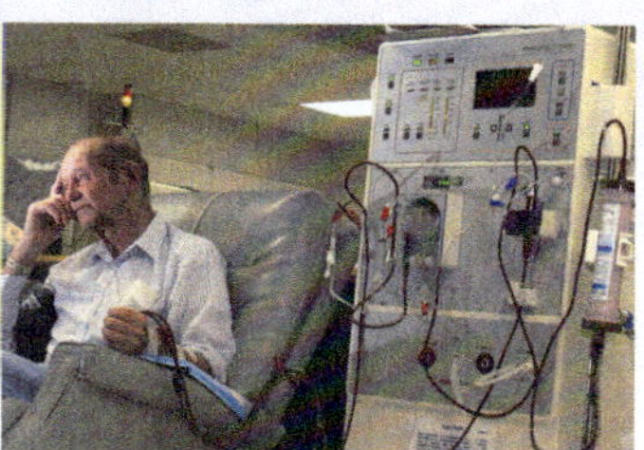

The high cost of some medical treatments, such as dialysis, shown here, has led to the issue of rationing medical care.

7 Modern medical technology is marvelous. People walk around with the hearts, kidneys, livers, lungs, and faces of deceased people. Eventually, perhaps, surgeons will be able to transplant brains. The costs are similarly astounding. Our national medical bill runs more than $2 trillion a year. Frankly, I can't understand what a trillion of anything is. I've tried, but the number is just too high for me to grasp. Now there are two of these trillions to pay each year. Where can we get such fantastic amounts? How long can we continue to pay them? These questions haunt our medical system, making the question of medical rationing urgent.

8 The nation's medical bill will not flatten out. Rather, it is destined to increase. Medical technology, including new drugs, continues to advance—and to be costly. And we all want the latest, most advanced treatment. Then there is the matter that people are living longer and the number of elderly is growing rapidly. It is the elderly who need the most medical care, especially during their last months of life.

9 The dilemma is harsh: If we ration medical treatment, many sick people will die. If we don't, we will indebt future generations even further.

—Henslin, *Sociology: A Down-to-Earth Approach,* p. 577

1. **Preview.** Preview the reading using the guidelines on p. 7 and then answer the following questions.
   a. When does rationing of medical care become necessary?
   b. What is a reason for rationing medical care?

2. **SQ3R.** Write at least three questions for the Q step of SQ3R. Answer them after completing the reading.
3. **Textbook Features.** What points in this selection might the photo on page 181 help you remember when you are studying? What kinds of emotions does the photo evoke?
4. **Vocabulary.**
   a. Identify the important new terms that are introduced in the reading.
   b. Define each of the following words and phrases as used in the reading: *metastatic* (par. 1), *far-fetched* (par. 4), *distills* (par. 4), *astounding* (par. 7), *indebt* (par. 9)
5. **Applying Chapter Skills.** Complete the diagram based on paragraph 4 of the selection.

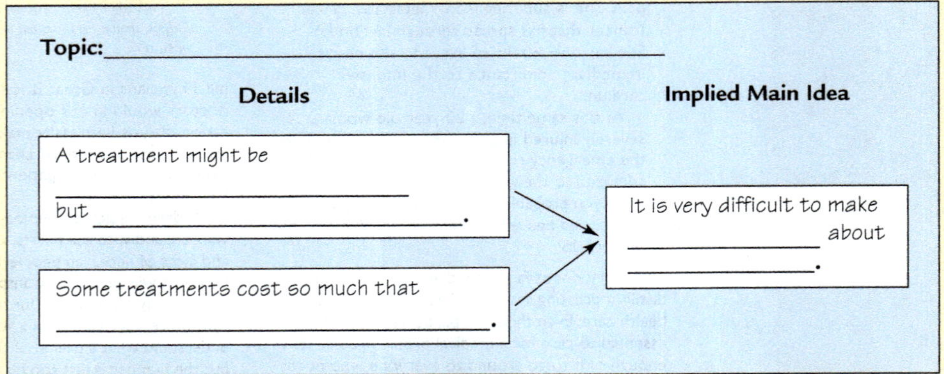

6. **Essay Question.** Write an answer to the following essay question. To test your memory, write it without referring to the excerpt.
   What are the dilemmas involved when there is not enough of a medical treatment to go around? What examples can you offer of this situation?
7. **Thinking Critically.** Use your critical thinking skills to answer each of the following questions.
   a. What are some ways that decisions about rationing of health care could be made? What system makes the most sense to you?
   b. How do you make rationing decisions about things like money, food, and so on within your own household?
   c. What other kind of visual could the author have included with this selection to further enhance or explain the topic? Explain how it would do so.

Part B: Your College Textbook

Choose a chapter that you have been assigned to read in a textbook for one of your other courses. Choose one or two paragraphs and write down the general idea and specific ideas contained in the selection you've chosen.

SELF-TEST SUMMARY

To test yourself, cover up the Answer column with a sheet of paper and answer each question listed in the left column. Evaluate each of your answers as you work by sliding the paper down and comparing your answer with what is printed in the Answer column.

	Question	Answer
GOAL 1	What is implied meaning?	An implied meaning is not stated outright but is instead suggested by the writer, and the reader comes to the conclusion.
GOAL 2	How do you use the idea of general and specific ideas?	A general implied meaning is the overall concept behind the paragraph. Specific details contained in the paragraph support this unstated idea.
GOAL 3	How do you locate an implied main idea?	Locate the topic and then think about what the most important thing is that the writer wants you to know about it.
GOAL 4	How can you find implied main ideas in visuals?	Determine the purpose of the visual; look for a single impression; add up facts and details to find trends and patterns.
GOAL 5	How can you think critically about visuals?	Authors often include visuals as support for the implied main idea. Determine whether the images reflect the author's opinions or beliefs.

Copyright © 2012 by Pearson Education

PRACTICE TEST 5-1

NAME ______________ SECTION ______________

DATE ______________ SCORE ______________

Implied Main Ideas

***Directions:** After reading each paragraph, complete the diagram that follows by filling in each blank line.*

1. The constellation [group of stars] that the Greeks named Orion, the hunter, was seen by the ancient Chinese as a supreme warrior called *Shen*. Hindus in ancient India also saw a warrior, called *Skanda*, who rode a peacock. The three stars of Orion's belt were seen as three fishermen in a canoe by Aborigines of northern Australia. As seen from southern California, these three stars climb almost straight up into the sky as they rise in the east, which may explain why the Chemehuevi Indians of the California desert saw them as a line of three sure-footed mountain sheep.

—adapted from Bennett et al., *The Solar System*, p. 40

Topic: ______________

Details

The constellation that the Greeks called ______ was called ______ by the Chinese.

Hindus called the constellation ______ and saw it as a warrior who rode ______.

The ______ of northern Australia saw the stars of Orion's belt as fishermen in a canoe.

The Chemehuevi Indians of the ______ ______ saw the stars as a line of sure-footed mountain ______.

Implied Main Idea

People of many cultures gave different ______ to the Orion constellation and saw different shapes.

2. Recently experts have begun to focus on "sitting behavior," a term used to describe sedentary activities. Recent studies point out the troubling amount of time that adults spend sitting. For about 15 hours or more each day, the only body parts that many of us move are our hands on computer keyboards or cell phones. New research indicates that there is a dose-response association between sitting time and mortality from all causes and form cardiovascular disease (CVD), independent of leisure-time activity. In fact, some people are so prone to sitting that they spend large parts of their day subconsciously seeking their next place to sit down.

—Donatelle, *Health*, p. 300

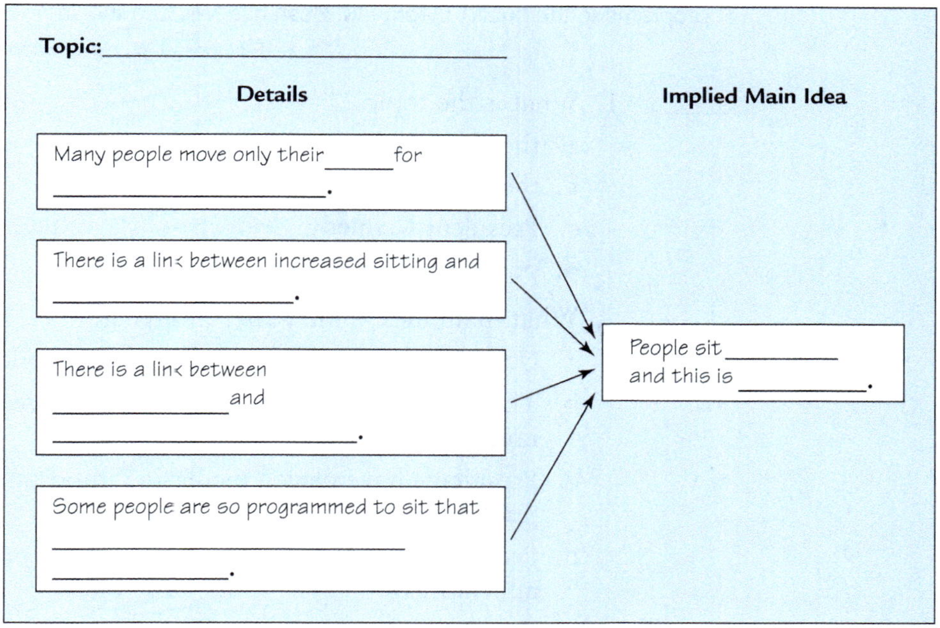

Topic: ______________________________

Details

Many people move only their _____ for ______________________.

There is a link between increased sitting and ____________________.

There is a link between ______________ and ________________________.

Some people are so programmed to sit that ____________________________ ______________.

Implied Main Idea

People sit __________ and this is ____________.

Copyright © 2012 by Pearson Education

PRACTICE TEST 5-2

NAME ______________________ SECTION ______________________

DATE ______________________ SCORE ______________________

Implied Main Ideas

***Directions:** After reading each paragraph, select the choice that best answers each of the questions that follow.*

Paragraph A

John Kennedy, the first "television president," held considerably more public appearances than did his predecessors. Kennedy's successors, with the notable exception of Richard Nixon, have been even more active in making public appearances. Indeed, they have averaged more than one appearance every weekday of the year. Bill Clinton invested enormous time and energy in attempting to sell his programs to the public. George W. Bush has followed the same pattern.

—Edwards et al., *Government in America,* p. 422

_______ 1. What is the topic?

a. the presidency
b. the effects of television
c. President Kennedy
d. public appearances of the president

_______ 2. What main idea is the writer implying?

a. U.S. presidents all enjoy being in the public eye.
b. The successors of President Kennedy have tried to imitate him.
c. Presidents have placed increasing importance on making public appearances.
d. Presidents spend too much time making public appearances.

Paragraph B

When speaking on the telephone be sure to speak clearly, enunciating carefully. It is also a good practice to speak just a bit slower than if you were talking with someone face-to-face. When responding to an answering machine or voice mail, be brief but to the point. Give your name, telephone number, and a brief explanation of why you called. State what time would be best to return your call. It is also helpful to give your phone number a second time as a conclusion to your message.

—adapted from Cook, Yale, and Marqua, *Tourism: The Business of Travel,* p. 370

_______ 3. What is the topic?

a. telephone manners
b. public speaking
c. telemarketing
d. customer service

_______ 4. What is the writer saying about the topic?

a. People today have terrible phone manners.
b. Telephone manners are not as important as those used in face-to-face conversations.
c. Speaking on the telephone requires clarity, brevity, and conciseness.
d. Telephone messages should be kept to a minimum.

Paragraph C

All the nutrients in the world are useless to humans unless oxygen is also available. Because the chemical reactions that release energy from foods require oxygen, human cells can survive for only a few minutes without oxygen. Approximately 20% of the air we breathe is oxygen. It is made available to the blood and body cells by the cooperative efforts of the respiratory and cardiovascular systems.

—adapted from Marieb, *Human Anatomy & Physiology,* p. 9

_______ 5. What is the topic?

a. humans
b. nutrients
c. oxygen
d. the respiratory system

_______ 6. What main idea is the writer implying?

a. All chemical reactions require oxygen.
b. Oxygen is vital to human life.
c. Less than a fourth of the air we breathe is oxygen.
d. The respiratory system and the cardiovascular system work together.

_______ 7. Which one of the following details does *not* support the paragraph's implied main idea?

a. All the nutrients in the world are useless to humans.
b. The chemical reactions that release energy from foods use oxygen.
c. Plants release oxygen into the air through the process of photosynthesis.
d. The respiratory and cardiovascular systems supply oxygen to the blood and body cells.

Copyright © 2012 by Pearson Education

Paragraph D

People's acceptance of a product may be largely determined by its packaging. In one study the very same coffee taken from a yellow can was described as weak, from a dark brown can as too strong, from a red can as rich, and from a blue can as mild. Even your acceptance of a person may depend on the colors worn. Consider, for example, the comments of one color expert: "If you have to pick the wardrobe for your defense lawyer heading into court and choose anything but blue, you deserve to lose the case. . . . " Black is so powerful it could work against the lawyer with the jury. Brown lacks sufficient authority. Green would probably elicit a negative response.

—adapted from DeVito, *Messages: Building Interpersonal Communication Skills,* p. 161

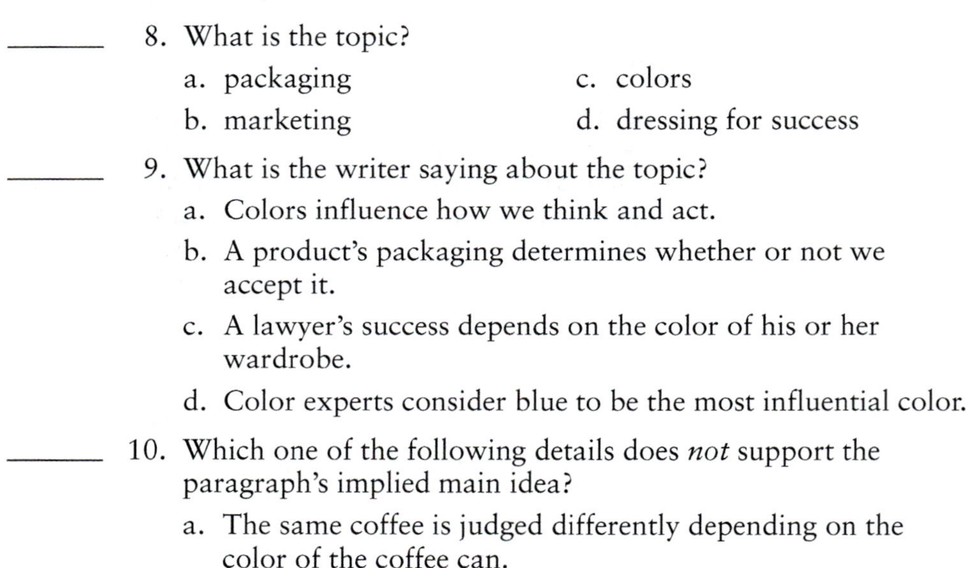

_______ 8. What is the topic?

a. packaging
b. marketing
c. colors
d. dressing for success

_______ 9. What is the writer saying about the topic?

a. Colors influence how we think and act.
b. A product's packaging determines whether or not we accept it.
c. A lawyer's success depends on the color of his or her wardrobe.
d. Color experts consider blue to be the most influential color.

_______ 10. Which one of the following details does *not* support the paragraph's implied main idea?

a. The same coffee is judged differently depending on the color of the coffee can.
b. The colors a person is wearing may influence your opinion of that person.
c. Lawyers who wear blue in court deserve to be defeated.
d. Green is not considered a good color to wear in the courtroom.

NAME ______________________ SECTION ______________________

DATE ______________________ SCORE ______________________

MASTERY TEST 5-1

Implied Main Ideas

Directions: *After reading each paragraph, select the choice that best completes each of the statements that follow.*

Paragraph A

The highest-quality women's fashion shoes, such as Manolo Blahnik, Robert Clegerie, Patrick Cox, Ferragamo, Christian Louboutin, Bruno Magli, Andrea Pfister, Prada, Sergio Rossi, and Stuart Weitzman, are made by hand in Italy with the finest leathers. Some women's manufacturers, such as Magli and Ferragamo, also make men's shoes. Italian manufacturers such as Borri and Lorenzo Banfi specialize in high-quality men's shoes. Most high-end U.S. shoe manufacturers contract production in Italian factories. Traditional shoe production involves various measurements for length and width combinations. The full range of women's shoe sizes includes 103 width and length combinations between sizes 5 and 10. Shoes for the U.S. market are made according to U.S. sizing specifications. European shoes have only one width, whereas European shoes exported to the United States are usually made available in four widths. Two to three hundred operations can go into the production of a finely made fashion shoe. If a shoe is made in a factory, 80 different machines could be involved in its production. Shoe parts must be joined together for a smooth, perfect fit.

—Frings, *Fashion,* pp. 281–282

______ 1. The implied main idea of the paragraph is that

a. U.S.-made shoes are inferior to Italian shoes.

b. leather quality affects the cost of shoes more than workmanship does.

c. Americans buy more shoes than Europeans.

d. traditional shoe production is a complex process.

______ 2. The statement that can be reasonably inferred from the details given in the paragraph is that

a. shoes sold in Europe have fewer size options than those sold in America.

b. men's shoes are more expensive than women's.

c. most inexpensive American shoes are made in China.

d. shoemakers are true artisans.

Copyright © 2012 by Pearson Education

_______ 3. Factory-made shoes can require

a. 200 employees.

b. 103 widths.

c. 80 different machines.

d. 300 different machines.

_______ 4. A consumer looking to buy a high-quality shoe should look for one that

a. comes in a wide variety of sizes.

b. is factory made.

c. is made to U.S. size specifications.

d. is made in Italy.

_______ 5. One detail that does not support the main idea of this paragraph is

a. Some women's shoe manufacturers also make men's shoes.

b. 200 to 300 operations can go into the making of a shoe.

c. 80 different machines can be involved in the production of a shoe.

d. Various measurements are involved in making shoes.

Paragraph B

Who controls the market—companies or consumers? This question is even more complicated as new ways of buying, having, and being are invented every day. It seems that the "good old days" of *marketerspace,* a time when companies called the shots and decided what they wanted their customers to know and do, are dead and gone. Many people now feel empowered to choose how, when, or if they will interact with corporations as they construct their own *consumerspace.* In turn, companies need to develop and leverage brand equity in bold new ways to attract the loyalty of these consumer "nomads." People still "need" companies—but in new ways and on their own terms.

—adapted from Solomon, *Consumer Behavior,* p. 19

_______ 6. The implied main idea of this paragraph is that

a. the marketplace should return to the "good old days."

b. companies should work on increasing consumer loyalty.

c. companies still control the marketplace.

d. consumers have gained power in the marketplace.

_______ 7. According to the paragraph, the power in the marketplace has shifted from

a. consumers to corporations.

b. corporations to consumers.

c. buyers to sellers.

d. traditional brick-and-mortar stores to Internet businesses.

_______ 8. The term *marketerspace* is defined as a time when

a. people developed new ways of buying, having, and being.

b. people felt empowered about their interactions with corporations.

c. companies decided what they wanted their customers to know and do.

d. companies developed and leveraged brand equity in bold new ways.

_______ 9. When the author states that "People still 'need' companies," he means that

a. companies offer products that people want.

b. people need companies as employers.

c. people need companies to show them what they want.

d. companies convince people to buy unnecessary products.

_______ 10. As used in the paragraph, the term *nomads* refers to someone who

a. travels a lot.

b. is a native of a desert region.

c. has immigrated from another country.

d. moves from one product brand to another.

Copyright © 2012 by Pearson Education

NAME ______________________ SECTION ______________

DATE ______________________ SCORE ______________

Implied Main Ideas

Directions: *Read the following selection from a U.S. government textbook. Then read each statement and decide whether it is an implied idea that can reasonably be concluded from the information presented in the selection. If the statement is reasonable, write R in the space provided; if it is not reasonable, write NR.*

Amending the Constitution

Gregory Lee Johnson knew little about the Constitution, but he knew he was upset. He felt that the buildup of nuclear weapons in the world threatened the planet's survival, and he wanted to protest presidential and corporate policies concerning nuclear weapons. Yet he had no money to hire a lobbyist or to purchase an ad in a newspaper. So he, along with some other demonstrators, marched through the streets of Dallas, chanting political slogans and stopping at several corporate locations to stage "die-ins" intended to dramatize the consequences of nuclear war. The demonstration ended in front of Dallas City Hall, where Gregory doused an American flag with kerosene and set it on fire.

Burning the flag violated the law, and Gregory was convicted of "desecration of a venerated object," sentenced to one year in prison, and fined $2,000. He appealed his conviction, claiming the law that prohibited burning the flag violated his freedom of speech. The U.S. Supreme Court agreed in the case of *Texas v. Gregory Lee Johnson.*

Gregory was pleased with the Court's decision, but he was nearly alone. The public howled its opposition to the decision, and President George H. W. Bush called for a constitutional amendment authorizing punishment of flag desecraters. Many public officials vowed to support the amendment, and organized opposition to the amendment was scarce. However, an amendment to prohibit burning the American flag did not obtain the two-thirds vote in each house of Congress necessary to send a constitutional amendment to the states for ratification.

Instead, Congress passed a law—the Flag Protection Act—that outlawed the desecration of the American flag. The next year, however, in *United States v. Eichman,* the Supreme Court found the act an impermissible infringement on free speech.

After years of political posturing, legislation, and litigation, little has changed. Burning the flag remains a legally protected form of political expression despite the objections of the overwhelming majority of the American public. Gregory Johnson did not prevail because he was especially articulate, nor did he win because he had access to political resources such as money or powerful supporters. He won because of the nature of the Constitution.

—Edwards, *Government in America*, p. 31

_______ 1. The American flag is a symbol that inspires deep emotions.

_______ 2. Johnson participated in the demonstration in order to challenge the law against flag burning.

_______ 3. Johnson believed nuclear weapons would have dangerous and deadly consequences.

_______ 4. Johnson believed the protest could change people's minds or awareness about nuclear weapons.

_______ 5. If Johnson had burned a flag inside his own home, it is unlikely he would have been convicted.

_______ 6. President George H. W. Bush disagreed with Johnson's opinion on nuclear weapons.

_______ 7. It takes fewer votes for Congress to pass a law than a Constitutional amendment.

_______ 8. The Congressional vote for a Constitutional amendment accurately reflected public opinion about flag burning.

_______ 9. The Supreme Court thought that flag burning was something that should be encouraged.

_______ 10. The Constitutional protection of free speech also includes actions that convey messages.

Copyright © 2012 by Pearson Education

MASTERY TEST 5-3

NAME ____________ SECTION ____________

DATE ____________ SCORE ____________

READING SELECTION

Friendship for Guys (No Tears!)

Jeffrey Zaslow

In this essay, which originally appeared in *The Wall Street Journal*, the author explores the differences in male and female friendships. Read it to find out what characterizes men's interactions and relationships.

Vocabulary Preview

These are some of the difficult words in this essay. The definitions here will help you if you can't figure out the meanings from the sentence context or word parts.

paradigm (par. 2) model or pattern

trajectories (par. 8) paths

platonic (par. 10) free from physical desire

jocular (par. 11) characterized by jokes and good humor

therapeutic (par. 12) helpful for healing

1 Every summer for 25 years, Mark Vasu has gotten together for a weekend getaway with old friends from Duke University. The 15 men, who graduated in 1984, gather in the same cabin in Highlands, N.C. "It's a judgment-free, action-packed, adventure-based weekend," says Mr. Vasu. "We go hiking, whitewater rafting, rock climbing, fly-fishing." What they don't do is sit around as a group, the way women do, sharing their deepest feelings.

2 Male friendships like these are absolutely typical, but don't assume they're inferior to female friendships. "If we use a women's paradigm for friendship, we're making a mistake," says Geoffrey Greif, a professor at the University of Maryland's School of Social Work, who has studied how 386 men made, kept and nurtured friendships. Men might not be physically or emotionally expressive, he says, but we derive great support from our friendships. Researchers say women's friendships are face to face: They talk, cry together, share secrets. Men's friendships are side by side: We play golf. We go to football games.

3 For several years, I've reported on the friendships women share, first for this column and then for "The Girls From Ames," a book about the 40-year friendship of 11 women from Ames, Iowa. And though I envy women's easy intimacy, I also know it wouldn't work for me and my friends.

4 I've played poker with the same guys every Thursday night for 18 years. We rarely talk about our lives. We talk about cards, betting, bluffing. I used to say that my poker buddies don't even know my kids' names. But then I wondered

if I was exaggerating. So one night I turned to my left at the poker table and casually asked my friend Lance: "Hey Lance, could you name my children?" He shrugged, paused to think, then smiled sheepishly. "I could rename them," he said. Dr. Greif isn't surprised by my story. In his poker game, he says, if a man were to reveal that he lost his job or that his wife left him, the other guys would say, "Gee, dude, that's too bad. Want us to deal you out this hand?"

5 Since 1978, Mark Leonard has played on a softball team with eight pals he grew up with in East Northport, N.Y. When they get together, they reminisce about shared experiences, like the time they were asked to leave an all-you-can-eat dinner at Beefsteak Charlie's because they had consumed every piece of meat in the restaurant. "Our conversations deal with the doing of things rather than the feeling of things," says Mr. Leonard.

6 In his research, Dr. Greif found that men generally resist high-maintenance relationships, whether with spouses, girlfriends or male pals. When picking friends, "men don't want someone who is too needy," he says, A third of the men in his study said they learned positive things from female friendships, but 25% had a negative impression of women as friends, citing issues such as "cattiness" and "too much drama." And women are more likely than men to hold grudges toward friends, according to Dr. Greif's 2009 book, "Buddy System."

7 Studies show that in their late 20s and 30s, women have a harder time staying in touch with old friends. Those are the years when they're busy starting careers and raising children, so they don't have time to gather for reunions. Money is tighter, too. But around age 40, women start reconnecting. Before the 1990s, researchers assumed this was because they had more time for friendship in their 40s, as their children became self-sufficient. But now researchers consider this middle-aged focus on friendship to be a life stage; as women plan the next chapter of their lives, they turn to friends for guidance and empathy.

8 Men, meanwhile, tend to build friendships until about age 30, but there's often a falloff after that. Among the reasons: Their friendships are more apt to be hurt by geographical moves and differences in career trajectories. Recent studies, however, are now finding that men in their late 40s are turning to what Dr. Grief calls "rusted" friends—longtime pals they knew when they were younger. The Internet is making it easier for them to make contact with one another.

9 A woman from Wisconsin wrote to me recently to say that she effortlessly shares intimate feelings with her friends. That's in great contrast to her husband. He recently went on a fishing trip to Canada with four longtime friends. And so she wondered: What did they talk about for a whole week? She knew one of the men had problems at work. Another's daughter was getting married. The third man has health problems. Her husband said none of those issues came up. She couldn't believe it. She told him: "Two female strangers in a public restroom would share more personal information in five minutes than you guys talked about in a week!"

Copyright © 2012 by Pearson Education

10 But again, it's a mistake to judge men's interactions by assuming we need to be like women. Research shows that men often open up about emotional issues to wives, mothers, sisters and platonic female friends. That's partly because they assume male friends will be of little help. It may also be due to fears of seeming effeminate or gay. But it's also an indication that men compartmentalize their needs; they'd rather turn to male friends to momentarily escape from their problems. The new buzzword is "bromance."

11 Frank Alessandra, 44 years old, remains close with five guys he grew up with in Denville, N.J. "As men, we feel the need to camouflage our sensitivity," he says, "but that doesn't mean we're not sensitive." Timothy Smith, 55, of St. Charles, Ill., has been gathering with seven male friends each summer for 18 years. They bring their children, but their wives stay home. Without mothers around, the kids live a pirate adventure; they get to eat junk food, bathe irregularly, and jump off a cliff into a lake. They also get to see how their jocular dads treasure old friendships.

12 Larry Schulsinger, 51, remains close with his six childhood friends from North Miami Beach, Fla. Though they have since moved elsewhere, they made a pledge long ago to meet up each fall at Miami Dolphins away games. Now, when they're together, the conversations feel to him like scenes from the movie "Diner." They razz each other about their teen years as bellhops at Miami Beach hotels. They rarely discuss serious issues. "I wouldn't talk about my insecurities with the guys," says Mr. Schulsinger, a consultant. "All my real insecurities—about work, finances, the kids—those I share with my wife." A lot is left unspoken among Mr. Schulsinger's friends, but the love is there. One of his friends recently lost both parents, and without telling anyone, he started writing down his childhood memories of the group. He filled 150 pages and found it therapeutic to reminisce about those days when his parents were alive, and his friends were just a bike ride away.

13 Men often have their own quieter ways to show their feelings. Dan Miller, a member of Mr. Leonard's longstanding softball team, had bone cancer as a boy and walked with a crutch. He served as the team manager, Mr. Leonard says, "but we made sure he got at least one official at-bat each season, so he'd be in the scorebook." The guys have fond memories of Dan getting a hit and using his bat as a crutch to make his way to first base. They'd kid him about that—with great affection—even after Dan had to have his leg amputated. Dan died from cancer in 2001 at age 40, and in his final months, his teammates went to Atlanta, where he lived, to reminisce with him about softball and a thousand other memories.

14 Mr. Leonard says he and his friends all have issues in their lives, and they sometimes acknowledge when they're going through tough times. "We'll say, 'Yes. We understand. It's really hard. Now let's go play some baseball.'"

—Jeffrey Zaslow, "Friendship for Guys (No Tears!)." Reprinted by permission of THE WALL STREET JOURNAL, Copyright © 2010 Dow Jones and Company, Inc. All Rights Reserved Worldwide. License number 2526790449255/2526790813565.

Directions: Select the choice that best completes each of the following statements.

CHECKING YOUR COMPREHENSION

_______ 1. The central thought of this selection is that
   a. friendship is less valuable to men than it is to women.
   b. men must learn to model their friendships on female relationships.
   c. men's friendships are different from women's friendships.
   d. men use their male friendships for escaping problems rather than sharing them.

_______ 2. Research on male and female friendships indicates that
   a. men have learned positive and negative things from female friendships.
   b. men generally resist relationships that are high-maintenance.
   c. women are more likely than men to hold grudges toward friends.
   d. all of the above.

_______ 3. In one of the examples described in the article, a man and his male friends have gathered with their children for a "pirate adventure" every summer for 18 years. The man in this example is named
   a. Mark Vasu.
   b. Geoffrey Greif.
   c. Timothy Smith.
   d. Frank Alessandra.

_______ 4. According to researchers, women start reconnecting with friends around age 40 because they
   a. have more time for friendship as their children become self-sufficient.
   b. are going through a life stage as they plan the next chapter of their lives.
   c. have fewer financial constraints after establishing their careers.
   d. are hoping to expand their network of professional contacts.

Copyright © 2012 by Pearson Education

_______ 5. The topic sentence of paragraph 13 begins with the words
   a. "Men often have."
   b. "The guys have fond memories."
   c. "They'd kid him."
   d. "Dan died from cancer."

USING WHAT YOU KNOW ABOUT IMPLIED MAIN IDEAS

_______ 6. The main idea of paragraph 2 is that
   a. male friendships are inferior to female friendships.
   b. men are not physically or emotionally expressive.
   c. female friends talk, cry together, and share secrets.
   d. men's and women's friendships are different.

_______ 7. The main idea of paragraph 4 is that
   a. the author has had the same group of friends for 18 years.
   b. the author's poker buddies do not know his kids' names.
   c. male friends rarely talk about their lives.
   d. men are not very sympathetic to each other.

_______ 8. The main idea of paragraph 8 is that men
   a. find it difficult to form new friendships.
   b. tend to build friendships up until age 30.
   c. maintain their friendships through the Internet.
   d. lose track of friends when they move.

_______ 9. The main idea of paragraph 9 focuses on the
   a. relationship between husbands and wives.
   b. problems facing a group of male friends.
   c. contrast between how males and females share feelings.
   d. different activities in male and female friendships.

_______ 10. The main idea of paragraph 12 is that Larry Schulsinger and his group of childhood friends
   a. meet every year at Miami Dolphins games.
   b. spend their time together teasing each other about their youth.

c. refuse to share their insecurities with anyone but their wives.

d. have a loving friendship despite rarely discussing serious issues with each other.

USING CONTEXT CLUES AND WORD PARTS

_______ 11. In paragraph 2, the word **derive** means

a. decrease. c. gain.
b. conclude. d. aspire.

_______ 12. In paragraph 5, the word **reminisce** means

a. recall. c. reason.
b. reject. d. reveal.

_______ 13. In paragraph 7, the word **empathy** means

a. alarm. c. direction.
b. understanding. d. mistrust.

_______ 14. In paragraph 9, the word **effortlessly** means

a. without trying. c. carefully.
b. on purpose. d. secretly.

_______ 15. In paragraph 11, the word **camouflage** means

a. complicate. c. dispute.
b. emphasize. d. hide.

REVIEWING DIFFICULT VOCABULARY

Directions: *Complete each of the following sentences by inserting a word from the Vocabulary Preview on page 194 in the space provided. Use each word only once.*

16. Despite majoring in different fields, the two friends' career _______________ were remarkably similar after college.

17. Once the business part of the meeting had concluded, the mood in the room became more _______________.

18. Michael's new bistro was based on a _______________ that he observed while working as a chef in several successful restaurants.

Copyright © 2012 by Pearson Education

19. Swimming is considered one of the most ________________ exercises for people with arthritis.
20. The senator and her campaign manager insisted that their relationship was strictly ________________.

THINKING CRITICALLY

1. Why did the author begin the article by telling about Mark Vasu's experience?
2. How would you describe the author's attitude toward this subject? How well do you think his approach fits the subject matter?

QUESTIONS FOR DISCUSSION

1. What differences have you observed in male friendships as compared to female friendships? Discuss whether your observations are consistent with what the author states in this selection.
2. Have you kept in touch with childhood friends? Why or why not?
3. Discuss how important a role the Internet plays in maintaining your current friendships and reconnecting with old friends. Are there people whose friendships would be lost to you if not for the Internet?

WRITING ACTIVITIES

1. What did you think of the title for this article? Try to come up with at least two alternative titles that fit the content of the selection.
2. Brainstorm about the meaning of friendship. What qualities are most important to you in a friend? What makes a friendship last over many years? What are the advantages of platonic friendships with members of the opposite sex? Write a brief essay expressing your ideas about friendship.
3. Evaluate this friendship classification developed by a PhD student: http://www.stanford.edu/~pgbovine/types-of-friends.htm Write a paragraph about whether you agree with this classification. How do you categorize your friends?

CHAPTER 5

Working with Implied Main Ideas

RECORDING YOUR PROGRESS

Test	Number Right		Score
Practice Test 5-1	______	× 5 =	______%
Practice Test 5-2	______	× 10 =	______%
Mastery Test 5-1	______	× 10 =	______%
Mastery Test 5-2	______	× 10 =	______%
Mastery Test 5-3	______	× 5 =	______%

GETTING MORE PRACTICE myreadinglab

To get more practice with Implied Main Ideas, go to http://www.myreadinglab.com and click on

> Study Plan
> Reading Skills
> Main Ideas

EVALUATING YOUR PROGRESS myreadinglab

To measure your progress after reading and viewing the information in the Review Materials section, complete the Practices and Tests in the Activities section. You can check your scores by clicking on the Gradebook tab.

Then, based on your performance in this chapter and/or on the MyReadingLab Practices and Tests, write your own evaluation.

YOUR EVALUATION: ______________________________

____

____

____

____

Copyright © 2012 by Pearson Education

THINKING ABOUT

Organizing Information

The Microsoft electronic calendar shown on this page is just one example of ways to keep track of commitments and organize your time. Others may include a print desk calendar or a pocket calendar. Each is a method of organizing commitments and making your life run smoothly.

Just as there are several ways to keep track of time commitments, there are several ways to keep track of information when you read academic assignments.

CHAPTER 6

Organizing Information

Why Keep Track of Information?

GOAL 1

Understand the importance of organizing information

As you plan a vacation, you often begin to collect all sorts of information—newspaper articles on various cities, brochures, restaurant suggestions from friends, and so forth. If you don't keep track of the various pieces of information, you soon discover that they are hard to find and thus not very useful. For a trip to Texas, for instance, you might decide to sort what you've collected by city, putting everything for San Antonio in one large envelope, everything for Dallas in another envelope, and so forth.

When you read, the ideas and details you are learning about also become more useful if you can organize them in some way. In the preceding chapters, you discovered how to find main ideas and the details that support them. This chapter will show you five ways to keep track of this kind of information: (1) highlighting, (2) marking, (3) outlining, (4) mapping, and (5) summarizing. You may decide to use only a few of these methods, or you may decide to use different ones for different kinds of reading assignments. Whatever approach you take, keep in mind that all of these methods can help you remember what you have read—an important skill for studying and taking tests in college.

LEARNING GOALS

GOAL 1
Understand the importance of organizing information

GOAL 2
Highlight and mark textbooks effectively

GOAL 3
Use outlining

GOAL 4
Draw maps

GOAL 5
Summarize information

GOAL 6
Think critically about information

Copyright © 2012 by Pearson Education

Highlighting and Marking Textbooks

Highlight and mark textbooks effectively

myreadinglab

To practice highlighting and marketing textbooks, go to
> Study Plan
> Reading Skills
> Highlighting and Notetaking

Highlighting and marking important facts and ideas as you read are effective ways to keep track of information. They are also big time-savers for college students. Suppose it took you four hours to read an assigned chapter in sociology. One month later you might need to review that chapter to prepare for an exam. If you did not highlight or mark the chapter the first time, then you would have to spend another four hours rereading it. However, if you had highlighted and marked as you read, you could review the chapter fairly quickly.

Highlighting Effectively

Here are a few basic suggestions for highlighting effectively:

1. **Read a paragraph or section first.** Then go back and highlight what is important.
2. **Highlight important portions of any topic sentence.** Also highlight any supporting details you want to remember (see Chapter 4).
3. **Be accurate.** Make sure your highlighting reflects the content of the passage.
4. **Highlight the right amount.** If you highlight too little, you may miss valuable information. On the other hand, if you highlight too much, you are not zeroing in on the most important ideas, and you will wind up rereading too much material when you study. As a general rule of thumb, highlight no more than 20 to 30 percent of the material.

Read the following paragraph. Notice that you can understand its meaning from the highlighted parts alone.

> The results of resistance training in men and women are quite different. Women don't normally develop muscle to the same extent that men do. The main reason for the difference between the sexes is that men and women have different levels of the hormone testosterone in their blood. Before puberty, testosterone levels in blood are similar for both boys and girls. During adolescence, testosterone levels in boys increase dramatically, about ten-fold, but testosterone levels in girls are unchanged. Women's muscles will become larger as a result of resistance training exercise but typically not to the same degree as in adult males.
>
> —Donatelle, *Health: The Basics*, p. 286

EXERCISE 6-1 Using Highlighting

Directions: *Read the following paragraph, which has been highlighted two different ways. Look at each highlighted version and then answer the questions that follow.*

Example 1

Chemistry begins defining **matter** by dividing it into two broad types, *pure substances* and *mixtures*. In **pure substances**, only a single type of matter is present. **Mixtures** occur when two or more pure substances are intermingled with each other. For example, table salt is a pure substance. So is water. And so is table sugar. If you put salt and sugar in a jar together and shake, however, you have a mixture. Dissolve sugar in water and you have another mixture. Some things that you might not think of as mixtures actually do fit the definition—a rock, for example. In most rocks, you'll see a mixture of different minerals, each a different pure substance.

—Russo and Silver, *Introductory Chemistry Essentials*, pp. 3–4

Example 2

Chemistry begins defining **matter** by dividing it into two broad types, *pure substances* and *mixtures*. In **pure substances**, only a single type of matter is present. **Mixtures** occur when two or more pure substances are intermingled with each other. For example, table salt is a pure substance. So is water. And so is table sugar. If you put salt and sugar in a jar together and shake, however, you have a mixture. Dissolve sugar in water and you have another mixture. Some things that you might not think of as mixtures actually do fit the definition—a rock, for example. In most rocks, you'll see a mixture of different minerals, each a different pure substance.

1. The topic sentence begins with the word ________________.
2. Is Example 1 or Example 2 the better example of effective highlighting?

   ____
3. Why isn't the highlighting in the other example effective?

   ____
4. According to the writer, what two broad types of matter are there in chemistry?

   a. ________________

   b. ________________

Copyright © 2012 by Pearson Education

Marking to Record Ideas

Although highlighting can be very helpful, sometimes you may want to circle a word, ask a question, or write some other kind of note to yourself as you read. In these instances, try making notes in the margin in addition to highlighting.

Here are just a few ways to use marking:

1. **Circle words you do not know.**
2. **Mark definitions with "def."**
3. **Make notes to yourself**—such as "good example," "test question," "reread," or "ask instructor."
4. **Put question marks next to confusing words/passages.**

In the following passage a student taking a marketing course has used marking as well as highlighting.

> With so many stores competing for customers, how do consumers pick one over another? As with products, stores may be thought of as having "personalities." Some stores have very clearly defined images (either good or bad). Others tend to blend into the crowd. They may not have anything distinctive about them and may be overlooked for this reason. This personality, or **store image**, is composed of many different factors. Store features, coupled with such consumer characteristics as shopping orientation, help to predict which shopping outlets people will prefer. Some of the important dimensions of a store's profile are location, merchandise suitability, and the knowledge and congeniality of the sales staff.
>
> What does this mean?
>
> Test question?
>
> def.
>
> Because a store's image is now recognized as a very important aspect of the retailing mix, store designers pay a lot of attention to **atmospherics**, or the conscious designing of space and its various dimensions to evoke certain effects in buyers. These dimensions include colors, scents, and sounds. A store's atmosphere in turn affects purchasing behavior—one recent study reported that the extent of pleasure reported by shoppers five minutes after entering a store was predictive of the amount of time spent in the store as well as the level of spending there.
>
> —adapted from Solomon, *Consumer Behavior*, p. 301

Notice how the student has used marking to circle a word and a phrase she's not sure of, to point out a definition, and to call attention to a possible test question.

EXERCISE 6-2 Using Highlighting and Marking

Directions: *Read the following paragraphs. Highlight and mark the paragraphs in a way that would help you remember the material and study it later.*

The gradual hearing loss that occurs as you age (presbycusis) is a common condition. However, the number of people experiencing hearing loss at younger ages is gradually increasing.

Each day you are surrounded by a variety of sounds in your environment. Most sounds occur at safe levels that do not affect hearing. However, sounds that are too loud or last for a long time can damage sensitive structures called hair cells in the inner ear. The result is noise-induced hearing loss (NIHL).

Hair cells convert sound energy into electrical signals that travel to the brain. Once damaged, hair cells cannot grow back. Scientists once believed that the force of vibrations from loud sounds caused the damage to hair cells. Recent studies, however, have shown that exposure to harmful noise triggers the formation of molecules that can damage or kill hair cells.

NIHL can be caused by a single exposure to a quick, intense sound such as an explosion, or by long-term exposure to loud sounds over an extended period of time, such as noise generated in a woodworking shop. The loudness of sound is measured in decibels. Sources of noise that can cause NIHL range from 120 to 150 decibels. Examples include motorcycles, firecrackers, and small firearms.

Long or repeated exposure to sounds at or above 85 decibels can also cause hearing loss. The louder the sound, the shorter the time period before NIHL can occur. Sounds of less than 75 decibels, even after long exposure, are unlikely to cause hearing loss.

The good news is that NIHL is 100 percent preventable. In order to protect yourself, you must understand the hazards of noise and how to practice good hearing health in everyday life.

—Badasch and Chesebro, *Health Science Fundamentals,* p. 425

Outlining

Use outlining

myreadinglab

To practice outlining, go to
> Study Plan
> Reading Skills
> Outlining and Summarizing

Making an outline is another good way to keep track of what you have read. **Outlining** involves listing major and minor ideas and showing how they are related. When you make an outline, follow the writer's organization. An outline usually follows a format like the one below:

I. Major topic
  A. First major idea
    1. First key supporting detail
    2. Second key supporting detail

Copyright © 2012 by Pearson Education

B. Second major idea
 1. First key supporting detail
  a. Minor detail or example
  b. Minor detail or example
 2. Second key supporting detail

II. Second major topic
 A. First major idea

Suppose you had just read a brief essay about your friend's vacation in San Francisco. An outline of the essay might begin like this:

I. Favorite places
 A. Chinatown
  1. Restaurants and markets
   a. Fortune cookie factory
   b. Dim sum restaurants
  2. Museums
   a. Chinese Culture Center
   b. Pacific Heritage Museum
 B. Fisherman's Wharf
  1. Pier 39
   a. Street performers
   b. Sea lions sunning themselves on the docks
  2. Ghiradelli Square

Notice that the most important ideas are closer to the left margin. The rule of thumb to follow is this: The less important the idea, the more it should be indented.

Here are a few suggestions for using the outline format:

1. **Don't worry about following the outline format exactly.** As long as your outline shows an organization of ideas, it will work for you.
2. **Use words and phrases or complete sentences,** whichever is easier for you.
3. **Use your own words, and don't write too much.**
4. **Pay attention to headings.** Be sure that all the information you place underneath a heading explains or supports that heading. In the outline above, for instance, the entries "Chinatown" and "Fisherman's Wharf" are correctly placed under the major topic "Favorite Places." Likewise, "Pier 39" and "Ghiradelli Square" are under "Fisherman's Wharf," since they are located in the Wharf area.

Read the following paragraph about homeschooling, and then study its outline.

> With the increase in comprehensive online learning providers, a growing number of parents are choosing to educate their children at home. The number of homeschooled students rose from an estimated 300,000 in 1990 to more than a million just a decade later. Common reasons for homeschooling include avoiding the negative influences of public schools, concern with the quality of public school education, and a desire to include religious teachings in the curriculum. Although most studies agree that there is little difference in student achievement between homeschooled and public-schooled students, three factors appear to influence academic achievement: Students who are homeschooled by more educated parents do better than those who are taught by less educated parents; students who are homeschooled by more conservative parents do better on standardized tests than those taught by more liberal parents; and children of parents who homeschool due to family needs have lower levels of achievement than those who are homeschooled for other reasons. However, the primary factor directly linked to student achievement can best be attributed to the approach and teaching style of the parent. For example, in the case of students who are taught by more conservative parents and do better on standardized tests than those taught by more liberal parents, this is most likely attributed to the conservative teaching style of teaching specific knowledge, whereas the more liberal parent might teach in an experimental or less formal approach, which would not be rewarded or recognized by standardized testing.
>
> —Kunz, *Think Marriages & Families*, p. 207

In this outline, the major topic of the paragraph is listed first. The writer's main ideas are listed as A, B, and C. Supporting details are then listed under the ideas. When you look at this outline, you can easily see the writer's most important points.

I. There is an increase in the number of parents who choose to homeschool their children.
   A. Reasons for homeschooling
      1. Avoiding the negative influences of public schools
      2. Concern about the quality of public school educations
      3. Desire to include religious teachings in the curriculum
   B. There is little difference between home and public schooling, but students' academic achievement is impacted by the parents
      1. Students homeschooled by educated parents do better than those taught by less educated parents
      2. Students homeschooled by conservative parents do better on standardized tests than those taught by liberal parents
      3. Students homeschooled because of family needs achieve at lower levels than students homeschooled for other reasons.

Copyright © 2012 by Pearson Education

C. Student achievement is linked to the parents' approach and teaching styles
    1. Conservative parent-teachers have students who achieve better on standardized tests due to the conservative teaching style of specific knowledge
    2. Liberal parent-teachers have students who do not do as well on standardized tests because of a less formal or experiential approach

EXERCISE 6-3 Using Outlines

Directions: *After reading the passage and the incomplete outline that follows, fill in the missing information in the outline.*

CLEARANCE AND CONVICTION RATES

The efficiency of our criminal justice system is determined by varying standards. To a great extent, police effectiveness is still judged by rates of arrest, of either an entire agency or an individual investigator. Although it may not always be fair or even logical to judge police effectiveness by this standard alone, it continues to be the criterion used by much of the public.

As a national average, police are successful in clearing by arrest approximately 20 percent of all serious felonies reported to their agencies. Police departments judge solution rate by counting clearances; that is, the number of cases in which a known criminal offense has resulted in the arrest, citation, or judicial summoning of an individual in connection with the offense. The success of a particular investigation is not, however, a uniform factor among all crimes. Some investigations have a naturally higher probability of success than others. For example, criminal homicide investigations generally involve perpetrators who know their victims and who make little or no real effort to avoid apprehension. In addition, the extreme seriousness of the crime dictates maximum investigative effort, with an exhaustive search for forensic evidence. On the other hand, there is traditionally a much lower rate of arrest in cases of burglary. Many factors contribute to this unfortunate fact, including heavy caseloads and the large amount of stolen property that is unidentifiable when recovered. The main reason for the low rate of clearance is, however, the lack of a suspect identification, as this type of criminal purposely avoids contact with victims or witnesses.

Of those cases successfully concluded by an arrest, an unfortunately large number are not carried onward into the judicial process (see Figure A). National studies indicate that approximately 40 percent of all felony arrests brought by police for prosecution are rejected in some manner. Some investigations are either dropped outright by a prosecutor prior to court examination or dismissed by a judge in one of the various judicial screenings. Prosecutors tend to reject cases because of problems of insufficient evidence,

FIGURE A **Typical outcome of 100 felony crime investigations resulting in arrest and brought for prosecution.**

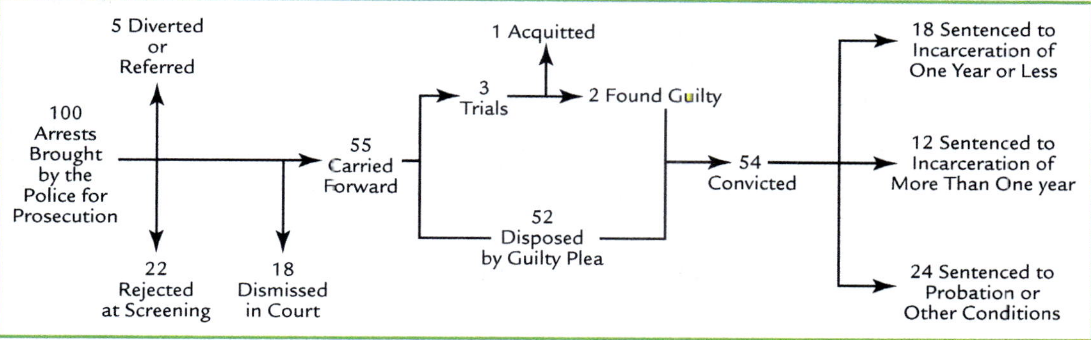

(*Source:* U.S. *Department of Justice, Bureau of Justice Statistics.*)

whereas judges tend to dismiss cases because of legal violations relating to due process. However, those cases that are carried forward to the trial stage are typically strong, as evidenced by only 2 percent not resulting in conviction.

Such data can be very helpful to the investigator, demonstrating that, in many cases, evidence linking a suspect to an offense is not located, collected, or processed effectively. Although it is true that certain types of investigations are inherently difficult in this regard, there is considerable room for improvement. On the positive side, research indicates that the screening process is quite effective in predicting which cases will result in conviction.

—Gilbert, *Criminal Investigation,* pp. 64–65

I. Police effectiveness is judged by rates of arrests
II. 20% of felonies are cleared by arrest
  A. Criminal homicide has a higher rate of clearance
    1. Perpetrators know their victims
    2. ____________________
  B. Burglary cases have a lower rate of arrests.
    1. There are heavy caseloads
    2. ____________________
    ____
    3. ____________________
    ____
III. 40% of arrests are not moved forward into the judicial process
  A. ____________________
  B. Judges can dismiss cases due to legal violations of due process
  C. ____________________

Copyright © 2012 by Pearson Education

Mapping

Draw maps

In Chapter 4 you learned a little bit about **mapping** (p. 133), which is a visual method of organizing information. It involves drawing diagrams to show how ideas in a paragraph or chapter are related. Some students prefer mapping to outlining because they feel it is freer and less tightly structured.

Maps can take many forms. You can draw them in any way that shows the relationships between ideas. Figures 6-1 and 6-2 (p. 213) show two sample maps of the paragraph about homeschooling. Look at the maps and then look

FIGURE 6-1 Sample hand-drawn map

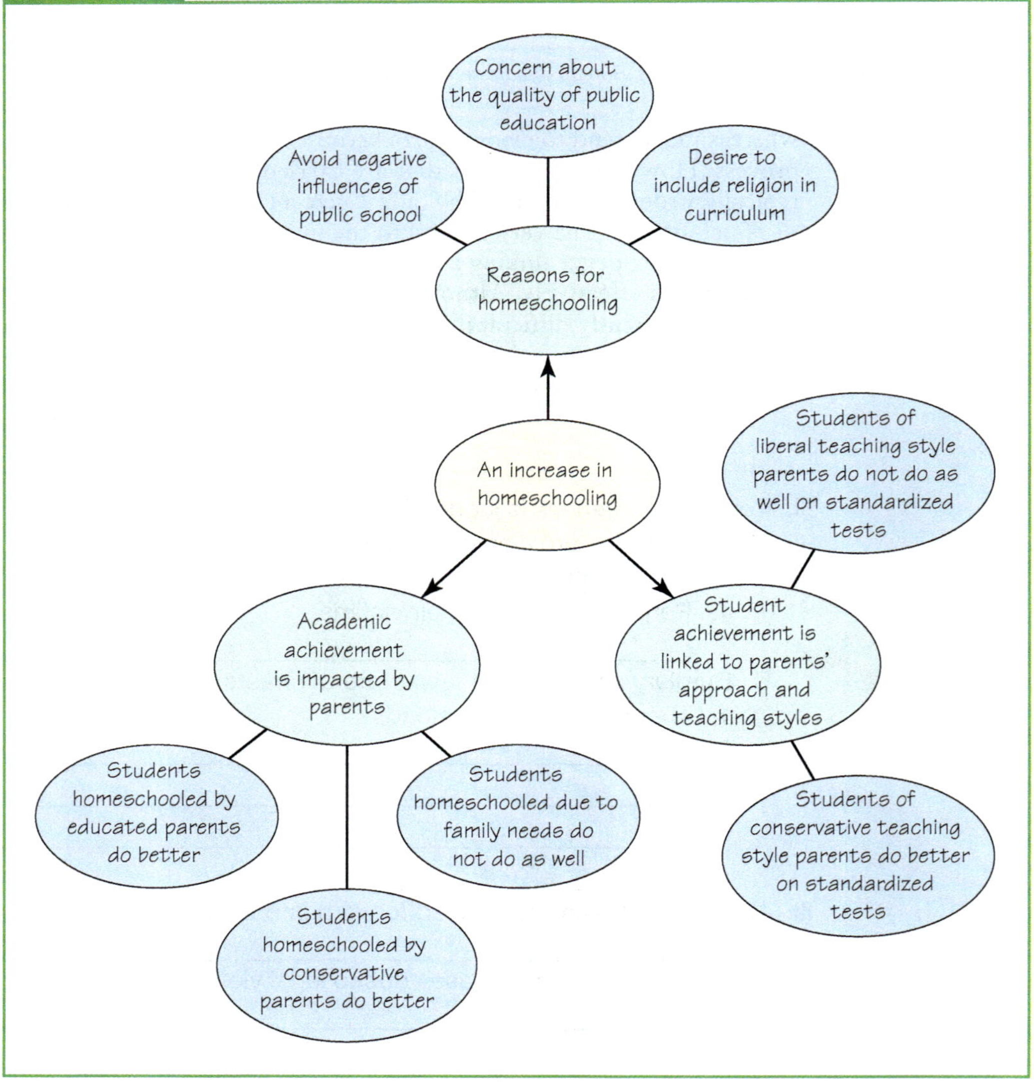

Concern about the quality of public education
Avoid negative influences of public school
Desire to include religion in curriculum
Reasons for homeschooling
An increase in homeschooling
Students of liberal teaching style parents do not do as well on standardized tests
Academic achievement is impacted by parents
Student achievement is linked to parents' approach and teaching styles
Students homeschooled by educated parents do better
Students homeschooled due to family needs do not do as well
Students of conservative teaching style parents do better on standardized tests
Students homeschooled by conservative parents do better

FIGURE 6-2 Sample computer-drawn map

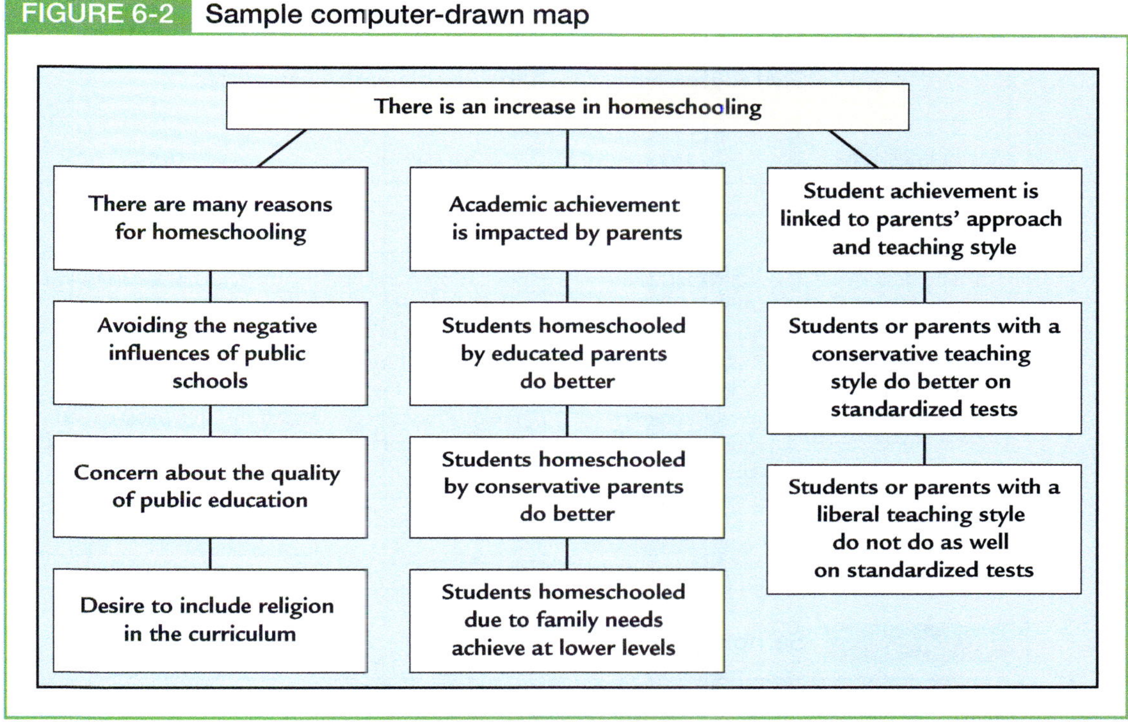

again at the outline of the homeschooling paragraph. Notice how the important information is included by each method—it's just presented differently.

As you draw a map, think of it as a picture or diagram that shows how ideas are connected. You can hand draw maps or use a word processor. Use the following steps, which can be seen in Figures 6-1 and 6-2:

1. **Identify the overall topic or subject.** Write it in the center or at the top of the page.
2. **Identify major ideas that relate to the topic.** Using a line, connect each major idea to the central topic.
3. **As you discover supporting details that further explain an idea already mapped, connect those details with new lines.**

Once you are skilled at drawing maps, you can become more creative, drawing different types of maps to fit what you are reading. For example, you can draw a *time line* (see Figure 6-3, p. 214) to show historical events in the order in which they occurred. A time line starts with the earliest event and ends with the most recent. Another type of map is one that shows a process—the steps involved in doing something (see Figure 6-4, p. 214). When you study chronological order and process in Chapter 7 (p. 254), you will discover more uses for these kinds of maps.

Copyright © 2012 by Pearson Education

FIGURE 6-3 Sample time line

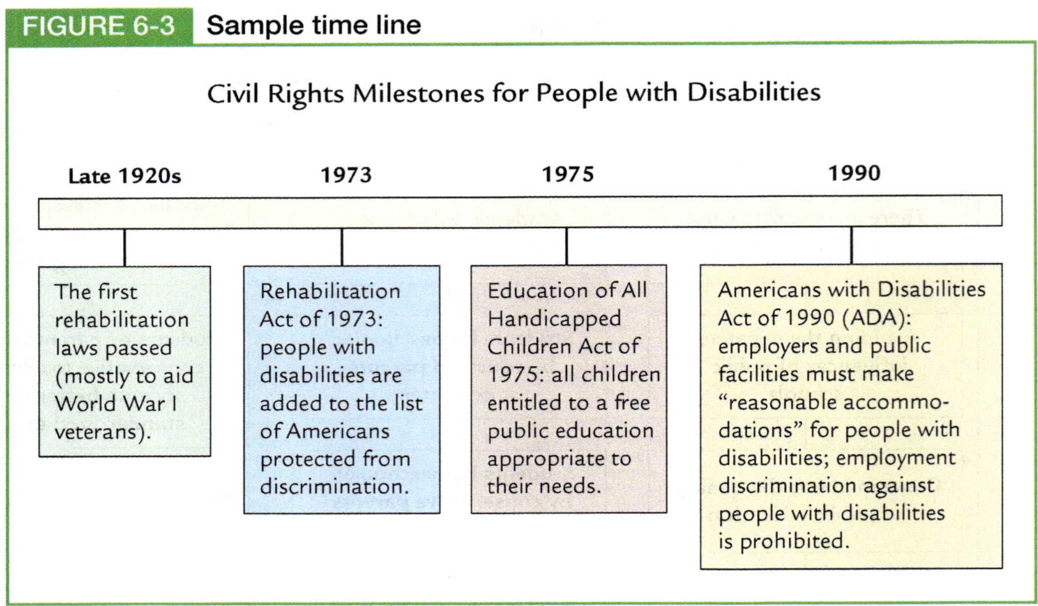

FIGURE 6-4 Sample process map

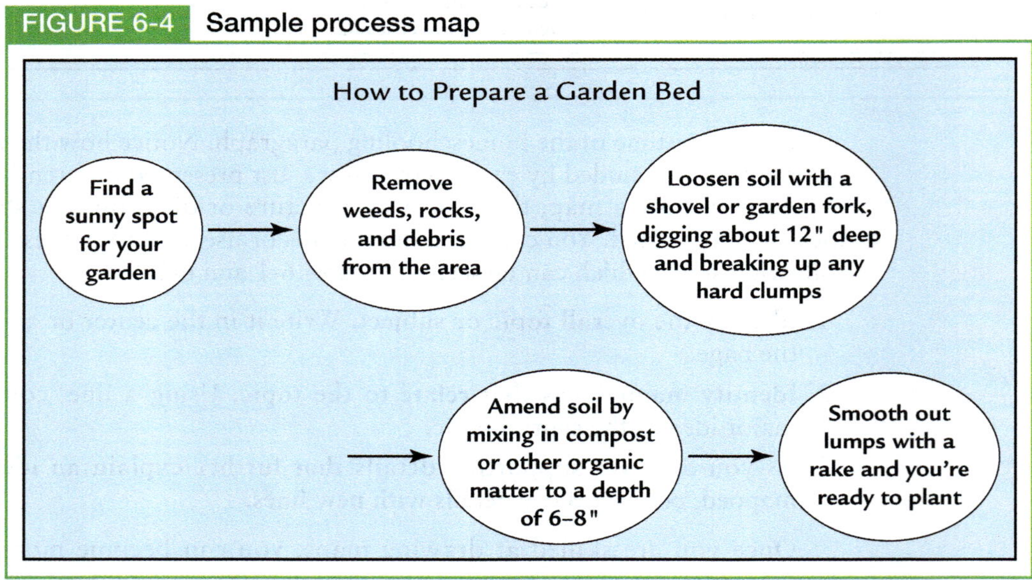

EXERCISE 6-4 Understanding Maps

Directions: *Read the paragraph and complete the map that follows, filling in the writer's main points in the spaces provided. Then answer the question that follows the map.*

Because complaints are often preludes to conflict in the workplace, they need to be listened to and responded to appropriately. Here are some suggestions for dealing with complaints. First, let the person know that you're open to complaints; you view them as helpful sources of information, and you're listening. (Be careful not to fall into the trap of seeing someone who voices a complaint as someone to avoid.) Second, try to understand both the thoughts and the feelings that go with the complaint. Express not only your concern about the problem but also your understanding of the frustration this person is feeling. Third, respect confidentiality. Let the person know that the complaint will be treated in strict confidence or that it will be revealed only to those he or she wishes. Fourth, ask the person what he or she would like you to do. Sometimes all a person wants is for someone to hear the complaint and appreciate its legitimacy. Other times, the complaint is presented in hopes that you will do something specific. Finally, thank the person for voicing the complaint, and assure him or her of your intention to follow up.

—adapted from DeVito, *Messages*, p. 317

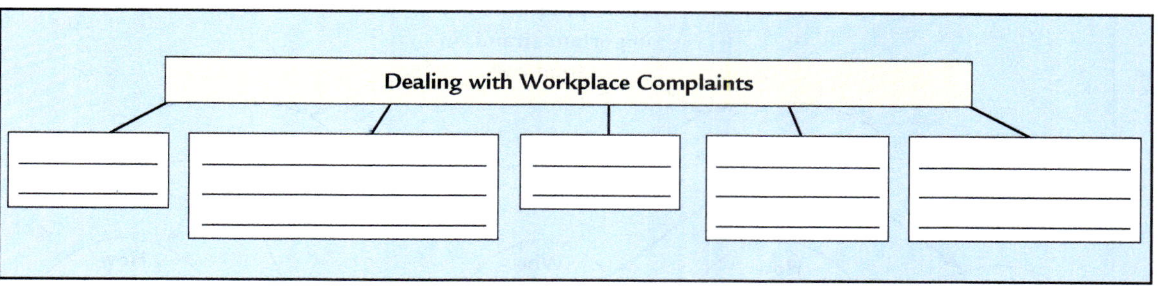

1. What five transition words does the writer use to introduce the main points?

   a. ________ b. ________ c. ________ d. ________ e. ________

EXERCISE 6-5 Using Maps

Directions: *After reading the following paragraphs, complete the map of the passage. Fill in the writer's main points as well as some supporting details.*

TWO TYPES OF ORGANISMS THAT RELEASE NUTRIENTS

Among the most important strands in a food web are the detritus feeders and decomposers. The detritus feeders are an army of mostly small and often unnoticed animals and protists that live on the refuse of life: molted exoskeletons, fallen leaves, wastes, and dead bodies. (Detritus means "debris.") The network of detritus feeders is complex; in terrestrial ecosystems it includes

Copyright © 2012 by Pearson Education

earthworms, mites, centipedes, some insects, land-dwelling crustaceans, nematode worms, and even a few large vertebrates such as vultures. These organisms consume dead organic matter, extract some of the energy stored in it, and excrete it in a further decomposed state. Their excretory products serve as food for other detritus feeders and for decomposers.

The decomposers are primarily fungi and bacteria (the black coating or gray fuzz you may notice on decaying tomatoes and bread crusts are fungal decomposers). Decomposers digest food outside their bodies by secreting digestive enzymes into the environment. They absorb the nutrients they need, and the remaining nutrients are released to the environment.

—Audesirk, Audesirk, and Byers, *Life on Earth*, pp. 584–585

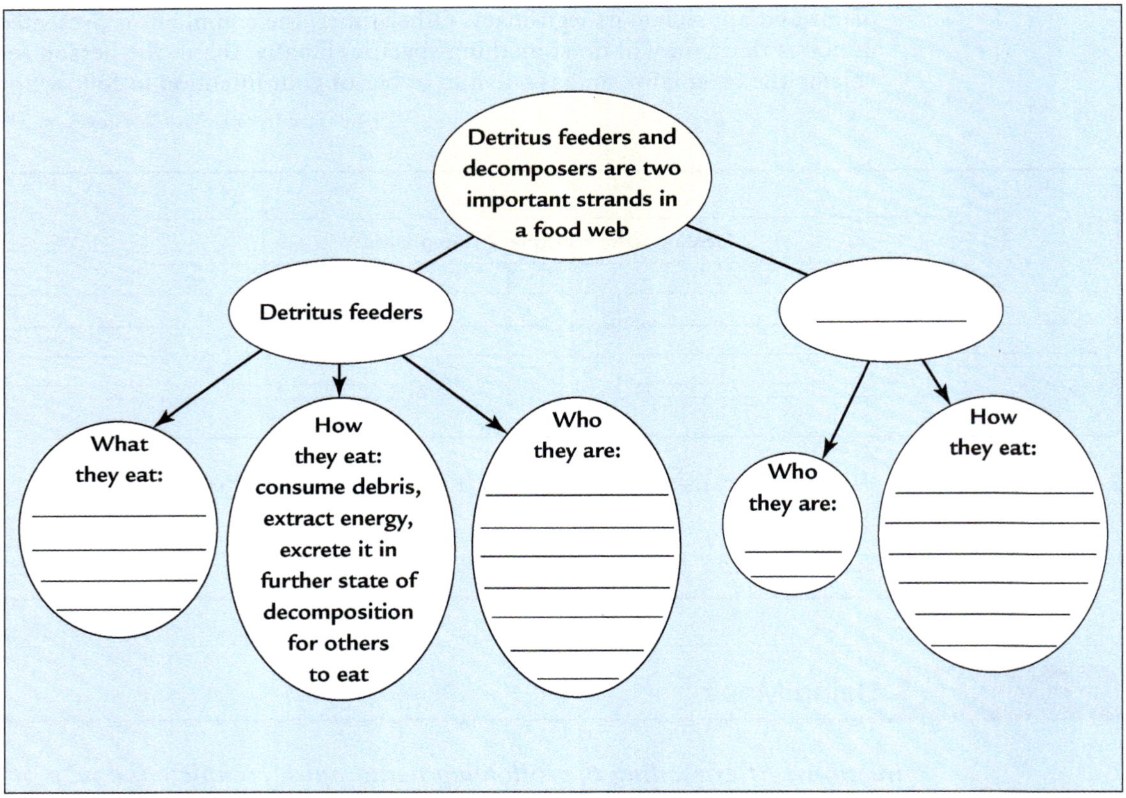

Detritus feeders and decomposers are two important strands in a food web

Detritus feeders

What they eat: ____________

How they eat: consume debris, extract energy, excrete it in further state of decomposition for others to eat

Who they are: ____________

____

Who they are: ____________

How they eat: ____________

Summarizing

Summarize information

Summarizing is another good way to remember and keep track of information. A **summary** is a brief statement that pulls together the most important ideas in something you have read. It is much shorter than an outline and contains less detailed information. At times, you may want to summarize a paragraph, an essay, or even a chapter.

myreadinglab
To practice summarizing, go to
> Study Plan
> Reading Skills
> Outlining and Summarizing

To write a good summary you need to understand the material and identify the writer's major points. Here are some tips to follow:

1. **Underline each major idea in the material.**
2. **Write one sentence that states the writer's most important idea.** This sentence will be the topic sentence of your summary.
3. **Be sure to use your own words rather than those of the author.**
4. **Focus on the author's major ideas,** not on supporting details.
5. **Keep the ideas in the summary in the same order in which they appear in the original material.**

Read the following summary of "Clearance and Conviction Rates," which appeared in Exercise 6-3 on page 210.

> Police effectiveness is usually judged by arrest rates. Police make arrests in 20 percent of all serious felonies. A clearance is a case concluded with an arrest, citation, or judicial summons. There is a higher chance of clearance in homicide cases and less in burglary. In cases where there are arrests, 40 percent are rejected by prosecutors or judges. Cases that do go to trial result in 98 percent conviction rates. The justice system's screening process is effective in predicting which cases will be successful.

Notice that this summary contains only the most important ideas. Details are not included.

EXERCISE 6-6 Using Summaries

A. Directions: *Indicate whether each of the following statements is true (T) or false (F).*

_______ 1. When writing a summary, you should focus on the author's major ideas.

_______ 2. The ideas in a summary should be in the same order as in the original material.

_______ 3. A summary is usually much longer than an outline.

_______ 4. A summary should be in your own words rather than those of the author.

B. Directions: *After reading the following paragraphs, select the choice that best summarizes each one.*

_______ 5. The tourist potential of any spot depends upon its "three A's": accessibility, accommodations, and attractions. The rich bird life on the islands of Lake Nicaragua, the lions of Kenya, and

Copyright © 2012 by Pearson Education

the tropical vegetation in many countries are important tourist destinations. Overall, the countries best endowed for tourism have both natural and cultural attractions, pleasant climates, good beaches, and reasonably well-educated populations. Political stability is a necessity. Despite Africa's wealth of ecological and cultural attractions, political instability and lack of accommodations have restricted its income to only 2.2 percent of global tourist dollars.

—adapted from Bergman and Renwick, *Introduction to Geography*, pp. 495–496

a. The tourist potential of a place depends upon its accessibility, accommodations, and attractions. Important tourist destinations include Lake Nicaragua, Kenya, and tropical countries. However, despite Africa's many attractions, its income is only 2.2 percent of global tourist dollars due to political instability and lack of accommodations.

b. Tourists typically want to visit places that offer the three A's. They also want pleasant weather, nice beaches, and an educated population.

c. A country's ability to attract tourism is determined by how accessible it is and by the accommodations and attractions it provides. Countries that are tourist destinations offer a variety of activities, mild weather, attractive beaches, and a population that is educated and politically stable.

d. Tourists are interested in places that offer political stability, excellent beaches, nice weather, and well-educated people. A tourist spot has to have natural and cultural attractions and a variety of accommodations.

_______ 6. The common cold is responsible for more days lost from work and more uncomfortable days spent at work than any other ailment. Caused by any number of viruses (some experts claim there may be over 200 different viruses responsible for the common cold), colds are always present to some degree among people throughout the world. In the course of a year, Americans suffer over 1 billion colds. Cold viruses are carried in the nose and throat most of the time. These viruses are held in check until the host's resistance is lowered. It is possible to "catch" a cold—from the airborne droplets of another person's sneeze or from skin-to-skin or mucous membrane contact—though recent studies indicate that the hands may be the greatest avenue of colds and transmission of other viruses. Although many people believe that a cold results from exposure to cold weather or from getting chilled or overheated, experts believe that such things have little or no effect on cold development. Stress, allergy disorders that affect the nasal passages, and menstrual cycles do, however, appear to increase susceptibility.

—adapted from Donatelle, *Health: The Basics,* p. 350

a. More workers are affected by the common cold than by any other illness. Colds are caused by viruses and result from exposure to another person's virus through the air or by physical contact. Stress, nasal allergies, and certain stages of the menstrual cycle may make people more susceptible to colds.

b. People who suffer from the common cold often miss work or are uncomfortable at work. Experts say that over 200 different viruses may be responsible for the common cold, which is always present in people all over the world. In America, people suffer over 1 billion colds every year.

c. The common cold is caused by different viruses that are carried in the nose and throat most of the time. These viruses wait until a person's resistance is low; then the person may catch a cold from someone else, through either a sneeze or some other contact.

d. Cold viruses exist all over the world, and Americans suffer more than 1 billion colds each year. More than 200 different viruses may be responsible for causing the common cold.

Thinking Critically About Information

Think critically about information

We live in a society bombarded with information. Everywhere you look, you will see written materials, from newspapers and magazines to billboards and Web sites. Some experts estimate that the amount of information available to society is increasing by 66 percent every year.

That's a lot of information for a person to take in. So how do you cut through the clutter to find and learn the information you need? Here are some suggestions.

- **Practice selective reading.** You do not have to read everything you see. (College assignments are the exception, of course.) Learn to quickly skim material to see if it interests you and then read the material that does.
- **Understand the goal of what you are reading.** Is it to educate you or to convince you of something? In advertising, lovely words and images are used to make products seem desirable. In the news, politicians rant and rave about the issues. Evaluate the purpose of what you are reading by asking yourself what the writer's goal is.
- **Adjust your reading speed to match the task.** If you are reading an article in *People* magazine, you probably can skim through it quickly. However, if you

Copyright © 2012 by Pearson Education

are filling out paperwork for financial aid or medical claims, you will want to read the forms slowly and carefully to make sure you are doing everything right.

- **Read the "fine print."** When dealing with important paperwork, look to see if important information is buried in large amounts of text or in small print so that you'll be less likely to read it. Never sign anything without reading it completely first.

EXERCISE 6-7 Thinking Critically About Information

Directions: *Read the passage and then answer then question that follows.*

HIDDEN INFORMATION

Banks and credit card companies make a huge amount of money each year by charging interest to their customers. When you use a credit card, you are actually borrowing money from the credit card company. Unless you pay the borrowed amount back within one month, you start paying interest charges. By law, credit card companies are required to tell you on your credit card statement how much interest they are charging you.

Have you ever looked at your credit card statement? It is filled with information and can have pages of "fine print" (that is, very small print) with the information required by law. How many people take the time to read this information? Not many. The credit card companies have effectively buried important information that they don't want you to know.

The back side of your credit card statement is filled with tiny print. Somewhere in the middle it says, "You are not responsible for paying for any purchases made if your credit card is stolen." You receive a phone call from the credit card company offering you "protection against unauthorized use of your card." If you pay them $99 a year, they will cover any purchases that are made if your card is stolen. Should you pay the $99 for the protection plan? Why or why not?

____

____

____

EXERCISE 6-8 Thinking Critically About Advertisements

Directions: *Use your critical thinking skills to answer the following questions.*

1. Think about the following two advertisements. Advertisement A says, "Each year millions of homes are broken into! For just $40 per month, sign up for our alarm system service to protect

your home and valuables." Advertisement B says, "What happens when the power goes out? Homes are robbed and looted, and your family is in danger. Buy one of our emergency flashlights today to make sure your family is safe."

What emotion are the advertisers using to try to sell you a product or service? ___________________

2. You go to the drugstore to buy some painkillers. A bottle of 100 brand-name capsules costs $10. The generic drugstore brand costs $3 for 100 capsules. You read the back of the packages and see that both products have "acetaminophen 25g" listed as the active ingredient. Should you buy the brand name that you know, even though it's much more expensive?

____

____

TEXTBOOK CHALLENGE

TIPS for Reading in Health Fields

When reading health textbooks, pay attention to

- **Cause and effect.** Links between disease or illnesses and the things that create or influence them are often discussed in health textbooks.
- **Scientific thought.** Courses in health fields encourage students to ask questions and seek explanations.
- **New terminology.** Specialized words make up a considerable amount of what you will need to learn as you study health fields.

Copyright © 2012 by Pearson Education

Part A: Analyzing a Textbook Excerpt

This excerpt was taken from a health textbook chapter titled *Living Well: Promoting Healthy Behavior Change.* Read the excerpt and follow the directions on p. 223.

GENDER DIFFERENCES AND HEALTH

1 You don't have to be a health expert to know that there are physiological differences between men and women. Though much of the male and female anatomy is identical, researchers are discovering that the same diseases and treatments can affect men and women very differently. Many illnesses—for example, osteoporosis, multiple sclerosis, diabetes, and Alzheimer's disease—are much more common in women, even though rates for these diseases seem to be increasing in men. Why these differences? Is it simply a matter of lifestyle? Clearly it is much more complicated than that. Consider the following:

2 • The size, structure, and function of the brain differs in women and men, particularly in areas that affect mood and behavior and in areas used to perform tasks. Reaction time is slower in women, but accuracy is higher.

3 • Bone mass in women peaks when they are in their twenties; in men, it increases gradually until age 30. At menopause, women lose bone at an accelerated rate, and 80 percent of osteoporosis cases are women.

4 • Women's cardiovascular systems are different in size, shape, and nervous system impulses; women have faster heart rates.

5 • Women's immune systems are stronger than men's, but women are more prone to autoimmune diseases (disorders in which the body attacks its own tissues, such as multiple sclerosis, lupus, and rheumatoid arthritis). Men and women experience pain in different ways and may react to pain medications differently.

6 Differences do not stop there, according to a report by the Society for Women's Health Research:

7 • When consuming the same amount of alcohol, women have a higher blood alcohol content than men, even allowing for size differences.

8 • Women who smoke are 20 to 70 percent more likely to develop lung cancer than men who smoke the same number of cigarettes.

9 • Women are more likely than men to suffer a second heart attack within 1 year of their first heart attack.

10 • The same drug can cause different reactions and different side effects in women and men—even common drugs like antihistamines and antibiotics.

11 • Women are two times more likely than men to contract a sexually transmitted infection and are ten times more likely to contract HIV when having unprotected intercourse.

12 • Depression is two to three times more common in women than in men, and women are more likely than men to attempt suicide; however, men are more likely to succeed at suicide.

13 Surprisingly, although countless disparities in health have long been recognized, researchers largely ignored the unique aspects of women's health until the 1990s, when the National Institutes of Health (NIH) funded a highly publicized 15-year, $625 million study. Known as the Women's Health Initiative (WHI), this study was designed to focus research on the uniqueness of women when it came to drug trials, development of surgical instruments, and other health issues, rather than assuming that women were just like the men who had been studied. This research and the follow-up studies are providing invaluable information about women's health risks and potential strategies for prevention, intervention, and treatment.

—Donatelle, *Access to Health*, p. 14

1. **Preview.** Preview the reading using the guidelines on p. 7 and then answer the following questions.
   a. What are some of the basic ways men and women are different when it comes to health?
   b. When and how did things begin to change in the way women's health is studied?
2. **SQ3R.** Write at least three questions for the Q step of SQ3R. Answer them after completing the reading.
3. **Textbook Features.** What important function do the bulleted lists serve that help you to understand the main point of the selection?
4. **Vocabulary.**
   a. Identify the important new terms that are introduced in the reading.
   b. Define each of the following words as used in the reading:
   physiological (par. 1), *accelerated* (par. 3), *autoimmune* (par. 5), *disparities* (par. 13), *invaluable* (par. 13)
5. **Applying Chapter Skills.** Draw a map to organize the information presented in this selection.
6. **Essay Question.** Write an answer to the following essay question. To test your memory, write it without referring to the excerpt.
   Explain how and why diseases and treatments differ for men and women.
7. **Thinking Critically.** Use your critical thinking skills to answer each of the following questions.
   a. If you read this excerpt selectively by looking only at the bulleted facts presented in this selection, would you have a good grasp of the author's message? Why or why not? What does that make you think about the usefulness of bullets in textbooks?
   b. Why do you think medical research focused primarily on men until recently?
   c. What other differences exist among people that might require a more personalized approach to medicine? How do you envision medicine changing in the future?

Part B: Your College Textbook

Choose a chapter that you have been assigned to read in a textbook for one of your other courses. Highlight and mark the chapter.

Copyright © 2012 by Pearson Education

SELF-TEST SUMMARY

To test yourself, cover up the Answer column with a sheet of paper and answer each question listed in the left column. Evaluate each of your answers as you work by sliding the paper down and comparing your answer with what is printed in the Answer column.

	Question	Answer
GOAL 1	How can you keep track of information when reading?	Information can be tracked using highlighting and marking, outlining, mapping, and summarizing.
GOAL 2	How can you highlight effectively?	Identify what is important in each paragraph by ■ Reading first, then highlighting ■ Using heading as a guide ■ Developing a highlighting system ■ Highlighting as few words as possible
GOAL 3	What is outlining?	Outlining is a method of organizing information to show the relative importance of ideas.
GOAL 4	What is mapping?	Mapping is the process of drawing diagrams to show connections between a topic and its related ideas.
GOAL 5	What is involved in summarizing?	Summarizing involves selecting a passage's most important ideas and recording them in condensed, abbreviated form.
GOAL 6	How can you think critically about information?	Read selectively, understand the goals of the material, adjust your reading speed to the task to allow you to track information, and read the fine print.

NAME ______________________ SECTION ______________________

DATE ______________________ SCORE ______________________

PRACTICE TEST 6-1

Summarizing

Directions: *After reading the following passage, select words and phrases from the box that follows the selection to complete the summary. Each word or phrase should be used only once. Not all words or phrases in the box will be used.*

On Visiting an Art Museum, (Or How to Enjoy Looking at Art Without Being Overwhelmed by Museum Fatigue)

Art museums can be mind-expanding or sleep-inducing, depending on how you approach them. It is a mistake to enter a museum with the belief that you should like everything you see—or even that you should see everything that is there. Without selective viewing, the visitor to a large museum is likely to come down with a severe case of museum exhaustion.

It makes sense to approach an art museum the way a seasoned traveler approaches a city for a first visit: Find out what there is to see. In the museum, inquire about the schedule of special shows, then see those exhibitions and outstanding works that interest you. Museums are in the process of rethinking their buildings and collections in order to meet the needs of changing populations and changing values. It is not unusual to find video exhibits, performances of all kinds, and film showings as part of regular museum programming.

If you are visiting without a specific exhibition in mind, follow your interests and instincts. Browsing can be highly rewarding. Zero in on what you feel are the highlights, savoring favorite works and unexpected discoveries.

Don't stay too long in a museum. Take breaks. Perhaps there is a garden or café in which you can pause for a rest. The quality of your experience is not measured by the amount of time you spend in the galleries or how many works you see. The most rewarding experiences can come from finding something that "speaks" to you, then sitting and enjoying it in leisurely contemplation.

—Preble and Preble, *Artforms,* p. 110

Copyright © 2012 by Pearson Education

mind-expanding	selective viewing	exhaustion	overwhelmed
art museum	sleep-inducing	offer	too long
overload	highlights	instincts	breaks
outstanding works	speaks	special exhibitions	

Summary

When you are visiting an ________________, you should practice ________________. Find out what the museum has to ________________. Decide what ________________ and ________________ appeal to you. Follow your ________________ and focus on the ________________. Don't stay ________________ in the museum, and take frequent ________________. Find art that ________________ to you and take time to enjoy it.

NAME ______________________ SECTION ______________________

DATE ______________________ SCORE ______________________

PRACTICE TEST 6-2

Outlining

Directions: *After reading the passage, fill in the missing information in the outline that follows.*

Gangs as Formal Organizations

Inner-city gangs provide a good example of a formal organization. According to a study of 37 different gangs comprising Chicano, Jamaican, Irish, African American, and other ethnic groups, certain basic elements are common to all gang organizations. First, like all organizations, gangs are organized to achieve specific goals—such as securing money, protecting members, gaining prestige in a neighborhood, and providing alternatives to mainstream low-pay, dead-end jobs.

Second, all gangs have defined organizational structures that take three basic forms. Many of the larger ones subscribe to a *hierarchical model* of organization, with a president or "godfather," a vice-president in charge of administrative tasks, a warlord whose job it is to maintain order within ranks, and a treasurer who collects and manages the gang's finances. A second type, favored by Chicano gangs, which are often smaller and more cohesive than those hierarchically arranged, is the *horizontal organizational model*. It, too, has four offices but they have roughly equal authority and different individuals may assume duties based on preference and need. The *influential model* has neither formal written duties for leaders nor formal titles, but relies instead on charismatic authority. According to gang members, leaders appear "naturally," perhaps because of superior fighting skills, mediating abilities, or some other unique talent that gang members deem important.

—adapted from Thompson and Hickey, *Society in Focus,* p. 147

I. Gangs are organized to ______________________
   A. Secure money
   B. ______________________
   C. ______________________
   D. Provide alternatives to dead-end jobs

II. Gangs have defined organizational structures
   A. ______________________
      1. President or "godfather"
      2. Vice-president—administrative tasks
      3. ______________________
      4. ______________________

Copyright © 2012 by Pearson Education

B. Horizontal model
    1. Four offices
        a. ______________________________
        b. Different members may assume duties based on ______________________________
C. Influential model
    1. No formal written duties or titles for leaders
    2. Natural, charismatic authority established by:
        a. ______________________________
        b. Mediating abilities
        c. ______________________________

NAME ________________ SECTION ________________

DATE ________________ SCORE ________________

MASTERY TEST 6-1

Mapping

***Directions:** After reading the following passage from a marketing textbook, select the choice that best completes each of the statements that follow. Then fill in the missing information in the map on page 231.*

The Product Life Cycle

The life of a product may be measured in months or years. The humble zipper is an example of a product that has managed to live an exceptionally long life. Invented in the 1800s for use on high-buttoned shoes, the zipper did not make its way onto a pair of trousers until the 1930s; basically unchanged nearly seventy years later, the zipper continues to be an essential part of our wardrobes. From zippers to zip drives, the life of a product can be divided into four separate stages: introduction, growth, maturity and decline.

The first stage of the product life cycle is **introduction,** when customers get their first chance to purchase the good or service. During this early stage, a single company usually produces the product. If the product is accepted and profitable, competitors will follow with their own versions. The goal during this stage is to get first-time buyers to try the product. Sales increase at a steady but slow pace. The company does not make a profit during this stage for two reasons: research and development costs and heavy spending for advertising and other promotional costs. How long the introduction stage lasts depends on a number of factors, including marketplace acceptance and producer willingness to support the product during its start-up.

Not all products make it past the introduction stage. For a new product to be successful, consumers must first know about it. Then they must believe that the product is something they need. Thus, marketing during this stage often focuses on informing consumers about the product, how to use it, and its benefits. Overall, 38 percent of all new products fail.

The second stage in the product life cycle, the **growth stage,** sees a rapid increase in sales while profits increase and peak. The goal here is to encourage brand loyalty by convincing the market that this brand is superior to others in the category. When competitors appear, marketers must use heavy advertising and other types of promotion. Price competition may develop, driving profits down.

The **maturity stage** of the product life cycle is usually the longest. Sales peak and then begin to level off and even decline while profit margins narrow. Competition grows intense when remaining competitors fight for a piece of a shrinking pie. Because most customers have already accepted the product, sales are often to replace a "worn-out" item or to take advantage of product improvements. To remain competitive and maintain market share during the

Copyright © 2012 by Pearson Education

maturity stage, firms may tinker with the marketing mix by adding "bells and whistles" to their products' features, or they may try to attract new users of the product.

The **decline stage** of the product life cycle is characterized by a decrease in sales. Often this is because new technology has made the product obsolete, as when computers caused the decline of the typewriter. Although a single firm may still be profitable, the market as a whole begins to shrink, profits decline, and suppliers pull out. In this stage, there are usually many competitors with no one having a distinct advantage. A firm's major product decision in the decline stage is whether or not to keep the product. Once the product is no longer profitable, it drains resources from the firm—resources that could help develop new products.

—adapted from Solomon and Stuart, *Marketing: Real People, Real Choices,* pp. 266–269

_____ 1. The topic of this passage is
   a. the zipper.
   b. new products.
   c. competition.
   d. the product life cycle.

_____ 2. The longest stage of the product life cycle usually is the
   a. introduction stage.
   b. growth stage.
   c. maturity stage.
   d. decline stage.

_____ 3. The two stages in which profits typically peak are the
   a. introduction and growth stages.
   b. growth and maturity stages.
   c. introduction and maturity stages.
   d. maturity and decline stages.

_____ 4. The primary goal during the introduction stage of a product is to
   a. get first-time buyers to try the product.
   b. encourage brand loyalty by convincing buyers that a particular brand is better than others in the category.
   c. persuade buyers to replace worn-out items or take advantage of product improvements.
   d. decide whether or not to keep the product.

_______ 5. In the last paragraph, the topic sentence begins with the words
   a. "The decline stage."
   b. "Often this."
   c. "Although a single."
   d. "Once the product."

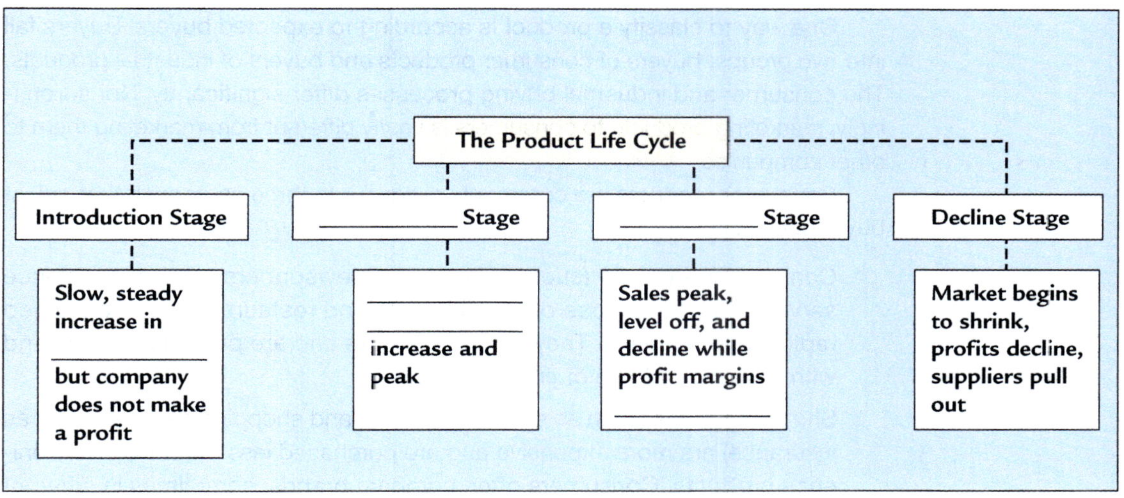

Copyright © 2012 by Pearson Education

MASTERY TEST 6-2

NAME ______________________ SECTION ______________________

DATE ______________________ SCORE ______________________

Outlining

Directions: *After reading the passage, fill in the missing information in the outline that follows.*

Classifying Goods and Services

One way to classify a product is according to expected buyers. Buyers fall into two groups: buyers of consumer products and buyers of industrial products. The consumer and industrial buying processes differ significantly. Not surprisingly, marketing products to consumers is vastly different from marketing them to other companies.

Consumer products are commonly divided into three categories that reflect buyer behavior:

- Convenience goods (such as milk and newspapers) and convenience services (such as those offered by fast-food restaurants) are consumed rapidly and regularly. They are inexpensive and are purchased often and with little expenditure of time and effort.
- Shopping goods (such as stereos and tires) and shopping services (such as insurance) are more expensive and are purchased less often than convenience products. Consumers often compare brands, sometimes in different stores. They may also evaluate alternatives in terms of style, performance, color, price, and other criteria.
- Specialty goods (such as wedding gowns) and specialty services (such as catering for wedding receptions) are extremely important and expensive purchases. Consumers usually decide on precisely what they want and will accept no substitutes. They will often go from store to store, sometimes spending a great deal of money and time to get a specific product.

Depending on how much they cost and how they will be used, industrial products can be divided into two categories: expense and capital items.

- Expense items are any materials and services that are consumed within a year by firms producing other goods or supplying other services. The most obvious expense items are industrial goods used directly in the production process (for example, bulkloads of tea processed into tea bags).
- Capital items are permanent (expensive and long-lasting) goods and services. All these items have expected lives of more than a year and typically up to several years. Expensive buildings (offices, factories), fixed equipment

(water towers, baking ovens), and accessory equipment (computers, airplanes) are capital goods. Capital services are those for which long-term commitments are made. These may include purchases for employee food services, building and equipment maintenance, or legal services. Because capital items are expensive and purchased infrequently, they often involve decisions by high-level managers.

—Ebert and Griffin, *Business Essentials,* pp. 266–267

I. Consumer products

A. Convenience goods and services
1. Examples: milk, newspapers, fast-food places
2. Consumed ______________________
3. Inexpensive
4. Purchased ______________________
5. Little expenditure of time and effort

B. Shopping goods and services
1. Examples: stereos, tires, insurance
2. More ______________________
3. Purchased less often
4. Brands ______________________
5. Alternatives evaluated
   a. Style
   b. Performance
   c. Color
   d. Price
   e. Other criteria

C. ______________________
1. Examples: wedding gowns, caterers
2. Very important and expensive
3. No substitutes
4. Large expenditure of ______________________

II. Industrial products

A. Expense items
1. Materials and services consumed within 1 year
2. Goods used ______________________
3. Example: bulk tea packaged into teabags

Copyright © 2012 by Pearson Education

B. ____________________

1. Permanent goods and services lasting ____________________
2. Examples of goods
   a. Expensive buildings
   b. Fixed equipment
   c. Accessory equipment
3. Examples of services
   a. Employee food services
   b. Building/equipment maintenance
   c. Legal services
4. Decisions involve ____________________

NAME ______________ SECTION ______________

DATE ______________ SCORE ______________

MASTERY TEST 6-3

READING SELECTION

Employee Speech in the Digital Age

Dennis L. Wilcox and Glen T. Cameron

In this selection from a public relations textbook, the authors explore the challenges facing employers in the age of the Internet. Read the selection to find out how organizations are dealing with the digital communications of their employees.

Vocabulary Preview

These are some of the difficult words in this essay. The definitions here will help you if you can't figure out the meanings from the sentence context or word parts.

litigation (par. 1) legal action

avatar (par. 1) a graphical image that represents and is manipulated by a computer user

proprietary (par. 4) protected by trademark or legal ownership

netiquette (par. 9) a combination of *Internet* and *etiquette*, referring to the manners or rules of behavior on the Internet

netizen (par. 11) a combination of *Internet* and *citizen*, meaning someone who uses the Internet

cogs (par. 11) moving parts

1 A modern, progressive organization encourages employee comments and even criticisms. Many employee newspapers and e-bulletin boards even carry letters to the editor because they breed a healthy atmosphere of two-way communication and make company publications more credible. In an era of digital communications and increased legal litigation, however, organizations are increasingly setting guidelines and monitoring what employees say online. The following is a discussion of employee e-mail, surfing the Internet, blogging and even guidelines for being an "avatar" on sites such as Second Life.

Employee E-Mail

2 The monitoring of employee e-mail by management is well established. A survey by Forrester Consulting for Proofpoint, a maker of e-mail security products, found that almost 50 percent of large companies audit outbound e-mail by their employees. Another 32 percent had actually fired an employee within the last year for breaking e-mail rules.

Copyright © 2012 by Pearson Education

3 A number of court decisions have reinforced the right of employers to read employees' e-mail. Pillsbury, for example, fired a worker who posted an e-mail message to a colleague calling management "back-stabbing bastards." The employee sued, but the court sided with the company. In another case, Intel got a court injunction against a former employee who complained about the company in e-mails sent to thousands of employees. The Electronic Frontier Foundation, a group devoted to civil liberties in cyberspace, worried about violation of First Amendment rights. The company, however, contended that it wasn't a matter of free speech, but trespassing on company property.

4 Employers are increasingly monitoring employee e-mail for two reasons. First, they are concerned about being held liable if an employee posts a racial slur, engages in sexual harassment online, and even transmits sexually explicit jokes that would cause another employee to feel that the workplace was a "hostile" environment. Second, companies are concerned about employee e-mails that may include information that the organization considers proprietory such as trade secrets, marketing plans, and development of new products that would give the competition an advantage. In other words, you should assume that any e-mails you write at work are subject to monitoring and that you can be fired if you violate company guidelines.

Surfing the Internet

5 Employees should also be careful about using the World Wide Web at work. According to a recent survey by the American Management Association (AMA), more than 75 percent of American employers monitor personal web surfing at work. And more than 25 percent of the companies have actually fired someone for doing it. Other studies, of course, show that Web surfing at work for personal reasons is done by the majority of employees—and many even think of the Internet in the same context as using the lowly telephone.

6 Employers, of course, are concerned about loss of productivity when employees sit at their desks surfing the Internet or even playing video games. Potential liability, however, is another big factor. Companies can and do get sued for what their employees do online. Office workers accessing porn sites, instant messaging of smutty and racial jokes, and posting desktop wallpaper from *Playboy* magazine are all lawsuits waiting to happen when other workers are offended and even file complaints with the Equal Opportunity Employment Commission (EOEC). According to *Financial Times*, "a New Jersey court found that

> "A New Jersey court found that employers were not just permitted but actually obliged to monitor employee Internet use."
>
> —*Patti Waldmeir,* columnist for the *Financial Times*

employers were not just permitted but actually obliged to monitor employee Internet use."

Employee Blogs

7 Many organizations now encourage employees to have a blog as a way of fostering discussion on the Internet and getting informal feedback from the public. In some large companies, even top executives have a blog. In most cases, the blog prominently features their association with the business and gives information (and images) about the employer. As John Elasser, editor of *Public Relations Tactics,* says, "Some of that content may be innocuous; other types may be embarrassing or come back to haunt the company in litigation."

8 Consequently, it is important for the business to have a clear policy that provides guidelines for what rank-and-file employees, as well as executives, can say or not say on their blogs or a posting on another blog. The public relations staff often prepares the general guidelines and trains employees about such matters as the proper use of corporate trademarks, avoiding unfair criticism of other employees or the competition, the use of copyrighted material, or even what topics are particularly sensitive because of pending lawsuits or business negotiations. Bloggers also have an obligation to inform readers that they are employees of the organization, not just an interested average citizen.

9 Other general rules of netiquette are listed in Chapter 13. In addition, the Electronic Frontier Foundation has a "Legal Guide for Bloggers" at its Web site, www.eff.org/bloggers/lg.

Virtual Online Communities

10 A newer innovation is virtual online communities, such as Second Life, Entropia, Universe, and There.Com. Although these communities are used by gambling parlors and pornographers, they are also increasingly

Loss of worker productivity occurs when employees misuse office computers.

Copyright © 2012 by Pearson Education

home to multinational companies advertising their brands and hoping to promote communication among employees worldwide.

11 IBM, realizing the potential for hosting meetings with clients and partners, has published guidelines for more than 5,000 of its employees who inhabit Second Life and other worlds. Some of its basic rules are (1) don't discuss intellectual property with unauthorized people, (2) don't discriminate or harass, and (3) be a good netizen. IBM, whose employees are often parodied as cogs in matching navy suits, doesn't have a dress code for its employee avatars, but it does suggest being "sensitive to the appropriateness of your avatar or persona's appearance when you are meeting with IBM clients or conducting IBM business."

Directions: *Select the choice that best completes each of the following statements.*

CHECKING YOUR COMPREHENSION

_____ 1. The central thought of this selection is that organizations are
   a. limiting their employees' right to free speech on the Internet.
   b. becoming less likely to encourage employee comments and criticisms.
   c. establishing programs to teach employees about proper netiquette.
   d. increasing their oversight of what employees say and do online.

_____ 2. The main idea of paragraph 3 is that
   a. Pillsbury and Intel took legal action against employees over e-mail.
   b. the Electronic Frontier Foundation works to protect civil liberties in cyberspace.
   c. court decisions reinforce employers' rights to read their employees' e-mail.
   d. monitoring of employee e-mails is a violation of First Amendment rights.

_____ 3. The topic sentence of paragraph 4 begins with the words
   a. "Employers are."
   b. "First, they are."
   c. "Second, companies are."
   d. "In other words."

_______ 4. Reasons that employers are concerned about employee e-mail and Internet use include

a. loss of productivity.

b. potential liability for employees' words or actions.

c. possible leaks of proprietary information.

d. all of the above.

_______ 5. The main idea of paragraph 8 is that businesses should

a. never allow employees to blog about their employer.

b. have clear guidelines about employee blogs.

c. use blogs as a marketing and public relations tool.

d. require employee bloggers to conceal their company affiliation.

USING WHAT YOU KNOW ABOUT KEEPING TRACK OF INFORMATION

_______ 6. Of the following choices, the one that best summarizes paragraph 7 is

a. Many organizations encourage employees to foster discussion on the Internet and get informal feedback.

b. Many organizations encourage employee blogs as a way to foster discussion on the Internet and get informal public feedback. Most blogs feature the employee's association with the business and give information about the employer.

c. Many organizations now encourage employees to have a blog as a way of fostering discussion on the Internet and getting informal feedback from the public. In some large companies, even top executives have a blog. In most cases, the blog prominently features their association with the business and gives information and images about the employer.

d. Many organizations encourage employees to have a blog. According to John Elasser, editor of *Public Relations Tactics*, blog content may be embarrassing or come back to haunt the company in litigation.

Copyright © 2012 by Pearson Education

_______ 7. In paragraph 10, the most important group of words to highlight is

a. "Second Life, Entropia, Universe, and There.Com."
b. "gambling parlors and pornographers."
c. "virtual online communities" "home to multinational companies."
d. "hoping to promote communication."

Questions 8–10 refer to the following map of the selection.

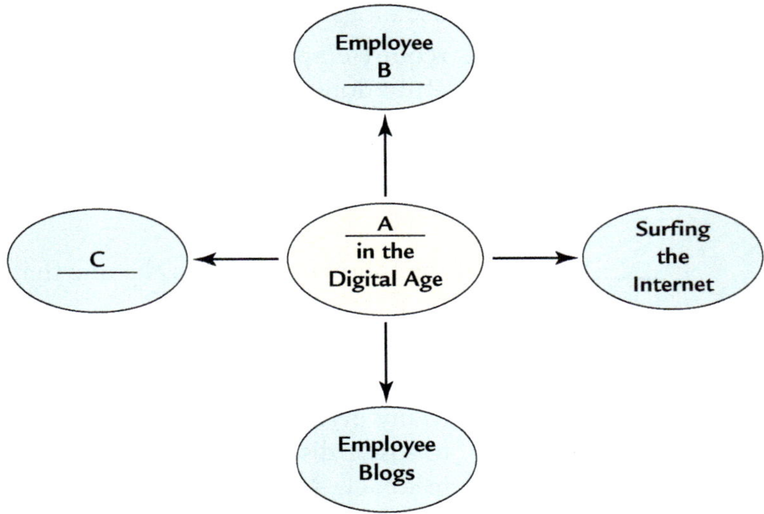

_______ 8. The best phrase to fill in the blank labeled A is

a. Monitoring E-mail.
b. Employee Speech.
c. Internet Use.
d. Corporate Policy.

_______ 9. The best word to fill in the blank labeled B is

a. E-mail.
b. Blogs.
c. Litigation.
d. Rights.

_______ 10. The best phrase to fill in the blank labeled C is

a. Rules of Netiquette.
b. Second Life.
c. Employee Avatars.
d. Virtual Online Communities.

USING CONTEXT CLUES AND WORD PARTS

_______ 11. In paragraph 1, the word **credible** means

a. optional.
b. believable.
c. recommended.
d. unrealistic.

_______ 12. In paragraph 2, the word **audit** means

a. approve.
b. revise.
c. increase.
d. review.

_______ 13. In paragraph 3, the word **contended** means

a. argued.
b. worried.
c. agreed.
d. ceased.

_______ 14. In paragraph 7, the word **innocuous** means

a. expensive.
b. disruptive.
c. harmless.
d. offensive.

_______ 15. In paragraph 11, the word **parodied** means

a. copied.
b. made fun of.
c. supported.
d. admired.

REVIEWING DIFFICULT VOCABULARY

Directions: *Complete each of the following sentences by inserting a word from the Vocabulary Preview on page 235 in the space provided. Use each word only once.*

16. After many years of feeling like ________________ in the huge corporation, Kaye and Anh-Vi left to form their own company.
17. The driver hoped to avoid ________________ by offering to pay for repairs to the other car.
18. Isaac spent so much time creating his ________________ that he missed several deadlines at work.
19. The company required new employees to sign an agreement stating that they would not share ________________ information.
20. Part of being a responsible ________________ involves practicing good ________________, such as not typing in all capital letters.

Copyright © 2012 by Pearson Education

THINKING CRITICALLY

1. How do the subheadings improve the readability of this selection? What guide questions can you form from each subheading to assist you in studying for a test over this material?
2. How would you describe the authors' approach to this subject? Consider how the selection might be different if it were written by someone who strongly objected to being monitored at work.
3. What is the effect of the image of employees playing video games? Why was it included?

QUESTIONS FOR DISCUSSION

1. Do you agree that employee comments and criticisms breed a healthy atmosphere at work? Why or why not?
2. Were you surprised at the percentages of employees who had been fired either for breaking e-mail rules (32 percent) or for surfing the Internet at work (25 percent)? Why or why not?
3. Discuss whether you think a company should be liable for what employees do online. Do you agree that employers are obliged to monitor employee Internet use?

WRITING ACTIVITIES

1. Create a list of ways to be a good netizen, including your own rules of proper netiquette.
2. Using what you learned in this chapter, create an outline based on this selection.
3. Have you ever created your own avatar? Write a paragraph describing your experience and your avatar.
4. Choose a category from this list of workplace privacy issues: http://www.privacyrights.org/fs/fs7-work.htm

   Write a paragraph that summarizes the rights of the employers and employees.

CHAPTER 6

Organizing Information

RECORDING YOUR PROGRESS

Test	Number Right		Score
Practice Test 6-1	________	× 10 =	________%
Practice Test 6-2	________	× 10 =	________%
Mastery Test 6-1	________	× 10 =	________%
Mastery Test 6-2	________	× 10 =	________%
Mastery Test 6-3	________	× 5 =	________%

GETTING MORE PRACTICE myreadinglab

To get more practice with Organizing Information, go to http://www.myreadinglab.com and click on

> Study Plan
> Reading Skills
> Note Taking and Highlighting and Outlining and Summarizing

EVALUATING YOUR PROGRESS myreadinglab

To measure your progress after reading and viewing the information in the Review Materials section, complete the Practices and Tests in the Activities section. You can check your scores by clicking on the Gradebook tab.

Then, based on your performance in this chapter and/or on the MyReadingLab Practices and Tests, write your own evaluation.

YOUR EVALUATION: ____

____

____

____

____

Copyright © 2012 by Pearson Education

THINKING ABOUT

Patterns of Organization

Study the photograph of the produce section of a market. How is the produce organized?

They are grouped together by type of fruit or vegetable to make it easy and convenient for shoppers to locate and select what they need to purchase. Are there other ways the produce could be organized?

Produce could be organized according to freshness, or by price, or by organic and non-organic.

C H A P T E R 7

Examining Basic Patterns of Organization

What Are Patterns of Organization?

GOAL 1
Identify patterns of organization

Just as there are several possible ways to organize produce at a market, there are several ways to organize a paragraph or essay. Writers use a variety of *patterns of organization,* depending on what they want to accomplish. These patterns, then, are the different ways that writers present their ideas.

To help you think a bit about patterns, complete each of the following steps:

1. Study each of the following drawings for a few seconds (count to ten as you look at each one).
2. Cover up the drawings and try to draw each from memory.
3. Check to see how many you had exactly correct.

myreadinglab

To practice examining the patterns of organization, go to
> Study Plan
> Reading Skills
> Patterns of Organization

LEARNING GOALS

GOAL 1 Identify patterns of organization

GOAL 2 Understand the example pattern

GOAL 3 Understand the definition pattern

GOAL 4 Understand the chronological order and process patterns

GOAL 5 Understand the listing pattern

GOAL 6 Think critically about the example pattern of organization

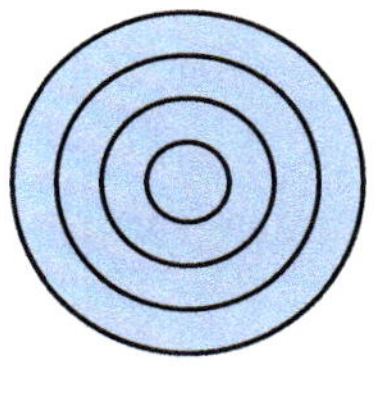

1

2

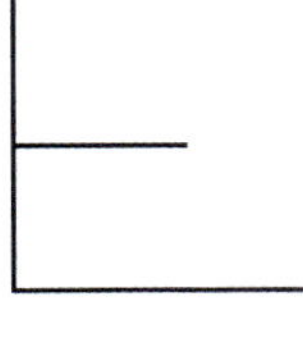

3

4

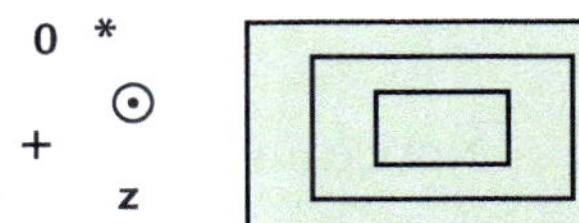

5

Copyright © 2012 by Pearson Education

You probably drew all but the fourth correctly. Why do you think you got that one wrong? How does it differ from the others?

Drawings 1, 2, 3, and 5 have patterns. Drawing 4, however, has no pattern; it is just a group of randomly arranged symbols.

From this experiment you can see that it is easier to remember drawings that have a pattern—a clear form of organization. The same is true of written material. If you can see how a paragraph or essay is organized, it is easier to understand and remember. In this chapter you will learn about some of the common patterns writers use and how to recognize them: (1) example, (2) definition, (3) chronological order and process, and (4) listing.

Example

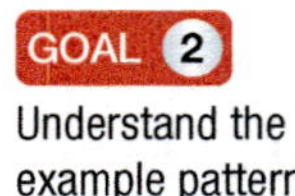

Understand the example pattern

One of the clearest ways to explain something is to give an example. This is especially true when a subject is unfamiliar. Suppose, for instance, you are taking a course in child psychology and your sister asks you to explain what aggressive behavior is in children. You might explain by giving examples of aggressive behavior, such as biting other children, striking playmates, and throwing objects at others. Through examples, your sister would get a fairly good idea of what aggressive behavior is.

When organizing a paragraph, a writer often states the main idea first and then follows it with one or more examples. The preceding paragraph takes this approach. The main idea in the topic sentence is supported by the example about explaining aggressive behavior to a sister. In some paragraphs, of course, a writer might use several examples. And in a longer piece of writing, a separate paragraph may be used for each example.

Here is one way to visualize the example pattern in a paragraph:

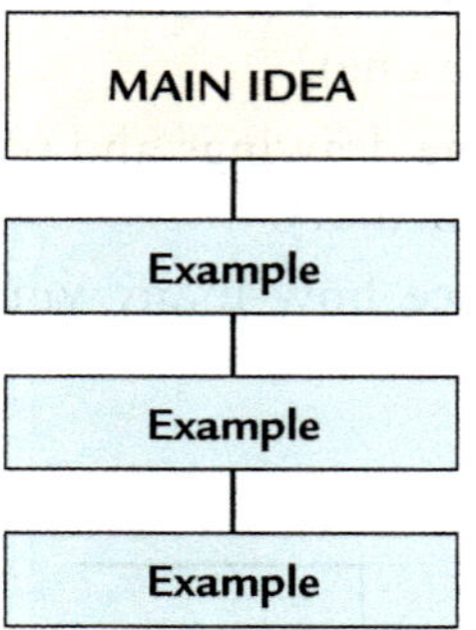

Notice how this example pattern is developed in the following paragraph.

> Many animals undergo a metamorphosis as they move from one developmental stage to the next in their growth cycle. A maggot transforms into a fly. A tadpole hatches from an egg and develops into an adult frog. A caterpillar changes from its larval form into a moth or a butterfly.

In the preceding paragraph, the writer explains metamorphosis through a variety of examples. You could visualize the paragraph as follows:

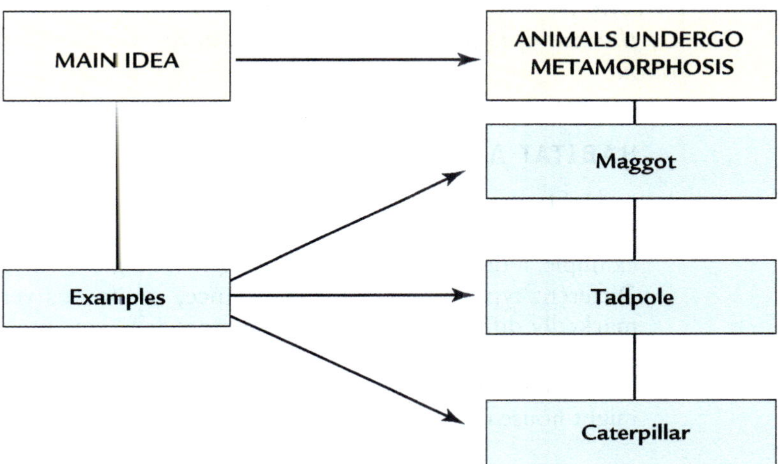

As you recall from Chapter 4, sometimes writers use transitional words—*for example, for instance,* or *such as*—to signal the reader that an example is to follow. The writer of the following paragraph uses transitions in this way:

> New technologies are helping to make alternative sources of energy cost-effective. In Pennsylvania and Connecticut, *for example,* the waste from landfills is loaded into furnaces and burned to generate electricity for thousands of homes. Natural sources of energy, *such as* the sun and the wind, are also becoming more attractive. The electricity produced by 300 wind turbines in northern California, *for instance,* has resulted in a savings of approximately 60,000 barrels of oil per year. Solar energy also has many applications, from pocket calculators to public telephones to entire homes, and is even used in spacecraft, where conventional power is unavailable.
>
> —adapted from Bergman and Renwick, *Introduction to Geography,* p. 356 and Carnes and Garraty, *The American Nation,* p. 916

Copyright © 2012 by Pearson Education

By using examples and transitions, the writer describes alternative sources of energy. Although writers don't always use transitions with examples, be on the lookout for them as you read.

EXERCISE 7-1 Understanding the Example Pattern

Directions: *The following paragraphs, all of which are about animal habitats, use the example pattern. Read each paragraph and answer the questions that follow.*

HABITAT AND NICHE

A. **Habitat** refers to the kind of place—defined by the plant community and the physical environment—where a species is biologically adapted to live. For example, a deciduous forest, a swamp, and a grassy field are types of habitats. Different types of forests (for instance, coniferous versus tropical) provide markedly different habitats and support different species of wildlife. Because some organisms operate on very small scales, we use the term *microhabitat* for things like puddles, sheltered spaces by rocks, and holes in tree trunks that might house their own small community.

—Wright, *Environmental Science*, pp. 56–57

1. What transition does the author use to introduce the examples of types of habitats? ____________________

2. List the three examples of habitats in the diagram below.

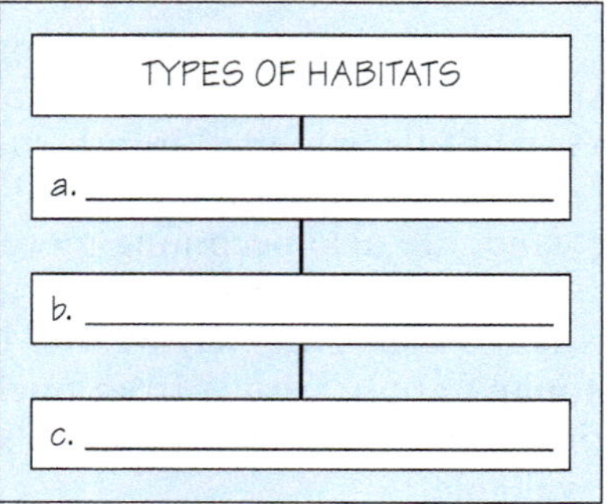

3. Does the topic sentence occur first, second, or last? ____________________

4. What transition does the author use to introduce an example of a type of forest? ____________________

5. What transition does the author use to introduce examples of microhabitats?

____

6. List the three examples of microhabitats.

   a. ____________________

   b. ____________________

   c. ____________________

B. Even when different species occupy the same habitat, competition may be slight or nonexistent because each species has its own niche. An animal's ecological **niche** refers to what the animal feeds on, where it feeds, when it feeds, where it finds shelter, how it responds to abiotic factors, and where it nests. Basically, the niche is the sum of all of the conditions and resources under which a species can live. Similar species can coexist in the same habitat, but have separate niches. Competition is minimized because potential competitors are using different resources. For example, woodpeckers, which feed on insects in deadwood, do not compete with birds that feed on seeds. Bats and swallows both feed on flying insects, but they do not compete because bats feed on night-flying insects and swallows feed during the day.

—Wright, *Environmental Science*, p. 57

7. Does the topic sentence of this paragraph occur first, second, or last?

____

8. What transition does the author use to introduce species that are not competing within a habitat? ____________________

9. Why is competition minimized between species that have different niches?

____

10. The author gives two examples of pairs of species that do not compete in the same habitat. List the pairs.

    a. ____

    b. ____

Copyright © 2012 by Pearson Education

Definition

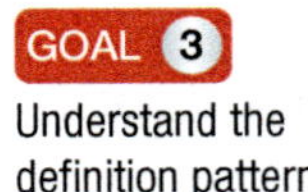

Understand the definition pattern

Another pattern writers follow is definition. Let's say that you see a game of lacrosse being played in your neighborhood and you mention this to a friend. Since your friend does not know what lacrosse is, you have to define it. Your definition should describe the sport's characteristics or features, explaining how it is different from other sports. Thus, you might define lacrosse as follows:

> Lacrosse was first played by Native Americans, making it the oldest sport in North America. Modern lacrosse is a fast-paced game played on a field by two teams of ten players each. During the game, players use the crosse—a long-handled stick with a webbed pouch—to maneuver a ball into the opposing team's goal. There are youth lacrosse teams for boys and girls, college and amateur teams for men and women, and professional teams for men.

This definition can be shown as follows:

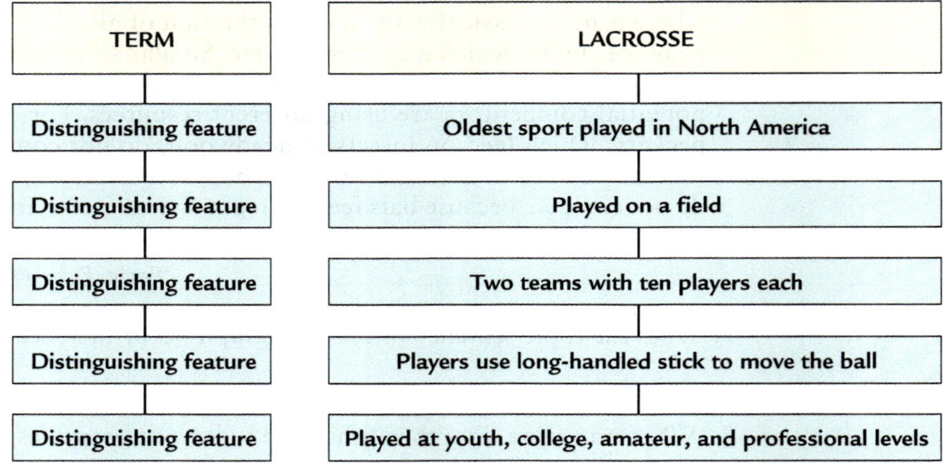

As you read passages that use the definition pattern, keep these questions in mind:

1. What is being defined?
2. What makes it different from other items or ideas?

Apply these questions to the following paragraph:

> **Humid subtropical climates** have several defining characteristics. They occur in latitudes between about 25 and 40 degrees on the eastern sides of continents and between about 35 and 50 degrees on the western sides. These climates are relatively warm most of the year but have at least

occasional freezing temperatures during the winter. Most humid subtropical climates have deciduous species of vegetation that lose their leaves in autumn and become dormant in winter. Eastern China, the southeastern U.S., and parts of Brazil and Argentina are the largest areas of humid subtropical climates.

—adapted from Bergman and Renwick, *Introduction to Geography,* p. 280

When you ask yourself the preceding questions, you can see, first of all, that *humid subtropical climates* are being defined. In addition, the definition lists four ways that humid subtropical climates are different from other climates: (1) they occur in latitudes between 25 and 40 degrees on the eastern sides of continents and between 35 and 50 degrees on the western sides, (2) they are warm most of the year but have some freezing temperatures during the winter, (3) they have deciduous species of vegetation that lose their leaves in autumn and become dormant in winter, and (4) the largest areas of humid subtropical climates are in eastern China, the southeastern United States, Brazil, and Argentina.

Combining Definition and Example

It is important to note that definitions are often combined with examples. For instance, if someone asks you to define the term *fiction writer,* you might begin by saying that a fiction writer is someone who creates novels and stories that describe imaginary people or events. You might also give some examples of well-known fiction writers, such as Ernest Hemingway or Stephen King. When definition and example are used together in this way, you can visualize the pattern as follows:

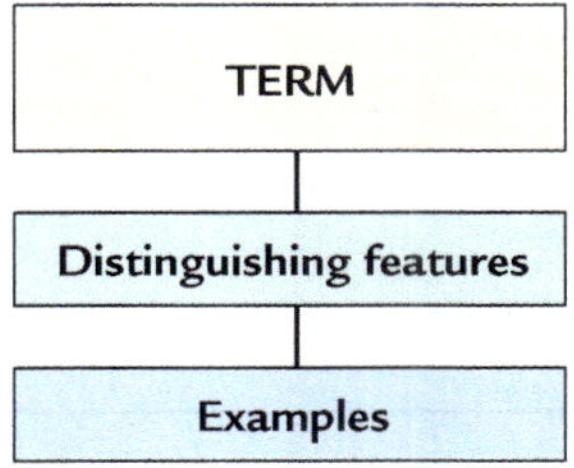

You will often encounter the definition and example pattern in your textbooks. An author will define a term and then use examples to explain it further, as shown in this passage from a health text:

Generally, positive stress, or stress that presents the opportunity for personal growth and satisfaction, is called **eustress.** Getting married, starting school, beginning a career, developing new friendships, and learning a new physical skill all give rise to eustress.

—Donatelle and Davis, *Access to Health,* p. 65

Copyright © 2012 by Pearson Education

First the authors define *eustress,* and then they provide several examples to make the definition more understandable. You have probably already noticed that textbook authors often put an important term in **boldfaced** type when they define it. This makes it easier for students to find definitions as they read or study for tests.

EXERCISE 7-2 Understanding the Definition Pattern

Directions: *Read each paragraph and answer the questions that follow.*

A. No time to socialize? Surely you can spare six minutes. That's how long potential couples usually spend getting acquainted while **speed dating**—an accelerated form of dating in which men and women choose whether to see each other again based on a very short interaction. Originally created for young Jewish singles in 1999, speed dating now provides homosexuals, heterosexuals, and a number of religious and ethnic groups with an opportunity to participate in quick, one-on-one dates with like-minded singles. Individuals spend six minutes talking to each date. If both individuals are interested, they are provided with each other's e-mail addresses.

—Kunz, *Think Marriages & Families*, p. 119

1. What term is being defined? ________________

2. The writer mentions several distinguishing features of this term. List three of them.

   a. ____

   ____

   b. ____

   c. ____

B. The patterns of stars seen in the sky are usually called constellations. In astronomy, however, the term constellation refers to a region of the sky. Any place you point in the sky belongs to some constellation; familiar patterns of stars merely help locate particular constellations. For example, the constellation Orion includes all the stars in the familiar pattern of the hunter, along with the region of the sky in which these stars are found.

—Bennett, *The Cosmic Perspective, Brief Edition*, p. 28

3. What term is being defined? ____________________

4. What example is given to illustrate the term being defined? ______________

5. What transitional phrase does the writer use? __________________________

C. The name "tale" is sometimes applied to any story, whether short or long, true or fictitious. But defined in a more limited sense, a **tale** is a story, usually short, that sets forth strange and wonderful events in more or less bare summary, without detailed character-drawing. "Tale" implies a story in which the goal is to reveal something marvelous rather than to reveal the character of someone. In the English folk tale "Jack and the Beanstalk," for instance, we take away a more vivid impression of the miraculous beanstalk and the giant who dwells at its top than of Jack's mind or personality.

—adapted from Kennedy and Gioia, *Literature*, p. 7

6. What term is being defined? _______________

7. What example is given to illustrate the term being defined?

____

8. What transitional phrase do the writers use? __________________________

D. The **nervous system,** the master controlling and communicating system of the body, has three overlapping functions: (1) It uses millions of sensory receptors to monitor changes occurring both inside and outside the body. These changes are called stimuli and the gathered information is called *sensory input*. (2) It processes and interprets the sensory input and decides what should be done at each moment—a process called *integration*. (3) It causes a response by activating our muscles or glands; the response is called *motor output*. An example will illustrate how these functions work together. When you are driving and see a red light ahead (sensory input), your nervous system integrates this information (red light means "stop"), and your foot goes for the brake (motor output).

—Marieb, *Human Anatomy & Physiology*, p. 387

9. What term is being defined? Enter it in the diagram on the next page.

10. In defining this term, the writer mentions three distinguishing features. List them in the diagram on the next page.

Copyright © 2012 by Pearson Education

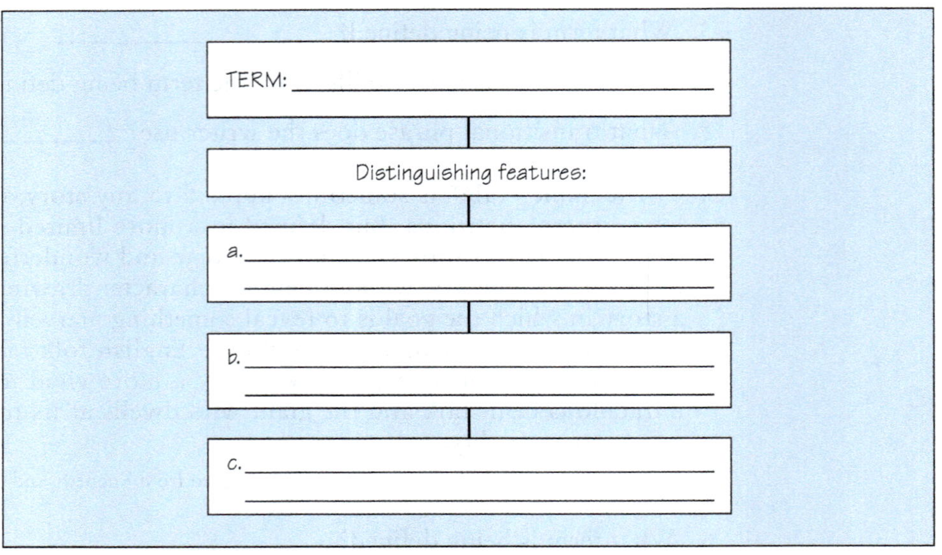

Chronological Order and Process

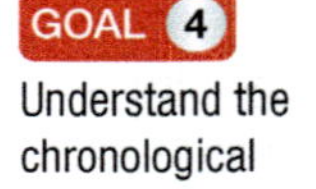

Understand the chronological order and process patterns

The terms **chronological order** and **process** both refer to the order in which something occurs or is done. When writers tell a story, they usually present events in chronological order. In other words, they start with the first event, continue with the second, and so on. For example, if you were telling a friend about finding a new part-time job, you would probably start by explaining how you found out about the job, continue by describing your interview, and end with the result—the manager was impressed with you and hired you on the spot. You would put events in order according to the *time* they occurred, beginning with the first event.

Common Transitions in Chronological Order and Process					
first	before	following	second	after	last
later	then	during	next	in addition	when
another	also	until	as soon as	finally	meanwhile

When you read stories for an English class or material in a history or political science text, you will often encounter chronological order. When writers use this pattern, they often include time transitions, such as *first, next,* and *finally* (see box). They may also use actual dates to help readers keep track of the sequence of events.

Example

Organized baseball teams first emerged in the 1840s, but the game only became truly popular during the Civil War, when it was a major form of camp recreation for the troops. After the war professional teams began to appear, and in 1876 teams in eight cities formed the National League. The American League followed in 1901. After a brief period of rivalry, the two leagues made peace in 1903, the year of the first World Series.

—adapted from Garraty and Carnes, *The American Nation,* p. 518

As you can see in this paragraph from a history text, the writers use chronological order to discuss the evolution of organized baseball. They use several phrases to show the reader the time sequence—*in the 1840s, during the Civil War, After the war, in 1876, in 1901,* and *in 1903*. As you read, look for such phrases as well as for time transitions.

Writers also follow a time sequence when they use the **process pattern**—when they explain how something is done or made. When writers explain how to put together a bookcase, how to knit a sweater, or how bees make honey, they use steps to show the appropriate order.

Example

To make a basic white sauce, follow a few easy steps. First, melt two tablespoons of butter over low heat. Next, add two tablespoons of flour and stir until the flour and butter are combined. Then add one cup of milk and continue stirring over low heat. Finally, when the mixture has thickened, add salt and pepper, or other seasonings, to taste.

This writer uses four time transitions—*first, next, then,* and *finally*—to make the order clear for the reader. Note that she also uses the word *steps* in the topic sentence. In the process pattern and in other patterns as well, the topic sentence often provides a clue as to the kind of pattern that will be used.

You can visualize and draw the chronological order and process patterns as follows:

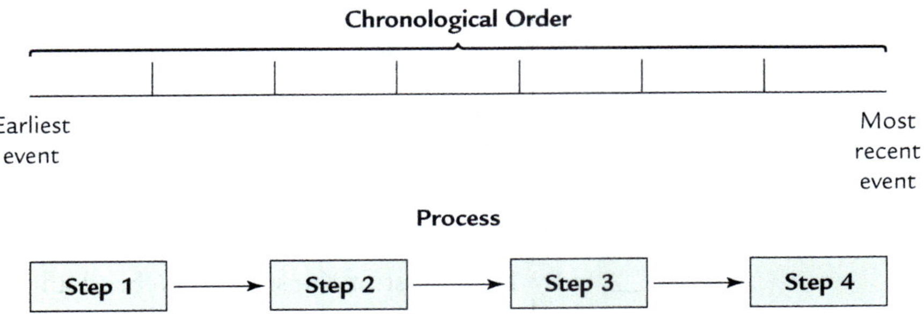

Sample maps showing chronological order and process appear in Chapter 6 (see Figures 6-3 and 6-4, p. 214).

Copyright © 2012 by Pearson Education

EXERCISE 7-3 Understanding Chronological Order and Process

Directions: *Using either chronological order or process, put each of the following groups of sentences in the correct order. For each sentence, write a number from 1 to 4 in the space provided, beginning with the topic sentence.*

1. _______ Rail travel originated in Europe in 1825, and four years later, North America welcomed the advent of passenger rail service.

   _______ Transcontinental service began in the United States in 1869 and in Canada in 1885.

   _______ Passenger rail service has been an important form of domestic transportation for more than 175 years.

   _______ In 1875 Fred Harvey introduced the golden age of passenger railroad service in the U.S., with the addition of dining cars and lodging facilities.

   —adapted from Cook, Yale, and Marqua, *Tourism: The Business of Travel,* p. 102

2. _______ Next, chemicals are released that attract even more platelets to the site.

   _______ Basically, once damage has occurred, blood elements called platelets immediately begin to cling to the injured site.

   _______ This rapidly growing pile-up of platelets initiates the sequence of events that finally forms a clot.

   _______ Blood clotting is a normal response to a break in the lining of a blood vessel.

   —adapted from Marieb, *Human Anatomy & Physiology,* p. 13

3. _______ A gold rush into Colorado in 1859 sent thousands of greedy prospectors across the Plains to drive the Cheyenne and Arapaho from land guaranteed them in 1851.

   _______ Thus it happened that in 1862, most of the Plains Indians rose up against the whites.

   _______ The American government showed no interest in honoring agreements with Indians.

   _______ By 1860 most of Kansas and Nebraska had been cleared, while other trouble developed in the Sioux country.

   —adapted from Garraty and Carnes, *The American Nation,* p. 455

4. _______ Once the defendant appears at the trial, the bail bond is refunded.

_______ When a person is arrested for a crime, he or she is taken to court and bail is set.

_______ The defendant is required to appear in person for the trial date, or the court keeps the entire bond that was posted.

_______ The person who is arrested (defendant) can pay the bail herself or himself, or a bail bondsperson can be paid a fee to post the bond, and the defendant is then released until trial.

5. _______ In the final stage, disorientation is often complete, and the person becomes completely dependent on others for eating, dressing, and other activities.

_______ These symptoms accelerate in the second stage, which also includes agitation and restlessness, loss of sensory perceptions, muscle twitching, and repetitive actions.

_______ During the first stage, symptoms include forgetfulness, memory loss, impaired judgment, increasing inability to handle routine tasks, disorientation, and depression.

_______ Alzheimer's disease is characteristically diagnosed in three stages.

—adapted from Donatelle and Davis, *Access to Health,* p. 533

Listing

Understand the listing pattern

Although writers often want to put events or items in a specific time sequence, sometimes they just want to list them. **Listing,** then, is used when a particular order isn't so important. If you were telling a friend about three places you would like to visit or three stores you like to shop at, you might just list them. It wouldn't matter which place or which store was listed first.

Example

The city of San Antonio, Texas, offers many attractions for visitors. One famous site is the Alamo, the eighteenth-century Spanish mission that had a historic role in Texas' revolution against Mexico. Another San Antonio highlight is much more modern: the River Walk, a shopping, dining, and entertainment promenade situated along the San Antonio River. For those interested in wildlife, the San Antonio Zoo and Aquarium houses more than 3,500 animals

Copyright © 2012 by Pearson Education

from 750 species. Visitors may also want to take in the serenity and beauty of the Japanese Tea Gardens next door to the zoo.

In the preceding paragraph, the writer might have put any of San Antonio's attractions first. The order simply depends on how the writer wants to present the material. Specific steps or time sequences are not important. Note, however, that the writer uses the transitions *another* and *also* to link the attractions together.

You can visualize the listing pattern as follows:

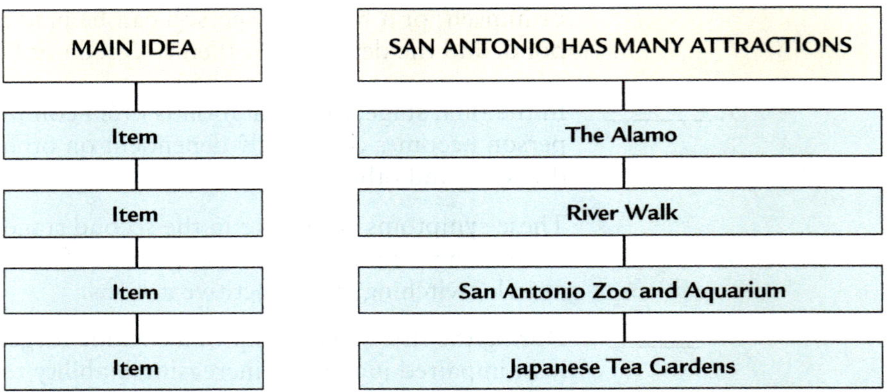

Textbook authors often use listing when they want to present information. The order is the way *they* want to present the material. It is not determined by time or steps.

Example

Precisely because the visual system is so complicated, it does not always work perfectly. For example, people with *myopia,* or nearsightedness, have difficulty focusing on distant objects. Myopia is usually caused by an eyeball that is too long to focus the image on the retina properly. Another visual problem is *hypermetropia,* or farsightedness, in which people have difficulty focusing on near objects. Such farsightedness usually results from an eyeball that is too short, or a lens that is too thin, to allow the image on the retina to focus properly. Finally, there is *astigmatism,* a defect in the curvature of the cornea or lens, causing blurriness. Astigmatism, like nearsightedness and farsightedness, can be corrected with eyeglasses (and sometimes with contact lenses).

—adapted from Kosslyn and Rosenberg, *Fundamentals of Psychology: The Brain, the Person, the World,* p. 102

The authors of this passage could have listed the visual problems in a different order. They might, for example, have discussed astigmatism first and myopia last. The decision was up to them because they were not talking about something related to time.

As in the paragraph about San Antonio, textbook writers also use transitions to link the items in a list. In the preceding example, the transitions *for example, another,* and *finally* tie together the three types of visual problems. Other transitions—such as *first* and *in addition*—are also used in the listing pattern.

EXERCISE 7-4 Understanding Listing

Directions: *After reading the paragraph, select the choice that best answers each of the questions that follow.*

The federal government has a handful of **government corporations.** These are not exactly like private corporations in which you can buy stock and collect dividends, but they *are* like private corporations—and different from other parts of the government—in two ways. First, they provide a service that *could be* handled by the private sector. Second, they typically charge for their services, though often at rates cheaper than those the consumer would pay to a private-sector producer. Government corporations include the Tennessee Valley Authority (TVA), which provides electricity to millions of Americans in Tennessee and neighboring states, and Comsat, a modern-day government corporation that sells time-sharing on NASA satellites. Of course, the government's largest and most well-known corporation is the U.S. Postal Service.

—adapted from Edwards et al., *Government in America,* pp. 478–479

_______ 1. The topic of the paragraph is

a. the U.S. Postal Service.

b. government corporations.

c. private corporations.

d. government regulations.

_______ 2. In the third and fourth sentences, the writers mention two ways that government corporations resemble private corporations. What pattern of organization do these sentences follow?

a. chronological order c. definition

b. process d. listing

_______ 3. In the last two sentences, the writers mention three government corporations. What pattern of organization do these sentences follow?

a. process c. example

b. chronological order d. definition

Copyright © 2012 by Pearson Education

4. Complete the following outline of the paragraph. Some items have been filled in for you.

I. Main idea: The federal government has several government corporations.
   A. Government corporations are similar to private corporations.
      1. ______________________________
      2. ______________________________
         ____
   B. There are three examples of government corporations.
      1. ______________________________
         ____
      2. Comsat is a modern-day government corporation that sells time-sharing on NASA satellites.
      3. ______________________________
         ____

Thinking Critically About the Example Pattern

Think critically about the example pattern of organization

The example pattern of organization often requires critical analysis. Why? By examining the examples authors provide, you may learn more about their motives and their viewpoints.

Consider the following excerpt from a textbook for hospitality and tourism students:

PARKS AND PRESERVES

Every park and preserve is a little bit different. They may range from famous urban parks such as Central Park in New York City or Hyde Park in London to forests and preserves such as Prince Albert National Park in Canada and Nairobi National Park in Kenya. Although they may be different in appearance and purpose, they are dedicated to protecting the natural beauty of landscapes, plants, and animals for future generations as well as providing visitors with open spaces for rest, relaxation, and recreation. Achieving this balance requires meeting the needs of visitors while maintaining the resources contained within the lands that have been set aside for public use. To serve all these needs, the potential impacts of all activities must be monitored and managed. For example, day-use areas and campsites that are accessible by motorized vehicles and have full sanitary facilities require more upkeep and labor than wilderness areas that are accessible by foot or on horseback only.

—Cook, Yale, and Marqua, *Tourism: The Business of Travel*, pp. 211–212

Notice that this paragraph contains two sets of examples. The first set includes the names of famous parks. The second set talks about the maintenance needs of different kinds of parks.

What does the authors' choice of examples tell us? At first, the examples may seem simple and straightforward. But look a little more deeply. Isn't it interesting that the authors have included parks from all over the globe? From these examples, you can tell that the authors are writing about *world* tourism, not just tourism within the United States. With their examples, the authors seem to be reminding us that the United States is not the only country that has created parks for its citizens and visitors.

Also notice the last sentence of the paragraph. The authors talk not only about campsites but also about day-use areas. Why have they chosen these examples? It seems that the authors are reminding the reader that there is more to a "park" than meets the eye. Many people think of parks as pretty areas with grass and ponds. By choosing these examples, the authors tell us that these are indeed important elements of the typical park, but they also remind us that parks must take human and sanitary needs into account.

EXERCISE 7-5 Analyzing the Example Pattern

Directions: *Read the paragraph and answer the questions that follow.*

GAME GENRES

Over the years, a number of standard game groupings—or *genres*, to borrow a term from literature and the movies—have developed. A game genre is a category that is used to group games that share the same kind of content, visual style, and gameplay actions. Some of these genres include action, adventure, vehicle, and sports. Each genre usually has several subgenres, with each subgenre providing a slightly different play experience. For example, the vehicle genre is sometimes divided into two separate categories: driving and flying.

—adapted from Moore and Sward, *Game Design and Development: An Introduction to the Game Industry*, p. 61

Copyright © 2012 by Pearson Education

1. Look at the genre examples the authors have included: action, adventure, vehicle, and sports. What do all of these genres have in common?

____

2. What are some other game genres not included in the list of examples? (Hint: Think about games like chess and checkers, as well as other games like Dungeons and Dragons.)

____

____

____

3. What does the authors' choice of examples tell you about their tastes in games?

____

____

EXERCISE 7-6 Analyzing the Example Pattern

Directions: *Read the paragraph and answer the questions that follow.*

HERBAL REMEDIES

People have been using herbal remedies for thousands of years. Herbs were the original sources for compounds found in approximately 25 percent of the pharmaceutical drugs we use today, including aspirin (white willow bark), the heart medication digitalis (foxglove), and the cancer treatment Taxol (Pacific yew tree plant). In addition, scientists continue to make pharmacological advances by studying the herbal remedies used in cultures throughout the world. With conventional scientists now recognizing the benefits of herbs, it is no wonder that more and more consumers are turning to herbal products.

—Donatelle, *Health: The Basics*, p. 511

1. What purpose does the author have for providing the examples in the second sentence of the paragraph?

____

____

2. If the author believed herbal remedies were not effective, what kinds of examples could she have provided?

____

____

____

____

TEXTBOOK CHALLENGE

TIPS for Reading in Literature

When reading literature, pay attention to

- **Literal meaning.** Before you can analyze a piece of literature you need to understand the plot, characters, and details.
- **Word choice.** Authors often rely on word choice to convey mood, emotion, and tone.
- **Message.** Works of literature usually make a point, express a viewpoint on life, or comment on a problem or issue. Looking for the work's message will help you interpret it.

Copyright © 2012 by Pearson Education

Part A: Analyzing a Textbook Excerpt

This excerpt was taken from a literature textbook chapter about fiction. Read the excerpt and follow the directions on p. 266.

WHAT IS FICTION?

1 The word *fiction* comes from the past participle of the Latin verb *fingere,* which means "to form" or "to craft"—and in many ways a fiction is indeed something that has been crafted. Usually, however, we use the word to refer to something that is not true. Nevertheless, for most writers, *fiction* continues to mean something that one crafts, painstakingly, from a diverse selection of raw materials, with language. The raw material of fiction—the stories it tells, the characters who act in them, and the places where they act—may be drawn from real life, the author's imagination, or some combination of the two. No matter the origin, crafting materials into fiction transforms those materials into artifact—another word from the Latin, meaning "made by art." As horror maestro Stephen King puts it, "Fiction is the truth inside the lie."

Fiction and History

2 In the classical world, the genre of fiction was contrasted to the genre of history in terms of the order in which events both real and imagined were told rather than in terms of imagined versus real events. Today many critics argue that the primary distinction between fiction and nonfiction is not the degree of truth each genre contains but the conventions and expectations, the way the events are presented to us. It is certainly possible to distinguish between truth and fiction most of the time: there are newspapers and histories that are credible most of the time, and there are plenty of genres of fiction that are totally imaginary. Nevertheless, when you read a newspaper headline while waiting in a supermarket checkout line that reads "Elvis Dug Up & It Isn't Him," you are not likely to believe a word of it. When you read a historical novel about the events of the French Revolution, by contrast, you will likely assume that most of the events described are true. And even in the most wildly speculative novel of science fiction, you may find that a particular character or detail strikes you as quite realistic—after all, much of science fiction, too, is drawn from the raw material of the world around us.

3 If we cannot judge fiction solely according to how much truth it contains, then how do we recognize it? As with all genres, we recognize it through a combination of its own presentation and self-labeling and our familiarity with generic conventions and expectations. The ancients assumed that history started at the beginning and recounted events in chronological order; fiction, by contrast, started wherever it believed the story could best be presented. These days, fiction often borrows the conventions of

> *Fiction is like a spider's web, attached ever so slightly perhaps, but still attached to life at all four corners. Often the attachment is scarcely perceptible.*
> —VIRGINIA WOOLF

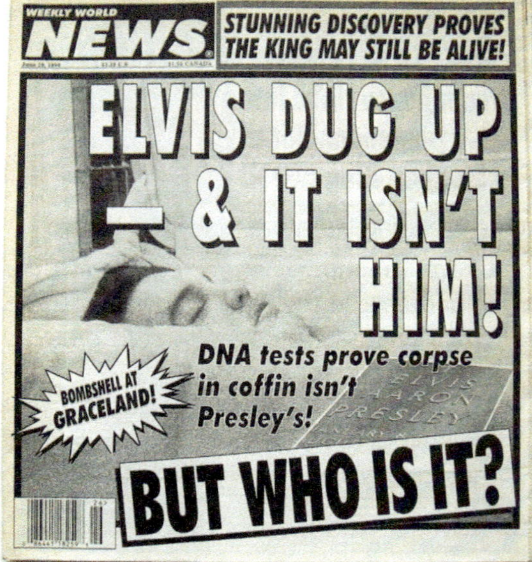

News as fiction: cover of the 29 June 1999 issue of the *Weekly World News,* a tabloid newspaper published between 1979 and 2007.

history and newspaper reporting, and history and reporting often borrow the conventions of fiction. Fiction is better at some things—character, psychology, suspense—while fact-based writing is better at others—recounting events, making broad historical connections, making its subject appear true-to-life—and writers in each genre use whatever tools work best for the story they have to tell.

Types of Fiction

4 There are two different ways to distinguish between types of fiction: in terms of genre (*romance, mystery, science fiction*) and in terms of the form of the text, which is usually determined according to length (*short story, novella, novel*).

5 In general, novels and novellas offer a much broader variety of formal and thematic combinations; short stories offer structural elegance and compression of effect. Because the majority of the fiction selections in this book are short stories, we outline the basic components of fiction through short story examples.

The Craft of Fiction

6 As an introduction to the craft of fiction, read the very short story by Padgett Powell that follows here. Born in 1952, Powell is the author of several novels, including *Edisto* and *Edisto Revisited,* and many short stories. He teaches creative writing at the University of Florida, Gainesville. Observe how "A Gentleman's C" manages to tell a moving story, develop two characters, and establish a setting in a scant 163 words.

PADGETT POWELL

A GENTLEMAN'S C

7 MY FATHER, TRYING TO FINALLY GRADUATE FROM college at sixty-two, came, by curious circumstance, to be enrolled in an English class I taught, and I was, perhaps, a bit tougher on him than I was on the others. Hadn't he been tougher on me than on other people's kids growing up? I gave him a hard, honest, low C. About what I felt he'd always given me.

8 We had a death in the family, and my mother and I traveled to the funeral. My father stayed put to complete his exams—it was his final term. On the way home we learned that he had received his grades, which were low enough in the aggregate to prevent him from graduating, and reading this news on the dowdy sofa inside the front door, he leaned over as if to rest and had a heart attack and died.

9 For years I had thought the old man's passing away would not affect me, but it did.

QUESTIONS FOR REFLECTION AND DISCUSSION

1. Who is the narrator of the story? What is his perspective on the events described?
2. Each paragraph narrates a different situation. What happens in each paragraph?
3. What has the author left out of the story in order to make it so short?
4. The author is in fact a professor of English and the events narrated may well be true, or they may be partially true, or they may be totally fabricated. What difference (if any) does the relation of the events to real life make in your attitude toward and understanding of the short story?
5. The final sentence is different in form and tone from the others. Characterize this difference and comment on the way it affects your understanding of the short story.
6. What is the meaning of the title and how does it relate to the story?

132 CHAPTER 4 ORGANIZING THE WORLD OF LITERATURE: THE CONVENTIONS OF GENRE

Copyright © 2012 by Pearson Education

—Pike and Acosta, *Literature: A World of Writing*, pp. 131–133

1. **Preview.** Preview the reading using the guidelines on p. 7 and then answer the following questions.
   a. How were fiction and history contrasted in the classical world?
   b. How is fiction categorized?
2. **SQ3R.** Write at least three questions for the Q step of SQ3R. Answer them after completing the reading.
3. **Textbook Features.** How does the quotation on p. 264 help you understand the definition of fiction?
4. **Vocabulary.**
   a. Identify the important new terms that are introduced in the reading.
   b. Define each of the following words and phrases as used in the reading: *artifact* (par. 1), *maestro* (par. 1), *conventions* (par. 2), *speculative* (par. 2), *dowdy* (par. 8)
5. **Applying Chapter Skills.** Complete the diagram based on the material in the selection.

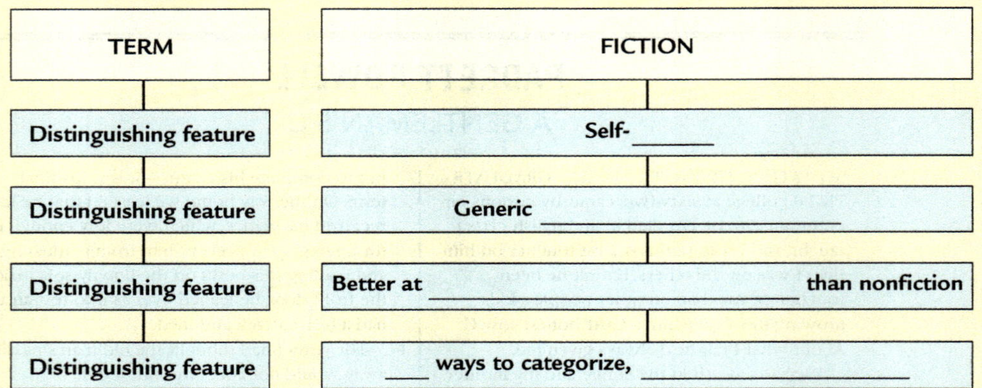

6. **Essay Question.** Write an answer to the following essay question. To test your memory, write it without referring to the excerpt.
   Define what fiction is, explain how to recognize it, and describe its features.
7. **Thinking Critically.** Use your critical thinking skills to answer each of the following questions.
   a. Answer the questions after the short story. How does answering the questions help you to understand the story more clearly?
   b. Think about a work of fiction you have read. Describe parts of it that could have been nonfiction.
   c. Why do you think the author chose to include the Elvis example in this selection? What point did it make?

Part B: Your College Textbook

Choose a chapter that you have been assigned to read in a textbook for one of your other courses. Choose a section of the chapter that uses the example, definition, chronological order/process, or listing pattern and create a chart to demonstrate the pattern.

SELF-TEST SUMMARY

To test yourself, cover up the Answer column with a sheet of paper and answer each question listed in the left column. Evaluate each of your answers as you work by sliding the paper down and comparing your answer with what is printed in the Answer column.

	Question	Answer
GOAL 1	What are the types of patterns of organization?	Patterns of organization include example, definition, combined definition and example, chronological order and process, and listing.
GOAL 2	What is the example pattern?	The example pattern supports a main idea by giving specific situations or instances that illustrate it.
GOAL 3	What is the definition pattern?	The definition pattern explains a term by giving its distinguishing features.
GOAL 4	What are the chronological order and process patterns?	The chronological order pattern presents information in the order in which it happened. The process pattern explains how something is done or how something works in the order in which it occurs.
GOAL 5	What is the listing pattern?	The listing pattern presents or names items in an order that is not determined by time or steps.
GOAL 6	Why are examples an important tool used by authors?	Writers selectively choose examples to support their motives and viewpoints.

Copyright © 2012 by Pearson Education

PRACTICE TEST 7-1

NAME ______________________ SECTION ______________________

DATE ______________________ SCORE ______________________

Identifying Patterns

Directions: *For each of the following statements, select the choice that best describes its particular pattern of organization.*

_______ 1. In a list of numbers, the **mode** is the number that occurs most often. For instance, if the ages of 5 children are 7, 10, 11, 8, and 10, then the mode is 10.

a. chronological order
b. process
c. definition and example
d. listing

_______ 2. If you want to improve your vocabulary, three reference sources that can help you are a collegiate dictionary, a subject area dictionary, and a thesaurus.

a. chronological order
b. process
c. definition and example
d. listing

_______ 3. The first step in solving word problems is to identify what is asked for. Then, locate the information that is provided to solve the problem.

a. chronological order
b. process
c. definition and example
d. listing

_______ 4. When treating a sprained ankle, you should first elevate the ankle to a comfortable position and apply ice to reduce the swelling. Next, wrap the ankle firmly with a cloth bandage. Try to keep it elevated, with ice on it, for 24 hours.

a. definition
b. process
c. example
d. listing

_______ 5. In late 1778, the British took Savannah. During the next year, most of the other settled areas of Georgia fell, followed by the surrender of Charleston, South Carolina, in 1780.

a. chronological order
b. process
c. definition
d. listing

_______ 6. Because of the language barrier, many new immigrants are unable to work in their former professions. For instance, Rima taught school in Lithuania, but in America she cleans houses.

a. chronological order
b. process
c. example
d. listing

_______ 7. There are four forces of nature: gravity, electromagnetism, strong nuclear force, and weak nuclear force.

a. chronological order
b. process
c. listing
d. definition

_______ 8. When a bill is vetoed by the president, he sends it back to the House or Senate and explains why he vetoed it. Congress can then override the veto with a two-thirds vote in both the House and the Senate.

a. example
b. process
c. definition
d. listing

_______ 9. An allergen is a substance that causes an allergic reaction. Common allergens include pollen, dust mites, mold spores, and pet dander.

a. chronological order
b. process
c. listing
d. definition and example

_______ 10. The explorers began their cross-country journey in early spring. By late fall, they had traveled nearly halfway to their destination.

a. chronological order
b. process
c. example
d. listing

Copyright © 2012 by Pearson Education

PRACTICE TEST 7-2

NAME ______________________ SECTION ______________________

DATE ______________________ SCORE ______________________

Identifying Patterns

Directions: *Read each of the passages and complete the exercises that follow.*

A. Factors that influence our behavior and our decisions to change our behavior can be divided into three general categories. One category is *predisposing factors,* such as our life experiences, knowledge, cultural and ethnic inheritance, and current beliefs and values. Factors that may predispose us to certain conditions include our age, sex, race, income, family background, educational background, and access to health care. For example, if your parents smoked, you are 90 percent more likely to start smoking than someone whose parents didn't.

Another category is *enabling factors.* These include skills or abilities; physical, emotional, and mental capabilities; and resources that make health decisions more convenient or difficult. Positive enablers encourage you to carry through on your intentions, whereas negative enablers work against your intentions to change. For example, if you would like to join a local gym but discover that the closest one is 4 miles away and costs $500 to join, those negative enablers may convince you to stay home.

Finally, *reinforcing factors* may influence you toward positive and/or negative behaviors. These include money, popularity, social support and appreciation from friends, and family interest and enthusiasm for what you are doing. If, for example, you are overweight and you lose a few pounds and your friends tell you how terrific you look, your positive behavior will be reinforced and you will be more likely to continue to diet.

—adapted from Donatelle and Davis, *Access to Health,* p. 25

1. Complete the following map by writing the three types of factors that influence behavior and behavior-change decisions.

MAIN IDEA: FACTORS THAT INFLUENCE BEHAVIOR AND THE DECISION TO CHANGE BEHAVIOR CAN BE DIVIDED INTO THREE CATEGORIES

a. **predisposing factors**

b. ______________________

c. ______________________

2. List three transitions used in the passage.

   a. ______________________

   b. ______________________

   c. ______________________

3. The two main patterns of organization used in this passage are listing and ______________________.

B. The process of digestion begins at the upper end of the gastrointestinal tract. The *mouth* is where food enters and where the processes of mechanical breakdown and digestion begin. In the mouth, food is chewed (a process called **mastication**) and mechanically broken down into smaller particles by the cutting and grinding actions of the teeth. The food is also mixed with **saliva,** which lubricates it and contains an enzyme which begins the digestion of carbohydrates by breaking down starch and glycogen.

From the mouth, the food-saliva mixture is propelled by the tongue into the **pharynx** (commonly known as the *throat*), a common passageway for food and air. From the pharynx, the passageways for food and air diverge. Whereas air enters the larynx and trachea and proceeds toward the lungs, food enters the esophagus, which runs parallel to the trachea.

The **esophagus** is a muscular tube whose primary function is to conduct food from the pharynx to the stomach. It can easily stretch to accommodate food as it is swallowed; when food is not present, however, it is normally collapsed.

—adapted from Germann and Stanfield, *Principles of Human Physiology,* pp. 606–607

4. Complete the following map.

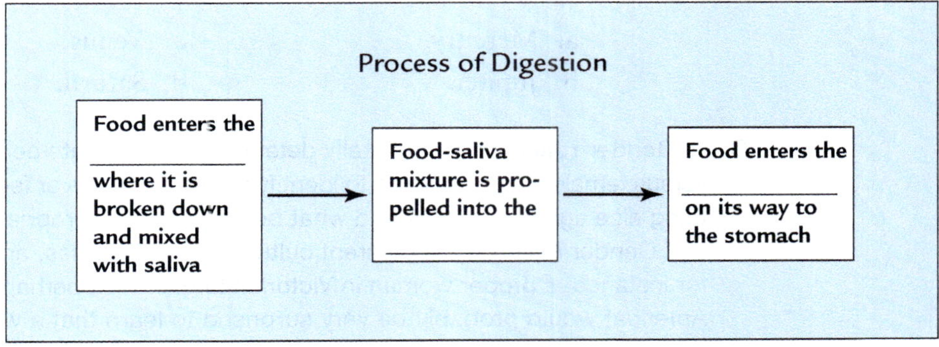

5. The organizational pattern used in this passage is ______________________.

Copyright © 2012 by Pearson Education

MASTERY TEST 7-1

NAME ______________________ SECTION ______________________

DATE ______________________ SCORE ______________________

Identifying Patterns

***Directions:** Read each of the following paragraphs and select the choice that best completes each of the statements that follow.*

A. Five planets are easy to see with the naked eye: Mercury, Venus, Mars, Jupiter, and Saturn. Mercury can be seen only infrequently, and then only just after sunset or before sunrise because it is so close to the Sun. Venus often shines brightly in the early evening in the west or before dawn in the east; if you see a very bright "star" in the early evening or early morning, it probably is Venus. Jupiter, when it is visible at night, is the brightest object in the sky besides the Moon and Venus. Mars is recognizable by its red color, but be careful not to confuse it with a bright red star. Saturn is easy to see with the naked eye, but because many stars are just as bright as Saturn, it helps to know where to look. (Also, planets tend not to twinkle as much as stars.) Sometimes several planets may appear close together in the sky, offering a particularly beautiful sight.

—Bennett et al., *The Solar System,* pp. 58–59

_______ 1. The main idea of this paragraph appears in the

a. first sentence.
b. third sentence.
c. fourth sentence.
d. last sentence.

_______ 2. The main pattern of organization used in this paragraph is

a. chronological order.
b. listing.
c. definition.
d. example.

_______ 3. The planet that often shines brightly in the early evening or early morning is

a. Mercury.
b. Jupiter.
c. Venus.
d. Saturn.

B. **Gender roles** are the culturally determined appropriate behaviors of males versus females. It is one thing to identify yourself as male or female, but something else again to understand what behaviors are appropriate for your gender. Gender roles vary in different cultures, social classes, and time periods; for instance, a proper woman in Victorian England (or, perhaps, 19th-century America) would probably be very surprised to learn that a woman can be a senator or the president of a major corporation today. Conceptions about gender roles develop early. Even preschool boys apparently believe that if they played with cross-gender toys (say, dishes instead of tools), their fathers would think that was "bad." Indeed, by age 2 children have apparently learned about gender role differences.

—adapted from Kosslyn and Rosenberg, *Fundamentals of Psychology: The Brain, the Person, the World,* p. 331

_______ 4. The main idea of this paragraph is that

a. gender roles have remained the same throughout history.

b. women can be politicians or presidents of corporations today.

c. the behaviors considered appropriate for males and females are known as gender roles and are culturally determined.

d. preschool boys should not play with cross-gender toys.

_______ 5. The main pattern of organization used in this paragraph is

a. chronological order.

b. listing.

c. process.

d. definition and example.

_______ 6. The transitional word or phrase that signals an example is to follow is

a. one.

b. for instance.

c. perhaps.

d. indeed.

C. The history of maps goes back thousands of years. In Babylonia, in approximately 2300 B.C., the oldest known map was drawn on a clay tablet. The map showed a man's property located in a valley surrounded by tall mountains. Later, around 1300 B.C., the Egyptians drew maps that detailed the location of Ethiopian gold mines and that showed a route from the Nile Valley. The ancient Greeks were early mapmakers as well, although no maps remain for us to examine. It is estimated that in 300 B.C. they drew maps showing the earth to be round. The Romans drew the first road maps, a few of which have been preserved for study today. Claudius Ptolemy, an Egyptian scholar who lived around 150 A.D., drew one of the most famous ancient maps. He drew maps of the world as it was known at that time, including 26 regional maps of Europe, Africa, and Asia.

_______ 7. The main idea of the paragraph appears in the

a. first sentence.

b. second sentence.

c. third sentence.

d. last sentence.

Copyright © 2012 by Pearson Education

_______ 8. The pattern of organization used in this paragraph is

a. process.
b. definition.
c. chronological order.
d. example.

_______ 9. Of the following phrases, the only one that is *not* used as a transition in this paragraph is

a. thousands of years.
b. Later.
c. in 300 B.C.
d. around 150 A.D.

_______ 10. According to this passage, the first road maps were drawn by the

a. Babylonians.
b. Egyptians.
c. Greeks.
d. Romans.

NAME ______________________ SECTION ______________________

DATE ______________________ SCORE ______________________

MASTERY TEST 7-2

Identifying Patterns

***Directions:** After reading the excerpt below, taken from a textbook about the Internet, select the choice that best completes each of the statements that follow.*

Viruses, Trojans, and Worms

1 Computer security experts worry about software that can be used maliciously to put computer users at risk. Over the years, they have found it useful to distinguish different classes of software that are often associated with security problems. Mainstream news outlets tend to call such software a *virus*. However, many fast-spreading troublemakers are actually *worms*, and one of the most insidious forms of software attack is the *Trojan horse*.

2 A **virus** is an executable program that attaches itself to a host program and whose purpose is to replicate itself via files that are transferred from one computer to another. They can propagate through a host program. Some viruses are benign, doing nothing more than leaving the equivalent of their initials on a file somewhere. Others, however, are extremely destructive, capable of destroying files or even entire file systems.

3 A **Trojan horse** is an executable program that slips into a system under the guise of another program. To qualify as a Trojan horse, the program must do something that is undocumented and intended by the programmer that the user would not approve of. Deception is a key characteristic of all Trojan horses. You think that you've installed only a particular program, but you end up getting more than you expected. Some Trojan horses, for instance, are designed to record every key that you hit, such as the credit card account number that you use when online shopping. Your keystrokes might be monitored by the program's author in real time, or they might be saved and sent back to the program's author at a later time.

4 A **worm** is very similar to a virus but differs in its reproductive habits. Whereas viruses propagate via shared floppies or other media and need a host program in order to propagate, a worm depends on active network connections in order to multiply and needs many different hosts that are running the same software. Sophisticated worms can have multiple segments that run on different machines, do different things, and communicate with each other over a network. Some are programmed to act maliciously, whereas others are merely resource hogs that pull down entire networks by tying up too much memory or too many CPU cycles.

Copyright © 2012 by Pearson Education

5 If you can't remember how these three differ from each other, just remember that everyone who uses computers is vulnerable to attack and must take precautions. There are some steps that you can take to protect your system. Once you know the ropes, good computer security doesn't have to take a lot of your time.

—adapted from Lehnert, *Light on the Web,* pp. 32–33

______ 1. The general subject of this passage is

a. problems with antivirus software.

b. computer software security troublemakers.

c. evaluation of computer services.

d. propagation of computer viruses.

______ 2. The main pattern of organization used throughout this selection is

a. process.

b. chronological order.

c. definition.

d. listing.

______ 3. The main idea of paragraph 1 is that

a. mainstream news outlets tend to call all problems viruses.

b. three kinds of software are associated with security problems.

c. *virus* is the general name for software that causes security problems.

d. the Trojan horse is one of the worst forms of software attack.

______ 4. The main idea of paragraph 2 appears in the

a. first sentence.

b. second sentence.

c. third sentence.

d. last sentence.

______ 5. The best synonym for the word **benign** as used in paragraph 2 is

a. destructive.

b. obvious.

c. humorous.

d. harmless.

_______ 6. The two patterns of organization used in paragraph 3 are
   a. definition and listing.
   b. listing and process.
   c. definition and example.
   d. example and chronological order.

_______ 7. A transitional phrase that signals an example in paragraph 3 is
   a. to qualify.
   b. a key characteristic.
   c. such as.
   d. a later time.

_______ 8. According to the selection, one distinguishing characteristic of a *worm* is that it
   a. depends on active network connections in order to multiply.
   b. does nothing more than leave its initials on a file.
   c. monitors keystrokes and sends them back to the program's author.
   d. actually improves the performance of the entire network.

_______ 9. The best synonym for the word **propagate** as used in paragraph 4 is
   a. change.
   b. multiply.
   c. damage.
   d. remove.

_______ 10. The main idea of paragraph 5 is that
   a. you should be able to identify each type of software threat.
   b. not every computer is vulnerable to attack.
   c. good computer security can be expensive.
   d. everyone who uses a computer should take precautions.

Copyright © 2012 by Pearson Education

MASTERY TEST 7-3

NAME ______________________ SECTION ______________________

DATE ______________________ SCORE ______________________

READING SELECTION

Lifestyle Changes

Richard T. Wright and Dorothy F. Boorse

Have you ever wondered what you can do to help bring about solutions to environmental problems? In this selection from an environmental science textbook, the authors describe lifestyle changes that can have a positive impact on the environment.

Vocabulary Preview

These are some of the difficult words in this essay. The definitions here will help you if you can't figure out the meanings from the sentence context or word parts.

sustainable (par. 2) capable of being continued with minimal long-term environmental effects

alleviating (par. 7) offering relief

adept (par. 7) skillful

urban blight (par. 8) a run-down area of a city

photochemical smog (par. 8) air pollution produced by the action of sunlight on hydrocarbons, nitrogen oxides, and other pollutants

exploited (par. 9) used selfishly or unjustly

inundated (par. 9) flooded

1 What are some of the lifestyle changes that are needed to solve environmental problems, and are they in fact occurring? We should be encouraged and inspired by the literally millions of people in all walks of life who are acutely aware of the problems and who are making outstanding efforts to bring about solutions. Every pathway toward solutions that we have mentioned represents the work of thousands of dedicated professionals and volunteers, ranging from scientists and engineers to businesspeople, lawyers, and public servants. Indeed, we are all involved, whether we recognize it or not. Simply by our existence on the planet, everything we do—the car we drive, the products we use, the wastes we throw away, virtually every choice we make and action we take—has a certain environmental impact and a certain consequence for the future. Therefore, it is not a matter of choosing to have an effect, but a matter of what and how great that effect will be. It is a

matter of each of us asking ourselves: Will I be part of the problem or part of the solution? The outcome will depend on how each of us responds to the challenges ahead.

2 There are a number of levels on which we can participate to work toward a sustainable society:

- Individual lifestyle choices
- Political involvement
- Membership and participation in nongovernmental environmental organizations
- Volunteer work
- Career choices

3 *Lifestyle choices* may involve such things as switching to a more fuel-efficient car or walking or using a bicycle for short errands; recycling paper, cans, and bottles; retrofitting your home with solar energy; starting a backyard garden and composting and recycling food and garden wastes into your soil; putting in time at a soup kitchen to help the homeless; choosing low-impact recreation, such as canoeing rather than jet-skiing; and living closer to your workplace.

4 *Political involvement* ranges from supporting and voting for particular candidates to expressing your support for particular legislation through letters or phone calls. In effect, you are exercising your citizenship on behalf of the common good.

5 *Membership in nongovernmental environmental organizations* can enhance both lifestyle changes and political involvement. As a member of an environmental organization, you will receive, and can help disseminate, information, making you and others more aware of specific environmental problems and things you can do to help. Also, your membership and contribution serve to support the lobbying efforts of the organization. A lobbyist representing a million-member organization that can follow up with thousands of phone calls and letters (and, ultimately, votes) can have a powerful impact.

6 In cases where enforcement of the existing law has been the weak link, some organizations, such as the Public Interest Research Groups, the Natural Resources Defense Council, and the Environmental Defense Fund, have been highly influential in bringing polluters or the government to court to see that the law is upheld. Again, this can be done only with the support of members.

7 Another form of involvement is *joining a volunteer organization.* Many effective actions that care for people and the environment are carried out by groups that depend on volunteer labor. Political organizations and virtually all NGOs depend highly on volunteers. Many helping organizations, such as those dedicated to alleviating hunger and to building homes for needy families (Fig. A),

Copyright © 2012 by Pearson Education

are adept at mobilizing volunteers to accomplish some vital tasks that often fill in the gaps left behind by inadequate public policies.

8 Finally, you may choose to devote your *career* to implementing solutions to environmental problems. Environmental careers go far beyond the traditional occupations of wildlife ranger and park manager. Many lawyers, journalists, teachers, research scientists, engineers, medical personnel, agricultural extension workers, and others are focusing their talents and training on environmental issues or hazards. Business and job opportunities exist in pollution control, recycling, waste management, ecological restoration, city planning, environmental monitoring and analysis, nonchemical pest control, the production and marketing of organically grown produce, the manufacture of solar and wind energy components, and so on. Some developers concentrate on rehabilitation and the reversal of urban blight, as opposed to contributing more to urban sprawl. Some engineers are working on the development of pollution-free vehicles to help solve the photochemical smog dilemma of our cities. Indeed, it is difficult to think of a vocation that cannot be directed toward promoting solutions to environmental problems.

9 Human society is well into a new millennium, and it promises to be an era of rapid changes unprecedented in human history. Will we just survive, or will we thrive and become a sustainable global society? We are engaged in an environmental revolution—a major shift in our worldview and practice from seeing the natural world as resources to be exploited to seeing it as life's supporting structure that needs our stewardship. You are living in the early stages of this revolution, and we invite you to be one of the many who will make it happen. We close with two quotes:

> Imagine a future of relentless storms and floods; islands and heavily inhabited coastal regions inundated by rising sea levels; fertile soils rendered barren by drought and the desert's advance; mass migrations of environmental refugees; and armed conflicts over water and precious natural resources.

FIGURE A: HABITAT FOR HUMANITY VOLUNTEERS By using charitable contributions and volunteer labor, Habitat for Humanity creates quality homes—more than 300,000 built throughout the world by 2009—that needy families can afford to buy with no-interest mortgages, enabling the money to be recycled to build more homes. Prospective home buyers participate in the construction and may gain valuable skills in the process.

Then think again—for one might just as easily conjure a more hopeful picture: of green technologies; livable cities; energy-efficient homes, transport and industry; and rising standards of living for all the people, not just a fortunate minority. The choice between these competing visions is ours to make.

—*Kofi Annan, former Secretary General of the United Nations*

No one could make a greater mistake than he who did nothing because he could do only a little.

—*Edmund Burke, Irish orator, philosopher and politician (1729–1797)*

Directions: *Select the choice that best completes each of the following statements.*

CHECKING YOUR COMPREHENSION

_______ 1. The purpose of this selection is to
- a. argue for stricter enforcement of environmental protection laws.
- b. explore the causes and effects of urban blight and urban sprawl.
- c. discuss the sources of photochemical smog and global climate change.
- d. describe lifestyle changes that are needed to create a sustainable society.

_______ 2. The topic of paragraph 1 is
- a. pollution.
- b. scientists and engineers.
- c. environmental problems and solutions.
- d. political involvement.

_______ 3. According to the authors, individual lifestyle choices that contribute to a sustainable society include
- a. driving a more fuel-efficient car.
- b. recycling paper, cans, and bottles.
- c. living closer to your workplace.
- d. all of the above.

_______ 4. The main idea of paragraph 5 is stated in the
- a. first sentence.
- b. second sentence.
- c. third sentence.
- d. last sentence.

Copyright © 2012 by Pearson Education

_______ 5. The main idea of paragraph 8 is that

a. traditional environmental careers include wildlife ranger and park manager.

b. a variety of career choices can promote solutions to environmental problems.

c. lawyers and engineers often focus their training on environmental issues or hazards.

d. business and job opportunities are available in pollution control and recycling.

USING WHAT YOU KNOW ABOUT BASIC PATTERNS

_______ 6. The overall pattern of organization followed in this selection is

a. chronological order.
b. listing.
c. process.
d. definition.

_______ 7. In paragraph 3, the transitional word or phrase that signals an example is to follow is

a. may involve.
b. such as.
c. rather than.
d. and.

_______ 8. In paragraph 7, the transitional word that indicates a continuation of the listing pattern is

a. Another.
b. Many.
c. virtually.
d. such as.

_______ 9. The main pattern used in paragraph 8 to describe careers that promote solutions to environmental problems is

a. definition.
b. chronological order.
c. process.
d. listing.

_______ 10. All of the following groups are given as examples of organizations that help uphold environmental laws *except*

a. the Public Interest Research Groups.

b. the Natural Resources Defense Council.

c. Habitat for Humanity.

d. the Environmental Defense Fund.

USING CONTEXT CLUES AND WORD PARTS

_______ 11. In paragraph 1, the word **acutely** means

a. partially.
b. intensely.
c. likely.
d. rarely.

_______ 12. In paragraph 3, the word **retrofitting** means

a. installing on an existing structure.
b. continuing on the same route.
c. causing damage to a structure.
d. avoiding change.

_______ 13. In paragraph 5, the word **disseminate** means

a. disagree.
b. interrupt.
c. disrupt.
d. spread.

_______ 14. In paragraph 8, the word **vocation** means

a. discussion.
b. travel.
c. career.
d. problem.

_______ 15. In paragraph 9, the word **unprecedented** means

a. typical.
b. never seen before.
c. slow-moving.
d. unnecessary.

REVIEWING DIFFICULT VOCABULARY

Directions: *Complete each of the following sentences by inserting a word from the Vocabulary Preview on page 278 in the space provided. Use each word only once.*

16. During her internship at the mayor's office, Lauren became _______________ at writing press releases.

17. The company was _______________ with hundreds of resumes after advertising two openings.

18. The deposed king denied that he had _______________ his country's workers and its natural resources.

19. Habitat for Humanity has helped transform areas known for _______________ into appealing neighborhoods.

Copyright © 2012 by Pearson Education

20. Volunteers in the urban center work toward ________________ hunger and providing social services for families in need.

THINKING CRITICALLY

1. Describe your reaction to the photograph that accompanies this selection. What concept in the selection is illustrated by this photograph?
2. Consider the authors' decision to close this selection with quotes from Kofi Annan and Edmund Burke. Do you think the quotes are effective? Why or why not?
3. How objective or biased do you think the authors of this selection are? How do you know where they stand on the issues?

QUESTIONS FOR DISCUSSION

1. Would you consider making any of the lifestyle changes discussed in this selection? Discuss which changes you are most likely to put into practice.
2. Discuss your response to the authors' invitation to join the "environmental revolution" (par. 9). Have you have seen evidence of a major shift in our worldview?
3. How did this selection make you think differently about your impact on the planet?

WRITING ACTIVITIES

1. Write a paragraph giving your answer to the authors' question in paragraph 9: "Will we just survive, or will we thrive and become a sustainable global society?"
2. Think about the term *sustainability* as it applies to your city, town, or college campus. In what ways is your community sustainable? Write a paragraph describing what your community has already done and what you would like to see it do to improve its sustainability.
3. Try these ecological footprint calculators: http://www.footprintcalculator.org/ and http://www.myfootprint.org/

   Write about your experience with these tools. Consider the following questions: How do your results compare? Which test did you prefer and why? What were the results? What can you do to reduce your ecological footprint?

CHAPTER 7

Examining the Basic Patterns of Organization

RECORDING YOUR PROGRESS

Test	Number Right		Score
Practice Test 7-1	________	× 10 =	________%
Practice Test 7-2	________	× 10 =	________%
Mastery Test 7-1	________	× 10 =	________%
Mastery Test 7-2	________	× 10 =	________%
Mastery Test 7-3	________	× 5 =	________%

GETTING MORE PRACTICE myreadinglab

To get more practice with Patterns of Organization, go to http://www.myreadinglab.com and click on

> Study Plan
> Reading Skills
> Patterns of Organization

EVALUATING YOUR PROGRESS myreadinglab

To measure your progress after reading and viewing the information in the Review Materials section, complete the Practices and Tests in the Activities section. You can check your scores by clicking on the Gradebook tab.

Then, based on your performance in this chapter and/or on the MyReadingLab Practices and Tests, write your own evaluation.

YOUR EVALUATION: ____

____

____

____

____

Copyright © 2012 by Pearson Education

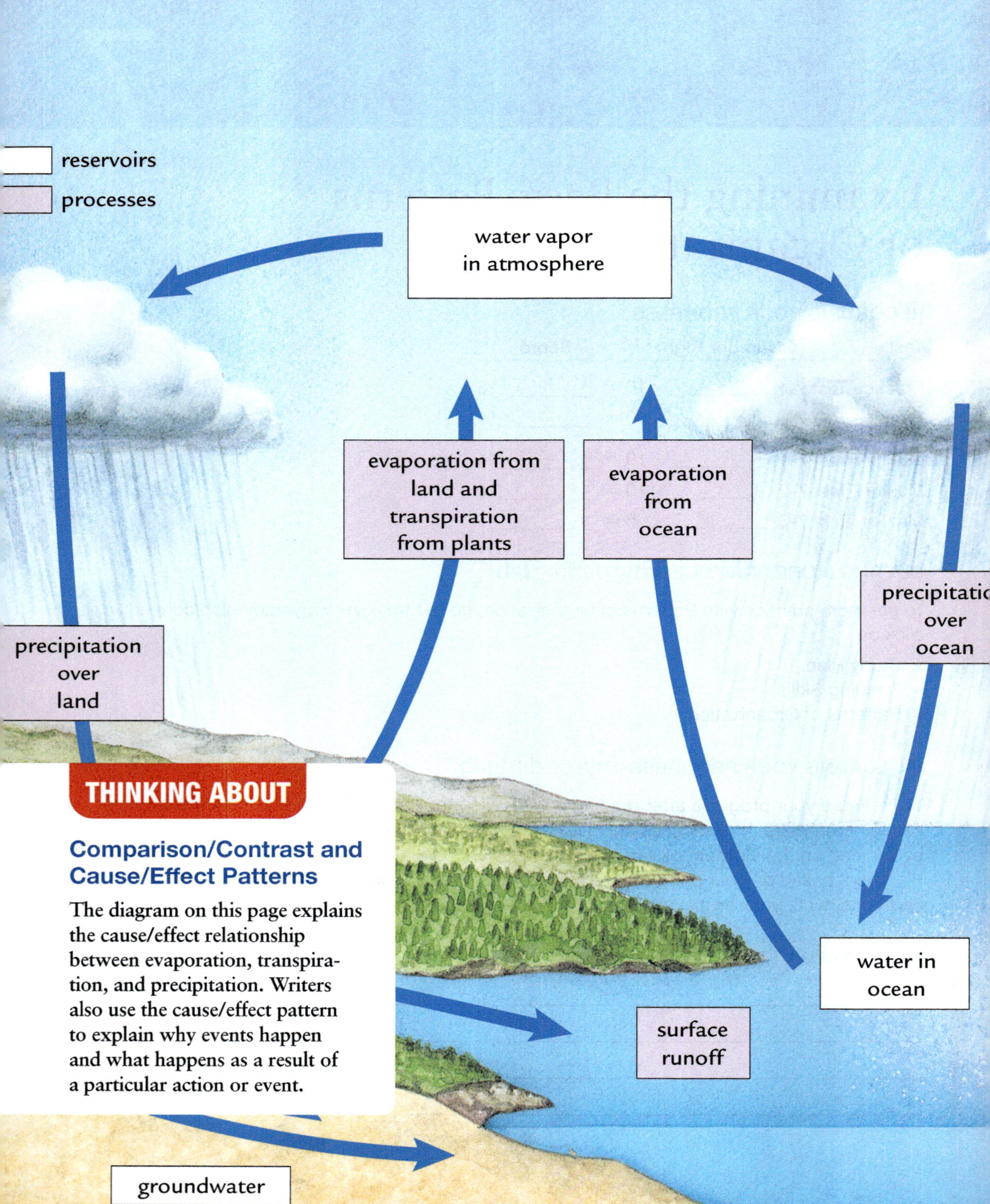

THINKING ABOUT

Comparison/Contrast and Cause/Effect Patterns

The diagram on this page explains the cause/effect relationship between evaporation, transpiration, and precipitation. Writers also use the cause/effect pattern to explain why events happen and what happens as a result of a particular action or event.

CHAPTER 8

Examining Comparison/Contrast and Cause/Effect Patterns

LEARNING GOALS

GOAL 1 Understand comparison/contrast patterns

GOAL 2 Learn how cause/effect patterns are used

GOAL 3 Identify other useful thought patterns

GOAL 4 Think critically about comparison/contrast and cause/effect

Comparison/Contrast Patterns

GOAL 1 Understand comparison/contrast patterns

To practice examining the patterns of organization, go to
- Study Plan
- Reading Skills
- Patterns of Organization

You use comparison and contrast every day. For example, when you decide which pair of shoes to buy, where to apply for a part-time job, or what topic to choose for a research paper, you are thinking about similarities and differences.

Writers use comparison or contrast to explain how something is similar to or different from something else. **Comparison** treats similarities, whereas **contrast** emphasizes differences. For example, a writer who is *comparing* two U.S. presidents would focus on their shared features: experience in politics, leadership characteristics, and commitment to fulfill the duties of the office. But a writer who is *contrasting* the two presidents would discuss how they differ in foreign policy, education, family background, and so forth.

As you read, you will find passages that only compare, some that only contrast, and some that do both.

Copyright © 2012 by Pearson Education

EXERCISE 8-1 Understanding Comparison/Contrast Patterns

Directions: *Choose one of the following subjects: two musical groups, two jobs, two professors, or two cities. Then, using the box below as a guide, make a list of five similarities and five differences.*

Example

Subject: two restaurants

Items A and B: Blue Mesa and Chico's

Similarities	Differences
1. Both specialize in Mexican food.	1. Blue Mesa is much more expensive than Chico's.
2. Both serve lunch and dinner.	2. Chico's is a chain, while Blue Mesa is a single restaurant.
3. Both are located on the east side of town.	3. Only Chico's offers takeout.
4. Both employ college students.	4. Blue Mesa is closed on Mondays, while Chico's is open every day.
5. Both have a special menu for children.	5. Only Blue Mesa accepts reservations.

Subject: ______________________________

Items A and B: ______________________________

Similarities	Differences
1.	1.
2.	2.
3.	3.
4.	4.
5.	5.

Comparison

A writer who is concerned only with similarities may identify the items to be compared and then list the ways they are alike. The following paragraph describes apparent similarities between two planets, Earth and Mars.

> Early telescopic observations of Mars revealed several uncanny resemblances to Earth. The Martian rotation axis is tilted about the same amount as Earth's, and on both planets a day lasts about 24 hours. In addition, Mars has polar caps, which we now know to be composed primarily of frozen carbon dioxide, with smaller amounts of water ice. Telescopic observations also showed seasonal variations in surface coloration over the course of the Martian year (about 1.9 Earth years). All these discoveries led to the perception that Mars and Earth were at least cousins, if not twins. By the early 1900s, many astronomers—as well as the public—envisioned Mars as nearly Earth-like, possessing water, vegetation that changed with the seasons, and possibly intelligent life.
>
> —adapted from Bennett et al., *The Cosmic Perspective,* p. 249

Such a pattern can be diagrammed as follows:

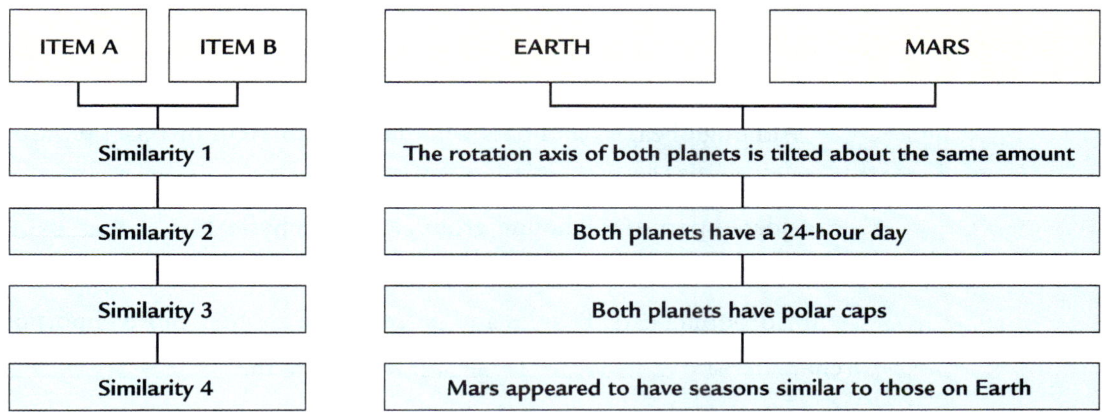

Look at the paragraph again, and notice the clues the writers provide about what kind of pattern they are following. In the first sentence—the topic sentence—the phrase *several uncanny resemblances* tells you that the paragraph will be about the similarities between Earth and Mars. The writers also use the words *same* and *both,* which signal that a comparison is being made. As you read, be on the lookout for words that indicate comparison or contrast.

When writers use comparison or contrast, sometimes they also include transitions to introduce each important point they are making. In the paragraph about Earth and Mars, for example, the writers use the transitions *in addition* and *also* to help the reader follow the main points of the comparison. Although

Copyright © 2012 by Pearson Education

such transitions are not always used in comparison and contrast, you will often find them in longer selections.

Transitions in Comparison and Contrast

To Show Similarities		To Show Differences	
alike	likewise	unlike	in contrast
same	both	different	despite
similar	just as	difference	nevertheless
similarity	each	on the other hand	however
like	in common	instead	but

EXERCISE 8-2 Using Comparison Transitions

Directions: *Select the comparison word or phrase from the box below that best completes each sentence in the paragraph. Write each answer in the space provided. Use each choice only once.*

same	in common	both	similarity	alike

Although beagles and basset hounds are different breeds, they are ________________ in many ways. They are ________________ considered part of the hound group, and the physical ________________ between the two breeds is apparent in their coloring and their typically long, drooping ears. Beagles and bassets have another, more important characteristic ________________: they share the ________________ friendly and sociable disposition, especially when it comes to children.

Contrast

The following paragraph was written to point out only the differences between two types of tumors:

Not all tumors are **malignant** (cancerous); in fact, most are **benign** (non-cancerous). Benign and malignant tumors differ in several key ways. Benign tumors are generally composed of ordinary-looking cells enclosed in a fibrous shell or capsule that prevents their spreading to other body areas. Malignant tumors, in contrast, are usually not enclosed in a protective capsule and can therefore spread to other organs. Unlike benign tumors, which merely expand to take over a given space, malignant cells invade surrounding tissue, emitting clawlike protrusions that disrupt chemical processes within healthy cells.

—adapted from Donatelle, *Health: The Basics,* p. 324

Such a pattern can be diagrammed as follows:

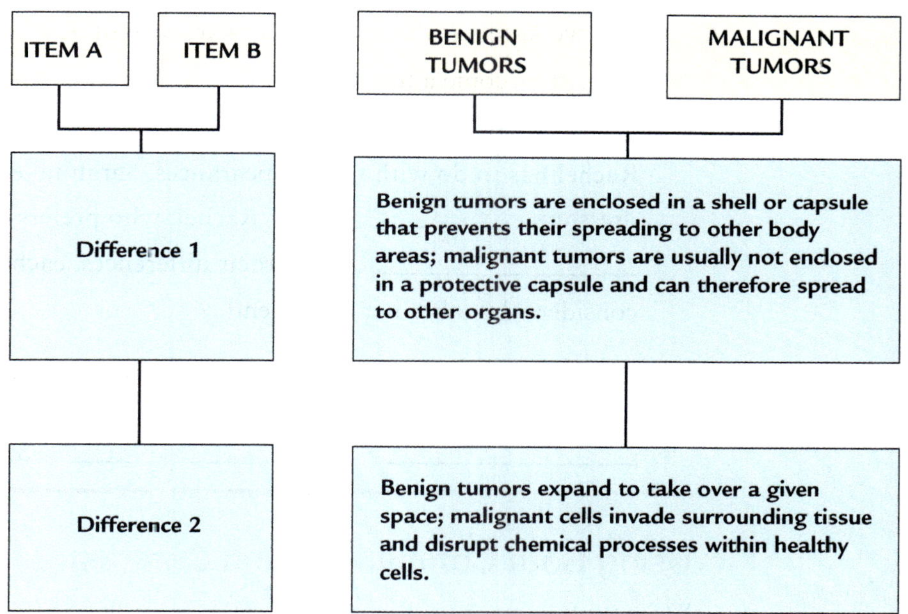

Look at the preceding paragraph again, and circle the contrast clues you can find (use the box on p. 290 to help you). Did you circle the following words and phrases: *differ, in contrast,* and *unlike*?

EXERCISE 8-3 Using Contrast Transitions

A. *Directions:* *Select the contrast word or phrase from the box below that best completes each sentence in the paragraph. Write each answer in the space provided. Use each choice only once.*

Copyright © 2012 by Pearson Education

contrast	difference	however	on the other hand
different	unlike	but	

Sarah and Rachel may be sisters, but their friends and family agree that the girls couldn't be more ________________. To begin with, Sarah has a very active social life; Rachel, ________________, is content to curl up at home with a good book. Another ________________ between the two sisters is their attitude toward school. Rachel loves school and plans to become a teacher, ________________ Sarah is happiest outside of the classroom. One last ________________ between Sarah and Rachel has to do with their appearances. Sarah takes every opportunity to dress up, ________________ Rachel, who prefers jeans and a sweatshirt. ________________, despite their differences, each of the two girls considers the other her best friend.

B. Directions: *List the three transitions that the writer uses to introduce her three main points.*

1. ________________ 2. ________________ 3. ________________

Using Both Comparison and Contrast

Writers often want to discuss similarities as well as differences. They might, for instance, want to compare *and* contrast two popular modern novelists, Stephen King and Danielle Steele; two presidents, George W. Bush and Barack Obama; or two national parks, Yosemite and Yellowstone.

When writers use comparison and contrast together, they may discuss everything about their first item (say, Stephen King) and then discuss everything about their second item (say, Danielle Steele). Often, though, writers move back and forth from item to item, discussing similarities and differences as they go along. This pattern is shown in the following paragraph, which compares and contrasts the Senate and the House of Representatives.

Congress is bicameral, meaning that it is made up of two houses, the Senate and the House of Representatives. According to the Constitution, all members of Congress must be residents of the states that they have been elected to represent. The Constitution also specifies that representatives must be at least 25 years old and American citizens for 7 years, whereas senators must be at least 30 and American citizens for 9 years. The roles of majority and minority leaders are similar in both houses, and both use committees to review bills and to set their legislative agenda. Despite these similarities, there are many important differences between the two houses. First, the term of office is two years for representatives but six years for senators. Further, each state is guaranteed two senators but its number of representatives is determined by the state's population; thus, the House of Representatives has 435 members and the Senate has 100. Another difference involves procedure: the House places limits on debate, whereas the Senate allows unlimited debate, which sometimes leads to a filibuster.

EXERCISE 8-4 Using Comparison and Contrast

***Directions:** After reading the preceding paragraph, select the choice that best answers each of the following questions.*

_______ 1. Although the writer is comparing and contrasting the two houses of Congress, what other pattern (from Chapter 7) does she use in the first sentence of the paragraph?

a. example
b. definition
c. process
d. listing

_______ 2. The writer uses many words to indicate similarities and differences. Which of the following is *not* used as a contrast word?

a. whereas
b. but
c. further
d. difference

3. The paragraph includes many similarities and differences between the House of Representatives and the Senate. List some of the similarities and differences below.

The House of Representatives and the Senate

Similarities	Differences
1. ____________________	1. ____________________
____________________	____________________
2. ____________________	____________________
____________________	2. ____________________
3. ____________________	____________________
____________________	3. ____________________
	____________________
	4. ____________________
	____________________

Copyright © 2012 by Pearson Education

Cause/Effect Patterns

GOAL 2
Learn how cause/effect patterns are used

myreadinglab
To practice examining cause/effect patterns, go to
> Study Plan
> Reading Skills
> Patterns of Organization

Writers use the **cause/effect** pattern to explain why an event or action causes another event or action. For example, if you are describing a skiing accident to a friend, you would probably follow a cause/effect pattern. You would tell what caused the accident and what happened as a result.

When a single cause has multiple effects, it can be visualized as follows:

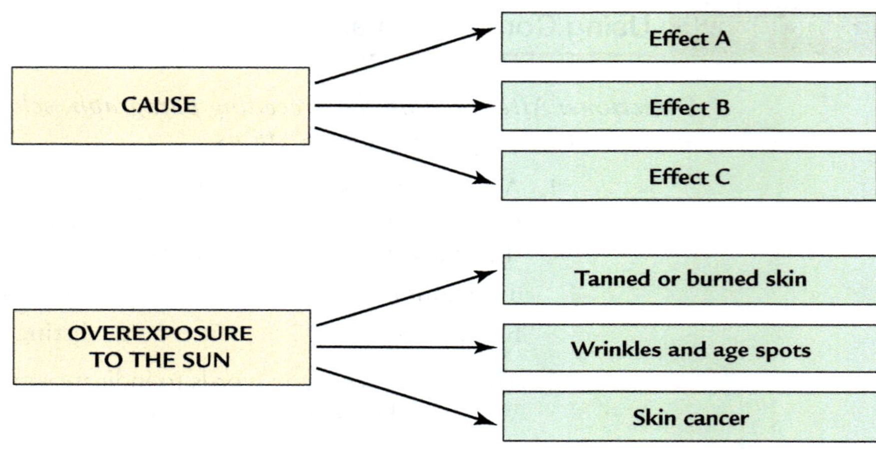

Sometimes, however, multiple causes result in a single effect. This kind of cause/effect pattern can be visualized this way:

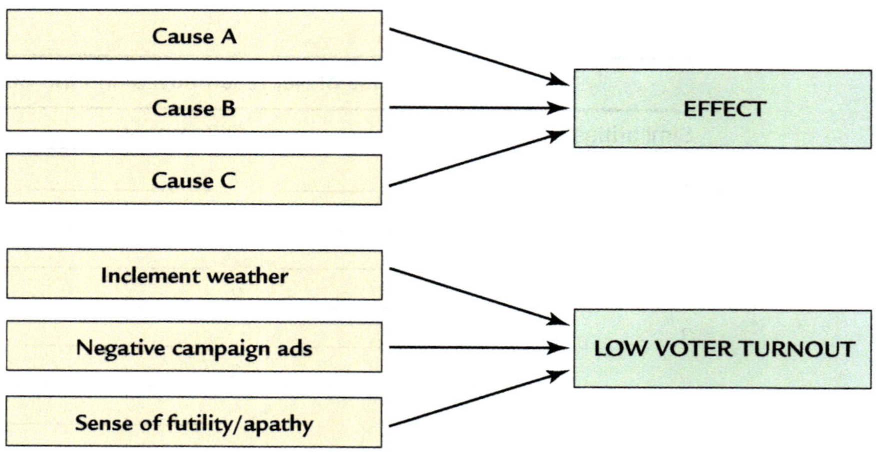

Read the following paragraph, which discusses the multiple causes of a single effect.

> Although ulcers are commonly associated with stress, they can be brought on by other risk factors. Chronic use of aspirin and other nonsteroidal anti-inflammatory drugs increases the risk of ulcer because these agents suppress the secretion of both mucus and bicarbonate, which normally protect the lining of the GI tract from the effects of acid and pepsin. The risk of ulcer is also increased by chronic alcohol use or the leakage of bile from the duodenum into the stomach, both of which can disrupt the mucus barrier. Surprisingly, ulcers are usually not associated with abnormally high rates of stomach-acid secretion; more often than not, acid secretion is normal or even below normal in most people with ulcers.
>
> —adapted from Germann and Stanfield, *Principles of Human Physiology*, p. 622

EXERCISE 8-5 Understanding Cause/Effect Patterns

Directions: *After reading the preceding paragraph, answer each of the following questions.*

1. What effect is the writer discussing? ____________________
2. List four causes described by the authors.
   a. ____________________
   b. ____________________
   c. ____________________
   d. ____________________

As you worked on Exercise 8–5, did you notice that the topic sentence tells the reader that the paragraph will be about causes, referred to as *risk factors?* Topic sentences often provide this important clue in a cause/effect paragraph, so pay close attention to them.

Writers often use specific words to show why one event is caused by another. Look at the following statement:

> Shirley accidentally drove past the exit for her dentist's office. Consequently, she was late for her appointment.

The word *consequently* ties the cause—missed the exit—to the effect—being late. Here is another example:

> Deion was not in class all week because he had the flu.

Copyright © 2012 by Pearson Education

In this sentence the word *because* ties the effect—Deion was absent—to the cause—he had the flu. In both of these examples, the cause and effect words help explain the relationship between two events. As you read, watch for words that show cause and effect; some common ones are listed in the box below.

Transitions in Cause and Effect			
cause	since	effect	one result is
because	due to	consequently	therefore
because of	reasons	as a result	thus

EXERCISE 8-6 Using Cause/Effect Transitions

A. Directions: *After reading the following paragraph, select the cause/effect word in the box below that best completes each sentence in the paragraph. Write your answer in the space provided. Not all words will be used.*

consequently	effects	reasons
because of	cause	result

Although it was a frightening experience, Bill's heart attack last year has had several positive ________________. First, Bill realized that his diet had to change. He has eliminated the high-fat, high-sodium foods that were a major ________________ of his health problems, replacing them with healthy, low-fat foods that he can prepare at home. Another aspect of Bill's life that has changed ________________ his heart attack is his attitude toward exercise. He used to drive everywhere; now he walks whenever possible. In addition, he has started an exercise program approved by his doctor. As a ________________, he looks and feels better than he has in years. Finally, Bill's heart attack served as a powerful reminder of the importance of his family. ________________, he has adjusted his work schedule so that he is able to spend more time with the people he loves.

B. Directions: *After reading the preceding paragraph, answer the following questions.*

1. What cause is being discussed? ______________________________
2. What three effects does the writer mention?
   a. ______________________________
   b. ______________________________
   c. ______________________________
3. Does the topic sentence tell you that this will be a cause/effect paragraph?

   ____
4. Aside from the cause and effect words, list four transitions that the writer uses to lead the reader through the information.

   a. __________ b. __________ c. __________ d. __________

Other Useful Thought Patterns

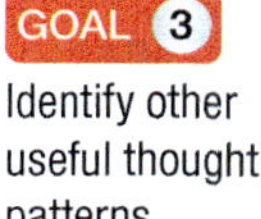

Identify other useful thought patterns

The patterns presented in Chapter 7 and in this chapter are the most common. However, writers do not limit themselves to these six patterns. Especially in academic writing, you may find one or more of the patterns described in the next pages.

Classification

A common way to explain something is to divide the topic into parts and explain each part. For example, you might explain the kinds of courses taken in college by dividing the courses into such categories as electives, required basic courses, courses required for a specific major, and so on and then describing each category. Textbook writers use the classification pattern to explain a topic that can easily be divided into parts. These parts are selected on the basis of common characteristics. For example, a psychology textbook writer might explain human needs by classifying them into two categories, primary and secondary. Or in a chemistry textbook, various compounds may be grouped or classified according to common characteristics, such as the presence of hydrogen or oxygen. In the following paragraph, the authors describe three types of business strategy.

Three types of strategy are usually considered by a company. The purpose of **corporate strategy** is to determine the firm's overall attitude toward growth and the way it will manage its businesses or product lines. A company may

Copyright © 2012 by Pearson Education

decide to *grow* by increasing its activities or investment or to *retrench* by reducing them. **Business** (or **competitive**) **strategy,** which takes place at the level of the business unit or product line, focuses on improving the company's competitive position. At the level of **functional strategy,** managers in specific areas decide how best to achieve corporate goals by being as productive as possible.

—adapted from Ebert and Griffin, *Business Essentials,* p. 117

Words that signal the classification patterns are shown below.

Transitions for Classification			
another	another kind	classified as	include
is composed of	one	types of	

Statement and Clarification

Many writers make a statement of fact and then proceed to clarify or explain that statement. For instance, a writer may open a paragraph by stating that "The best education for you may not be the best education for someone else." The remainder of the paragraph would then discuss that statement and make its meaning clear by explaining how educational needs are individual and based on one's talents, skills, and goals. In the following paragraph the author makes a statement about computer hackers and then elaborates on the issue.

In recent years, computer hackers have become a serious problem. It is very difficult to catch the culprits because the virus programs they introduce often affect a system afterwards. In fact, very few hacking incidents get reported and even fewer of the hackers get caught. According to the San Francisco–based Computer Security Institute (CSI), only about 17% of companies report hacking incidents because of the fear of adverse publicity, copycat hacking and loss of customer confidence. Out of those reported cases, normally an infinitesimal number of those responsible are caught.

—adapted from Bandyo-Padhyay, *Computing for Non-Specialists,* p. 260

Words associated with this pattern are listed below.

Transitions for Statement and Clarification				
in fact	in other words	clearly	evidently	obviously

Summary

A summary is a condensed statement that provides the key points of a larger idea or piece of writing. The summaries at the end of each chapter of many textbooks provide a quick review of the chapter's contents. Often writers summarize what they have already said or what someone else has said. For example, in a psychology textbook you will find many summaries of research. Instead of asking you to read an entire research study, the textbook author will summarize the study's findings. Other times a writer may repeat in condensed form what he or she has already said as a means of emphasis or clarification. In the following paragraph from a sociology text, the author summarizes a general principle of human behavior.

> To sum up, the minimax strategy is a general principle of human behavior that suggests that humans try to minimize costs and maximize rewards. The fewer costs and the more rewards we anticipate from something, the more likely we are to do it. If we believe that others will approve an act, the likelihood increases that we will do it. In short, whether people are playing cards with a few friends or are part of a mob, the principles of human behavior remain the same.
>
> —adapted from Henslin, *Sociology: A Down-to-Earth Approach,* p. 637

Words associated with this pattern are listed below.

Transitions for Summary			
in summary	in conclusion	in brief	to summarize
to sum up	in short	on the whole	

Addition

Writers often introduce an idea or make a statement and then supply additional information about that idea or statement. For instance, an education textbook may introduce the concept of homeschooling and then provide in-depth information about its benefits. The addition pattern is distinct from the listing pattern discussed in Chapter 7. This pattern is often used to expand, elaborate, or discuss a single idea in greater detail. The listing pattern enumerates items. In the following paragraph, the authors introduce the concept of a transnational organization and then describe one in depth.

> Perhaps the most commonly cited **example from the world of management** of a transnational organization is **Nestlé**. Although Nestlé is headquartered in Vevey, Switzerland, its arena of daily business activity is truly the

Copyright © 2012 by Pearson Education

world. Nestlé has a diversified list of products that include instant coffee, cereals, pharmaceuticals, coffee creamers, dietetic foods, ice cream, chocolates, and a wide array of snack foods. Its recent acquisition of the French company Perrier catapulted Nestlé into market leadership in the mineral water industry. Additionally, Nestlé has more than 210,000 employees and operates 494 factories in 71 countries worldwide, including the United States, Germany, Portugal, Brazil, France, New Zealand, Australia, Chile, and Venezuela. Moreover, of Nestlé's sales and profits, about 35 percent come from Europe, 40 percent from North and South America, and 25 percent from other countries. As with most transnational organizations, Nestlé has grown by acquiring companies rather than by expanding its present operations.

—adapted from Certo et al., *Modern Management*, p. 127

Words associated with this pattern are shown below.

Transitions for Addition			
furthermore	additionally	also	besides
further	in addition	moreover	again

Spatial Order

Spatial order is concerned with physical location or position in space. Spatial order is used in disciplines in which physical descriptions are important. A photography textbook may use spatial order to describe the parts of a camera. An automotive technology textbook may use spatial order to describe disc brake operation. In the following paragraph from a physiology textbook, the authors use spatial order to describe the human chemoreceptors for taste.

We can taste food because chemoreceptors in the mouth respond to certain chemicals in food. The chemoreceptors for taste are located in structures called **taste buds**, each of which contains 50–150 receptor cells and numerous support cells. At the top of each bud is a pore that allows receptor cells to be exposed to saliva and dissolved food molecules. Each person has over 10,000 taste buds, located primarily on the tongue and the roof of the mouth, but also located in the pharynx.

—Germann and Stanfield, *Principles of Human Physiology*, pp. 303–304

Words associated with this pattern are listed below.

Transitions for Spatial Order			
above	below	besides	next to
in front of	behind	inside	outside
opposite	within	nearby	

EXERCISE 8-7 Understanding Other Patterns

Directions: *After reading each paragraph, select the pattern from the box below that best describes the organization of the paragraph.*

classification	summary	addition
statement and clarification	spatial order	

1. All languages have four key characteristics. First, they have phonology. Phonemes are the basic units of speech, and they are arranged in sequences to form words. Second, languages have grammar. Grammar is a set of rules for combining words that is based on the relationships among parts of speech. Third, languages have semantics, which specify meaning. The semantics of a word arise from its morphemes, small elements of meaning. Fourth, languages have pragmatics, the indirect or implied aspects of meaning. Pragmatics play a key role in understanding whether a question is actually a request, and whether a statement ending with a rising pitch is actually a question.

—adapted from Kosslyn and Rosenberg, *Fundamentals of Psychology: The Brain, the Person, the World*, p. 197

Organization pattern: ____________________

2. The **meninges** are three connective tissue membranes that lie just external to the central nervous system organs. The leathery **dura mater,** meaning "tough mother," is the strongest of the meninges. Where it surrounds the brain, it is a two-layered sheet of fibrous connective tissue. Its more superficial layer, the *periosteal layer,* is attached to the inner surface of the skull. The deeper *meningeal layer* forms the true external covering of the brain and continues in the vertebral canal as the dural sheath of the spinal cord. The brain's two dural layers are fused together except in certain areas, where they separate to enclose dural sinuses that collect venous blood from the brain and direct it into the internal jugular veins of the neck.

—adapted from Marieb, *Anatomy and Physiology,* pp. 402–403

Organization pattern: ____________________

3. In this chapter, we looked at listening and criticism and offered suggestions for making your listening and your criticism more effective. To sum up, criticism helps to (1) identify a speaker's strengths and weaknesses, (2) identify standards for evaluating different kinds of public speeches, and (3) show that the audience is concerned about the speaker's progress. In short, criticism is crucial to mastering the principles of public speaking.

—adapted from DeVito, *The Essential Elements of Public Speaking,* p. 46

Organization pattern: ____________________

Copyright © 2012 by Pearson Education

4. Economic conditions determine spending patterns by consumers, businesses, and governments. Thus, they influence every marketer's plans for product offerings, pricing, and promotional strategies. Among the more significant economic variables, marketers are concerned with inflation, interest rates, recession, and recovery. In other words, they must monitor the general business cycle, which typically features a pattern of transition from periods of prosperity to recession to recovery (return to prosperity).

—Ebert and Griffin, *Business Essentials*, p. 254

Organization pattern: ______________________________

5. Introducing a surprise element in an advertisement can be particularly effective in aiding recall. In addition, mystery ads, in which the brand is not identified until the end of the ad, are more effective at building associations in memory between the product category and that brand—especially in the case of relatively unknown brands

—adapted from Solomon, *Consumer Behavior*, p. 89

Organization pattern: ______________________________

Thinking Critically About Comparison/Contrast and Cause/Effect

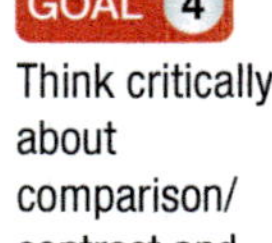

Think critically about comparison/contrast and cause/effect

In this chapter you learned to recognize several patterns of organization used by writers. Here is another important reason for mastering them: In many of your college courses, you'll be taking essay exams. These exams require you to think and write using these patterns. Consider the following typical essay questions:

How are the medical systems of England and Sweden similar? How are they different?

Although the words are not used, this is actually a comparison/contrast question. To get full credit for your answer, you have to compare and contrast the English and Swedish medical systems.

Discuss at least three causes of the United States Civil War.

This essay question is actually a cause/effect question. The effect is the Civil War, and you must discuss at least three causes of it.

College instructors love comparison/contrast and cause/effect questions because they require you to think deeply (critically) about the topic. If you can discuss why something happened, you probably have a good understanding of it. If you understand how two things are similar and how they are different, you probably have a good understanding of them.

Consider the first question above. To say that the English and Swedish medical systems are similar because they are both in Europe does not demonstrate any understanding of how those systems work. But to say that both systems provide basic health care for all citizens at no cost does show a good understanding of them.

When you are writing about cause and effect, be sure to focus on meaningful and significant causes and effects. In answering the question about the Civil War, you could convincingly argue that differing attitudes toward slavery was one cause. But you would not receive credit for saying, "One cause of the Civil War was the South's desire to separate from the North," because that reason does not offer any insight into *why* the North and the South went to war.

EXERCISE 8-8 Analyzing the Comparison and Contrast Patterns

Directions: *Read the essay question that follows. Then write an X next to the three best comparison or contrast statements.*

Compare and contrast the lifestyle of two U.S. cities—New York City and San Francisco.

_______ New York and San Francisco are similar in that both have mass transit systems.

_______ San Francisco has fewer one-way streets than New York City.

_______ Both New York and San Francisco are located near major waterways.

_______ Both San Francisco and New York are currently very Democratic cities where Republicans are a distinct minority.

_______ New York City was founded earlier than San Francisco.

_______ While New York experiences wild temperature swings, San Francisco has a much more moderate climate.

_______ Housing in San Francisco is more readily available than in New York.

EXERCISE 8-9 Analyzing the Cause and Effect Patterns

Directions: *Read the essay question that follows. Then write an X next to the three best statements of effect.*

List three large-scale effects that American Idol *has had on American society.*

Copyright © 2012 by Pearson Education

_______ *American Idol* has led to thousands of young people to feel that there is a popular outlet for their interests and talents.

_______ For a long time, Americans were moving away from network TV and watching more cable TV. *American Idol* has brought Americans back to network TV.

_______ *American Idol* has made its creator, Simon Cowell, a multimillionaire.

_______ The people without talent on the *American Idol* auditions have been a good source of humor for society.

_______ *American Idol* has proven that the generation gap can be bridged, as parents and their children watch the show and vote together.

_______ *American Idol* has made a star of Ryan Seacrest, the show's host/emcee.

_______ *American Idol* has led to friends across the United States sending one another millions of text messages while the show is being broadcast.

TEXTBOOK CHALLENGE

TIPS for Reading in History

When reading history textbooks, pay attention to

- **Sequence of events.** History textbooks emphasize time lines and historical context of events.
- **Long-term effects.** Courses in history focus on the influence events have on later occurrences.
- **Motivation.** History courses emphasize not only what happened, but why people acted as they did.

Part A: Analyzing a Textbook Excerpt

This excerpt was taken from a history textbook chapter about politics. Read the excerpt and follow the directions on pp. 307–308.

WHETHER TO VOTE: A CITIZEN'S FIRST CHOICE

suffrage
The legal right to vote, extended to African Americans by the **Fifteenth Amendment**, to women by the **Nineteenth Amendment**, and to people over the age of 18 by the **Twenty-sixth Amendment**.

1 Over two centuries of American electoral history, federal laws have greatly expanded **suffrage**—the right to vote. In the election of 1800, only property-owning White males over the age of 21 were typically allowed to vote. Now virtually everyone over the age of 18—male or female, White or non-White, rich or poor—has the right to vote. The two major exceptions concern noncitizens and convicted criminals.

2 Interestingly, as the right to vote has been extended, proportionately fewer of those eligible have chosen to exercise that right. In the past 120 years, the 80 percent turnout in the 1896 election was the high point of electoral participation. In 2008, 61 percent of adult citizens voted in the presidential election.

DECIDING WHETHER TO VOTE

3 Realistically, when over 125 million people vote in a presidential election, as they did in 2008, the chance of one vote affecting the outcome is very, very slight. Once in a while, of course, an election is decided by a small number of votes, as occurred in Florida in 2000. It is more likely, however, that you will be struck by lightning during your lifetime than participate in an election decided by a single vote.

4 Not only does your vote probably not make much difference to the outcome, but voting is somewhat costly. You have to spend some of your valuable time becoming informed, making up your mind, and getting to the polls. If you carefully calculate your time and energy, you might rationally decide that the costs of voting outweigh the benefits. Indeed, the most frequent response given by nonvoters in the 2004 Census Bureau survey on turnout was that they could not take time off from work or school that day. Some scholars have therefore proposed that one of the easiest ways to increase American turnout levels would be to move Election Day to Saturday or make it a holiday, as practiced in many other countries.

5 Economist Anthony Downs, in his model of democracy, tries to explain why a rational person would ever bother to vote. He argues that rational people vote if they believe that the policies of one party will bring more benefits than the policies of the other party. Thus, people who see policy differences between the parties are more likely to join the ranks of voters. If you are an environmentalist and you expect the Democrats to pass more environmental legislation than the Republicans, then you have an additional incentive to go to the polls. On the other hand, if you are truly indifferent—that is, if you see no difference whatsoever between the two parties—you may rationally decide to abstain.

political efficacy
The belief that one's **political participation** really matters—that one's vote can actually make a difference.

6 Another reason why many people vote is that they have a high sense of **political efficacy**—the belief that ordinary people can influence the government. Efficacy is measured by asking people to agree or disagree with statements such as "I don't think public officials care much what people like me think." Those who lack strong feelings of efficacy are

Copyright © 2012 by Pearson Education

being quite rational in staying home on Election Day because they don't think they can make a difference. Yet even some of these people will vote anyway, simply to support democratic government. In this case, people are impelled to vote by a sense of civic duty. The benefit from doing one's **civic duty** is the long-term contribution made toward preserving democracy.

civic duty
The belief that in order to support democratic government, a citizen should always vote.

WHY TURNOUT IN THE UNITED STATES IS SO LOW COMPARED TO OTHER COUNTRIES

7 Despite living in a culture that encourages participation, Americans have a woefully low turnout rate compared to other democracies. The figure below displays the most recent election turnout rates in the United States and a variety of other nations.

8 There are several reasons given for Americans' abysmally low turnout rate. Probably the reason most often cited is the American requirement of voter registration. The governments of many (but not all) other democracies take the responsibility of seeing to it that all their eligible citizens are on the voting lists. In America, the responsibility for registration lies solely with the individual. If we were like the Scandinavian countries, where the government registers every eligible citizen, no doubt our turnout rate would be higher.

9 A second difference between the United States and other countries is that the American government asks citizens to vote far more often. Whereas the typical European voter may cast two or three ballots in a four-year period, many Americans are faced with a dozen or more separate elections in the space of four years. Furthermore, Americans are expected to vote for a much wider range of political offices. With one elected official for every 442 citizens and elections held somewhere virtually every week, it is no wonder that it is so difficult to get Americans to the polls. It is probably no coincidence that the one European country that has a lower turnout rate—

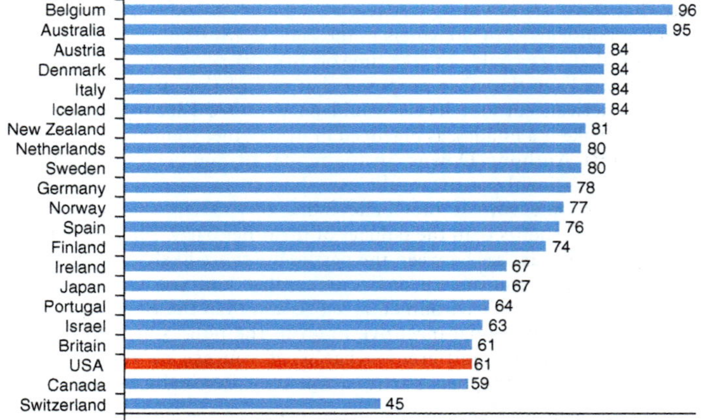

314 Part 2 People and Politics

Switzerland—has also overwhelmed its citizens with voting opportunities, typically asking people to vote three times every year.

10 Third, the stimulus to vote is low in the United States because the choices offered Americans are not as starkly different as in other countries. The United States is quite unusual in that it has always lacked a major left-wing socialist party. When European voters go to the polls, they are deciding on whether their country will be run by parties with socialist goals or by conservative (and in some cases religious) parties. The consequences of their vote for redistribution of income and the scope of government are far greater than the ordinary American voter can imagine.

11 Finally, the United States is one of the few democracies that still vote mid-week, when most people are working. Article I, Section III of the U.S. Constitution allows Congress to determine the timing of federal elections. In the 1840s, Congress established the first Tuesday after the first Monday in November as the date for presidential elections. Americans have become quite accustomed to Tuesday elections, just as they are used to other outdated practices such as the nonmetric system for weights and measures. States continue to set primary election dates on Tuesday, even though they are perfectly free to pick any day of the week for these contests. Comparative research has shown that countries that hold elections on the weekend have higher turnout, but so far there has been no groundswell to change the American practice of holding elections on Tuesday.

Questions for Discussion

- Some people would like the United States to emulate other countries and have the government register everyone who is eligible to vote. Others oppose this European-style system, believing that this would lead to an intrusive big government that would require everyone to have a national identity card. What do you think?
- Do you think American turnout rates would be better if we followed the lead of most other democracies and held elections on the weekend? Do you think young Americans, in particular, would be more likely to vote if elections were held on the weekend? Why or why not?

—Edwards, *Government in America*, pp. 312–314

1. **Preview.** Preview the reading using the guidelines on p. 7 and then answer the following questions.
   a. What kind of trend is there with respect to the number of people voting?
   b. How is voting costly to voters?
   c. Why do people vote?
2. **SQ3R.** Write at least three questions for the Q step of SQ3R. Answer them after completing the reading.

Copyright © 2012 by Pearson Education

3. **Textbook Features.** What new information does the bar graph on p. 306 offer that is not included elsewhere? How would you use the definitions in the margins when studying?
4. **Vocabulary.**
   a. Identify the important new terms that are introduced in the reading.
   b. Define each of the following words as used in the reading:
   proportionately (par. 2), *impelled* (par. 6), *woefully* (par. 7), *abysmally* (par. 8), *stimulus* (par. 10), *groundswell* (par. 11)
5. **Applying Chapter Skills.** Complete the cause and effect diagram below.

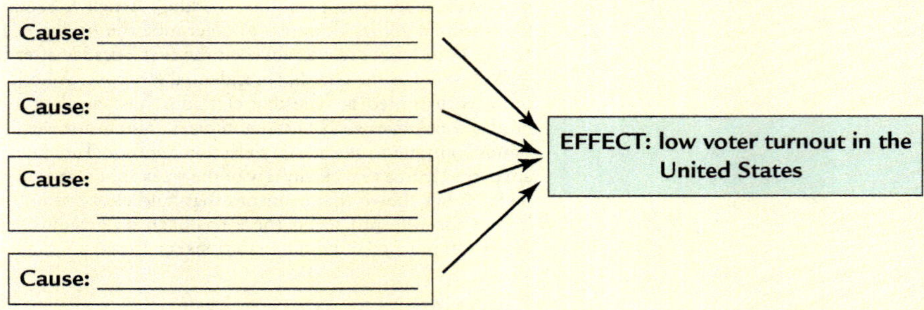

6. **Essay Question.** Write an answer to the following essay question. To test your memory, write it without referring to the excerpt.
   Discuss the factors that determine whether citizens vote. How do people decide whether to vote, and what considerations do they weigh?
7. **Thinking Critically.** Use your critical thinking skills to answer each of the following questions.
   a. Do you think there are other reasons in addition to those listed in the chapter that might cause people to choose to vote or not vote? What are they?
   b. The selection compares U.S. voting rates with European voting rates and focuses on explaining why U.S. turnout is so low. If the selection were written to discuss why European voting turnout is so high, do you think additional evidence would need to be offered? Why or why not?
   c. What affects your decision to vote? Explain how you decide whether you will vote in an election.

Part B: Your College Textbook

Choose a chapter that you have been assigned to read in a textbook for one of your other courses. Identify sections of the chapter that use comparison/contrast, cause/effect, classification, statement and clarification, summary, addition, or spatial order organization patterns. Circle the transitions that indicate the patterns.

SELF-TEST SUMMARY

To test yourself, cover up the Answer column with a sheet of paper and answer each question listed in the left column. Evaluate each of your answers as you work by sliding the paper down and comparing your answer with what is printed in the Answer column.

	Question	Answer
GOAL 1	What is the difference between comparison and contrast?	Comparison is used to show how two or more things are similar to each other. Contrast is used to show how they are different from each other.
GOAL 2	How are cause/effect patterns used?	Cause/effect patterns explain why one action or event causes another.
GOAL 3	What other useful patterns might you encounter?	Other useful patterns include classification, statement and clarification, summary, addition, and spatial order.
GOAL 4	How can comparison/contrast and cause/effect patterns help you succeed in college?	Many exams rely on these patterns; understanding them will enable you to answer questions more easily and more accurately.

Copyright © 2012 by Pearson Education

PRACTICE TEST 8-1

NAME ______________________ SECTION ______________________
DATE ______________________ SCORE ______________________

Mapping and Outlining Patterns

Directions: *After reading each paragraph, complete the map or outline that follows.*

A. Comedy is often divided into two varieties—"high" and "low." **High comedy** relies more on wit and wordplay than on physical action for its humor. It tries to address the audience's intelligence by pointing out the pretension and hypocrisy of human behavior. High comedy also generally avoids derisive humor. Jokes about physical appearances would, for example, be avoided. **Low comedy** explores the opposite extreme of humor. It places greater emphasis on physical action and visual gags, and its verbal jokes do not require much intellect to appreciate. Low comedy does not avoid derisive humor; rather it revels in making fun of whatever will get a good laugh. Drunkenness, stupidity, lust, senility, trickery, insult, and clumsiness are inexhaustible staples for this kind of comedy.

—adapted from Kennedy and Gioia, *Literature*, pp. 885–886

Contrasting High and Low Comedy

Difference #1 ______________ relies more on wit and wordplay.

Difference #2 ______________ tries to speak to the audience's intellect by pointing out certain aspects of human behavior.

Difference #3 ______________ usually avoids derisive humor, including jokes about physical appearance.

Difference #4 ______________ emphasizes physical action and visual jokes, not intellect.

Difference #5 ______________ takes delight in making fun of anything for a good laugh.

For cells to be brought to a cancerous state, two things are required: Their accelerators must get stuck and their brakes must fail. The control mechanisms that *induce* cell division must become hyperactive, and the mechanisms that *suppress* cell division must fail to perform. You may have heard a couple of terms used to describe the genetic components of this process. There are normal genes that induce cell devision, but that when mutated can cause cancer; these are the stuck-accelerator genes, called oncogenes. Then, there are genes that normally suppress cell division but that can cause cancer by acting like failed brakes. These are tumor suppressor genes. Note that *both* kinds of genes must malfunction for cancer to get going; indeed, it usually takes a long succession of genetic failures to induce cancer. This is why cancer is most often a disease of the middle-aged and elderly: It can take decades for the required series of mutations to fall into line in a single cell, such that it becomes cancerous.

—Krough, *Biology*, p. 172

I. How cancer cells develop from regular cells
  A. Their accelerators get stuck
    1. Mechanisms that induce ________________ become hyperactive
    2. Normal cells that induce cell division can mutate and cause cancer—these are called ________________
  B. Their brakes fail
    1. Mechanisms that suppress cell division ________________
    2. Cells that normally suppress cell division fail to work and cause cancer—these are called ________________
  C. Both kinds of genes must malfunction for ________________
    1. It can take decades for all the necessary mutations to happen
    2. ____

Copyright © 2012 by Pearson Education

PRACTICE TEST 8-2

NAME ______________________ SECTION ______________________

DATE ______________________ SCORE ______________________

Identifying Patterns

Directions: *After reading each paragraph, select the choice that best completes each of the statements that follow.*

A. The three major types of managerial styles are autocratic, democratic, and free rein. Managers who adopt an **autocratic style** generally issue orders and expect them to be obeyed without question. The military commander prefers and usually needs the autocratic style on the battlefield. Because no one else is consulted, the autocratic style allows for rapid decision making. Another managerial style is the **democratic style.** Managers who adopt this generally ask for input from subordinates before making decisions but retain final decision-making power. For example, the manager of a technical group may ask other group members to interview job applicants, but the manager will ultimately make the hiring decision. Managers who adopt a **free-rein style** typically serve as advisers to subordinates who are allowed to make decisions. The chairperson of a volunteer committee to raise funds for a new library may find a free-rein style most effective.

—adapted from Ebert and Griffin, *Business Essentials,* pp. 212–213

_______ 1. The organizational pattern of this paragraph is

a. process.

b. cause/effect.

c. spatial order.

d. classification.

_______ 2. The purpose of the paragraph is to

a. describe different managerial styles.

b. summarize the qualities of good managers.

c. explain the effects of different managerial styles.

d. show which managerial style is best.

_______ 3. A transitional word or phrase that signals the writers' pattern is

a. another.

b. because.

c. for example.

d. however.

_______ 4. A manager who involves subordinates in decision making but retains final decision-making power is using the style known as

a. autocratic.

b. military.

c. democratic.

d. free rein.

_______ 5. One characteristic of the autocratic style is that it allows for

a. rapid decision making.

b. employee creativity.

c. input from subordinates.

d. decisions by subordinates.

B. Most of the asteroids, rocky objects that orbit stars, found outside the asteroid belt [regions in which asteroids are heavily concentrated]—including the Earth-approaching asteroids that pass near Earth's orbit—are probably "impacts waiting to happen." But asteroids can safely congregate in two stable zones outside the main belt. These zones are found along Jupiter's orbit 60 degrees ahead of and behind Jupiter. The asteroids found in these two zones are called the *Trojan asteroids,* and the largest are named for the mythological Greek heroes of the Trojan War. The Trojan asteroids are stable because of a different type of orbital resonance with Jupiter. In this case, any asteroid that wanders away from one of these zones is nudged back into the zone by Jupiter's gravity. The existence of such orbital resonances was first predicted by the French mathematician Joseph Lagrange more than 200 years ago—135 years before the discovery of the first asteroid in such an orbit. It is possible that the population of Trojan asteroids is as large as that of main-belt asteroids, but the greater distance to the Trojan asteroids makes them more difficult to study or even to count from Earth.

—adapted from Bennett et al., *The Cosmic Perspective,* p. 326

_______ 6. The topic of this paragraph is

a. Earth's orbit.

b. asteroids.

c. the Trojan War.

d. Jupiter.

Copyright © 2012 by Pearson Education

______ 7. The organizational pattern of this paragraph is

a. comparison/contrast.

b. classification.

c. spatial order.

d. cause/effect.

______ 8. All of the following transitional words from the paragraph signal the writers' pattern *except*

a. outside.

b. into.

c. behind.

d. but.

______ 9. One characteristic of asteroids outside the main belt is that they

a. are totally unstable.

b. are found only near Earth's orbit.

c. can congregate safely in two zones along Jupiter's orbit.

d. immediately crash into each other.

______ 10. This paragraph is concerned primarily with

a. differences between Trojan asteroids and main-belt asteroids.

b. similarities between Trojan asteroids and main-belt asteroids.

c. general characteristics of all types of asteroids.

d. the physical position of asteroids outside the main belt.

NAME ______________________ SECTION ______________________

DATE ______________________ SCORE ______________________

MASTERY TEST 8-1

Recognizing Patterns

Directions: *After reading the following passage, select the choice that best completes each of the statements that follow.*

Folk Culture and Popular Culture

1 Today's rapid pace of cultural change requires us to distinguish between folk culture and popular culture. The term **folk culture** refers to a culture that preserves traditions. Folk groups are often bound by a distinctive religion, national background, or language, and folk cultures are conservative and resistant to change. Most folk-culture groups are rural, and relative isolation helps these groups maintain their integrity. Folk-culture groups, however, also include urban neighborhoods of immigrants struggling to preserve their native cultures in their new homes.

2 Cultural geographers have identified a surprising number of folk cultures across the United States. Folk geographic studies in the U.S. range from studies of songs, foods, medicine, and folklore to objects of folk material culture as diverse as locally produced pottery, clothing, tombstones, farm fencing, and even knives and guns. In addition, houses, barns, and other structures are built in distinct architectural styles that reveal the origins of their builders.

3 In North America the Amish provide an example of a folk culture. The Amish stand out because they wear plain clothing and shun modern education and technology. They prosper by specializing their farm production and marketing their produce, but they severely curtail the choice of goods that they will accept in return.

4 In contrast to folk culture, **popular culture** is the culture of people who embrace innovation and conform to changing norms. Popular culture may originate anywhere, and it tends to spread rapidly, especially wherever people have time, money, and inclination to indulge in it.

5 Popular material culture usually means mass culture—that is, items such as clothing, processed food, books, CDs, and household goods that are mass produced for mass distribution. Popular culture is largely defined by consumption, so it is usually more closely related to social class, as defined by income and education, than folk cultures are. The consumer items people buy are largely determined by what they can afford.

—adapted from Bergman and Renwick, *Introduction to Geography,* pp. 215–217

Copyright © 2012 by Pearson Education

_____ 1. The primary purpose of this passage is to
   a. describe the history of folk groups in America.
   b. explain how geographers study different cultural groups.
   c. contrast the characteristics of folk culture and popular culture.
   d. give geographical locations for folk groups in America.

_____ 2. Popular material culture usually refers to items such as
   a. houses and other structures.
   b. locally produced pottery.
   c. farm fencing.
   d. consumer goods that are mass produced.

_____ 3. According to this passage, the Amish stand out because they
   a. wear plain clothing and shun modern education and technology.
   b. will accept anything in exchange for the goods they market.
   c. build in distinct architectural styles.
   d. strive to adapt to changing norms.

_____ 4. One transitional word or phrase in the passage that signals the writers' pattern is
   a. however.
   b. in addition.
   c. in contrast.
   d. largely defined.

_____ 5. In paragraph 3, the word **curtail** means
   a. want.
   b. limit.
   c. promote.
   d. change.

Directions: *For items 6–10, write F next to each characteristic of folk culture and P next to each characteristic of popular culture.*

_____ 6. Preserves traditions and resists change

_____ 7. Embraces innovation

_____ 8. Originates anywhere and spreads rapidly

_____ 9. Mostly rural

_____ 10. More closely related to social class

NAME ______________ SECTION ______________
DATE ______________ SCORE ______________

MASTERY TEST 8-2

Analyzing Patterns

Directions: *After reading the following passage, select the choice that best completes each of the statements that follow.*

1 At about the turn of the nineteenth century, George Bernard Shaw wrote a famous essay comparing the two foremost stage stars of the day—Eleonora Duse and Sarah Bernhardt. Shaw's comparison is a useful springboard for a discussion of the different kinds of film stars. Bernhardt, Shaw wrote, was a bravura personality, and she managed to tailor each different role to fit this personality. This is what her fans both expected and desired. Her personal charm was larger than life, yet undeniably captivating. Her performances were filled with brilliant effects that had come to be associated with her personality over the years. Duse, on the other hand, possessed a more quiet talent, less dazzling in its initial impact. She was totally different with each role, and her own personality never seemed to intrude on the playwright's character. Hers was an invisible art: Her impersonations were so totally believable that the viewer was likely to forget it *was* an impersonation. In effect, Shaw was pointing out the major distinctions between a **personality star** and an **actor star.**

2 Personality stars commonly refuse all parts that go against their type, especially if they're leading men or leading ladies. Performers like Tom Hanks almost never play cruel or psychopathic roles, for example, because such parts would conflict with their sympathetic image. If a star is locked into his or her type, any significant departure can result in box-office disaster. For example, when Pickford tried to abandon her little girl roles in the 1920s, her public stayed at home: They wanted to see Little Mary or nothing. She retired in disgust at the age of forty, just when most players are at the peak of their powers.

3 On the other hand, many stars prefer to remain in the same mold, playing variations on the same character type. John Wayne was the most popular star in film history. From 1949 to 1976, he was absent from the top ten only three times. "I play John Wayne in every part regardless of the character, and I've been doing okay, haven't I?" he once asked. In the public mind, he was a man of action—and violence—rather than words. His **iconography** is steeped in a distrust of sophistication and intellectuality. His name is virtually synonymous with masculinity—though his persona suggests more of the warrior than the lover, a man's man rather than a lady's man. As he grew older, he also grew more human, developing his considerable talents as a comedian by mocking his own macho image. Wayne was fully aware of the enormous influence a star can wield in transmitting values, and in many of his films, he embodied a right-wing ideology that made him a hero to conservative Americans, including Ronald Reagan, Newt Gingrich, Oliver North, and Pat Buchanan.

—Giannetti, *Understanding Movies,* pp. 260–264

Copyright © 2012 by Pearson Education

_______ 1. The topic of the passage is

a. leading men and masculinity.
b. George Bernard Shaw.
c. types of film stars.
d. box-office disasters.

_______ 2. In paragraph 1, the author compares and contrasts

a. typecasting roles.
b. personality stars and actor stars.
c. the success of different types of performances.
d. qualities of impersonations.

_______ 3. In addition to comparison/contrast, the author uses the organizational pattern known as

a. example.
b. chronological order.
c. cause/effect.
d. spatial order.

_______ 4. Mary Pickford lost her audience when she

a. began to work for another studio.
b. played a psychopathic character.
c. abandoned the role audiences expected her to play.
d. became too old to play her popular role.

_______ 5. John Wayne used his roles to help popularize

a. Westerns.
b. macho images.
c. intellectuality.
d. right-wing values.

_______ 6. In paragraph 3, the word **synonymous** means

a. tougher than.
b. the same as.
c. misunderstood for.
d. exaggerated as.

Directions: *For items 7–10, write a P next to each actor who is or was a personality star and an A next to each actor who is or was an actor star.*

_______ 7. Tom Hanks

_______ 8. Sarah Bernhardt

_______ 9. Eleonora Duse

_______ 10. John Wayne

NAME ______________________ SECTION ______________________

DATE ______________________ SCORE ______________________

MASTERY TEST 8-3

READING SELECTION

Global Warming

Edward F. Bergman and William H. Renwick

In this selection from a geography textbook, the authors discuss what is known and unknown about global warming. Read the selection to find out about the potential consequences of global warming.

Vocabulary Preview

These are some of the difficult words in this essay. The definitions here will help you if you can't figure out the meanings from the sentence context or word parts.

emissions (par. 1) substances discharged into the air

evapotranspiration (par. 5) evaporation plus transpiration, equaling the total amount of water transferred from the Earth into the atmosphere

photosynthesis (par. 7) the process by which green plants and other organisms make carbohydrates from carbon dioxide and water using light energy from the sun

commodity (par. 8) any product manufactured or grown

ecosystems (par. 9) communities of plants and animals together with their environment

1 During the twentieth century, Earth's temperature increased slightly less than 1°C (1.8°F) (Figure A). Throughout the 1990s the body of scientific evidence linking this temperature rise to emissions of CO_2 accumulated rapidly, so that today few scientists doubt that increased CO_2 is the principal cause of global warming. The future of global warming is always uncertain, but the consensus is that unless output of CO_2 slows dramatically, world average temperature could rise by a few degrees celsius in the next century.

2 Despite this scientific consensus, there are many uncertainties. One is that we do not know how rapidly atmospheric CO_2 content will increase. That will depend on whether we continue to expand our use of fossil fuels as we have in the past. Another uncertainty is that we are not sure how water in the atmosphere, which plays a major role in regulating climate, will be affected by the increased levels of greenhouse gases.

3 Thus, we have only limited knowledge of how global warming will affect specific regions. Will storm tracks shift? How will a place's current levels of rainfall, snowfall, and temperature change? Will the seasons change? How will plants and animals be affected? How large an effect will this have on sea level, worldwide energy use, and food supply?

Copyright © 2012 by Pearson Education

FIGURE A World surface temperature history of the last 148 years, based on records of measured temperatures

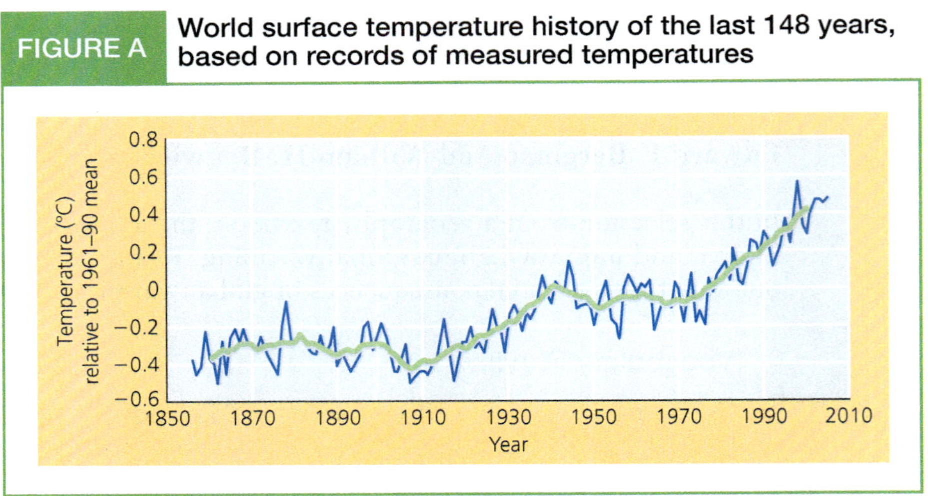

Temperatures are shown relative to the average for 1961–1990. The trend shows three distinct periods of warming, from about 1855–1880, 1910–1945, and 1975–2005. The total warming over the period of record is about 1°C (1.8°F).

The consequences of global warming

4 One serious effect of global warming that is widely believed to be likely is a worldwide rise in sea level of perhaps 1 to 5 meters (3 to 16 feet). People living near coasts would face danger from rising seas. The danger would not be from constant inundation, because sea level would rise very gradually over years, allowing people time to relocate, raise structures, or build dikes. The danger would be from occasional severe storms that would cause sudden flooding farther inland, such as happened in hurricane Katrina. The Dutch have shown that well-built dikes can hold back the sea, but poorer countries cannot afford such protection.

5 Another possibility is that climate change could reduce water supply in some regions. Consider a mid-latitude environment such as eastern Nebraska that averages 60 centimeters (24 inches) precipitation and 55 centimeters (22 inches) evapotranspiration. The 5 centimeters (2 inches) of precipitation that is not transpired by plants flow into streams and rivers. A small increase in evapotranspiration, due to a warmer climate, could sharply reduce water flow to the region's streams and rivers. Semiarid regions and densely populated subhumid areas depend on river flow for irrigation, drinking water, and waste removal. These areas might suffer severe water shortages if warming increases evapotranspiration and decreases river flow. However, if this warming brings greater precipitation, agriculture may be

helped rather than harmed. Agricultural production might be especially helped in areas currently receiving little precipitation. Warming could also lengthen the growing season in high-latitude areas and make agriculture possible in areas of Canada and Siberia where today it is not. A third possibility is that warming will increase storminess.

Should we attempt to halt global warming?

6 Although global warming is in progress and humans are significant contributors to the problem, we have not reached global consensus on how we should try to stop it or if we should stop it at all. Those who argue for immediate action emphasize the potentially severe consequences of warming in some areas. But it is hard to convince people to spend money to prevent an event that occurs over long periods of time rather than in the short term.

7 Reducing carbon dioxide concentrations will be difficult because we depend on fossil fuels in our daily lives, and energy producers employ many people and earn billions of dollars each year. Significantly reducing fossil-fuel use is possible only if we consume less energy or shift to alternative energy sources. An alternative to reducing fossil-fuel use is to try to trap and store (*sequester*) CO_2. Several alternatives are being discussed, from storing CO_2 in the deep ocean or underground to increasing photosynthesis by fertilizing plants in the ocean. Any of these alternatives would be expensive. Would people prefer to cut back on their use of coal-generated electricity or spend money on new ways to produce electricity? Either alternative is expensive and inconvenient.

8 Another reason for not acting to curb global warming is the belief that it may be easier to adapt to climatic change than to prevent it. People already adjust to changing weather, commodity prices, and technology from year to year, so why shouldn't we be able to adjust to climate change, too? The United States refused to join the Kyoto Protocol, an international treaty that would limit CO_2 emissions on the grounds that a strategy of adapting to global warming would be less costly and more effective than attempting to reduce it.

9 We must remember, though, that humans are not the only life on the planet. We are only one form of life and one part of many interacting ecosystems. Some animals and plants could not adapt to a climate change, and thus *our* human-environment interaction might be responsible for the extinction of other species. Is the possibility that we can adapt to climate change sufficient reason not to halt our contribution to global warming?

Copyright © 2012 by Pearson Education

Directions: Select the choice that best completes each of the following statements.

CHECKING YOUR COMPREHENSION

_____ 1. The central thought of this selection is that
- a. most scientists do not agree on the principal cause of global warming.
- b. global warming has not been proven to be related to human activity.
- c. average global temperatures have varied widely over millions of years.
- d. there are uncertainties about climate change and how we should respond to it.

_____ 2. The main idea of paragraph 2 is expressed in the
- a. first sentence.
- b. second sentence.
- c. third sentence.
- d. last sentence.

_____ 3. Figure A indicates that the world surface temperature was about 0.2 degrees *below* the mean in
- a. 1850.
- b. 1910.
- c. 1930.
- d. 1990.

_____ 4. Potential consequences of global warming include
- a. a worldwide rise in sea level of 1 to 5 meters.
- b. a reduced water supply in some regions.
- c. an increase in storminess.
- d. all of the above.

_____ 5. The main idea of paragraph 7 is that
- a. people cannot agree on how or whether to stop global warming.
- b. the energy industry employs many people and earns billions of dollars.
- c. several alternatives to reducing fossil-fuel use are being considered.
- d. reducing carbon dioxide concentrations will be difficult and expensive.

USING WHAT YOU KNOW ABOUT PATTERNS

_______ 6. The main pattern of organization followed in paragraph 2 is

a. example.

b. listing.

c. comparison/contrast.

d. process.

_______ 7. When the authors describe the consequences of global warming, the overall pattern they are following is

a. chronological order.

b. classification.

c. comparison/contrast.

d. cause/effect.

_______ 8. The transitional word or phrase that signals the cause/effect pattern in paragraph 5 is

a. such as.

b. due to.

c. however.

d. also.

_______ 9. In paragraph 5, the *cause* that the authors are discussing is

a. climate change.

b. water supply.

c. precipitation.

d. storminess.

_______ 10. In paragraphs 7–9, the *effect* of not acting to curb global warming might be

a. our daily dependence on fossil fuels.

b. the expense of alternative energy sources.

c. the belief that adapting to climate change is easier than preventing it.

d. the extinction of other species.

Copyright © 2012 by Pearson Education

USING CONTEXT CLUES AND WORD PARTS

_______ 11. In paragraph 1, the word **accumulated** means

a. added up.

b. altered.

c. lost.

d. declined.

_______ 12. In paragraph 5, the word **semiarid** means

a. overly dry.

b. not completely dry.

c. not at all dry.

d. completely dry.

_______ 13. In paragraph 5, the prefix of the word **subhumid** means

a. against.

b. apart.

c. below.

d. extra.

_______ 14. In paragraph 7, the word **consume** means

a. use.

b. waste.

c. eat.

d. gain.

_______ 15. In paragraph 7, the definition context clue given for the word **sequester** is

a. alternative.

b. reducing.

c. trap and store.

d. cut back.

REVIEWING DIFFICULT VOCABULARY

Directions: *Match each of the following words in column A from the Vocabulary Preview on page 319 with its meaning in column B.*

	Column A	Column B
_______	16. emissions	a. the total amount of water transferred from the earth into the atmosphere
_______	17. evapotranspiration	b. any product manufactured or grown
_______	18. photosynthesis	c. substances discharged into the air
_______	19. commodity	d. communities of plants and animals together with their environment
_______	20. ecosystems	e. the process by which green plants and other organisms make carbohydrates from carbon dioxide and water using light energy from the sun

THINKING CRITICALLY

1. What do you already know about the causes and effects of global warming? Did the information in this selection confirm or clarify any information you may have had?
2. Do you think the author is trying to influence your opinions in this selection? Why or why not?
3. How did the graph (Figure A) help you understand the subject? What trends can you see illustrated in the graph?

QUESTIONS FOR DISCUSSION

1. According to consensus, world average temperature could rise by a few degrees in the next century. Do you think this would affect your daily life enough to want to make changes now?
2. Discuss the possible positive consequences of climate change described in paragraph 5, such as improved agricultural conditions in some parts of the world. Do you think a potential benefit such as this outweighs the potential harm?

Copyright © 2012 by Pearson Education

3. What do you think is the best approach to global warming? Consider the options set forth in this selection, including consuming less energy, shifting to alternative energy sources, and adapting to climate change.

WRITING ACTIVITIES

1. Write a paragraph in response to the authors' question: Should we attempt to halt global warming?
2. In your opinion, which of the alternatives to reducing fossil-fuel use described in paragraph 7 seems most likely to succeed? Write a paragraph explaining your answer.
3. Do you agree with the reasoning behind the United States' decision not to join the Kyoto Protocol? Write a paragraph explaining your answer.
4. Watch one of these videos about the climate and oceans: http://climate.nasa.gov/ClimateReel/

   Compose a paragraph that summarizes the video and expresses your opinions, concerns, and suggestions related to this topic.

CHAPTER 8

Examining Comparison/Contrast and Cause/Effect Patterns

RECORDING YOUR PROGRESS

Test	Number Right		Score
Practice Test 8-1	________	× 10 =	________%
Practice Test 8-2	________	× 10 =	________%
Mastery Test 8-1	________	× 10 =	________%
Mastery Test 8-2	________	× 10 =	________%
Mastery Test 8-3	________	× 5 =	________%

GETTING MORE PRACTICE

PEARSON myreadinglab

To get more practice with Examining Patterns, go to http://www.myreadinglab.com and click on

> Study Plan
> Reading Skills
> Patterns of Organization

EVALUATING YOUR PROGRESS

PEARSON myreadinglab

To measure your progress after reading and viewing the information in the Review Materials section, complete the Practices and Tests in the Activities section. You can check your scores by clicking on the Gradebook tab.

Then, based on your performance in this chapter and/or on the MyReadingLab Practices and Tests, write your own evaluation.

YOUR EVALUATION: ____

____

____

____

____

Copyright © 2012 by Pearson Education

PART II

Critical Reading Skills

Copyright © 2012 by Pearson Education

THINKING ABOUT

Inference and Author's Purpose

What is happening in the photograph on this page? Most likely you said that an athlete has just won a race, but how did you know? No doubt, you used clues in the photograph such as the runner's attire, the finish line ribbon, and so forth.

What was the photographer's purpose in taking this photograph? That is, what did he or she want to show or emphasize? The smile on the athlete's face and his gestures are obvious and noticeable in the photograph. The photographer's purpose, then, may be to show the elation of victory. As you read text, you will also need to pick up on clues and "go beyond simple facts." This chapter will show you how to make inferences as you read and analyze the author's purpose.

C H A P T E R 9

Making Inferences and Analyzing the Author's Purpose

LEARNING GOALS

GOAL 1 Understand inference

GOAL 2 Make reasonable inferences

GOAL 3 Make inferences about graphics

GOAL 4 Learn to determine a writer's purpose

GOAL 5 Understand style and audience

GOAL 6 Examine denotative and connotative meanings

What Is Inference?

Understand inference

Just as you use inference when you study a photograph, you also use it when you try to figure out why a friend is sad or what an author's message is in a particular piece of writing. An **inference** is an educated guess or prediction about something unknown based on available facts and information. It is the logical connection that you draw between what you observe or know and what you do not know.

Here are a few everyday situations. Make an inference for each.

- A well-dressed man walks toward the front of your lecture hall on the first day of class.
- You see a young woman in a shopping mall wearing a wedding ring pushing a baby in a stroller with two young children following her.

In the first situation, a good inference might be that the man is the instructor because he is not dressed like the average student. However, it is possible that the man is a student who has an important appointment right after class. In the second situation, one inference is that the woman was married very young and had three children in a row; another possibility is that she is married but is just babysitting the children.

Copyright © 2012 by Pearson Education

When you make inferences about what you read, you go beyond what a writer says and consider what he or she *means*. You have already done this, to some extent, in Chapters 2 and 5 as you inferred the meanings of words from context (see pp. 49–59) and figured out implied main ideas (see pp. 165–193). Thus you know that writers may directly state some ideas but hint at others. It is left to the reader, then, to pick up on the clues or suggestions and to figure out the writer's unstated message. This chapter will show you how to do so.

How to Make Inferences

Make reasonable inferences

Making an inference is a thinking process. As you read, you are following the writer's thoughts. You are also alert for ideas that are suggested but not directly stated. Because inference is a logical thought process, there is no simple, step-by-step procedure to follow. Each inference depends on the situation, the facts provided, and the reader's knowledge and experience.

> **myreadinglab**
> To practice making inferences, go to
> > Study Plan
> > Reading Skills
> > Inference

However, here are a few guidelines to keep in mind as you read. These will help you get in the habit of looking beyond the factual level.

1. **Be sure you understand the literal meaning.** Before you can make inferences, you need a clear grasp of the facts, the writer's main ideas, and the supporting details.
2. **Notice details.** Often a particular detail provides a clue that will help you make an inference. When you spot a striking or unusual detail, ask yourself: Why did the writer include this piece of information? Remember that there are many kinds of details, such as descriptions, actions, and conversations.
3. **Add up the facts.** Consider all the facts taken together. Ask yourself: What is the writer trying to suggest with this set of facts? What do all these facts and ideas point toward?
4. **Look at the writer's choice of words.** A writer's word choice often suggests his or her attitude toward the subject. Notice, in particular, descriptive words, emotionally charged words, and words that are very positive or negative.
5. **Understand the writer's purpose.** An author's purpose, which is discussed later in this chapter, affects many aspects of a piece of writing. Ask yourself: Why did the author write this?
6. **Be sure your inference is supportable.** An inference must be based on fact. Make sure there is sufficient evidence to justify any inference you make.

Keep the preceding guidelines in mind as you read the following article about the Susan G. Komen Foundation and KFC chicken.

GREED, CANCER AND PINK KFC BUCKETS

1 We live in a world of profound contradictions. Some things are just unbelievably strange. At times I feel like I've found a way to adapt to the weirdness of the world, and then along comes something that just boggles my mind.

2 The largest grassroots breast cancer advocacy group in the world, a group called "Susan G. Komen for the Cure," has now partnered with the fast food chain KFC in a national "Buckets for the Cure" campaign. The program began last month and runs through the end of May.

3 KFC is taking every chance it can manufacture to trumpet the fact that it will donate 50 cents to Komen for every pink bucket of chicken sold.

4 For its part, Komen is announcing on its website that "KFC and Susan G. Komen for the Cure are teaming up . . . to . . . spread educational messaging via a major national campaign which will reach thousands of communities served by nearly 5,000 KFC restaurants."

5 Educational messaging, indeed. How often do you think this "messaging" provides information about the critical importance a healthy diet plays in maintaining a healthy weight and preventing cancer? How often do you think it refers in any way to the many studies that, according to the National Cancer Institute's website, "have shown that an increased risk of developing colorectal, pancreatic, and breast cancer is associated with high intakes of well-done, fried or barbecued meats?"

6 If you guessed zero, you're right.

7 Meanwhile, the American Institute for Cancer Research reports that 60 to 70 percent of all cancers can be prevented with lifestyle changes. Their number one dietary recommendation is to: "Choose predominantly plant-based diets rich in a variety of vegetables and fruits, legumes and minimally processed starchy staple foods." Does that sound like pink buckets of fried chicken?

8 Pardon me for being cynical, but I have to ask, if Komen is going to partner with KFC, why not take it a step further and partner with a cigarette company? They could sell pink packages of cigarettes, donating a few cents from each pack while claiming "each pack you smoke brings us closer to the day cancer is vanquished forever."

9 Whose brilliant idea was it that buying fried chicken by the bucket is an effective way to fight breast cancer? One breast cancer advocacy group, Breast Cancer Action, thinks the Komen/KFC campaign is so egregious that they call it "pinkwashing," another sad example of commercialism draped in pink ribbons. "Make no mistake," they say, "every pink bucket purchase will do more to benefit KFC's bottom line than it will to cure breast cancer."

10 One thing is hard to dispute. In partnering with KFC, Susan B. Komen for the Cure has shown itself to be numbingly oblivious to the role of diet in cancer prevention.

11 Of course it's not hard to understand KFC's motives. They want to look good. But recent publicity the company has been getting hasn't been helping. For one thing, the company keeps taking hits for the unhealthiness of its food.

Copyright © 2012 by Pearson Education

Just last month, KFC came out with its new Double Down sandwiches. The products were derided by just about every public health organization for their staggering levels of salt, calories and artery-clogging fat.

12 Then there's the squeamish matter of the treatment of the birds who end up in KFC's buckets, pink or otherwise. People for the Ethical Treatment of Animals (PETA) has an entire website devoted to what they call Kentucky Fried Cruelty, but you don't have to be an animal activist to be horrified by how the company treats chickens, if you lift the veil of the company's PR and see what actually takes place.

13 When PETA sent investigators with hidden cameras into a KFC "Supplier of the Year" slaughterhouse in Moorefield, West Virginia, what they found was enough to make KFC choke on its own pink publicity stunts. Workers were caught on video stomping on chickens, kicking them and violently slamming them against floors and walls. Workers were also filmed ripping the animals' beaks off, twisting their heads off, spitting tobacco into their eyes and mouths, spray-painting their faces, and squeezing their bodies so hard that the birds expelled feces—all while the chickens were still alive.

14 Dan Rather echoed the views of many who saw the footage when he said on the CBS Evening News, "There's no mistaking what the video depicts: cruelty to animals, chickens horribly mistreated before they're slaughtered for a fast-food chain."

15 KFC, naturally, did everything they could to keep the footage from being aired, but their efforts failed. In fact, the video from the investigation ended up being broadcast by TV stations around the world, as well as on all three national evenings news shows, *Good Morning America*, and every one of the major cable news networks. Plus, more than a million people subsequently watched the footage on PETA's website.

16 It wasn't just animal activists who condemned the fast food chain for the level of animal cruelty displayed at KFC's "Supplier of the Year" slaughterhouse. Dr. Temple Grandin, perhaps the meat industry's leading farmed-animal welfare expert, said, "The behavior of the plant employees was atrocious." Dr. Ian Duncan, a University of Guelph professor of applied ethology and an original member of KFC's own animal-welfare advisory council, wrote, "This tape depicts scenes of the worst cruelty I have ever witnessed against chickens . . . and it is extremely hard to accept that this is occurring in the United States of America."

17 KFC claims, on its website, that its animal-welfare advisory council "has been a key factor in formulating our animal welfare program." But Dr. Duncan, along with five other former members of this advisory council, say otherwise. They all resigned in disgust over the company's refusal to take animal welfare seriously. Adele Douglass, one of those who resigned, said in an SEC filing reported on by the *Chicago Tribune* that KFC "never had any meetings. They never asked any advice, and then they touted to the press that they had this animal-welfare advisory committee. I felt like I was being used."

18 You can see why KFC would be eager to jump on any chance to improve its public image, and why the company would want to capitalize on any opportunity to associate itself in the public mind with the fight against breast cancer. What's far more mystifying is why an organization with as much public trust as Susan B. Komen for the Cure would jeopardize public confidence in its authenticity. As someone once said, it takes a lifetime to build a reputation, but only 15 minutes to lose it.

—Robbins et al., "KFC Buckets," HuffingtonPost.com

Of course you've realized the author is outraged by the idea of the Komen foundation partnering with KFC and believes KFC has its own self-interest at heart in promoting the pink buckets. Let's look at some of the clues the writer gives that lead to this inference.

- **Literal meaning and facts:** The author discusses the mission of the Komen foundation, the type of food KFC sells, reports about KFC abuse of animals, and the dietary recommendations surrounding cancer wellness.
- **Descriptive details:** The selection describes how KFC donates only 50 cents per bucket to the Komen foundation and describes the bad publicity KFC has recently gotten, including details about the cruelty to the chickens used in their food.
- **Word choice:** The author uses the term *pinkwashing* to show disdain for the way both organizations are acting. He describes KFC food as "artery-clogging" and having "staggering" levels of unhealthy ingredients. He uses vivid imagery to show how KFC workers treat the birds.
- **Writer's purpose:** The author wrote this to call attention to the hypocrisy displayed by both KFC and Komen Foundation. An organization committed to curing breast cancers is pairing with a company that produces food that actually increases cancer risk. KFC has an image problem and is using the Komen Foundation to make it look good.

EXERCISE 9-1 Understanding Inferences

Directions: *Read each of the following passages. Based on the information contained in the passage, use inference to determine whether the statements that follow it are likely to be true (T) or false (F). Write your answer in the space provided.*

A. "TARGETING INNER-CITY CONSUMERS"

Cigarette, beer, and fast-food marketers have generated controversy in recent years by their attempts to target inner-city minority consumers. For example, McDonald's and other chains have drawn criticism for pitching their high-fat, salt-laden fare to low-income, urban residents. Similarly,

Copyright © 2012 by Pearson Education

R.J. Reynolds took heavy flak in the early 1990s when it announced plans to market Uptown, a menthol cigarette targeted toward low-income blacks. It quickly dropped the brand in the face of a loud public outcry and heavy pressure from African-American leaders.

—adapted from Armstrong and Kotler, *Marketing: An Introduction*, p. 192

_______ 1. R.J. Reynolds withdrew its ads because it was concerned about the risk of lung cancer among low-income blacks.

_______ 2. Low-income urban consumers are fast food consumers.

_______ 3. McDonald's salt-laden foods include burgers and fries.

_______ 4. These companies have never in the past targeted any specialized groups.

_______ 5. Due to the outcry, McDonald's began offering healthier choices.

B. "IS LAUGHTER THE BEST MEDICINE?"

Lucy went to the hospital to visit Emma, a neighbor who had broken her hip. The first thing Lucy saw when the elevator door opened at the third floor was a clown, with an enormous orange nose, dancing down the hall, pushing a colorfully decorated cart. The clown stopped in front of Lucy, bowed, and then somersaulted to the nurses' station. A cluster of patients cheered. Most of them were in wheelchairs or on crutches. Upon asking for directions, Lucy learned that Emma was in the "humor room," where the film *Blazing Saddles* was about to start.

Since writer Norman Cousins's widely publicized recovery from a debilitating and usually incurable disease of the connective tissue, humor has gained new respectability in hospital wards around the country. Cousins, the long-time editor of the *Saturday Review,* with the cooperation of his physician, supplemented his regular medical therapy with a steady diet of Marx brothers movies and *Candid Camera* film clips. Although he never claimed that laughter alone effected his cure, Cousins is best remembered for his passionate support of the notion that, if negative emotions can cause distress, then humor and positive emotions can enhance the healing process.

—Zimbardo and Gerrig, *Psychology and Life,* p. 501

_______ 6. The clown was at the hospital to celebrate a patient's birthday.

_______ 7. *Blazing Saddles* and Marx brothers movies would be found in the comedy section of a video store.

_______ 8. Cousins believed that humor should be only a part of a person's health-care plan.

_______ 9. Lucy watched the movie with Emma.

_______ 10. Emma probably used a wheelchair or crutches to reach the humor room.

EXERCISE 9-2 Using Inferences

Directions: *After reading the following selection, select the choice that best completes each of the statements that follow.*

AVATAR FANTASY LIFE: THE BLURRING LINES OF REALITY

1 Dissatisfied with your current life? Would you like to become someone else? Maybe someone rich? Maybe someone with no responsibilities? You can. Join a world populated with virtual people and live out your fantasy.

2 For some, the appeal is strong. *Second Life*, one of several Internet sites that offer an alternative virtual reality, has exploded in popularity. Of its 8 million "residents," 450,000 spend twenty to forty hours a week in their second life.

3 To start your second life, you select your avatar, a kind of digital hand puppet, to be your persona in this virtual world. Your avatar comes in just a basic form, although you can control its movements just fine. But that bare body certainly won't do. You will want to clothe it. For this, you have your choice of outfits for every occasion. Although you buy them from other avatars in virtual stores, you have to spend real dollars. You might want some hair, too. For that, too, you'll have your choice of designers. And again, you'll spend real dollars. And you might want to have a sex organ. There is even a specialty store for that.

4 All equipped the way you want to be?

5 Then it is time to meet other avatars, the virtual personas of real-life people. In this virtual world, they buy property, open businesses, and interact with one another. They share stories, talk about their desires in life, and have drinks in virtual bars.

6 Avatars flirt, too. Some even date and marry.

7 For most people, this second life is just an interesting game. They come and go, as if playing *Tomb Raider* or *World of Warcraft* now and then. Some people, though, get so caught up in their virtual world that their real world shrinks in appeal, and they neglect friends and family. That is, they neglect their real friends and family, but remain attentive to their virtual friends and family. As the virtual replaces the real, the virtual becomes real and the real fades into nonreality.

—Henslin, *Sociology: A Down-to-Earth Approach*, p. 153

Copyright © 2012 by Pearson Education

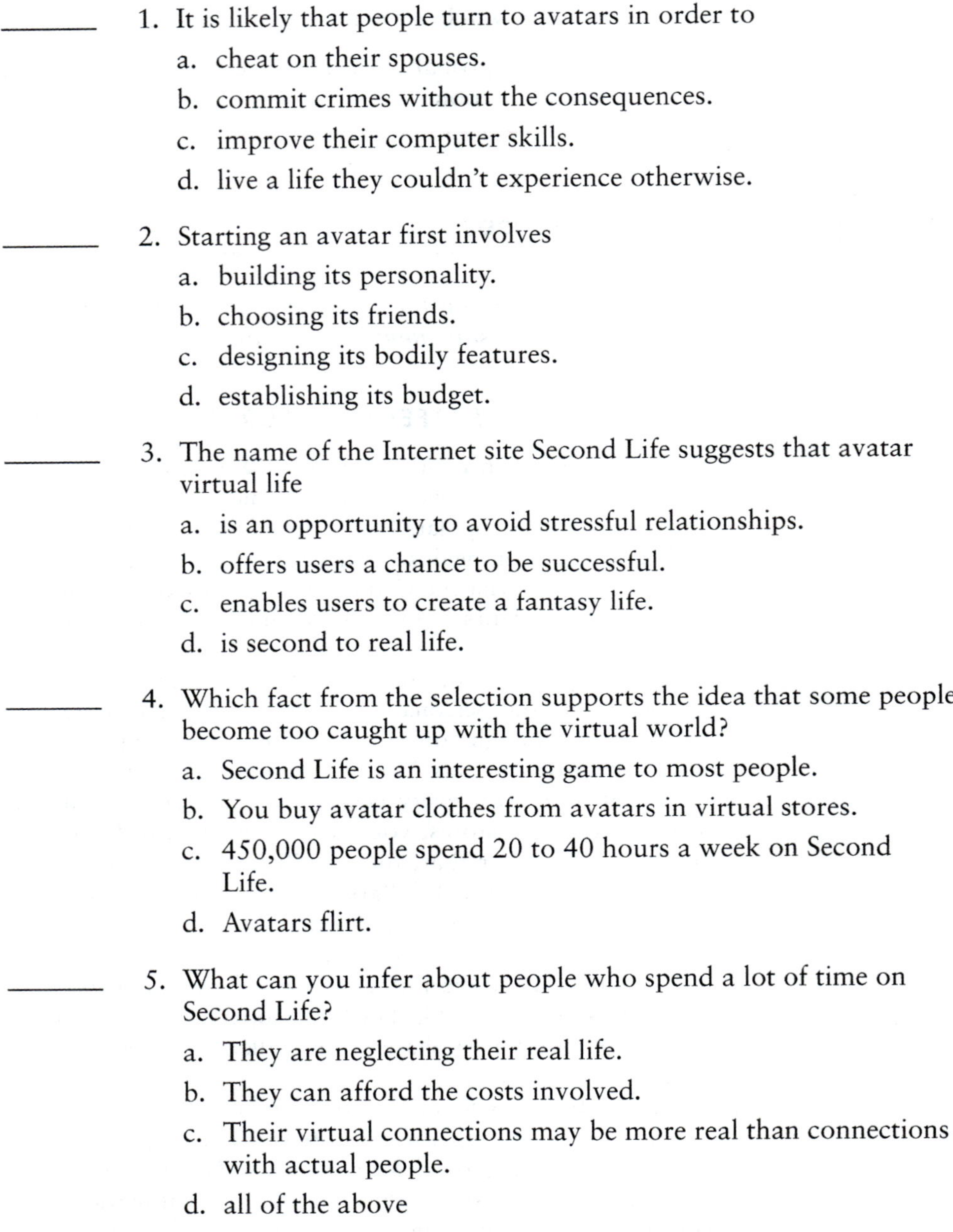

_______ 1. It is likely that people turn to avatars in order to

a. cheat on their spouses.
b. commit crimes without the consequences.
c. improve their computer skills.
d. live a life they couldn't experience otherwise.

_______ 2. Starting an avatar first involves

a. building its personality.
b. choosing its friends.
c. designing its bodily features.
d. establishing its budget.

_______ 3. The name of the Internet site Second Life suggests that avatar virtual life

a. is an opportunity to avoid stressful relationships.
b. offers users a chance to be successful.
c. enables users to create a fantasy life.
d. is second to real life.

_______ 4. Which fact from the selection supports the idea that some people become too caught up with the virtual world?

a. Second Life is an interesting game to most people.
b. You buy avatar clothes from avatars in virtual stores.
c. 450,000 people spend 20 to 40 hours a week on Second Life.
d. Avatars flirt.

_______ 5. What can you infer about people who spend a lot of time on Second Life?

a. They are neglecting their real life.
b. They can afford the costs involved.
c. Their virtual connections may be more real than connections with actual people.
d. all of the above

Making Inferences About Graphics

Make inferences about graphics

Graphics present a large amount of information in compact form. However, it is your responsibility as a reader to interpret this volume of information. In textbooks, on occasion, the accompanying print text will offer some of the ideas the author wants to emphasize by including the graphic. If this text is available, always read it before closely studying the graphic. Other times, however, the author does not provide commentary and the interpretation is solely up to you. The form of the graphic often suggests what the author is trying to show about the data it presents. The chart below lists several types of graphics and suggests the purpose of each.

Type of Graphic	Purpose
Tables	Tables often classify information. A table may classify the number of calories required based on age, gender, and activity level, for example. Tables also allow you to make comparisons easily.
Bar Graphs	Bar graphs often make comparisons between quantities or amounts. A bar graph may compare the rates of extinction of birds and mammals over 400 years.
Circle Graphs	Circle graphs show part–whole relationships. A circle graph may show how the population of the United States is divided among various racial/ethnic groups.
Linear Graphs	A linear graph plots information along vertical and horizontal axes, with one or more variables plotted on each. A linear graphs allows you to make comparisons between the variables. A linear graph may track the number of divorces from 1890 to 2010, allowing you to observe increases and decreases in the divorce rate in various decades.
Diagrams	A diagram explains an idea, object, or process by outlining it in visual form, showing parts or steps. A diagram may show how the food chain works or how the AIDS virus spreads, for instance.

Copyright © 2012 by Pearson Education

EXERCISE 9-3 Analyzing Graphics

Directions: Interpret each of the following graphics by identifying its purpose and the trends it shows.

1. **CommuniCo: A Corporation's Preferred Communication Media**

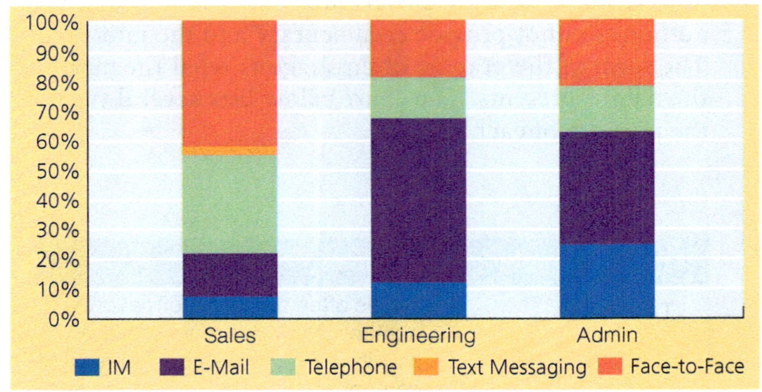

Courtland L. Bovée and John V. Thill, *Business Communication Today*, Ninth Edition, © 2008, Figure 12.8d (p. 376). Reproduced in print and electronic formats by permission of Pearson Education, Ins. Upper Saddle River, New Jersey.

Purpose: ______________________________

Trends: ______________________________

2. **How Americans Spend Their Free Time**

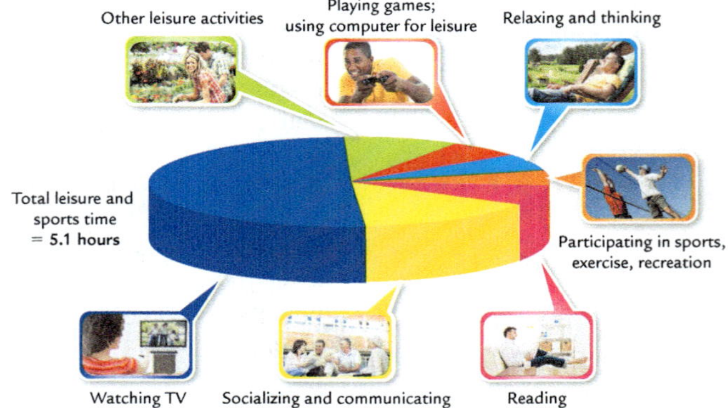

Note: Data include all persons age 15 and over. Data include all days of the week.

Source: Bureau of Labor Statistics.

—Baird, *Think Psychology*, p. 280

Purpose: ______________________________

Trends: ______________________________

Understanding a Writer's Purpose

Learn to determine a writer's purpose

myreadinglab
To practice understanding a writer's purpose, go to
> Study Plan
> Reading Skills
> Purpose and Tone

Writers have many different reasons or purposes for writing. These purposes affect their style of writing, the language they use, and the details they include. Once you understand a writer's purpose, it becomes easier to make inferences about a particular piece of writing.

Read the following statements and try to decide why each was written:

1. Maria Montessori founded her first school for young children in Italy in 1906. Today there are thousands of Montessori schools throughout the world.
2. *New Baked Fat-Free Spicy Chips.* Finally a tasty snack without the fat. We bake them instead of frying and add your favorite spices. Try a bag today.
3. Children tell it like it is . . . sometimes to the embarrassment of their parents.
4. In case of an emergency, remain calm and proceed in an orderly manner to the nearest exit.

The statements above were written (1) to give information, (2) to persuade you to buy chips, (3) to amuse you and make a comment on human behavior, and (4) to give instructions.

In each of the examples, the writer's purpose was fairly clear, as it will be in most textbooks, newspaper articles, and reference books. However, in many other types of writing, authors have less obvious purposes. In these cases, an author's purpose must be inferred.

Suppose a writer says, "The recent actions of the president of the United States should be closely examined." You cannot tell whether the writer's purpose is to criticize presidential actions, or to suggest that the actions should be studied carefully and used in making future policy decisions.

Sometimes a writer wants to express an opinion indirectly or to encourage readers to think about a particular issue or problem. Writers achieve their purposes by controlling what they say and how they say it.

EXERCISE 9-4 Identifying the Author's Purpose

Directions: *Based on the title of each of the following articles, predict the author's purpose.*

1. Changing Habits: How Online Shopping Can Change Your Life

____

2. I Got Straight A's, but I Wasn't Happy

____

3. Animals Can't Speak: We Must Speak for Them

____

Copyright © 2012 by Pearson Education

4. Guns Don't Kill People: People Kill People

____

5. What the Bible Says About the End of the World

____

6. Sources of Drug Information

____

7. Holy Week in Spain

____

8. Two Famous Twentieth-Century Composers

____

9. Internet Scams: You Could Be Next

____

10. Biofuels: A Look to the Future

____

Considering Style and Intended Audience

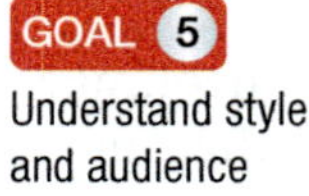

Understand style and audience

Are you able to recognize a friend just by his or her voice? Can you identify family members by their footsteps? You are able to do so because each person's voice and footsteps are unique. Have you noticed that a piece of writing has unique characteristics as well? One selection may include many examples; another may have few. One may have relatively short sentences, whereas another may use long, complicated ones. The characteristics that make a piece of writing unique are known as **style**. By changing style, writers can create different effects.

Writers may vary their styles to suit their intended audiences. For example, someone writing an article on the latest medical research for a newspaper or general magazine, such as *Time* or *Newsweek,* would use fairly straightforward language and would be careful to explain or define any uncommon medical or technical terms. The same person, writing for medical doctors in *JAMA: The Journal of the American Medical Association* could assume that readers would be familiar with the subject and thus would use more sophisticated language and details.

Depending on the group of people for whom an author is writing, he or she may change the level of language, choice of words, and method of presentation.

EXERCISE 9-5 Identifying Intended Audience

Directions: *After reading each of the following statements, select the choice that best describes the audience for whom each was written.*

_______ 1. Don't worry. Many youngsters experience a case of hives sometime during childhood. Usually the hives last for three to four days and then disappear. You may never know what caused them.

a. medical students
b. pediatricians
c. parents
d. pharmacists

_______ 2. The abortion debate has taken away resources and attention from other important issues such as high Caesarian rates, poor child-care options, and employer discrimination against working mothers.

a. pregnant teenagers
b. high-school health instructors
c. scientists performing stem cell research
d. people interested in women's rights

_______ 3. Now available—homeworkhelper.com—let our experts instantly provide you with "almost perfect" homework.

a. parents looking for a tutor
b. teachers who need lesson plan ideas
c. students who have trouble completing their homework assignments on time and well
d. guidance counselors looking for resources for students

_______ 4. Theories of music origin come in two basic varieties: structural models and functional models. Structural models look to the acoustic properties of music as outgrowths of homologous precursor functions, whereas functional models look to the adaptive roles of music as determinants of its structural design features.

a. students of music
b. pop music stars
c. piano tuners
d. professors of music history

_______ 5. As a computer user, you can save money on costly service visits and calls by learning to troubleshoot and fix simple problems yourself.

a. network administrators
b. computer store managers
c. computer hackers
d. computer owners who are unfamiliar with simple computer problems

Copyright © 2012 by Pearson Education

Analyzing Language: Denotation and Connotation

Examine denotative and connotative meanings

You already know that writers use different words to achieve different purposes. A reporter writing an objective newspaper account of a murder might use very different words than would a brother of the slain person. In this section you will learn more about the meanings of words and how they are clues to a writer's purpose.

Which of the following would you like to be: shrewd, brainy, tricky, smart, ingenious, sly, or resourceful? Each of these words has the same basic meaning: "clever and quick-witted." But each has a different *shade* of meaning. *Ingenious* suggests being skillful and original in idea formation. *Sly,* on the other hand, suggests secrecy, mischief, and deceit.

This example shows that words have two levels of meaning—a literal meaning and an additional shade of meaning. These two levels of meaning are called denotation and connotation. A word's **denotation** is the meaning stated in the dictionary—its literal meaning. A word's **connotation** is the additional implied meanings that a word may take on. A word's connotation often carries either a positive or negative, favorable or unfavorable, impression. The words *tricky* and *sly* have a negative connotation because they imply deception and dishonesty. *Smart* and *resourceful* have a positive connotation because they suggest intelligence and creativity.

Here are a few more examples. Would you prefer to be described as *old* or *mature?* As *centered* or *self-absorbed?* As *fun* or *amusing?* Notice that each pair of words has a similar denotation, but each word within the pair has a different connotation.

Depending on the words they choose, writers can suggest favorable or unfavorable impressions of the person, object, or event they are describing. For example, through the writer's choice of words, the two sentences below create two entirely different impressions. As you read them, underline the words that have a positive or negative connotation.

- The war protesters stormed through the streets, causing major traffic gridlock.
- The peace march spanned several blocks as motorists looked on.

It is important to pay attention to a writer's choice of words, especially when you are reading persuasive material. Often a writer may communicate subtle or hidden messages or encourage you to feel positive or negative toward the subject.

Read the following paragraph from Martin Luther King Jr.'s "Letter from Birmingham Jail" and, as you read, underline the words that have a strong positive or negative connotation.

> We have waited for more than 340 years for our constitutional and God-given rights. The nations of Asia and Africa are moving with jetlike

speed toward gaining political independence, but we still creep at horse-and-buggy pace toward gaining a cup of coffee at a lunch counter. I guess it is easy for those who have never felt the stinging darts of segregation to say, "Wait." But when you have seen vicious mobs lynch your mothers and fathers at will and drown your sisters and brothers at whim; when you have seen hate-filled policemen curse, kick, and even kill your black brothers and sisters; when you see the vast majority of your 20 million Negro brothers smothering in an airtight cage of poverty in the midst of an affluent society; when you suddenly find your tongue twisted and your speech stammering as you seek to explain to your six-year-old daughter why she can't go to the public amusement park that has just been advertised on television, and see tears welling up in her eyes when she is told that Funtown is closed to colored children, and see ominous clouds of inferiority beginning to form in her little mental sky, and see her beginning to distort her personality by developing an unconscious bitterness toward white people . . . then you will understand why we find it difficult to wait.

—King, "Letter from Birmingham Jail," *Why We Can't Wait,* p. 363

EXERCISE 9-6 Analyzing Connotative Meanings

Directions: *For each of the following pairs of words, underline the word with the more positive connotation.*

1. fictitious — false
2. persistent — stubborn
3. absentminded — preoccupied
4. decontaminate — cleanse
5. nasty — disagreeable
6. disturbance — riot
7. whimsical — scatterbrained
8. flimsy — fragile
9. bother — harass
10. old-fashioned — antiquated

Copyright © 2012 by Pearson Education

CRITICAL THINKING CHALLENGE

In this section is an excerpt from a blog on which to practice your critical thinking skills. Review the "Tips for Reading Blogs" and use the steps below to guide your reading and your response.

TIPS for Reading Blogs

When reading blogs, be sure to

- **Understand the blogger's purpose.** Determine what the main reason or intent of the blog is and use this to help you evaluate what it says.
- **Separate fact from opinion.** Bloggers are usually not fact-checked by anyone, so it is up to the reader to evaluate the information presented.
- **Follow links.** Bloggers often include links to other Web sites where you can find more information, get background information, and read related blogs.

Thinking Critically as You Read

1. **Reading, Highlighting, and Annotating.** As you read, highlight the key ideas. Write marginal notes to record your thinking as you read. Include comments, reactions, questions, opposing ideas, and so forth.
2. **Summarizing.** (Refer to Chapter 6, page 216.) Write a one-paragraph summary of the reading.
3. **Thinking Critically.**
   a. Identify at least three words that have strong connotative meanings. (See Chapter 2, page 69 and Chapter 9, page 344.)
   b. Evaluate the writer's main ideas. Identify at least three facts and three opinions. (See Chapter 3, page 105.)
   c. Study the writer's choice of supporting details. Does his choice suggest an emphasis, bias, or a particular viewpoint toward the topic? (See Chapter 4, page 139.) If so, please explain.
   d. Study the visual that accompanies the reading. What does it contribute to the reading? What does the writer's choice of this visual suggest about his position on or attitude toward the topic? (See Chapter 5, page 175.)
   e. What thought pattern is used to organize the reading? How does the writer use the pattern to organize his ideas? Choose a different pattern from that used in the reading. Consider how this pattern might have affected the reading's content and/or your response to the reading.

'Green Exercise' Better than Just Plain Exercise

By Keith Goetzman

The sight of open, untrashed green space while exercising is a balm for our minds and bodies, a group of U.K. researchers has concluded. In a study published in the *International Journal of Environmental Health Research*, five groups of 20 subjects exercised on a treadmill while watching a series of scenes projected on a wall.

Four types of scenes were tested—"rural pleasant," "rural unpleasant," "urban pleasant" and "urban unpleasant." The subjects' blood pressure and two psychological measures—self-esteem and mood—were measured before and after the treadmill sessions. The researchers write:

There was a clear effect of both exercise and different scenes on blood pressure, self-esteem and mood. Exercise alone significantly reduced blood pressure, increased self-esteem, and had a positive significant effect on 4 of 6 mood measures. Both rural and urban pleasant scenes produced a significantly greater positive effect on self-esteem than the exercise-only control. This shows the synergistic effect of green exercise in both rural and urban environments. By contrast, both rural and urban unpleasant scenes reduced the positive effects of exercise on self-esteem. The rural unpleasant scenes had the most dramatic

effect, depressing the beneficial effects of exercise on three different measures of mood. It appears that threats to the countryside depicted in rural unpleasant scenes have a greater negative effect on mood than urban unpleasant scenes.

So: Exercise in itself is a good thing. Exercise in pleasant surroundings is an even better thing. The researchers muse on the societal implications of this:

We conclude that green exercise has important implications for public and environmental health. A fitter and emotionally more content population would clearly cost the economy less as well as reducing individual human suffering. . . . Thus increasing support for and access to a wide range of green exercise activities for all sectors of society should produce substantial economic and public health benefits. Such support could include the provision and promotion of healthy walks projects, exercise on prescription, healthy school environments, healthy travel to school projects, green views in hospitals, city farms and community gardens, urban green space, and outdoor leisure activities in the countryside.

The interesting thing to me is that none of the subjects actually went outdoors—they simply looked at images of the outdoors. If the mere sight of green space makes us feel better, just imagine what it does when you incorporate all the sensory intangibles of the physical experience: a fresh breeze, fragrant wildflowers, wildlife sightings, clouds rolling past, perhaps a beautiful sunrise or sunset. Maybe for their next study, the researchers will get people off their treadmills and onto their feet or bicycles.

In the meantime, I'm going to bicycle home past a mixture of "urban pleasant" and "urban unpleasant" scenes and on my weekend seek out a nice long, uninterrupted stretch of "rural pleasant."

(Thanks, EcoVelo.)

—Goetzman, *Utne Reader*

Copyright © 2012 by Pearson Education

f. What is the author's purpose for writing? (See Chapter 9, page 341.)

g. What conclusion does the author want you to draw about exercising outdoors? What facts support this idea?

h. What inference does the author want you to draw about green exercise and public health and health costs? What facts support this in the selection?

4. **Responding to Ideas**
Write a paragraph sharing your reactions and response to one or more of the ideas presented in the reading. Refer to your marginal notes.

SELF-TEST SUMMARY

To test yourself, cover up the Answer column with a sheet of paper and answer each question listed in the left column. Evaluate each of your answers as you work by sliding the paper down and comparing your answer with what is printed in the Answer column.

	Question	Answer
GOAL 1	What is inference?	Inferences are logical conclusions drawn from what you read or observe.
GOAL 2	How can you make reasonable inferences?	Make inferences by understanding the literal meaning, noticing details, adding up the facts, examining word choice, understanding the writer's purpose, and examining supporting evidence.
GOAL 3	How do you interpret graphics?	Interpret graphics by examining the title, studying the organization, identifying the variables, noting the scale of measurement, identifying trends and patterns, and reading the source and footnotes.
GOAL 4	What is a writer's purpose?	A writer's purpose is the author's reason for writing.
GOAL 5	How are style and intended audience related?	Writers adjust their writing style to suit their intended audience.
GOAL 6	What are denotative and connotative meaning?	A denotative meaning is the literal, dictionary definition of a word. Connotative meanings are the additional implied meanings a word can have.

Copyright © 2012 by Pearson Education

PRACTICE TEST 9-1

NAME ______________________ SECTION ______________________

DATE ______________________ SCORE ______________________

Inference and Author's Purpose

***Directions:** After reading the following passage, select the choice that best completes each of the statements that follow.*

Scar

The mark on my face made me who I am

1 Growing up, I had a scar on my face—a perfect arrow in the center of my cheek, pointing at my left eye. I got it when I was 3, long before I knew that scars were a bad thing, especially for a girl. I knew only that my scar brought me attention and tenderness and candy.

2 As I got older I began to take pride in my scar, in part to stop bullies from taunting me, but mainly to counter the assumption that I should feel embarrassed. It's true, I was embarrassed the first couple of times someone pointed at my cheek and asked "What's that?" or called me Scarface. But the more I heard how unfortunate my scar was, the more I found myself liking it.

3 When I turned 15, my parents—on the advice of a plastic surgeon—decided it was time to operate on what was now a thick, shiny red scar.

4 "But I don't mind the scar, really," I told my father as he drove me home from the local mall, explaining that I would have the surgery during my summer vacation. "I don't need surgery." It had been years since I'd been teased. And my friends, along with my boyfriend at the time, felt as I did—that my scar was unique and almost pretty in its own way. After so many years, it was a part of me.

5 "You do need surgery," my father said, his eyes on the road, his lips tight.

6 "But I like it," I told him. "I don't want to get rid of it."

7 "You need surgery," he said again, and he lowered his voice. "It's a deformity."

8 I don't know what hurt more that day: hearing my father call my scar a deformity or realizing that it didn't matter to him how I felt about it.

9 I did have plastic surgery that summer. They cut out the left side of the arrow, leaving a thinner, zigzag scar that blended into the lines of my face when I smiled. The following summer they did the same to the right side of the arrow. Finally, when I was 18, the surgeon sanded my cheek smooth.

10 In my late 20s, I took a long look at my scar, something I hadn't done in years. It was still visible in the right light, but no one asked me about it anymore. I examined the small steplike pattern and the way it made my cheek dimple when I smiled. As I leaned in awkwardly toward the mirror, I felt a sudden sadness.

11 There was something powerful about my scar and the defiant, proud person I became because of it. I have never been quite so strong since they cut it out.

—Audet, "Scar," from *The Sun,* p. 96

_______ 1. The central thought of the reading is that

a. the author's scar contributed to her self-identity and gave her power.

b. parents should not make decisions for their children.

c. people really do not notice deformities.

d. beauty is in the eye of the beholder.

_______ 2. The writer's primary purpose is to

a. provide autobiographical information.

b. explain how she feels about her scar.

c. give a general overview of plastic surgery.

d. criticize her father.

_______ 3. What does the author mean when she says "scars were a bad thing, especially for a girl"?

a. Faces reveal the inner person.

b. Girls poke fun at other girls.

c. Beauty is important for girls and a scar is thought to detract from beauty.

d. Boys do not care about how they look.

_______ 4. The meaning of the word **taunting** in paragraph 2 is

a. complimenting.

b. arguing with.

c. teasing.

d. accompanying.

_______ 5. This article seems written primarily for which of the following audiences?

a. plastic surgery patients

b. audiences interested in personal stories

c. children with serious physical disabilities

d. parents who make decisions for their children

_______ 6. The connotation of the word **deformity** (paragraph 7) is

a. strong and forceful act.

b. frequently recurring problem.

c. unsightly, unpleasant disability.

d. unfortunate accident.

Copyright © 2012 by Pearson Education

_______ 7. Which word best describes the author's attitude toward her scar?

a. positive

b. negative

c. uncertain

d. hateful

_______ 8. Based on the reading, the author is likely to agree that

a. plastic surgeons should be more sensitive to their patients' needs.

b. parents seldom have their children's best interest in mind.

c. disabled people should be pitied.

d. disabilities can be a source of strength.

_______ 9. The father probably wanted his daughter to have surgery because he

a. thought she would look better without the scar.

b. thought the scar disturbed her.

c. blamed himself that she had a scar.

d. knew she would be happier in the long run.

_______ 10. The author helps readers make inferences about the father's attitude toward the scar by

a. examples.

b. opinion of others.

c. dialogue.

d. comparisons.

NAME ______________________ SECTION ______________________
DATE ______________________ SCORE ______________________

Inference and Author's Purpose

***Directions:** After reading the following passage, select the choice that best completes each of the statements that follow.*

Remembrance of Foods Past

Thriving in old age isn't simply a matter of nutrition—it's a matter of taste

1 Everywhere we look another edible schoolyard is sprouting. In the most progressive schools, children are bringing their produce into the cafeteria to clean it and cook it. Junk food and soda vending machines are disappearing; some districts even outlaw lunchtime visits to fast-food restaurants.

2 The national concern for our children is important, and it's one that I share. When my daughter was small I tried to get the local school district to allow more than 20 minutes for lunch; the kids would wolf down their food in eagerness for a few extra minutes of recess. These days my daughter is lucky enough to be at a college where healthy eating is considered part of the larger education. But I am still thinking about institutional meals—except now at the other end of the age spectrum.

3 Last spring my mother had to enter long-term care. She is someone who always cared passionately about food. In her hands a simple roast chicken was transformed into a dish that both embodied longing and fulfilled desire. And oh, her sweet and sour meatballs! Now she can no longer command her kitchen; she is presented with three generic meals a day. I recognize that the trays are put together with an eye to variety as well as nutrition. But even in her diminished state she discerns what tastes good and what does not, and she responds accordingly.

4 This experience is shared by many people who find themselves in institutional care at the end of their lives. Yet hardly anyone is speaking about better food for the elderly. Their eating habits are not a public health issue, like type 2 diabetes or childhood obesity. But providing pleasure through food is not frivolous; what and how we eat are crucial to the quality of our lives.

5 The nutritionists who work from charts to devise nutritionally sound menus, balanced in the standard American way with that sacred trinity of protein, vegetable, and starch, are missing something. Although this kind of quantitative analysis serves patients' physical needs, it falls very short on their mnemonic ones—their rich memories. Swedish studies have shown that the foods served in old-age homes make a huge difference in the way people feel, even those suffering from dementia. Familiar foods can stimulate memories and improve cognition. The aromas and flavors of times past enable us to reconnect with the world, reawakening appetite not only for food but for life.

Copyright © 2012 by Pearson Education

6 Standardized cooking is admittedly more efficient, and individualized attention would require additional expense. But we're caring for people here, not manufacturing something. It should not be too much for caregivers to ask a few more questions when they are assessing each person. *What are your culinary traditions? Do you have any comfort foods? How do you feel about broccoli and beets?* These questions are so basic that no one ever thinks to ask them, but a meal that triggers a positive emotional response can make an enormous difference in a person's day.

7 Thriving in old age is not simply a question of calorie counts and nutritional supplements. People of all ages deserve to enjoy their meals. Food should not be seen solely as sustenance, a means to keep people alive, but also as an opportunity to connect people in their declining years with memories they hold close.

—Goldstein, from *Gastronomica* and *Utne Reader,* pp. iii–iv

_______ 1. In paragraph 1, the word **progressive** means

a. well-funded.
b. rural.
c. forward-thinking.
d. high-achieving.

_______ 2. The central thought of the entire passage is that

a. familiar foods can help the elderly.
b. school lunches need improvement.
c. the elderly are often overlooked or ignored.
d. homemade meals are more nutritional than institutional food.

_______ 3. In paragraph 3, the connotation of the word **generic** is

a. distasteful.
b. costly.
c. healthy and nutritional.
d. plain and boring.

_______ 4. The author's purpose is to

a. discuss trends in school meal preparation.
b. advocate for more personalized meals for the elderly in institutions.
c. complain about the quality of care in long-term institutions.
d. share her own food memories.

_______ 5. The article is primarily intended for

a. caregivers of the elderly.
b. elderly people.
c. schoolteachers.
d. government workers.

_______ 6. The author discusses her mother's cooking skills in order to

a. explain where the author learned to cook.
b. calculate the cost of serving long-term care residents.
c. show how important food is to her mother.
d. criticize the nutritional value of institutional meals.

_______ 7. In paragraph 5, the word **mnemonic** means

a. physical needs.
b. related to skills.
c. having to do with memories.
d. emotional needs.

_______ 8. The author discusses schools where produce is grown and served to show

a. the danger of junk foods.
b. cost savings.
c. the increasing awareness of the importance of healthy foods in our society.
d. long-term care institutions how to improve.

_______ 9. The studies cited in paragraph 5 show that

a. dementia is treatable.
b. cognition influences life expectancy.
c. meals containing protein, vegetables, and starch are appropriately balanced.
d. familiar foods improve life for the elderly.

_______ 10. The author believes that food

a. should be prepared with closer attention to personal nutritional needs.
b. provides both nutrition and pleasure.
c. can influence performance in schools.
d. has become an overemphasized focus of Americans' lives.

Copyright © 2012 by Pearson Education

MASTERY TEST 9-1

NAME ______________________ SECTION ______________________

DATE ______________________ SCORE ______________________

Inference and Author's Purpose

A. Directions: *Study the photograph below and then use inference to answer the questions that follow.*

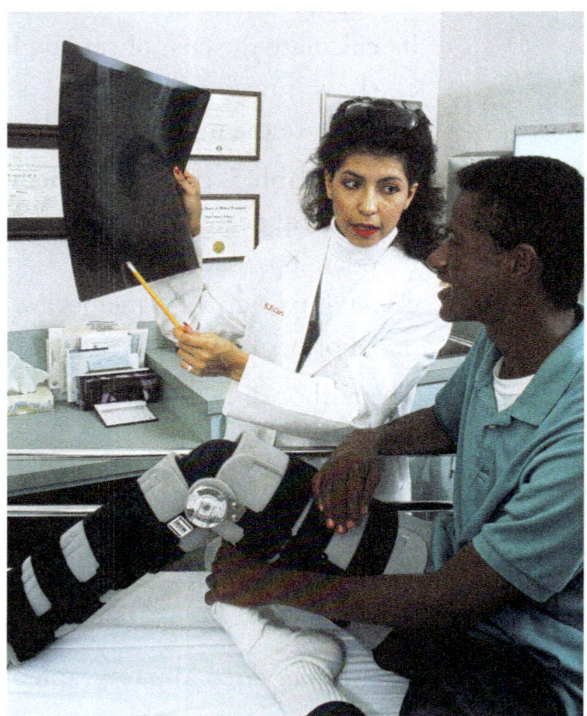

1. What is the relationship between the people in the photo?

____

2. What are the two people doing in the picture?

____

3. How might the man have come to be in this situation?

____

4. What details in the photo suggest that it was taken in a health-care setting?

____

B. Directions: *After reading the following passage, select the choice that best answers each of the questions that follow.*

Eat It Raw

Raw food is not just for hippies anymore. It is being embraced by hip-hop stars and New York restaurateurs.

The raw-food diet, once the exclusive domain of '70s food faddists, is making a comeback for the same reasons it flourished 30 years ago: health and politics. Many find it helpful in relieving a variety of maladies—including allergies, fibromyalgia, obesity, gum disease, and mood swings—while others see raw food as a way to resist the unhealthy products of an industrialized food system. No matter how you slice it, excitement about a diet of uncooked food is running high.

"Anecdotally, there's been a definite rise in interest in raw-foods diets," says nutritionist Suzanne Havala Hobbs, adjunct assistant professor at the University of North Carolina–Chapel Hill's School of Public Health. "There's been a lot of information out about celebrities that are eating raw foods, and naturally many younger people are interested in trying it out. There's also been a wave of raw-foods cookbooks and restaurants." Hobbs, who also serves as nutrition advisor to the Baltimore-based Vegetarian Resource Group, is currently conducting a research survey on the topic, called the Raw Foods Project.

A raw-food diet consists of foods that have not been processed or heated above 118 degrees Fahrenheit. These might include fresh fruits, vegetables, cold-pressed oils, sprouted grains, nuts, seeds, and even organic wine—but not meat or fish. According to June Butlin in *Positive Health*, a proper raw-food diet provides high levels of natural, essential nutrients such as fiber, essential oils, antimicrobials, plant hormones, bioflavonoids, vitamins, minerals, chlorophyll, digestive enzymes, and antioxidants.

—Olson, *Utne Reader*, pp. 20–22

_______ 5. The central thought of the passage is that

a. a raw-food diet is the *most* healthy diet.

b. interest in eating raw foods is growing in the United States.

c. raw foods improve mental health.

d. the Raw Foods Project is studying the nutrition of raw foods.

Copyright © 2012 by Pearson Education

_______ 6. Which of the following words or phrases has a somewhat negative connotative meaning?

a. people

b. restaurants

c. food faddists

d. degrees Fahrenheit

_______ 7. Which would *not* be part of a raw-food diet?

a. cold-pressed olive oil

b. fresh squeezed orange juice

c. sunflower seeds

d. bran muffin

_______ 8. Which describes the audience for whom this article was written?

a. students studying nutrition

b. business people seeking new opportunities

c. mothers looking for new dinner ideas

d. people interested in alternative lifestyles and diets

_______ 9. The phrase "unhealthy products of an industrialized food system" refers to

a. standard packaged grocery store food.

b. raw food.

c. all health foods.

d. sugar-free and fat-free foods.

_______ 10. This reading is an excerpt from a longer article. You can expect the rest of the article to

a. discuss other alternative diets.

b. provide personal testimonies from people on a raw-food diet.

c. explain why a raw-food diet is bad for you.

d. teach you how to start a raw-food café.

NAME ______________ SECTION ______________
DATE ______________ SCORE ______________

MASTERY TEST 9-2

Inference and Author's Purpose

Directions: *After reading the following article, select the choice that best completes each of the statements that follow.*

Working Moms: Don't Feel So Guilty

1 A study finds that children of career women do not lag behind their peers if their parents are attentive—and can afford quality child care.

2 As a working mother of two young boys, I found myself riveted by these recent headlines: "Study Links Working Mothers to Slower Learning" and "Study of Working Moms Finds Children Lag in Early Years." Oh, great, I thought. More ammunition for the ongoing guilt-slinging at working mothers.

3 The stories reported that three Columbia University researchers analyzed data from a three-year child-care study of 1,000 families in 10 cities. They found that 3-year-olds scored a significant six points less on the Bracken Test, which assesses children's knowledge of colors, letters, numbers, shapes, and comparisons, if their mothers worked more than 30 hours a week by the time the child was 9 months old. Considering that 75% of women are back on the job by a child's ninth month, myself included, I figured other working mothers were also assessing the damage they had inflicted on their children.

4 But first, consider the following: The women most likely to fret about this study are those who don't need to worry. They're likely to be highly educated, highly paid professionals, and their children tend to do well in school, notes Ellen Galinsky, president of the Families & Work Institute in New York.

5 These women also have the most flexible work and babysitting arrangements. Many have the option to work from home a couple of days a week or delay their return to the office. And they also are likely to have the resources to purchase high-quality child care. "For the woman who has the best child care possible and who is sensitive to her child when she is home," there is no difference between her children and those of mothers who stay home, says Jane Waldfogel, an associate professor of social work who is a co-author of the study.

6 One thing the study didn't account for was the father's contribution. In our family, my husband easily carries 50% of the home-life load, which definitely helps decrease my stress and increase my "maternal sensitivity"—my ability to be responsive to my children, which, along with quality of child care, number of hours in child care, and home environment, were the areas the researchers examined. While this study didn't include the impact of a father's efforts, Jeanne Brooks-Gunn, professor of child development and another co-author, is now

Toddi Gutner, "Working Moms: Don't Feel So Guilty." Reprinted from the September 23, 2002 issue of *Bloomberg Businessweek* by special permission. Copyright © 2002 by Bloomberg L.P.

Copyright © 2012 by Pearson Education

researching the effects of shared caregiving on children under 3 who have two working parents. "The more shared caregiving there is among couples, the less likely there would be a negative effect on the children," she says.

7 Another thing to keep in mind is that studies are just that. They're helpful, but they don't account for many real-world situations. That means no working mother should second-guess the decisions she has made based on research findings.

8 What these study results can do is help with broader national policy decisions. The goal is to give women with lower incomes work flexibility and child-care arrangements similar to those enjoyed by higher-earning professionals. At this point, the debate returns to how best to increase quality child-care options, improve family-leave policies, and offer more part-time and flextime opportunities. Since the U.S. has among the worst work-family policies of all Western industrialized countries, those policies are certainly worth changing.

9 Yet while policy prescriptions may be useful for government planning, it's important for women to separate the public from the personal. If working moms don't focus on what is best for them and their families, they will only be adding stress to an already difficult job-vs.-home-life balance. And that does neither the mother, nor her children, any good.

—Gutner, *Bloomberg Businessweek*

_______ 1. The author of this article
   a. regrets she is forced to be a working mother.
   b. doesn't care if her children suffer because of her career.
   c. is concerned about the effect her career might have on her children.
   d. is confused about child-care studies.

_______ 2. The primary intended audience of this article is
   a. working moms who can afford quality child care.
   b. fathers whose wives work full-time.
   c. employers who hire women with young children.
   d. child-care center administrators.

_______ 3. One purpose of the article is to
   a. examine the validity of child-care studies.
   b. offer child-care solutions for low-income working mothers.
   c. help high-earning mothers feel less guilty about sending their children to day care.
   d. expose the difficulties of a two-income household with children.

_______ 4. Which of the following statements best summarizes the writer's attitude toward research cited in this article?

a. She mistrusts it.

b. She feels it is flawed and poorly designed research.

c. She feels it must be considered in light of family circumstances.

d. She feels family studies have little practical value.

_______ 5. The author implies but does not directly state that

a. women should not hold full-time jobs.

b. fathers should be involved in day-care selection.

c. children themselves determine the outcome of their day-care experiences.

d. it is the children of low-income women who suffer from day care.

_______ 6. In paragraph 2, what is suggested by the phrase "ongoing guilt-slinging at working mothers"?

a. Society doesn't approve of working mothers so it tries to make the mothers feel guilty.

b. Studies indicate that children of working mothers suffer in some way.

c. Working mothers make themselves feel guilty.

d. Children make their mothers feel guilty.

_______ 7. The author of this selection is most likely a woman who is

a. well educated and professionally employed.

b. low paid and poorly educated.

c. uncaring about her children.

d. a strong advocate for better employee benefits.

_______ 8. The author mentions the contributions of the father because

a. many working mothers are single.

b. fathers can take a lot of stress off working mothers at home.

c. most husbands do not contribute.

d. the study did not mention their contribution.

Copyright © 2012 by Pearson Education

_____ 9. The author feels that the research study should be used by
   a. mothers trying to decide if they should return to work.
   b. working mothers negotiating with their employers.
   c. policy makers, to create more options for low-income mothers.
   d. fathers trying to persuade their wives to stay home.

_____ 10. The author concludes by suggesting that
   a. only mothers can know what is good for their children.
   b. research studies do not apply to daily life.
   c. government officials do not care about the struggles of working women.
   d. professional women should fight to help less fortunate working moms.

NAME ______________________ SECTION ______________________

DATE ______________________ SCORE ______________________

MASTERY TEST 9-3

READING SELECTION

Boots on the Ground: A Day in the Life of a Border Sheriff

Melissa del Bosque

In this essay from *The Texas Observer*, the author describes her experience riding along with a Texas sheriff. Read the selection to find out more about the role of border sheriffs and their wider sphere of influence.

Vocabulary Preview

These are some of the difficult words in this essay. The definitions here will help you if you can't figure out the meanings from the sentence context or word parts.

celluloid (par. 4) as portrayed in a movie

coalition (par. 6) partnership or alliance

fodder (par. 6) raw material

assimilate (par. 20) become part of

rhetoric (par. 23) public speaking

1 "Y'all got here just in time. We're going to look for a body. Are you up for it? It's gonna get rough out there, but I can have you back by lunch."

2 It's 7 A.M. I've already driven two hours from El Paso with my husband, whom I've convinced to shoot photographs for my story. If it hadn't been for the Border Patrol checkpoint just outside of this dusty, half-abandoned town on Interstate 10, we might have missed Sierra Blanca altogether. Smack in the middle of the Chihuahuan Desert, we've arrived at the office of Arvin West, sheriff of Hudspeth County.

3 "Sure, I'm up for it," I say. My husband nods gamely.

4 West leads us out to his white SUV. He doesn't fit my celluloid idea of a Texas sheriff. He wears a white Stetson and Wrangler jeans, but is short, with a paunch. Instead of cowboy boots, he wears brown suede Wallaby boots. "I used to wear these in high school," he says, "and hell, they're comfortable. I'm getting too old for cowboy boots." West is 44. Half-Mexican, he jokes about growing up a "GMC," or "Gringo-Mexican combo," when Texas shops still displayed signs that read "No dogs, no Mexicans."

5 We set off south for the Rio Grande. The river has made West more than just a small-town sheriff. With 3,300 residents, his county straddles 98 miles of the Rio Grande. At 4,572 square miles, Hudspeth is twice the size of Delaware.

6 Since September 11, 2001, border counties like Hudspeth have played an outsized role in the contentious debates over border security and immigration

Copyright © 2012 by Pearson Education

reform. West and the Texas Border Sheriff's Coalition, which formed in 2005 and which he chairs, have shaped those debates. The sheriffs' congressional testimony has provided great fodder to many an anti-immigration politician. Their accounts of battling narcos and nabbing suspected terrorists have made them darlings of cable news. Members of Congress call on them to guide tours for political delegations and media, elaborating on the dire need for more equipment, money, and, as the sheriffs often put it, "boots on the ground."

7 Today West's people are looking for a Mexican man in his late 50s. He is a chronic alcoholic in poor health, the men traveling with him told Border Patrol after they were apprehended. By the time the group reached Hudspeth, the man was doubled over and vomiting. "Go ahead and I'll catch up," he told them.

8 That was two weeks earlier. This is West's third trip into the desert to look for the body and the second time he's requested help from a state helicopter. The search has already cost his department $12,000, which will come out of coalition money, West says.

9 Since 2006 the coalition has received $16.1 million in state and federal funds, while the 16 border sheriffs and their counties have received another $12.6 million from Operation Border Star, a border-security program launched by Governor Rick Perry. The money has allowed West to hire 6 more deputies for a total of 17. The department also has four new ATVs and six new Ford F-150 trucks.

10 What, I ask West, would immigration hard-liners think of his spending more than $12,000 of taxpayers' money searching for a chronic alcoholic immigrant? The sheriff seems startled, almost repulsed, by the question. "Of course we need to find him," he says. The man's daughter calls every day from New Mexico. "Wouldn't you want us to do everything that we could to find your loved one?" "Congress knows about as much about the border as that mesquite bush," West says, pointing to a straggly green plant about to be munched by a heifer.

11 West, like several other border sheriffs, has seen a lot of Washington since the coalition started. He has testified before Congress three times and been to Washington 13 times in the past four years. He's also found a loyal ally in Representative John Culberson, a Republican who represents west Harris County. Culberson is a full-out hawk on border security. In March 2009 he called for a "fast-reaction military force that can move up and down the border on the U.S. side" to fight the "undeclared war."

12 At least once, the congressman has used intelligence from West to send the anti-immigration movement into a frenzy. In November 2005 Culberson recounted to Fox News' *Hannity and Colmes* the tale of an "al-Qaida terrorist" he said had been taken into custody by West and locked up in a Brewster County jail. The terrorist was later whisked away by the FBI, Culberson said, telling Sean Hannity that he had obtained his information from West and Brewster County Sheriff Ronny Dodson.

13 I ask West about the story. It seems West's friend, sheriff of the Mexican town of Porvenir just across the river, had apprehended a fellow who was tracking migratory patterns of birds and writing down the information in Arabic in a diary. "I'm not saying the guy was a terrorist," West tells me as we bump through the desert, "but it seemed kind of strange that a guy of Arabic origin was keeping track of migratory animals in southwest Texas." He pauses. "Consequently or coincidentally, this was right before the bird flu broke out."

14 What became of the diarist? Mexican authorities called Border Patrol, West says, and Border Patrol called the FBI, but the man had "vanished from the face of the earth."

15 Parked up ahead with a trailer of ATVs are five of West's deputies: three young Latinos in their 30s, a Latino man in his 40s sporting a shirt reading "Hudspeth County Regulators," and a middle-aged Anglo with a belly and a mustache.

16 Two older, stone-faced Anglo men in Stetson hats stand silent and apart. West is summoned to their patch of desert. After a few minutes, he returns. "No pictures and they don't want to be interviewed," he says apologetically. One, he says, is from the Texas Rangers; the other is an Immigration and Customs Enforcement (ICE) agent.

17 West's deputies produce an ice chest full of sodas, Gatorade, and water. They offer brown paper bags filled with tinfoil-wrapped burritos. After eating, West climbs behind the wheel of an ATV called a "mule," which looks like the Humvee version of a golf cart. We head toward the last place the Mexicans saw their companion, a hunting cabin next to a creek.

18 The sheriff drives the mule with abandon. He rolls over six-foot ocotillo cactuses as if they were toothpicks. The deputies race around and ahead of one another on their ATVs, cracking jokes. The Ranger and the federal agent follow behind, crammed shoulder-to-shoulder in the front seat of their ATV.

19 About an hour later, we arrive at the hunting cabin, a tin-roofed shack near an old windmill. Finishing their Gatorades, the deputies fan out into the desert to look for the missing man. The sheriff goes inside the cabin. The white walls are covered with hundreds of names and dates going back to 1907. An old tin chest—containing cooking oil, soup cans, sardines, and dry goods—sits on the floor.

20 "You've got to have a heart for these people," West says. "Why can't we take the approach of the Bracero Program [which ran from the 1940s to the 1960s], where they can work here for so many years, and if they decide to assimilate and become American citizens, then allow them that opportunity?"

21 He sits back in an old wooden chair. "You are allowed to come and participate in the luxuries we have as American citizens, but if you violate our laws, then you are out of here. It's as simple as that."

22 If many Americans think "Texas-Mexico border" and envision a war zone, it's thanks in no small part to the stories spread by border sheriffs like West

Copyright © 2012 by Pearson Education

and Zapata County's Sheriff Sigifredo Gonzalez. In November 2005, shortly before the "al-Qaida terrorist" story started to spread, Gonzalez took NBC reporter Rita Cosby (wearing a bulletproof vest) down to the Rio Grande at night. He was armed with a pistol and an AR-15. He memorably told Cosby and her viewers that just on the other side of the river, drug lords were grinding up men and feeding the meat to dogs.

23 Lupe Treviño, sheriff of Hidalgo County, is among the coalition members who say that the inflammatory rhetoric has brought the border region nothing but a lot of headlines and bad publicity. "As an American, of course I am concerned about terrorism," Treviño says, "but do you think my deputies have time to post themselves on the river to look for Osama bin Laden?" His department receives a call for assistance every four minutes on average, he adds. "I'm not going to drop my homicides and my robbery investigations so that I can help Border Patrol keep terrorists out of the country."

24 It is getting late in the desert. "Let's go," West says, exiting the cabin. He hops into his ATV and motions for us to join him. "I want to show you Mexico," he says, hitting the gas. We crest a small butte, and the sun is hanging low. Suddenly the ATV makes a whump and then a thumping noise. Flat tire. "Dang," the sheriff says, pulling out a can of Fix-A-Flat. He shoots the white foam into the deflated tire. No luck. West kicks the dust with his Wallaby boot and radios for help.

25 Regrouped back at the trailer, the deputies begin loading the ATVs. They haven't found the body. It's nearly dark, but the men linger, elbows propped on truck beds, talking about sports and the weather. The stony-faced Ranger and the ICE agent dip into cans of chewing tobacco and spit into the dust. "You boys have to go home sometime, or your wives will divorce you," West says, guffawing. But he is in no hurry, either. His wife phoned earlier to remind him about a school function he'd promised to attend that evening.

26 "Do you have any other questions?" he asks hopefully. I can't think of any.

27 Two weeks later, I get an e-mail from West. The subject is "Body in Mountain." He wrote: "I just wanted to let you know we found the body. He was about two miles north east of the little house. We had to walk about a mile and a half to get him, but we made it for a bunch of old guys. The family can feel better knowing this information I guess. Take care and God Bless. Tu amigo, Sheriff West."

—del Bosque, *The Texas Observer*

Directions: *Select the choice that best completes each of the following statements.*

CHECKING YOUR COMPREHENSION

______ 1. The person who is the focus of this article can best be described as

a. a politician representing Texas.

b. an immigration lawyer.

c. the sheriff of a border town.

d. an agent from Immigration and Customs Enforcement (ICE).

_______ 2. The main idea of paragraph 6 is that border sheriffs

a. have more power than sheriffs in nonborder areas.

b. have an influential role in shaping immigration policies.

c. are trying to gain the attention of members of Congress and the media.

d. should spend their time on local crime rather than immigration issues.

_______ 3. On the day the reporter accompanied Sheriff West, most of their time was spent

a. reviewing the sheriff's congressional testimony in Washington, D.C.

b. discussing border security and immigration issues in the sheriff's office.

c. interviewing Texas Rangers and agents from ICE.

d. searching for a missing Mexican immigrant near the Texas-Mexico border.

_______ 4. All of the following statements about the Texas Border Sheriff's Coalition are true *except*

a. Sheriff West chairs the coalition.

b. Senator John Culberson wants to have the coalition disbanded.

c. members of the coalition have testified before Congress.

d. the coalition has received millions of dollars in state and federal funding.

_______ 5. Operation Border Star is

a. a border-security program launched by the governor of Texas.

b. an alliance of concerned citizens living in border towns.

c. a group of anti-immigration activists lobbying for reform.

d. a partnership formed between American and Mexican law enforcement agencies.

Copyright © 2012 by Pearson Education

USING WHAT YOU KNOW ABOUT INFERENCE AND THE WRITER'S PURPOSE

_______ 6. The audience that the author most likely intended this article for is

a. anti-immigration activists.

b. law enforcement officials.

c. social workers.

d. the general public.

_______ 7. The author's main purpose for writing this article is to

a. argue for stricter immigration policies.

b. criticize the actions of the Border Patrol.

c. describe the role and influence of a border sheriff.

d. explain changes in attitudes toward immigrants.

_______ 8. The phrase "boots on the ground" refers to

a. immigrants trying to cross the border illegally.

b. law enforcement personnel working in border areas.

c. reporters gathering information about immigration.

d. suspected terrorists and criminals in border towns.

_______ 9. A person who is described as a "hawk" on border security is one who

a. wants more aggressive enforcement.

b. opposes strict enforcement.

c. reports on immigration issues.

d. lobbies for more lenient immigration policies.

_______ 10. One inference you can make about this selection is that the author

a. wholeheartedly supports Sheriff West's efforts.

b. believes that Sheriff West enjoys his job.

c. considers herself an immigration hard-liner.

d. is emotional about the plight of immigrants.

USING CONTEXT CLUES AND WORD PARTS

_______ 11. In paragraph 3, the word **gamely** means
a. unhappily.
b. willingly.
c. carelessly.
d. uncomfortably.

_______ 12. In paragraph 6, the word **contentious** means
a. controversial.
b. pleasant.
c. sensible.
d. indifferent.

_______ 13. In paragraph 6, the word **dire** means
a. useless.
b. occasional.
c. misplaced.
d. desperate.

_______ 14. In paragraph 10, the word **repulsed** means
a. disgusted.
b. interested.
c. impressed.
d. fearful.

_______ 15. In paragraph 23, the word **inflammatory** means
a. painful.
b. arousing strong emotion.
c. hazardous.
d. ordinary.

REVIEWING DIFFICULT VOCABULARY

Directions: *Complete each of the following sentences by inserting a word from the Vocabulary Preview on page 363 in the space provided. Use each word only once.*

16. Several council members formed a ____________________ to oppose the mayor's agenda.

17. The comedian drew upon his childhood in Minnesota as ____________________ for his act.

18. Many immigrants strive to ____________________, while others hold onto the language and traditions of their native culture.

19. The actress's real-life personality was nothing like her ______________ persona.

20. After all the political ____________________ was over, it was time for us to cast our vote.

Copyright © 2012 by Pearson Education

THINKING CRITICALLY

1. What type of photograph could the author have included to make the reading selection more interesting or more informative?
2. Do you think the author is biased? Why or why not?
3. What can you infer about the author's opinion of Sheriff West? What details in the article help you make these inferences?

QUESTIONS FOR DISCUSSION

1. How does Sheriff West fit your idea of a Texas sheriff? How would you characterize his attitude toward illegal immigrants? Consider his actions and statements throughout the article.
2. What do you think the author wants you to believe or feel about the issues of border security and immigration?
3. Why did the author include the story about the alleged terrorist detained in southwest Texas (paragraphs 12–14)? What inferences can you make about her decision to include this information?

WRITING ACTIVITIES

1. Identify examples of connotative language in this article and analyze how the author's word choice affected your reading of the article.
2. Write a paragraph explaining your point of view toward immigration, especially as it relates to the border security issues described in this article.
3. Would you be willing to go along for the day with a border sheriff as this author did? How do you think it might change your opinion about the role of a sheriff? Write a paragraph explaining your answer.
4. Explore this Web site from PBS Frontline about one immigrant's experience. Write a paragraph or short essay that summarizes the story and explains how it relates it to the experiences of the border sheriff in the reading. http://www.pbs.org/frontlineworld/stories/mexico/

CHAPTER 9

Making Inferences and Analyzing the Author's Purpose

RECORDING YOUR PROGRESS

Test	Number Right		Score
Practice Test 9-1	________	× 10 =	________%
Practice Test 9-2	________	× 10 =	________%
Mastery Test 9-1	________	× 10 =	________%
Mastery Test 9-2	________	× 10 =	________%
Mastery Test 9-3	________	× 5 =	________%

GETTING MORE PRACTICE myreadinglab

To get more practice with Making Inferences and Analyzing the Author's Purpose, go to http://www.myreadinglab.com and click on

- Study Plan
- Reading Skills
- Inference and Purpose and Tone

EVALUATING YOUR PROGRESS myreadinglab

To measure your progress after reading and viewing the information in the Review Materials section, complete the Practices and Tests in the Activities section. You can check your scores by clicking on the Gradebook tab.

Then, based on your performance in this chapter and/or on the MyReadingLab Practices and Tests, write your own evaluation.

YOUR EVALUATION: ____

____

____

____

Copyright © 2012 by Pearson Education

THINKING ABOUT

Fact and Opinion

The newspapers and tabloids shown in this photograph of a newsstand display contain a wide variety of information. Some of these sources make sensational claims and report implausible events, while others report factual information in a clear and straightforward manner. How can you know which stories report factual information and which offer opinions and misleading information? This chapter will show you how to distinguish fact from opinion and, thereby, enable you to distinguish trustworthy sources from those that are not.

CHAPTER 10

Distinguishing Fact from Opinion

Is It Fact or Opinion?

GOAL 1
Understand the difference between fact and opinion

The ability to distinguish between fact and opinion is an important part of reading critically. You must be able to evaluate ideas you encounter and determine whether they are objective information from a reliable source or whether they are one person's expression of a personal belief or attitude.

myreadinglab
To practice distinguishing fact from opinion, go to
> Study Plan
> Reading Skills
> Critical Thinking

LEARNING GOALS

GOAL 1 Understand the difference between fact and opinion

GOAL 2 Identify writing that mixes fact and opinion

GOAL 3 Evaluate fact and opinion

GOAL 4 Understand informed opinion

Facts

Facts are statements that can be verified. They can be proven true or false. Statements of fact are objective—they contain information but do not tell what the writer thinks or believes about the topic or issue. The statement "My car payments are $250 per month." is a fact. It can be proven by looking at your car loan statement. Here are a few more statements of fact:

Examples

1. The Atlantic hurricane seasons lasts from June 1 to November 30. (You can check this by looking at the National Oceanic and Atmospheric Administration Web site or in various climate textbooks.)
2. In Washington State drivers must stop for pedestrians and bicyclists at crosswalks and intersections. (You can check this in the Washington State Drivers' Guide.)
3. Greenpeace is an organization dedicated to preserving the Earth's ability to support life in all its many forms. (You can check this by reading its mission statement or the "About Us" page on its Web site at http://www.greenpeace.org.)

Copyright © 2012 by Pearson Education

Opinions

Opinions are statements that express a writer's feelings, attitudes, or beliefs. They are neither true nor false. They are one person's view about a topic or issue. The statement "My car payments are too expensive." is an opinion. It expresses your feelings about the cost of your auto payments. Others may disagree with you, especially the company that sold you the car or another person who pays twice as much as you are paying. As you evaluate what you read, think of opinions as one person's viewpoint that you are free to accept or reject. Here are a few more examples of opinions:

Examples

1. Everyone should reduce their carbon footprint. (Those who do not believe in global warming or who are not convinced one person's actions can make a difference would disagree.)
2. The slaughter of baby seals for their pelts should be outlawed. (Hunters who make their living selling pelts would disagree.)
3. Population growth should be regulated through mandatory birth control. (People who do not believe in birth control would disagree.)

Here is a list of the types of statements that are often opinions:

- Positions on controversial issues (gun control, abortion, animal experimentation)
- Predictions about things in the future (predicting that there will be 10 major hurricanes next year; or speculating that the Federal Reserve Bank will reduce the interest rate by half a percent; or optimistically introducing a gubernatorial candidate as the "next governor")
- Evaluations of people, places, and things (a professor's teaching skills, a vacation spot, a movie)

EXERCISE 10-1 Identifying Facts and Opinions

Directions: *Indicate whether each of the following statements is a fact (F) or an opinion (O).*

_______ 1. Alligators provide no physical care for their young.

_______ 2. Humans should be concerned about the use of pesticides that kill insects at the bottom of the food chain.

_______ 3. There are 28 more humans living on the earth now than there were 10 seconds ago.

_______ 4. We must bear greater responsibility for the environment than our ancestors did.

_______ 5. Nuclear power is the only viable solution to our dwindling natural resources.

_______ 6. Between 1850 and 1900 the death rate in Europe decreased due to industrial growth and advances in medicine.

_______ 7. Dogs make the best pets because they can be trained to obey.

_______ 8. Solar energy is available wherever sunlight reaches the earth.

_______ 9. By the year 2020, many diseases, including cancer, will be preventable.

_______ 10. Hormones are produced in one part of the body and carried by the blood to another part of the body where they influence some process or activity.

Judgment Words

When a writer or speaker expresses an opinion he or she often uses words or phrases that can tip you off that a judgment or opinion is being offered. Here are a couple of examples.

Professor Rodriguez is a *better* teacher than Professor Harrigan.

The word *better* suggests someone is deciding who is more skilled than someone else. Many students disagree about the qualities that make a good teacher.

My sister's behavior at the party was *disgusting.*

The word *disgusting* reveals the author strongly disapproves and was sickened or horrified by the sister's behavior.

Here is a list of words that often suggest that the writer is interpreting, judging, evaluating, or expressing feelings.

Judgment Words				
bad	good	worthwhile	wonderful	frightening
worse	better	worthless	lovely	
worst	best	disgusting	amazing	

Copyright © 2012 by Pearson Education

EXERCISE 10-2 Locating Judgment Words

Directions: *For each of the following statements, underline the judgment word or phrase that suggests the statement is an opinion.*

1. Purchasing a brand new car is a terrible waste of money.
2. Many wonderful vegetarian cookbooks are available in bookstores.
3. Of all the film versions of Victor Hugo's novel *Les Miserables*, the 1935 version starring Charles Laughton is the best.
4. The introductory biology textbook comes with an amazing CD-ROM.
5. Volunteers for Habitat for Humanity are engaged in a worthwhile activity.

Mixing Fact and Opinion

Identify writing that mixes fact and opinion

Writers often mix fact and opinion within a piece of writing. They may mix fact and opinion within a paragraph or even within a single sentence. Some writers deliberately include some factual information to make their writing appear substantive and thereby encourage readers to accept their opinions along with the facts.

Mixed Paragraphs

Here is an example of a paragraph that mixes fact and opinion. The statements of opinion are highlighted.

> More people need to become aware of organ donation needs. 16 people die every day while waiting for an organ donation. 10,000 to 14,000 people eligible to be organ donors die each year, and fewer than half become donors. Organ donation currently is a voluntary system, with donors or their families required to take active steps to donate organs. Currently it is too hard for people to become donors. The United States needs to implement a system that automatically makes people organ donors unless they opt out of the program.

In this paragraph, the writer presents some factual information about organ donation but also offers opinions about the scarcity of donors.

To easily distinguish fact from opinion, ask yourself, "Is this information that can be verified, or is it what someone thinks about the topic?"

EXERCISE 10-3 Distinguishing Between Fact and Opinion

Directions: *Each of the following paragraphs contains both fact and opinion. Read each paragraph and label each sentence as fact or opinion.*

A. [1] Flowering plants that are native to the South include purple coneflower and rose verbena. [2] In the view of many longtime gardeners, these two plants are an essential part of the Southern landscape. [3] Trees that are native to the South include a variety of oaks, as well as flowering dogwoods and redbuds. [4] Dogwoods are especially lovely, with their white, pink, or coral blossoms announcing the arrival of spring. [5] For fall color, the deep red of the Virginia willow makes a spectacular show in the native Southern garden.

Sentences:

1. __________ 2. __________ 3. __________

4. __________ 5. __________

B. [1] Today, many companies provide child-care assistance, either on- or off-site, for their employees. [2] This suggests that employers are becoming aware that their workers' family concerns can affect the company's bottom line. [3] The Eli Lilly pharmaceutical company, for example, has built two child-development centers with a total capacity of more than 400 children. [4] In addition to assistance with daily child care, Bank of America reimburses employees for child-care expenses related to business travel. [5] It seems clear that other, less progressive employers will have to follow these companies' leads in order to attract and retain the best employees.

Sentences:

1. __________ 2. __________ 3. __________

4. __________ 5. __________

C. [1] Preparing a will is an important task that people ignore because they prefer not to think about their own death. [2] However, if you die without a will, the courts will determine how your assets should be distributed, as directed by state law. [3] Even more important than establishing a will, in my opinion, is expressing your willingness to be an organ donor upon your death. [4] Each year, twenty-five thousand new

Copyright © 2012 by Pearson Education

patients are added to the waiting list for organ transplants. [5] The legacy of an organ donor is far more valuable than any material assets put in a will.

Sentences:

1. ______________ 2. ______________ 3. ______________

4. ______________ 5. ______________

Mixed Sentences

Here is an example of a sentence that contains a mix of fact and opinion.

> Chronic back pain affects millions of Americans, but there are many more important conditions that need immediate attention from our health-care professionals.

In this sentence, *Chronic back pain affects millions of Americans* is a fact, and *but there are many more important conditions that need immediate attention from our health-care professionals* expresses an opinion.

In the following sentence, you can see that the author blends fact and opinion to convince the reader that an article on soy products is reputable.

> Dr. Athena Hunt, one of the best nutritionists, wrote an article titled, "Soy: The Amazing Miracle Bean."

EXERCISE 10-4 Finding Opinions in Mixed Sentences

Directions: *Underline the portion of each sentence that contains an opinion.*

1. Earthquake preparedness is vital in Southern California where earthquakes are the worst imaginable disaster that could occur there.
2. Senior citizens can benefit from having a pet since cats and dogs are so friendly.
3. Children should be in mixed-aged classrooms since all children develop at different rates.
4. Most documentary films are dull because they deal with real-life events.
5. Food banks are always in need of donations to meet their costs because nobody realizes what valuable services they provide.

6. Healthy eating habits are important, but most exercise regimes are a waste of time.
7. Christmas has become too commercial; decorations go up right after Halloween in some stores.
8. Tree sitters get a great deal of media attention because they are so strange.
9. Many families with young children are now taking cruise vacations since these are the best travel deals.
10. No one goes to see community theater productions because the actors are not professionals.

Evaluating Fact and Opinion

Evaluate fact and opinion

Not every fact needs to be independently checked in another source. When using reliable sources such as textbooks, encyclopedias, and scholarly journals, it is usually safe to assume that the author is presenting accurate information. For example, if you are reading about the Cuban Missile Crisis in *The Cold War Encyclopedia*, it is safe to assume that facts about those thirteen days in October 1962 are accurate.

However, when using less reliable and less trustworthy sources such as personal Web sites, letters to the editor, and popular magazines, it may be necessary to verify the information by checking more reliable sources. For example, if you are researching voting patterns for a term paper, and find an editorial in your local newspaper with statistics about a recent county election, you should verify these numbers. You can find out the official counts by contacting the local board of elections by phone or on the Internet.

Here are some tips to use when cross-checking facts in a second source:

- **Use a reliable source.** If you need help identifying a second source, ask your instructor or a librarian.
- **Find current sources.** Some information can change quickly.
- **Look at primary sources when possible.** For example, most American demographic information originally comes from the U.S. Census.

Because opinions are an expression of someone's personal attitudes or feelings, they cannot be verified as either true or false. However, you can evaluate how well the writer supports or justifies his or her opinions. For example, a writer may offer the opinion that plastic shopping bags are harmful to the

Copyright © 2012 by Pearson Education

environment. She may substantiate that attitude by explaining that the bags do not biodegrade and offering statistics that reveal the number of such bags going into landfills each year.

Writers may substantiate a statement of opinion in the following ways:

1. **Giving reasons.** A writer may support the opinion that school uniforms should not be required by stating that they are expensive and some parents cannot afford them.
2. **Offering personal experience that supports the opinion.** An author may support public school attendance because he went through public schools and ended up "fine."
3. **Presenting statistics.** A writer may, for example, try to prove that expensive housing drives families out of cities by citing census figures that show how the percentage of children is lowest in expensive urban cores such as San Francisco and Seattle.
4. **Offering examples.** For instance, a writer may explain clichés by giving examples of several, such as: "A step in time saves nine" and "Don't bite the hand that feeds you."

EXERCISE 10-5 Evaluating Support

Directions: *For each opinion, choose the type of information that the author could use to* best *support the opinion.*

_______ 1. Opinion: Parents should read to their children daily.

a. an example of a mother who reads Mother Goose stories to her child

b. an explanation that reading to children helps them see reading as fun

c. statistics that report how many children's books are published each year

d. the author's story of her children's reading preferences

_______ 2. Opinion: When teachers go on strike, the students suffer the most.

a. quotes from a wide variety of students who express distress and hurt

b. statistics that reflect the number of strikes that occur each year

c. an explanation of why teachers choose to strike

d. an interview with a teacher on strike

_______ 3. Opinion: The American prison system is doing a poor job of rehabilitating criminals.

a. an interview with a prison guard

b. statistics that show the numbers of inmates who are rearrested after release from prison

c. examples of prisoners who go on to productive crime-free lives after their incarceration

d. a list of the societal conditions that contribute to a person's tendency toward a life of crime

_______ 4. Opinion: Universities and colleges can do a great deal to stop underage drinking on campus.

a. descriptions of the activities and successes of anti-drinking campaigns at various schools across the country

b. interviews with students who have been punished for illegal drinking

c. data from research studies that address the negative effects of alcohol on college students

d. a list of Web sites that provide information for college students with alcoholism

_______ 5. Opinion: They'll never find a cure for the common cold.

a. statistics that show the number of people who get sick with a cold every year

b. examples of other diseases and conditions for which there are no cures

c. an interview with a doctor who treats patients suffering from the common cold

d. a description of the complex nature of the hundreds of cold viruses and the ease of transmission

Recognizing Informed Opinions

Understand informed opinion

The opinion of experts is known as informed opinion. For example, the surgeon general is regarded as an authority on the health of Americans, and his or her opinion on this subject is more trustworthy than that of casual observers or nonprofessionals.

Copyright © 2012 by Pearson Education

Here are a few examples of expert opinions.

Examples

Bill Gates, founder of Microsoft:

"I think it's fair to say that personal computers have become the most empowering tool we've ever created. They're tools of communication, they're tools of creativity, and they can be shaped by their user."

Jane Goodall, primate expert and ethologist:

"Chimps are in massive danger of extinction from dwindling habitats—forests are being cut down at an alarming rate."

Arthur Sullivan, attorney specializing in divorce/child custody:

"Don't buy your child lavish gifts or take him or her to special places. Such activities may make the judge suspicious. Live normally."

Textbook authors, too, often offer informed opinion. As experts in their fields, they may make observations and offer comments that are not strictly factual. Instead, they are based on years of study and research. Here is an example from an American government textbook:

> The Declaration of Independence quickly became one of the most widely quoted and revered documents in America. Filled with fine principles and bold language, it can be read as both a political tract and a philosophical treatise.
>
> —Edwards, *Government in America*, p. 34

The author of this statement has reviewed the available evidence and is providing his expert opinion on what the evidence indicates about how the Declaration of Independence is viewed.

Some authors are careful to signal the reader when they are presenting an opinion. Watch for words and phrases such as:

Opinion Words and Phrases			
apparently	this suggests	in my view	one explanation is
presumably	possibly	it is likely that	according to
in my opinion	it is believed	seemingly	

In the following excerpt from an autism support Web site, notice how the author carefully distinguishes factual statements from opinion by using qualifying words and phrases (highlighted) to express opinion.

1 The causes of Autism Spectrum Disorders such as Autism and Asperger's syndrome are the subject of much debate and research. Although a genetic cause is well established, many argue there are environmental causes as well.

Gastrointestinal problems such as bowel disturbances, diarrhea or constipation are a common feature of Autism and Asperger's. According to one theory, some children are unable to digest the protein in many cereals (gluten) or in milk (casein) completely. Casein and gluten proteins aren't properly broken down and lead to a build up of opioids in the body, leading to high pain tolerance, repetitive behaviors and lack of concentration. A gluten and casein-free diet is believed by some parents of autistic children to aid in reducing symptoms of Autism, Asperger's syndrome and other Autism Spectrum Disorders.

2 Dr. Karl Ludwig Reichelt claims to have found peptides from casein and gluten that worsen the symptoms of autistic children, many of whom have gastrointestinal disorders. These peptides are casomorphines and gluten exorphins, which influence the brain. The primary proponent of the possible link between digestive disorders and autism is Dr. Andrew Wakefield, a United Kingdom gastroenterologist who has described the disputed condition as autistic enterocolitis. According to Dr. Reichelt, significant improvement has been seen in the symptoms of some of his patients with Autism or Asperger's who had been put on a diet that omits these peptides. The diet is called the gluten-free, casein-free diet. Some physicians see diet as a central part of the treatment, but in addition to many other treatments at the same time.

—http://www.autism-help.org/intervention-casein-gluten-free.htm

EXERCISE 10-6 Understanding Informed Opinion

Directions: *Read each of the following statements. In each, underline the word or phrase that suggests that the author is offering an informed opinion.*

1. It seems clear that parents who would bring a young child to an R-rated movie are putting their own interests ahead of what's best for the child.
2. Voters rejected the proposed rapid transit system connecting the southern and northern suburbs, possibly because of racial issues.
3. According to the city superintendent of schools, school uniforms lead to improved behavior and fewer disruptions in the classroom.
4. One explanation for low attendance at professional sporting events is the high price of tickets.
5. It is believed that most people practice some form of recycling in their daily lives.

Copyright © 2012 by Pearson Education

CRITICAL THINKING CHALLENGE

In this section is an excerpt from a newspaper on which to practice your critical thinking skills. Review the "Tips for Reading Newspapers" and use the steps below to guide your reading and your response.

TIPS for Reading Newspapers

When reading newspapers, be sure to

- **Pay attention to the date line.** This information at the beginning of the article tells you the date the article was published and where the story took place. This allows you to place the information in context.
- **Take note of sources.** Newspaper articles are based on information the reporter gathered from others. Evaluate the sources and their knowledge about or involvement in the story at hand.
- **Ask yourself what is missing.** Reporters may not always address every side of every issue or investigate every aspect of a story.

Thinking Critically as You Read

1. **Reading, Highlighting, and Annotating.** As you read, highlight the key ideas. Write marginal notes to record your thinking as you read. Include comments, reactions, questions, opposing ideas, and so forth.
2. **Summarizing.** (Refer to Chapter 6, page 216.) Write a one-paragraph summary of the reading.
3. **Thinking Critically.**
   a. Identify at least three words that have strong connotative meanings. (See Chapter 2, page 69 and Chapter 9, page 344.)
   b. Evaluate the writer's main ideas. Identify at least three facts and three opinions. (See Chapter 3, page 105.)
   c. Study the writer's choice of supporting details. Does her choice suggest an emphasis, bias, or a particular viewpoint toward the topic? (See Chapter 4, page 139.) If so, please explain.

College Apologizes After Instructor Says Spanish Can't Be Spoken in Class

By Janine Zuñiga

CHULA VISTA—Administrators at a college in Chula Vista that is part of a national chain of higher education campuses across the country have apologized to students after an instructor told them that Spanish cannot be spoken in class.

The incident happened May 3 at Kaplan College. Jonathan Cedeño said he was in two medical assistant classes that day in which instructor Patricia Dussett said a school policy prohibited students from speaking anything but English at the campus. He said he confronted the teacher, who told him speaking Spanish could affect his grades and that students who ignored the rule might not get much-needed letters of recommendation.

"I told her that it wasn't right, that she was violating my rights, that we could speak whatever we wanted," Cedeño said.

The only reference to language in the school catalog states: "All courses are taught in English. Students must be able to speak, read and write English fluently. English abilities will be determined through the college administration's test and interview and completion of necessary documents."

Ron Iori, senior vice president of communications at Kaplan Higher Education, said the school's policy "broadly paraphrased says classes are taught in English but does not expressly forbid Spanish on campus." He said Kaplan officials visited the affected classes twice to apologize.

Some students said too much was made of the incident.

"Something very small became very big," said Mayra Barajas, 31-year-old medical billing and coding student. "We weren't even concentrating on school work anymore. It was getting to us. For about a week, it was very tense."

According to Barajas, "Ms. Dussett went into class and said, 'We're having a small problem with people speaking (Spanish) in class. . . . Out of respect for others who don't speak that language, it would be better that we all speak English during class.'"

Speaking Spanish was fine, Dussett said, during breaks, according to Barajas.

When the San Diego Chicano/Latino Concilio, a coalition of alumni, faculty, staff and students of colleges and universities in the region, learned about the incident at Kaplan, the group sent a letter to the college saying the coalition found it "especially reprehensible" that students who speak Spanish were told they would "be subject to a number of sanctions that include lower grades, denial of letters of recommendation, and even termination from the institution."

Iori said students will not be sanctioned for speaking Spanish.

Barajas said a day after the incident that campus director John Walker went into the same classrooms and apologized. Within days, Kaplan lawyers were dispatched to the campus to talk with students about the incident.

"They talked to almost everyone on campus," said student Maylin Cibrian, 20.

Students said Dussett was gone for a few days after the incident. Officials with Kaplan would not comment, saying any actions taken were a personnel matter. They also would not make Dussett available to be interviewed.

Cibrian said she has high regard for Dussett and was happy when she returned to class. While the instructor was gone, substitute teachers filled in, the students said.

"I know my class suffered when Ms. Dussett was asked not to come for a couple of days," Cibrian said.

Kaplan College is part of Kaplan Higher Education Corp., a division of Kaplan Inc., which is based in New York and a unit of the Washington Post Co. Kaplan Higher Education Corp., with headquarters in Chicago, serves 1 million students each year nationally and abroad, including online programs. The Chula Vista campus has about 230 students.

—© Copyright 2007 Union-Tribune Publishing Co., A Copley Newspaper Site.

Copyright © 2012 by Pearson Education

d. What thought pattern is used to organize the reading? How does the writer use the pattern to organize her ideas? Choose a different pattern from that used in the reading. Consider how this pattern might have affected the reading's content and/or your response to the reading.

e. What is the author's purpose for writing? (See Chapter 9, page 341.)

f. Which quote in the article is an informed opinion?

g. Locate and underline a judgment word or phrase used in the article.

h. How could you verify the college policy on Spanish?

4. **Responding to Ideas**
Write a paragraph sharing your reactions and response to one or more of the ideas presented in the reading. Refer to your marginal notes.

SELF-TEST SUMMARY

To test yourself, cover up the Answer column with a sheet of paper and answer each question listed in the left column. Evaluate each of your answers as you work by sliding the paper down and comparing your answer with what is printed in the Answer column.

	Question	Answer
GOAL 1	How do fact and opinion differ?	A fact is a verifiable statement. An opinion expresses a writer's beliefs, emotions, or attitudes and often uses judgment words.
GOAL 2	How do you distinguish fact from opinion?	Ask if the information is something that can be verified. If it can be, it is a fact.
GOAL 3	What types of sources are best used when verifying facts?	Primary sources that are reliable and current are best used for verifying facts.
GOAL 4	What is an informed opinion?	An informed opinion is an opinion offered by someone who is an expert about the topic.

Copyright © 2012 by Pearson Education

PRACTICE TEST 10-1

NAME ______________________ SECTION ______________________

DATE ______________________ SCORE ______________________

Identifying Fact and Opinion

A. Directions: *Indicate whether each of the following statements is a fact (F) or an opinion (O).*

English Learners in American Classrooms

[1] Bilingual education, perhaps the least understood program in our public schools, also turns out to be among the most beneficial. [2] Its effectiveness—both in teaching English and in fostering academic learning in English—has been validated in study after study.

[3] Yet U.S. media rarely report such findings. [4] All too often, bilingualism is portrayed as a political controversy rather than a set of pedagogical challenges, a conflict over immigration instead of an effort to turn language "problems" into classroom resources.

[5] In education, of course, there is no one-size-fits-all. [6] What works for one student or group of students will not necessarily work for others. [7] All things being equal, however, a large and consistent body of research shows that bilingual education is a superior way to teach English-language learners. [8] Building on—rather than discarding—students' native-language skills creates a stronger foundation for success in English and academics.

[9] This is a counterintuitive finding for many Americans, so it needs some explaining. [10] Why does bilingual education work? [11] Three reasons:

- [12] When students receive some lessons in their native language, the teacher does not need to "dumb down" instruction in simplified English. [13] So they have access to the same challenging curriculum as their English-speaking peers, rather than falling behind.
- [14] The more these students progress in academic subjects, the more contextual knowledge they acquire to make sense of lessons in English. [15] And the more "comprehensible input" they receive in English, the faster they acquire the language.
- [16] Reading provides a foundation for all learning. [17] It is much more efficiently mastered in a language that children understand. [18] As they acquire English, these literacy skills are easily transferred to the new language. [19] Once you can read, you can read!

[20] Finally, let's consider the alternative: all-English "immersion." [21] Independent studies have shown that after several years of such programs in California and Arizona, there has been no benefit for children learning English.

[22] In fact, the "achievement gap" between these students and fluent English speakers seems to be increasing.

[23] Unfortunately, so is the gap between research and policy. [24] Bilingual education has fallen out of favor politically for reasons that have nothing to do with its academic effectiveness. [25] If we seriously hope to integrate immigrants as productive members of our society, that will have to change.

—Jost, "Bilingual education vs. English immersion," *CQ Researcher*, p. 1045

_______ 1. Sentence 1

_______ 2. Sentence 7

_______ 3. Sentence 14

_______ 4. Sentence 21

_______ 5. Sentence 25

***B. Directions:** After reading the following editorial that appeared in the* Buffalo News, *select the choice that best completes each of the statements that follow.*

Let Student Athletes Pay Their Own Way

1 It seems like every day brings another newspaper, television or magazine story about Title IX [a federal law mandating equal public education sports programs for males and females] and how we should or should not fund high school and college athletics. Even though I am a proponent of sports participation on all levels by both males and females, I am sick of hearing this Title IX rhetoric. So, I have come up with the perfect solution to this problem: Eliminate all public funding for athletes and athletic teams.

2 In these current financial times, where our tax dollars are being spread thinner and thinner, I think money for amateur athletics should rank fairly low on our list of priorities. I am not advocating the elimination of high school and college sports. I am merely suggesting that we return to a time where student athletes paid their own way just as other extracurricular activity participants do.

3 If privately funded schools wish to give scholarships to people who run around tracks or kick soccer balls, more power to them. But I, as a taxpayer, don't feel that I should have to fund students for anything other than academics.

—Piechowicz, *Buffalo News*, p. B5

Copyright © 2012 by Pearson Education

_____ 6. The central thought of the article is that

a. athletics are a waste of time.

b. taxpayers should be consulted on how their tax dollars are spent.

c. Title IX has created a major problem within athletic programs.

d. taxpayers should not have to pay for student athletic programs.

_____ 7. Paragraph 2 contains

a. mostly opinion.

b. mostly fact.

c. an even mix of fact and opinion.

d. expert opinion.

_____ 8. Paragraph 3 contains

a. mostly fact.

b. all opinion.

c. a mix of fact and opinion.

d. unverifiable facts.

_____ 9. The first sentence of the editorial can be best verified by

a. contacting the author.

b. doing an Internet search for articles and stories about Title IX.

c. contacting television stations.

d. talking with a local news reporter.

_____ 10. The author could make a stronger case for his opinions by including

a. stories of athletes who benefit from Title IX.

b. facts about the added costs of operating athletic programs in high schools and colleges.

c. examples of school districts that ignore Title IX rulings.

d. facts about athletes who are graduates of colleges with strong athletic programs.

NAME ______________________ SECTION ______________________
DATE ______________________ SCORE ______________________

PRACTICE TEST 10-2

Identifying Fact and Opinion

A. Directions: *This passage was taken from the magazine* Nation. *It is written for a general audience. After reading the passage, select the choice that best completes each of the statements that follow.*

Food for All

1 There are many Americans who have the resources to buy healthy food and still are denied access to it. This denial of access has created "food deserts," a term I despise but use for the sake of argument. The trouble with the term "food deserts" is that it describes lack in a way that indicates that the solution is outside of the community labeled a desert. To change our food system, we need to change the way we talk about it.

2 There is a pervasive idea in the sustainable-food movement that simply returning to a food system of the past would right all that is wrong in the food world. However, history does not show that there has ever been a time when our food system was fair or just. Reflecting through my eyes, the eyes of an African-American woman, I see a system that from the earliest days of the founding of America was built on the annihilation of Native Americans and enslavement of Africans. There is room to expand the conversation about food to engage all Americans. Recently, the right to food has been inserted into the healthcare debate. Rightly so, since access to healthy foods is a missing component of the healthcare dialogue.

3 For too long our debates about food and healthcare have been traveling along separate paths, even though science has long proven that diet is a major contributor to chronic diseases. Food is also intimately tied to ideas of freedom and choice. Too often, the concept of choice is invoked in the dominant culture when it is related to all the things that destroy the moral fiber of communities. But when communities of color invoke choice, we are talking about freedom. In order to access the life, liberty and pursuit of happiness promised by the Declaration of Independence, one must be free.

4 I am often called a food-justice activist. However, I tend to look at myself as a freedom fighter. I believe that all communities should have access not just to food outcomes but to the production and distribution methods by which they get food. In other words, I don't just want access to the food in the store; I want access to the land that grows food so that I may grow my own. I want access to vacant land in urban communities to not only grow food but to grow soil. Fertile soil is the corner-stone of a vibrant community, urban or rural.

—Redmond, *Nation*

Copyright © 2012 by Pearson Education

_______ 1. The author begins the selection by using the term "food deserts" in order to

a. summarize her opinion.
b. create a dramatic impact.
c. provide contrast to the facts.
d. offer a derogatory opinion.

_______ 2. The author uses the phrase "reflecting through my eyes" (par. 2) because she

a. wants to explain what has influenced her opinion.
b. hopes to disguise the factors that have led her to her conclusions.
c. has factual evidence to support her statements.
d. is casting doubt on the facts.

_______ 3. This sentence: "For too long our debates about food and healthcare have been traveling along separate paths, even though science has long proven that diet is a major contributor to chronic diseases" (par. 3)

a. cannot be verified.
b. expresses an opinion.
c. mixes fact and opinion.
d. is a fact.

_______ 4. The Declaration of Independence is mentioned in paragraph 3

a. to provide expert evidence.
b. for dramatic effect.
c. as informed opinion.
d. to offer an opposing viewpoint.

_______ 5. The author's attitude toward the sustainable-food movement is that it is

a. offering false hope.
b. making a step in the right direction.
c. contributing to the problem.
d. diverting attention from more important issues.

NAME ______________________ SECTION ______________________

DATE ______________________ SCORE ______________________

PRACTICE TEST 10-2

B. Directions: *After reading the following excerpt, taken from a review of Al Gore's book* Our Choice: A Plan to Solve the Climate Crisis *titled "Is This Really Our Choice?" select the choice that best completes each of the statements that follow.*

Is This Really Our Choice, Review of *Our Choice: A Plan to Solve the Climate Crisis*

1 Al Gore's new book. *Our Choice: A Plan to Solve the Climate Crisis*, is an exercise in emotionally charged propaganda, calling for mankind to give up its standard of living and accept large increases in government power for the sake of the environment. Gore draws the conclusion, "The only meaningful and effective solutions to the climate crisis involve massive changes in human behavior." Characteristically missing from his argument is evidence that humans are a significant cause of global warming. Forgoing logical appeal, he instead targets readers' emotions, detailing supposed results of warming that threaten Earth's very existence.

2 The introduction presents readers with heart-wrenching scenes. There is a picture of an Eskimo woman whose house is tumbling down from melting permafrost; a photo of an offshore oil rig damaged by Hurricane Katrina (with the implication that SUV emissions generated the storm); a dazzling shot of sand dunes the UN claims are threatening fertile fields, owing to global warming; flood victims in Mexico wading forlornly in chesthigh water somehow caused by man's activities; and a helpless little girl refugee from a "climate-influenced" conflict in the Darfur region of Sudan. Throughout the rest of the book, Gore blames anthropogenic (human-caused) global warming for these and virtually all other human tragedies. Proof is apparently unnecessary and hinders our efforts to "get on with the job."

3 From an aesthetic point of view, *Our Choice* is a spectacular, high-budget book. Quality photographs embellish many pages, and the illustrations of things like geothermal systems and pebble-bed reactors are top notch. The book seems a cross between a coffee table–grade travel book and a copy of *Popular Mechanics*. Unfortunately, the publisher decided to include more than photographs and illustrations, and there is the rub. A large part of the text reads as if it were written by a staff of slick lawyers from the National Resources Defense Council or Greenpeace. It is pure environmentalist propaganda. Then there are the parts written by Gore himself, easy to identify since they sound punchy, just the way he speaks. However, quite a bit is written by engineers or other technical folk who aren't quite as extremist as Gore and his fellow activists. Even so, every page of the book will lead naïve readers astray through slyly administered misinformation.

4 Lies are so powerful by nature. A statement such as, "Military expenditures by the United States could be reduced by tens of billions of dollars per year if

Copyright © 2012 by Pearson Education

we switched to renewable sources of energy," is a hideous lie, easily told. To refute it would first require giving readers something of an education in the costs and nature of energy. The lie takes three seconds to produce and many hours to refute. (On a positive note, once someone knows the truth, the propagandist is vanquished in that person's mind forever.)

—Hiserodt, *The New American*, p. 30

______ 6. In the first paragraph, the word **propaganda** means

a. best-seller.

b. research experiment done to disprove a commonly held belief.

c. textbook.

d. statements made to attempt to sway public opinion.

______ 7. The author criticizes Gore for

a. offering conclusions without showing facts to back them up.

b. believing humans caused global warming.

c. offering incorrect statistics.

d. taking the position that the climate is changing in a drastic manner.

______ 8. In paragraph three, the phrase "from an aesthetic point of view" indicates the reviewer is

a. completely misinformed.

b. expressing an opinion.

c. evaluating fact.

d. unable to prove anything.

______ 9. In the third paragraph, the phrase "slyly administered misinformation"

a. expresses the reviewer's opinion.

b. mixes fact with the reviewer's opinion.

c. states a fact.

d. is based on clear research.

______ 10. The last paragraph of the review

a. is based only on the reviewer's opinion.

b. must be true because otherwise it wouldn't be published.

c. does not support the reviewer's opinion.

d. offers facts that need to be verified.

NAME ______________ SECTION ______________

DATE ______________ SCORE ______________

MASTERY TEST 10-1

Identifying Fact and Opinion

***Directions:** After reading the following excerpt from a social work textbook, select the choice that best completes each of the statements that follow.*

Social Work as a Profession

1 Social work is emerging as an important profession in the modern world. As we noted earlier, the National Association of Social Workers has 155,000 members. In December 1961, provision was made for professionally trained and experienced social workers to become members of the Academy of Certified Social Workers, which gave them additional professional status; more than 20,000 qualified. By 1998, some 59,000 were certified.

2 Social work today is utilized in a variety of settings and agencies. Some of the important ones are psychiatric, medical, marriage, and family counseling; the school; rehabilitation; corrections; public welfare; workplace; drug abuse; and child welfare. Schools of social work train a student to work in any agency, giving him or her the generic understandings, skills, and attitudes that make it possible to function adequately.

3 Social work is becoming more important because thousands of persons are benefiting from its services and are telling their friends and associates who have problems of its many values and services. People are not only being helped with personal and family problems but also with neighborhood, national and even international difficulties. A prominent American, upon returning from a trip abroad made the statement that what the United States needs most of all to improve its foreign policy and relations is to have trained social workers as State Department attachés where each of the official government representatives works and lives. Trained social workers in foreign countries would understand the people and work with them where they are, helping them to help themselves and interpreting the United States in a much more favorable light than in the past.

4 Current evidence indicates that social work is here to stay and that in the decades ahead it will likely grow and expand its services, helping even more people with personal, family and community problems, especially related to adequate social functioning.

—Farley, Smith, and Boyle, *Introduction to Social Work*, p. 13

______ 1. The first sentence

a. states a fact.

b. expresses an opinion.

c. cites a research study.

d. gives an example.

Copyright © 2012 by Pearson Education

_______ 2. The statistics in the first paragraph

a. cannot be verified.

b. do not add useful information to the passage.

c. create a historical backdrop for the rest of the passage.

d. provide evidence in support of the first sentence.

_______ 3. The first sentence in paragraph 2

a. states a fact.

b. expresses an opinion.

c. mixes fact and opinion.

d. cannot be verified easily.

_______ 4. The author lists the social work environments in order to

a. cite personal experiences with social work.

b. express an opinion.

c. give examples in support of the preceding sentence.

d. cite the results of research.

_______ 5. Paragraph 3 expresses

a. facts.

b. informed opinion.

c. unsupported opinion.

d. a mix of fact and opinion.

_______ 6. Paragraph 3 begins with a sentence that

a. states a fact.

b. provides examples from personal experience.

c. judges the people who need social workers.

d. mixes fact and opinion.

_______ 7. The statement made by a "prominent American"

a. expresses an informed expert opinion.

b. states an opinion.

c. states a verifiable fact.

d. mixes fact and opinion.

_______ 8. According to the author, American social workers could help U.S. foreign policy by

a. teaching U.S. government officials about the problems facing citizens of other countries.

b. helping the citizens of other countries.

c. sending citizens of other countries to see the U.S. official in their area.

d. convincing the citizens of other countries that the United States is a large nation with many problems.

_______ 9. Throughout the excerpt, the authors support their opinion that "social work is here to stay" by using

a. mostly solid, verifiable facts.

b. citations of research studies.

c. analysis and interpretation.

d. statistics, examples, and opinions.

_______ 10. Overall, the passage

a. describes the state of social work as a field.

b. gives an overview of a social worker's job description.

c. explains the main philosophies of the discipline of social work.

d. encourages students to become social workers.

Copyright © 2012 by Pearson Education

NAME ______________________ SECTION ______________________
DATE ______________________ SCORE ______________________

Identifying Fact and Opinion

A. Directions: *After reading the following excerpt from a reference book, select the choice that best completes each of the statements that follow.*

Organic Food

1 The reasons for eating organic foods vary, ranging from health issues to environmental concerns and from preferences for taste to nutritional advantages. Many do claim that organic foods taste better and are more nutritious. However, at the beginning of the twenty-first century, no scientific studies had substantiated that claim. Still, most would argue that the demands of the food processing industry to increase shelf life for conventional foods can have a real impact, at least on taste. In addition, reading the label on any food product can be a daunting prospect for consumers who are intimidated by the listing of chemical additives and unsure about their long-term health effects, even if they are deemed safe by law. Organic food choice represents a complex intersection of traditional perceptions, ideology, and scientific fact.

2 Many consumers also seek out organic foods as an alternative to the industrial agricultural complex and factory food production of conventional foods. While the early twenty-first-century trend, an estimated $10 billion in annual sales and rising, is great news for the organic food industry overall, hard-line organic food advocates are alarmed by a number of changes that are taking place. They feel that as organic foods become more mainstream, many of the traditions of organic farming will be left behind. The traditional small farm is beginning to lose out to the larger corporate farms and food companies. A number of traditional organic food product lines have already been bought up by the major food companies. Organic foods are no longer confined primarily to the natural food stores, either. Most large grocery store chains across the United States have been devoting specific sections to organic foods, often alongside other "health food" products. Organic foods can also be found mixed among the conventional foods as well, including organic microwaveable macaroni and cheese, potato chips, ketchup, and ready-to-eat bags of salad.

3 Traditional organic food producers feel that, even though the larger companies, often monopolizing and multinational, will follow the rule of the law when it comes to organic certification, the legislation is full of loopholes, with an oversight process that has little room for ongoing public response. In the end, the convenience of the widespread availability of organic foods may be

compromised with the ability to support local organic producers who still advocate for a world in which we "think globally and eat locally."

—Brenton and McIntyre, *The Oxford Encyclopedia of Food and Drink in America*, p. 219

_______ 1. The use of the word "claim" in paragraph 1 indicates
   a. a fact cannot be verified.
   b. the author agrees with the information.
   c. an opinion is being presented.
   d. research will be offered to support the opinion.

_______ 2. Sentence 4 in the first paragraph, which begins "Still, most would argue," is
   a. a fact that cannot be verified.
   b. the author's opinion.
   c. a mix of fact and opinion.
   d. a fact that should be verified.

_______ 3. In paragraphs 2 and 3, the word "feel" is used to
   a. convey emotion.
   b. demonstrate that an opinion is being discussed.
   c. show opposing viewpoints.
   d. weigh the evidence that is presented.

_______ 4. In paragraph 2, the portion of the second sentence that begins "While the early" and ends with " . . . sales and rising" is
   a. a verifiable fact.
   b. unnecessary information.
   c. a fact that cannot be verified.
   d. an opinion that is based on false information.

_______ 5. The best way to verify facts presented in this selection is to
   a. check with a friend.
   b. Google them.
   c. check the dictionary.
   d. consult a reference book about food history and trends.

Copyright © 2012 by Pearson Education

B. Directions: *After reading the following passage, select the choice that best completes each of the statements that follow.*

Screening Food Service Workers

1 Impressions of the prospective employee gained in the interview and from the follow-up of references are admittedly incomplete. They may be checked or replaced by tests of various type, the most common being intelligence, trade, and aptitude. A number of companies, including food services, have improved the results of their selection decisions by the use of psychological tests. These companies have found that the benefits derived from psychological testing far exceed the costs. An applicant's probable tenure, customer relations, work values, and safety record may be predicted with such tests. To be considered legal, all psychological test questions must be job related and legal to ask. In addition, all applicants must be asked the same questions, and scoring methods must be the same for all applicants.

2 The physical fitness of an applicant for a food service appointment is highly important. A health examination should be required of all food service workers. Only physically fit persons can do their best work. Quite as important is the need for assurance that the individual presents no health hazard to the food service. Managers are well aware of the devastation that might result from the inadvertent employment of a person with a communicable disease.

—Palaceo and Theis, eds., *West and Wood's Introduction to Food Service*, p. 403

______ 6. The first sentence of the excerpt

a. gives examples of hiring techniques.
b. judges the interviewer's style.
c. states a fact.
d. expresses an opinion.

______ 7. The author believes that tests

a. can provide useful information.
b. do not take the place of an interview.
c. should always be used in addition to an interview.
d. provide no useful information.

______ 8. In the first paragraph, sentence 3, which begins "A number of companies," expresses

a. an expert opinion.
b. an opinion.
c. a mix of fact and opinion.
d. a fact.

______ 9. The writer of the passage

a. expresses no doubts about using psychological tests in the hiring process.
b. feels there is no merit to even the best formulated tests.
c. holds no strong opinion about the tests.
d. recommends a certain type of test.

______ 10. In the second paragraph, the author

a. offers expert opinion from food service managers.
b. provides solid facts about food safety.
c. expresses a strong opinion regarding health testing for food service workers.
d. judges the quality of health monitoring programs in the food service industry.

Copyright © 2012 by Pearson Education

MASTERY TEST 10-3

NAME ______________________ SECTION ______________________
DATE ______________________ SCORE ______________________

READING SELECTION

Profanity Becoming Hard to Avoid

Michelle Park

This selection originally appeared as part of a week-long newspaper feature, in Pennsylvania's *Reading Eagle,* on the topic of civility, asking the question, "Is Courtesy Still Common?" Preview and then read this article, which explores how the use of crude language reflects a growing lack of civility.

Vocabulary Preview

These are some of the difficult words in this essay. The definitions here will help you if you can't figure out the meanings from the sentence context or word parts.

profanity (title) vulgar or obscene language
involuntary (par. 1) done against one's will or without choice
intimate (par. 4) private or personal
ironic (par. 4) contrary to what is expected
vigilant (par. 7) watchful

1 Apparently the woman seated in the New York City subway car didn't mind informing her fellow passengers that her boyfriend is inadequate in the bedroom. Because there she sat, loudly revealing the details of his performance—or lack thereof—to a person on her cell phone. Dr. Andrea D. Mitnick, an associate professor in the department of speech, communication and theater at Kutztown University, was one annoyed member of her involuntary audience. "There is no doubt that it (language) has become much, much cruder, much louder," said Mitnick, 59. "The kinds of conversation that used to be shared in private spaces, like a bedroom or a kitchen, are now being carried on in public spaces, like buses, subways. I think every single one of us is becoming more guilty of it all the time."

Changing standards

2 The standards for acceptable language are changing in our society. It is evident in the words we speak and the music, movies and television that win awards. Advertisements test the limits of good taste. Fine art, literature—even

greeting cards—employ profanities. "There was a much clearer sense of what was appropriate and where it was appropriate," Mitnick said. "The rules have changed." In the 1950s and 60s, Mitnick said, *suck* was considered a very dirty word. Today it's hard to avoid. Many profane terms—including the f-word—often are used in everyday conversation.

3 Dr. Michael Adams, an assistant professor of English at Indiana University in Bloomington, Ind., agreed. He said the f-word has lost much of its shock value because it is used so much. Most people would agree that there are instances in life where incivility is called for, said Adams, a former English department chairman at Albright College. Profane language, he said, is one way we draw the line.

What happened?

4 Why has our everyday language become cruder? It depends whom you ask. Many blame the media and parents. In the case of the woman who blared her intimate details on the subway last summer, Mitnick blames the cell phone. It is incredibly ironic, she said, that the very technology that enables people to be constantly connected with others can also result in their being disconnected with those around them. "The convenience of communication, the ability to whip out our cell phone . . . it seems to me outweighs anymore the notion where, 'wait, maybe I should do this where I'm not bothering anybody,'" Mitnick said.

A sign of disrespect

5 To Bill B. Leinbach of Birdsboro, using crude language is a sign of disrespect. When a group of teenagers walked by his house cursing loudly last year, he confronted them. How did the youths respond to the 72-year-old? "'Well, you go (expletive) yourself,'" Leinbach said they replied. "'Who the hell do you think you are? You ain't my parent.'" Leinbach blames their language on what they're hearing in the media and from adults who use the words.

A positive development

6 Though the use of profanity has increased, the public use of racial and ethnic slurs has decreased, said Gene F. Policinski, vice president and executive director of the First Amendment Center, which works to protect freedom of speech. While people believe we've become more coarse, slurs that were very common in the 1930s and 1940s are rarely heard now, Policinski said. "I don't see them as balancing, (but) it's worth noting both trends," he said. Every era sets its own level of acceptance, Policinski said, noting that 18th-century newspapers could use the word *bastard* without fear of offending anyone. Today it is considered rude.

Copyright © 2012 by Pearson Education

No turning back

7 Going back to the way language used to be, Mitnick said, is not a useful goal. "I don't want to go back, but I think there's certainly things that can be done to reduce incivility," she said. "I think we have to first of all be vigilant about monitoring our own behavior." Mitnick isn't proposing that everyone abandon the use of profanity; she uses it herself—and often. Instead, she suggests teaching appropriate behaviors at appropriate times. "Words count," she said. "Somehow, we seem to have forgotten that. They reflect who we are."

Directions: *Select the choice that best completes each of the following statements.*

CHECKING YOUR COMPREHENSION

_______ 1. The main purpose of this selection is to

a. criticize people who use profanity in public.
b. propose new standards for acceptable language.
c. discuss the increasing use of profanity in public.
d. describe the characteristics of people who use profanity.

_______ 2. According to this selection, the increasing use of crude language may be blamed on

a. the media.
b. parents and other adults.
c. the cell phone.
d. all of the above.

_______ 3. The person identified in the article as an assistant professor of English is named

a. Andrea D. Mitnick.
b. Michael Adams.
c. Bill B. Leinbach.
d. Gene F. Policinski.

_______ 4. A positive trend identified in the article is

a. a decrease in the use of profanity by teenagers.
b. a decrease in the public use of racial and ethnic slurs.
c. an increase in the standards of language used in advertisements.
d. an increase in the awareness of the shock value of certain words.

_______ 5. Dr. Mitnick suggests that the best way to reduce incivility is by

a. eliminating technology that lets people be constantly connected with others.

b. going back to the way language used to be.

c. teaching appropriate behaviors at appropriate times.

d. abandoning the use of profanity altogether.

USING WHAT YOU KNOW ABOUT FACT AND OPINION

_______ 6. All of the following types of information are used in this article *except*

a. examples.

b. reasons.

c. statistics.

d. personal experience.

_______ 7. In the first paragraph, an example of a word that suggests an opinion is

a. *apparently*.

b. *mind*.

c. *details*.

d. *performance*.

_______ 8. The author mentions Dr. Andrea Mitnick in order to

a. provide an informed opinion.

b. endorse freedom of speech.

c. present an opposing viewpoint.

d. illustrate disrespectful language.

_______ 9. Of the following statements from the selection, the one that is a fact is

a. "There is no doubt that language has become much, much cruder, much louder."

b. "I think every single one of us is becoming guilty of it all the time."

c. "Fine art, literature—even greeting cards—employ profanities."

d. "I think there's certainly things that can be done to reduce incivility."

Copyright © 2012 by Pearson Education

_______ 10. Of the following statements based on the selection, the one that is an informed opinion is

a. "Apparently the woman seated in the New York City subway car didn't mind informing her fellow passengers that her boyfriend is inadequate in the bedroom."

b. "Advertisements test the limits of good taste."

c. "Leinbach blames their language on what they're hearing in the media and from adults who use the words."

d. "I don't see them as balancing, but it's worth noting both trends."

USING CONTEXT CLUES AND WORD PARTS

_______ 11. In paragraph 1, the word **inadequate** means

a. distant.

b. misunderstood.

c. not enough.

d. essential.

_______ 12. In paragraph 3, the word **incivility** means

a. ability.

b. rudeness.

c. appearance.

d. kindness.

_______ 13. In paragraph 4, the word **blared** means

a. announced loudly.

b. compared.

c. hinted at.

d. preferred.

_______ 14. In paragraph 6, the word **slurs** means

a. forms.

b. errors.

c. speeches.

d. insults.

_______ 15. In paragraph 6, the word **coarse** means

a. bumpy.

b. pleasant.

c. crude.

d. insincere.

Directions: Complete each of the following sentences by inserting a word from the Vocabulary Preview on page 402 in the space provided. Use each word only once.

REVIEWING DIFFICULT VOCABULARY

16. In her new book, the movie star revealed ____________________ details about her relationship with a famous singer.
17. The song was banned on several radio stations because it contained so much ____________________.
18. Experts agree that parents must be ____________________ about the sites their children visit on the Internet.
19. It was ____________________ that the pastor's sermon on courtesy was repeatedly interrupted by the ringing of someone's cell phone.
20. When our taxi was hit by a truck, we were ____________________ witnesses to the accident.

THINKING CRITICALLY

1. Do you think the author is trying to influence your opinions in this selection? Why or why not?
2. What is the purpose of the headings used throughout the selection?
3. Evaluate the effectiveness of the title, "Profanity Becoming Hard to Avoid." What are some other titles that would work for this selection?

QUESTIONS FOR DISCUSSION

1. Do you agree that profanity is becoming hard to avoid? Why or why not?
2. In what situations is profanity considered appropriate or acceptable? Discuss circumstances in which you would be more likely to tolerate profane language.
3. Discuss the trends identified in paragraph 6. Why do you think the use of profanity has increased while the public use of racial and ethnic slurs has decreased?

Copyright © 2012 by Pearson Education

WRITING ACTIVITIES

1. Have you ever been an "involuntary audience" to another person's conversation? Write a paragraph describing how you reacted.
2. What makes a word offensive or obscene? Write your own definition of profanity, and explain why you consider certain language to be offensive, inappropriate, or unacceptable.
3. Think of a song, a movie, or a television show that you enjoy. Does it test the limits of good taste? Write a paragraph explaining your answer.
4. Read over the "Ten Commandments for Good Manners" from an etiquette consulting firm (http://www.courtesycounts.org/images/TenCommandments.pdf). Explain how each one does or does not apply to the topic of rude language and the use of cell phones in public.

CHAPTER 10

Distinguishing Fact from Opinion

RECORDING YOUR PROGRESS

Test	Number Right		Score
Practice Test 10-1	________	× 10 =	________%
Practice Test 10-2	________	× 10 =	________%
Mastery Test 10-1	________	× 10 =	________%
Mastery Test 10-2	________	× 10 =	________%
Mastery Test 10-3	________	× 5 =	________%

GETTING MORE PRACTICE PEARSON myreadinglab

To get more practice with Distingu shing Fact from Opinion, go to http://www.myreadinglab.com and click on

> Study Plan

> Reading Skills

> Critical Thinking

EVALUATING YOUR PROGRESS PEARSON myreadinglab

To measure your progress after reading and viewing the information in the Review Materials section, complete the Practices and Tests in the Activities section. You can check your scores by clicking on the Gradebook tab.

Then, based on your performance in this chapter and/or on the MyReadingLab Practices and Tests, write your own evaluation.

YOUR EVALUATION: ____

____

____

____

____

Copyright © 2012 by Pearson Education

THINKING ABOUT

Tone and Bias

The photographs on this page present two very different images of the celebrity, Britney Spears. Each conveys a quite different impression of her. The first presents Spears as an attractive, successful performer, while the second shows her as unattractive, making an unpleasant facial gesture.

Just as the two photographs of the same person can express very different attitudes, so can a writer create different impressions of his or her subject by choosing flattering or unflattering descriptive details and by using language that creates positive or negative impressions. In this chapter you will learn how to evaluate a writer's tone—his or her attitude toward the subject. You will also learn to uncover bias—the expression of an unfair preference for or dislike toward a subject.

CHAPTER 11

Analyzing Tone and Bias

LEARNING GOALS

GOAL 1 Evaluate a writer's tone

GOAL 2 Interpret irony and sarcasm

GOAL 3 Detect and analyze bias

Recognizing Tone

GOAL 1 Evaluate a writer's tone

myreadinglab
To practice recognizing tone, go to
> Study Plan
> Reading Skills
> Critical Thinking

The tone of a speaker's voice helps you interpret what he or she is saying. If a friend says to you, "Would you mind closing the door?" you can tell by her tone of voice whether she is being polite, insistent, or angry. Or if your brother asks, "Where did you get that coat?" he may mean that he wants to know where you bought it, or maybe he is being sarcastic and really dislikes it. You can tell by his tone of voice. The speaker's tone of voice, then, reveals the intended meaning. Writers also convey a tone, or feeling, through writing. **Tone** refers to the attitude or feeling a writer expresses about his or her subject. Think of tone as the feelings, mood, or emotions that a writer expresses through a piece of writing.

A writer can express a variety of different tones. In the following example, notice how each writer reveals a different attitude toward the same subject:

- We cannot trust our police chief; he is corrupt and completely ignorant of our community's problems.
- Our feelings of disappointment over the police chief's actions are overwhelming; we truly believed he would be the one to turn our community around, but he has betrayed us just like his predecessor.
- Is anyone really surprised by the scandal surrounding our police chief? Trusting a city official is like trusting a fox in a hen house.

In the first example, the writer is angry, in the second the writer is sad and disappointed, and in the third the writer is cynical.

Copyright © 2012 by Pearson Education

TABLE 11-1 Words Frequently Used to Describe Tone

abstract	condemning	flippant	irreverent	playful
absurd	condescending	forgiving	joyful	reverent
amused	convincing	formal	loving	righteous
angry	cynical	frustrated	malicious	sarcastic
apathetic	depressing	gentle	melancholic	satiric
arrogant	detached	grim	mocking	sensational
assertive	disapproving	hateful	nostalgic	serious
awestruck	disrespectful	humorous	objective	solemn
bitter	distressed	impassioned	obsequious	sympathetic
caustic	docile	incredulous	optimistic	tragic
celebratory	earnest	indignant	outraged	uncomfortable
cheerful	excited	indirect	pathetic	vindictive
comic	fanciful	intimate	persuasive	worried
compassionate	farcical	ironic	pessimistic	

As you can see, writers can express a wide range of tones. Table 11-1 lists words that are often used to describe tone. Here are six that are commonly used:

- **An instructive tone.** The writer values his or her subject and thinks it is important for the reader. Information about the subject is presented in a straightforward, helpful manner.

Example

When purchasing a piece of clothing, one must be concerned with quality as well as with price. Be certain to check for the following: double-stitched seams, matched patterns, and ample linings.

- **A sympathetic tone.** The writer reveals sympathy or sorrow toward the subject.

Example

The forlorn, frightened-looking child wandered through the streets alone, searching for someone who would show an interest in helping her find her parents.

- **A convincing tone.** The writer feels his or her ideas are correct and is urging the readers to accept them.

Example

Child abuse is a tragic occurrence in our society. Strong legislation is needed to control the abuse of innocent victims and to punish those who are insensitive to the rights and feelings of others. Write to your congressional representative today.

- **An entertaining tone.** The writer finds the subject light and amusing and wishes to share this with his or her readers.

Example

Gas prices are climbing again, which means some super-hard driving decisions in our family. Driving to the gym is definitely out—besides, walking builds character as well as muscle. And when Cousin Stanley comes to town, I hope he does not expect to be chauffeured around; walking may help him lose a couple of pounds that need to go. Of course, the 50-mile trek to Edgar's Easter Egg Extravaganza is a no-go this spring. Tough times = tough choices!

- **A nostalgic tone.** The writer is thinking about past times or events. The writer is often sentimental, recalling the past with happiness, sadness, or longing.

Example

Television is not what it used to be. There was a time when TV shows were truly entertaining and worthwhile. Wouldn't it be wonderful to see shows like *I Love Lucy* or *Batman* again?

- **An outraged tone.** The writer expresses anger and indignation toward something he or she finds offensive.

Example

It is appalling that people sit on bus seats talking loudly on their cell phones and expecting me to listen to their ignorant conversations. I'd like to grab their cell phones and throw them out the window.

A writer's tone is intended to rub off on you, so to speak. Tone is also directly tied to the author's purpose (see Chapter 9). A writer whose tone is humorous hopes you will be amused. A writer whose tone is convincing hopes you will accept his or her viewpoint.

EXERCISE 11-1 Understanding Tone

Directions: *Indicate whether the tone in each of the following statements is instructive (I), sympathetic (S), convincing (C) entertaining (E), outraged (O), or nostalgic (N).*

_______ 1. Try yoga for your back pain. Students of yoga agree that your discomfort will disappear while you gain strength and flexibility. Just five minutes a day to better back health.

_______ 2. I am sick of seeing billboards and signs plastered all over our beautiful countryside. These are visual pollution, and I never want to see another.

_______ 3. Most newcomers to our country are hoping for a better life. Unfortunately, before they can achieve that, they must face a myriad of problems. Seemingly endless bureaucracy and

Copyright © 2012 by Pearson Education

prejudice are just two of the major hurdles tragically placed in the way of these hardworking immigrants.

_______ 4. Yesterday, I saw a true sign of spring: a cute squirrel playing in the backyard. He was trying to get a piece of string that held up last summer's climbing peas. The squirrel tugged and tugged, spinning around and flipping, until he finally rolled the string into a ball. With this ball in his mouth, he gave one last tremendous pull that snapped the string from the post to which it had been tacked! With his mission accomplished, he scurried up the nearest tree with his treasure.

_______ 5. Parents need help raising their children. Since many families now have two income earners, mothers and fathers are increasingly turning to outside institutions and individuals for child care. Our government should assist these families with subsidies, health insurance, and parental leave in order to ensure stable futures for our country's youth.

_______ 6. Today's cameras come in many formats with a wide range of features. First, you must decide if you want to go digital. Then, you must consider your budget. Finally, you should try out a variety of models to find the best fit for you.

_______ 7. Public high school teachers work very hard at one of the most difficult jobs in our country. How do we reward them? We give them long hours and low salaries. No wonder so many teachers burn out quickly and turn to more lucrative jobs in the business world.

_______ 8. After four years of surpluses, the federal budget is now returning to deficit spending. Write your senators and representatives and let them know that this is unacceptable. We do not need surpluses to be spent on tax cuts that benefit the wealthiest Americans. What we do need is a government that sets a good fiscal example for its citizens.

_______ 9. Every living creature has different nutritional needs. For example, humans need water, oxygen, and a complicated combination of minerals, vitamins, and other substances. Other mammals have different needs. Even plants and microorganisms have their own set of nutritional requirements.

_______ 10. Public libraries have become much more than the quiet, relaxing places they used to be. Nowadays there is so much activity—there's free Internet access, games, and software. Some libraries even have espresso stands. I vote for a return to the good old days when a library meant books and only books.

Tone and Connotative Meanings

Look again at the examples of tone on pages 412–413. Notice that each writer uses particular words to convey tone. Often writers choose words that have a strong connotative or emotional meaning. (See Chapter 9 for a review of connotative meanings.) In the first example, the writer offers advice in a straightforward way, using the words *must* and *be certain*. In the second example, the writer wants you to feel sorry for the child and uses words such as *forlorn* and *frightened-looking*. In the third example, the writer tries to convince the reader that action must be taken to prevent child abuse. The use of such words as *tragic, innocent victims,* and *insensitive* establish this tone. In the fourth example, the writer uses exaggeration *(super-hard)* and silly expressions *(Edgar's Easter Egg Extravaganza)* to create humor.

EXERCISE 11-2 Recognizing Tone

Directions: *Select the word from the box below that best describes the tone of each of the following statements. Not all of the words will be used.*

optimistic—hopeful, positive
angry—extremely annoyed, mad
admiring—approving, holding a high opinion
cynical—distrustful, doubting
excited—feeling enjoyment and pleasure
humorous—amusing, making people laugh
disapproving—disliking, condemning
formal—serious, official
informative—factual
sarcastic—saying the opposite of what is meant
apathetic—lacking enthusiasm, energy, or interest

1. Taking a young child to a PG-13 movie is inappropriate and shows poor judgment on the part of the parents. ____________________
2. The brown recluse spider has a dark, violin-shaped marking on the upper section of its body. ____________________
3. The dedication and determination of the young men and women participating in the Special Olympics were an inspiration to everyone there. ____________________

Copyright © 2012 by Pearson Education

4. It does not matter to me which mayoral candidate wins the election, so I won't bother to vote. ____________________

5. Nobody is ever a complete failure; he or she can always serve as a bad example. ____________________

6. The councilman once again demonstrated his sensitivity toward the environment when he voted to allow commercial development in an area set aside as a nature preserve. ____________________

7. The success of the company's youth mentoring program will inspire other business groups to establish similar programs. ____________________

8. Professional athletes have no loyalty toward their teams or their fans anymore, just their own wallets. ____________________

9. We were thrilled to learn that next year's convention will be held in San Antonio—we've always wanted to see the Alamo! ____________________

10. To be considered for the president's student-of-the year award, an individual must demonstrate academic excellence as well as outstanding community service, and the individual must furnish no fewer than four letters of reference from faculty members. ____________________

Identifying Tone

It is sometimes difficult to find the right word to describe a writer's tone. To identify a writer's tone ask yourself the following questions:

- What feelings does the author reveal toward his or her subject?
- How is the writer trying to make me feel about the subject?
- What words reveal the writer's feelings toward the subject?

EXERCISE 11-3 Identifying with Tone

Directions: *Select the word from the box below that best describes the tone of each of the following statements. Not all of the words will be used.*

flippant	outraged	excited
awestruck	earnest	compassionate
sarcastic	worried	ironic

1. Our senator should be ousted from Congress. He no longer listens to the concerns of the people. He makes a mockery of the entire legislative process. ____________________
2. I still remember the first time I laid my eyes upon the New York City skyline. Having grown up in a rural town, I was amazed and a little frightened by the huge stretch of enormous buildings. ____________________
3. My niece is an aspiring actress, and I can't wait to see her star in the next production at the Children's Theatre. ____________________
4. It is scary that on some college campuses free thinking and critical debate are discouraged these days. What will happen if our students are not allowed to explore all sides of important issues? ____________________
5. As your best friend, I will do anything in my power to help you, so please let me know if there's anything I can do for you. ____________________

Tone: The Relationship Between the Writer and the Reader

Tone can also be used to help establish a relationship between reader and writer. Through tone a writer can establish a sense of a shared communication with the reader, drawing them closer together. Or a writer may establish a distance from the reader. In the excerpts that follow, notice how in the first passage a formality, or distance, is evident and, in the second, a familiarity and friendliness are created.

PASSAGE 1

At the time the dinosaurs reigned supreme among land animals, the first flowering on Earth occurred with the development of flowering plants, also known as **angiosperms.** Evolving between 180 and 140 Mya, the angiosperms eventually succeeded the gymnosperms as the most dominant plants on Earth.

Copyright © 2012 by Pearson Education

Today, there are about 700 gymnosperm species, but some 260,000 angiosperm species, with more being identified all the time. Angiosperms are not just more numerous than gymnosperms; they are vastly more diverse as well. They include not only magnolias and roses, but oak trees and cactus, wheat and rice, lima beans and sunflowers.

—Krogh, *Biology*, p. 366

PASSAGE 2

To begin evaluating a poem, first try to understand your own subjective response—don't pretend it doesn't exist. Admit, at least to yourself, whether the poem delights, moves, bores, or annoys you. Then try to determine what the poem seems designed to make you think and feel. Does it belong to some identifiable form or genre? (Is it, for instance, a love sonnet, narrative ballad, satire, or elegy?) How does its performance stack up against the expectations it creates? Considering those questions will give you some larger sense of perspective from which to evaluate the poem.

—Kennedy and Gioia, *Literature*, p. 789

Understanding how tone affects communication is particularly important for your writing classes, where you will be asked to choose a tone that is appropriate for your audience.

EXERCISE 11-4 Understanding Formal Versus Friendly Tone

***Directions:** Indicate whether each of the following statements is formal or friendly.*

1. Virus protection software helps to create a secure computing environment. The B-Safe program runs at all times and is constantly updated for maximum benefit. ____________________
2. Children who experience violence in the home are more likely to be the perpetrators of violence in school. Educators should be trained to recognize the signs of physical abuse in their students. ____________________
3. It takes stamina to keep up with technological advances. Just when you have mastered your VCR, it is time to get a DVD player. Right after you have finally gotten your scanner's software to run properly, you buy a digital

camera. Perhaps we need a device to help us keep track of all the changes and skills required to function in the modern world! ____________________

4. Becoming a professional magician takes a great deal of work. First, one must master the basic skills necessary for the core tricks. Then, there must be the development of complex, original illusions. Finally, the magician must begin the long process of working at clubs and parties until an agent who can foster a career notices him. ____________________

5. The aurora borealis, or northern lights, are a spectacular sight. If you ever hear that they are visible in your area, be sure to find a spot to look for this beautiful show in the sky. Do not miss the opportunity to see the effects of solar wind and geomagnetic activity in our atmosphere.

____

EXERCISE 11-5 Recognizing a Writer's Tone

Directions: *After reading each of the following passages, select the choice that best describes the writer's tone.*

_______ 1. Before you begin any knitting project, always check your gauge. Using the yarn and needles called for in the instructions, knit a two-inch swatch and then compare it with the scale given in the pattern. By making adjustments before beginning the project, you can avoid problems later on.

a. excited
b. instructive
c. sentimental
d. casual

_______ 2. After the helpless whales had beached themselves for a third time, the exhausted volunteers abandoned their rescue efforts and looked on grimly while the dying whales were euthanized.

a. persuasive
b. instructive
c. sympathetic
d. humorous

_______ 3. Use your frequent flyer programs to donate to charity. Your frequent flyer points may be used to help people with life-threatening medical conditions travel by plane to obtain the treatment they

Copyright © 2012 by Pearson Education

need, or to transport emergency relief personnel to the site of natural disasters, or simply to enable seriously ill children and their families to enjoy a trip to Disney World. You will be glad you helped others.

a. persuasive
b. angry
c. sympathetic
d. impersonal

_______ 4. "A boy can run like a deer, swim like a fish, climb like a squirrel, balk like a mule, bellow like a bull, eat like a pig, or act like a jackass, according to climate conditions. A boy is a piece of skin stretched over an appetite. However, he eats only when he is awake. Boys imitate their Dads in spite of all efforts to teach them good manners."

—former President Herbert Hoover; **http://www.hooverassoc.org**

a. persuasive
b. grim
c. logical
d. humorous

_______ 5. The handwritten letter is a vanishing art. Although the convenience of e-mail can't be beat, when someone sits down with pen and paper to write a good, old-fashioned letter, it reminds us of a simpler, more thoughtful time.

a. instructive
b. nostalgic
c. persuasive
d. angry

Understanding Irony and Sarcasm

Interpret irony and sarcasm

If while walking in a blinding snowstorm, a friend comments, "I really love this weather," you know that he means just the opposite. When someone says the opposite of what they mean, it is called **irony.** Here are a few examples:

- You want me to buy Girl Scout cookies? Sure, those will help me stay on my diet.
- Of course we should tear down this historic building for a parking lot. The city needs more pavement and less beautiful architecture.
- Oh, there's nothing better than waiting in line at the financial aid office!

Writers also use irony to humorously or lightly criticize, poke fun at, or indirectly comment on an issue or situation. Here is an example:

> Americans respond well to reality TV. We should hold our presidential elections this way—voters could just call in their votes after each debate.

In this example, the writer is suggesting that voter turnout would be better if our elections were held in the style of a reality TV show.

Sarcasm is a harsher, more bitter form of irony. Sarcasm is usually intended to ridicule, mock, or injure someone. Here is an example:

> When a woman at a dinner party told Winston Churchill he was drunk, he replied, "And you, madam, are ugly. But tomorrow I will be sober."

Here the humor is implied, but the meaning is clear. Here is another example:

> If you say to someone who has just come back from getting a haircut, "The barber shop was closed, huh?" you are making a sarcastic remark about the person's new hairdo.

EXERCISE 11-6 Recognizing Irony and Sarcasm

Directions: *Place a check mark in front of each statement that expresses irony or sarcasm.*

_______ 1. Violent crime is dropping due to the decrease in cocaine use.

_______ 2. Flight attendants have the most glamorous jobs—waitresses in the sky.

_______ 3. If you know your neighbor has an illegal immigrant working around the house, you should report it.

_______ 4. It is cruel and unusual punishment to force inmates at the Buffalo jail to shovel the snow. It is wrong to expect criminals to work or support themselves.

_______ 5. Gregory never says anything at our meetings; it's like working with a mummy.

Analyzing Bias

Detect and analyze bias

Suppose a classmate who is failing her psychology class tells you that the textbook for the course is difficult, that there are frequent unannounced quizzes, and that class participation is required. However, she fails to tell you that the instructor provides study guides for each textbook chapter, that students are allowed to retake quizzes to improve their grades, and that class participation often involves fun activities such as role-playing or simulated experiments. Obviously, the failing student is deliberately attempting to make her psychology class sound difficult and unappealing by presenting some facts and deliberately omitting others.

Copyright © 2012 by Pearson Education

What Is Bias?

When a writer or speaker deliberately presents a one-sided picture of a situation, it is known as bias. **Bias,** then, refers to an author's partiality, inclination toward a particular viewpoint, or prejudice. Now, think of a television commercial you have seen recently. Let's say it is for a particular model of car. The ad tells you its advantages—why you want to buy the car—but does it tell you its disadvantages? Does it describe ways in which the model compares unfavorably with competitors? Certainly not. Do you feel the ad writer is being unfair? Now let's say you know nothing about e-book readers and want to learn about them. You find an article titled "What you need to know about e-book readers." If the author of this article told you all the advantages of e-book readers, but none of their disadvantages, would you consider the article unfair? We expect advertisers to present a one-sided view of their products. In most other forms of writing, however, we expect writers to be honest and forthright. If a writer is explaining instant messaging he or she should explain it fully, revealing both strengths and weaknesses. To do otherwise is to present a biased point of view. You can think of bias as a writer's prejudice.

How to Detect Bias

To detect bias, ask the following questions:

- Is the author acting as a reporter—presenting facts—or as salesperson—providing only favorable information?
- Does the author feel strongly about or favor one side of the issue?
- Does the author seem to be deliberately creating a positive or negative image?
- Does the author seem emotional about the issue?
- Are there other views toward the subject that the writer does not recognize or discuss?

The author's language and selection of facts also provide clues about his or her bias. Specifically, words with strong connotative (emotional) meanings or words that elicit an emotional response on the part of the reader suggest bias.

In the following excerpt from a newspaper article, the author's choice of words (see highlighting) reveals his attitudes toward the police checkpoints.

> It started with a tip that checkpoints meant to nab drunken drivers were instead taking away cars, lots of them. The investigation confirmed those fears—and more.
>
> As a report in *The Bee* showed on Sunday, the sobriety stops have become cash cows for California police departments and towing firms—and they're fattening their wallets disproportionately at the expense of Latino motorists.

This hijacking of the checkpoints is an unfair, and likely illegal, corruption of what is an effective tool to keep dangerous drivers off California's highways.

Last year at DUI checkpoints statewide, officers impounded more than 24,000 vehicles from drivers caught without a license but made only 3,200 drunken driving arrests, according to the nonpartisan Investigative Reporting Program at the University of California, Berkeley.

To recover their cars, owners paid an average of $1,805 in towing fees and police fines—a total of more than $13 million statewide. In about 70 percent of seizures, the owners didn't bother to retrieve their vehicles, which then were sold at auction to pay the fees and fines, generating an additional $29 million. Finally, the officers running the checkpoints collected about $30 million in overtime last year.

California law allows police to impound the cars of unlicensed drivers for 30 days if they endanger public safety. But at some checkpoints witnessed by reporters, the seized vehicles appeared just fine. And while getting unlicensed—typically uninsured—motorists off the road is worthwhile, the punishment is out of whack with the crime, especially when DUI suspects typically don't lose their cars.

It's understandable, perhaps, that cash-strapped cities and towns are intoxicated by a revenue generator, especially when federal money often pays for the operations.

It apparently is up to the courts to step in and end this abuse. A case is pending before the 9th U.S. Circuit Court of Appeals that challenges the constitutionality of the California law, arguing that police can't seize vehicles when the only violation is driving without a license.

The appeals court should put this cash cow out to pasture.

—Car Seizure Law Invites Abuses, Views of the editorial board,
The Sacramento Bee, February 20, 2010, p. A10

EXERCISE 11-7 Recognizing Bias

Directions: *Place a check mark in front of each statement that reveals bias.*

_______ 1. Cities should be designed for the pedestrian, not the automobile.

_______ 2. There are more channels than ever before on cable television.

_______ 3. The current system of voter registration is a sham.

_______ 4. Professional sports have become elitist.

_______ 5. Space exploration costs millions of dollars each year.

Copyright © 2012 by Pearson Education

EXERCISE 11-8 Identifying Bias

Directions: *After reading each passage, select the choice that best answers each of the questions that follow.*

Al Gore's "The ice is melting!" rant deserves as much attention as Chicken Little's "The sky is falling!" The problem is he and other global-warming alarmists are getting as much attention as Chicken Little did. And while the fabled fowl was only trying to be helpful, the unscrupulous intent of global-warming alarmists is to set up an energy-regulating global government and an international carbon-trading market worth billions. Even though polar ice conditions are far from unusual or dangerous, these climate tycoons have far too much at stake to ever admit the sky isn't falling and humans aren't to blame. The public would do well to remember when Chicken Little's friends joined in her hysteria, they ended up as dinner in the fox's den. Unless countered through sound facts and reasoning, global-warming hysteria will end with much the same fate.

—Terrell, "Are the Polar Ice Caps Melting," *The New American,* February 15, 2010, p. 23

_______ 1. The author seems biased against

a. government energy regulations.
b. global-warming activists.
c. global markets.
d. corporations.

_______ 2. Which of the following phrases best reveals the author's bias?

a. "the fabled fowl"
b. "international carbon-trading market"
c. "polar ice conditions"
d. "global warming hysteria"

Plenty of statistics show a large number of offenders should never go to prison for nonviolent offenses. I, too, believe that the record should be expunged when the sentence is served. It is bad enough to have to pay back fines and court costs and perhaps child support that has accumulated during years in prison. To not be able to rent an apartment or get a job only ensures the person will soon return to prison. Criminologists have known for years that harsh punishments do not prevent crime. The plain fact is prisons are money-makers. Nothing is done for rehabilitation in the prisons, especially the private ones, which are only interested in the money. Frequently, the media, written and broadcast, are responsible for stirring up fear of being "soft on crime." Oklahomans should be thoroughly ashamed to have more women in prison than any other state. Rehabilitation programs work as do monitoring and community service.

—Morrow, "Letter to the Editor: Life After Prison," *Tulsa World,* April 2010, p. A16

_______ 3. The author's primary bias concerns the
   a. length of criminal sentences in general.
   b. imprisonment of nonviolent criminals.
   c. media portrayal of crime.
   d. cost of imprisonment.

_______ 4. Which of the following phrases expresses the author's bias?
   a. "offenders should never go to prison for nonviolent offenses"
   b. "soft on crime"
   c. "Oklahomans should be thoroughly ashamed"
   d. "more women in prison"

More than half of all video games are rated as containing violence, including more than 90% of games rated as appropriate for children 10 years or older. These games "provide an ideal environment in which to learn violence and use many of the strategies that are most effective for learning." The player is in the role of the aggressor and is rewarded for successful violent behavior. The games encourage repetitive and long playing to improve scores and advance to higher levels, and in some children and adolescents, promote addiction and an acceptance of violence as an appropriate means of solving problems and achieving goals.

—Masters, "Playing at War" *Women Against Military Madness Newsletter,* March 2010

_______ 5. The author is biased concerning
   a. the learning strategies children are exposed to.
   b. the violence in video games.
   c. how much time children spend playing video games.
   d. the way video games target young children.

_______ 6. Which phrase best suggests the author's bias?
   a. "ideal environment in which to learn violence"
   b. "encourage repetitive and long playing"
   c. "advance to higher levels"
   d. "promoting addiction"

Copyright © 2012 by Pearson Education

CRITICAL THINKING CHALLENGE

In this section is an excerpt from a magazine article on which to practice your critical thinking skills. Review the "Tips for Reading Magazine Articles" and use the steps below to guide your reading and response.

TIPS for Reading Magazine Articles

When reading magazine articles that address a specific audience, be sure to

- **Understand the audience.** You need to consider what their point of view is and how they would approach the topic.
- **Look for bias.** The author may slant the article to appeal to the interests and beliefs of the audience it is intended for.
- **Set aside your own bias.** You may have opinions about the particular audience the article is written for that could influence how you evaluate it.

Thinking Critically as You Read

1. **Reading, Highlighting, and Annotating.** As you read, highlight the key ideas. Write marginal notes to record your thinking as you read. Include comments, reactions, questions, opposing ideas, and so forth.
2. **Summarizing.** (Refer to Chapter 6, page 216.) Write a one-paragraph summary of the reading.
3. **Thinking Critically.**
   a. Identify at least two words that have strong connotative meanings. (See Chapter 2, page 69 and Chapter 9, page 344.)
   b. Evaluate the writer's main ideas. Identify at least three facts and three opinions. (See Chapter 3, page 105.)
   c. Study the writer's choice of supporting details. Does her choice suggest an emphasis, bias, or a particular viewpoint toward the topic? (See Chapter 4, page 139.) If so, please explain.
   d. Study the visual that accompanies the reading. What does it contribute to the reading? What does the writer's choice of this visual suggest about her position on or attitude toward the topic? (See Chapter 5, page 175.)

FEAR Itself

AIDS STIGMA DESTROYS CAREERS AND FRIENDSHIPS

by Regan Hofmann, from *POZ**

Stigma is one of the defining characteristics of HIV/AIDS, differentiating it from its biologically-parallel-but-socially-altogether-different retroviral kin. While we can discuss vaccinating children against HPV as we choke down our Cheerios, and we can sit comfortably in front of commercials for herpes drugs, the mere whisper of the word *AIDS* often causes all polite conversation to cease.

No one is imagining this. In 2007, the Foundation for AIDS Research sponsored a survey of Americans' attitudes about women living with HIV/AIDS. The survey found that more than half are uncomfortable having an HIV-positive woman as their dentist, doctor, or child care provider. Eighty-seven percent are uncomfortable dating someone who is HIV-positive. One in four was uncomfortable having an HIV-positive woman as a close friend.

It would be one thing if stigma stopped with an attitude, but in a recent survey on *POZ*'s website, 34 percent of respondents said that fear of stigma has prevented them from seeking care, treatment, and support. Imagine how many people don't get tested because of stigma. According to the Centers for Disease Control and Prevention, HIV-positive people who are unaware of their infection might account for 54 to 70 percent of all new sexually transmitted HIV infections in the United States. Stigma is a barrier to individual—and public—health.

While much of the impact of HIV-related stigma is quantifiable, however, it is, arguably, those aspects not captured by statistics that prove the most devastating. More than 1,000 people told *POZ* chilling stories of how stigma negatively affects their lives. Only a small group spoke of how they fight it, standing proud and strong despite society's desire to keep them down. The following are excerpts from the responses.

- When I told a very good friend of mine (we used to camp beside each other every weekend), he cried and said he would stand with me, support me, be there for me. I have never heard from him again, not a call, not even a note or e-mail.
- Most, if not all, of my negative experiences have been with, by, or in the presence of medical or dental personnel. . . . They look at me like I'm from outer space, and the quality of their care reflects it.
- I am a nurse by profession for 20 years. I told [human resources] the day I found out my HIV status [and] was put on administrative leave immediately and not called back or offered another job. [I had] impeccable credentials.
- I am basically unable to enter into any sort of romantic relationship. [I experience] quite a bit of social isolation—and it's just so tiresome.
- I must either turn a blind eye or tune people out, because I can honestly say in the 20-plus years of being positive, I have never had a bad experience. And I am very open about my status. . . . I have been able to educate others as a straight, white female (after they get over the shock first—folks don't think people like "me" get HIV/AIDS).
- For me it just feels like a very heavy weight I carry all the time. . . . Sometimes it gets very heavy. Rather than jeopardize [your] career, family, friendships, and security, you keep it secret. That's hard to do when you've lived an honest and truthful life.
- I have been asked not to share my water bottle with my 3-year-old nephew.
- I have been fortunate in the last 10 years to have not received a negative response from anyone I had to disclose to. However, I am extremely selective about whom I share this info with.

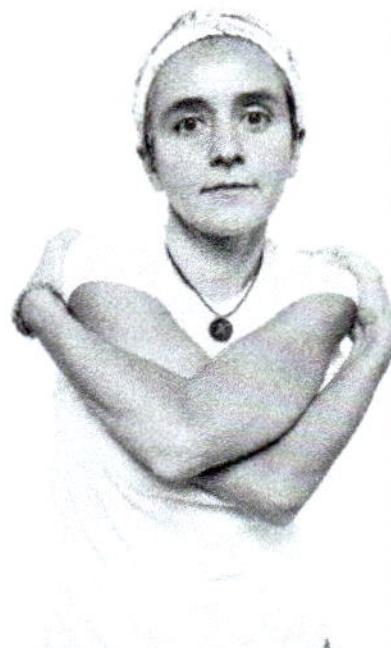

For her project INFECTED and AFFECTED, photographer Joan L. Brown asks people to show how they would fight, communicate love, and express the sadness surrounding HIV/AIDS stigma.

* *POZ* is a magazine for persons with a positive HIV status.

—Hofmann, *Utne Reader*

Copyright © 2012 by Pearson Education

e. What thought pattern is used to organize the reading? How does the writer use the pattern to organize her ideas? Choose a different pattern from that used in the reading. Consider how this pattern might have affected the reading's content and/or your response to the reading.

f. What is the author's purpose for writing? (See Chapter 9, page 341.)

g. What kind of tone does the author use in this article?

h. Given that the article is intended for an HIV-positive audience, what kind of bias do you think is present in the article?

i. Choose one of the quotations in the article and describe the tone of the speaker.

4. **Responding to Ideas**

Write a paragraph sharing your reactions and response to one or more of the ideas presented in the reading. Refer to your marginal notes.

SELF-TEST SUMMARY

To test yourself, cover up the Answer column with a sheet of paper and answer each question listed in the left column. Evaluate each of your answers as you work by sliding the paper down and comparing your answer with what is printed in the Answer column.

	Question	Answer
GOAL 1	What is a writer's tone?	Tone is the attitude or emotions the writer offers about the topic, often by using words with connotative meanings.
GOAL 2	What are irony and sarcasm?	Irony is a device in which the author says the opposite of what he or she means. Sarcasm is language used to mock or ridicule someone.
GOAL 3	How can bias be identified?	Authors with a bias present only one side of an argument, seem to have personal opinions about the topic, and deliberately create a positive or negative picture of the subject.

Copyright © 2012 by Pearson Education

PRACTICE TEST 11-1

NAME ______________________ SECTION ______________________

DATE ______________________ SCORE ______________________

Identifying Tone

Directions: *Indicate whether the tone in each of the following statements is instructive (I), sympathetic (S), convincing (C), entertaining (E), outraged (O), or nostalgic (N).*

_______ 1. When you see an automobile accident, call 911 immediately for assistance. If it is safe for you to do so, check the occupants of the vehicles for injuries. Stay until police arrive and identify yourself as a witness. The police will ask you to describe what you saw happen and will take your name and phone number in case your testimony is needed in a future investigation or in court.

_______ 2. Oil spills are devastating to the environment. These accidents cause massive damage to birds and marine mammals. Their sensitive bodies are simply not equipped to deal with the destructive effects of oil in their habitat.

_______ 3. Camping is a fun and educational experience for young children. They will delight in all the new sights and sounds of the forest and learn a great deal about our natural areas. Parents should not miss this important opportunity to enrich the lives of their children.

_______ 4. Regrettably, there are very few movies made these days that tell a good story. Most filmmakers simply rely on violence and special effects to attract viewers, disregarding character and plot development. Movies used to be so interesting, involved, and intellectual; now they are just visual candy.

_______ 5. Our government should make more of an investment in passenger trains. Many people do not like to fly and would rather have a leisurely railroad excursion. Also, trains use less fuel than airplanes and create less pollution. Finally, taking a train is much safer than flying. I am sure that most Americans would welcome a revival of train travel.

_______ 6. Who would ever think of taking a baby to a movie theater? Everyone there wants to hear the movie—not some burping, crying, sniveling baby. Do parents stupidly believe these babies will sleep through the whole movie? Send them to drive-in movies, or point them to the nearest video store!

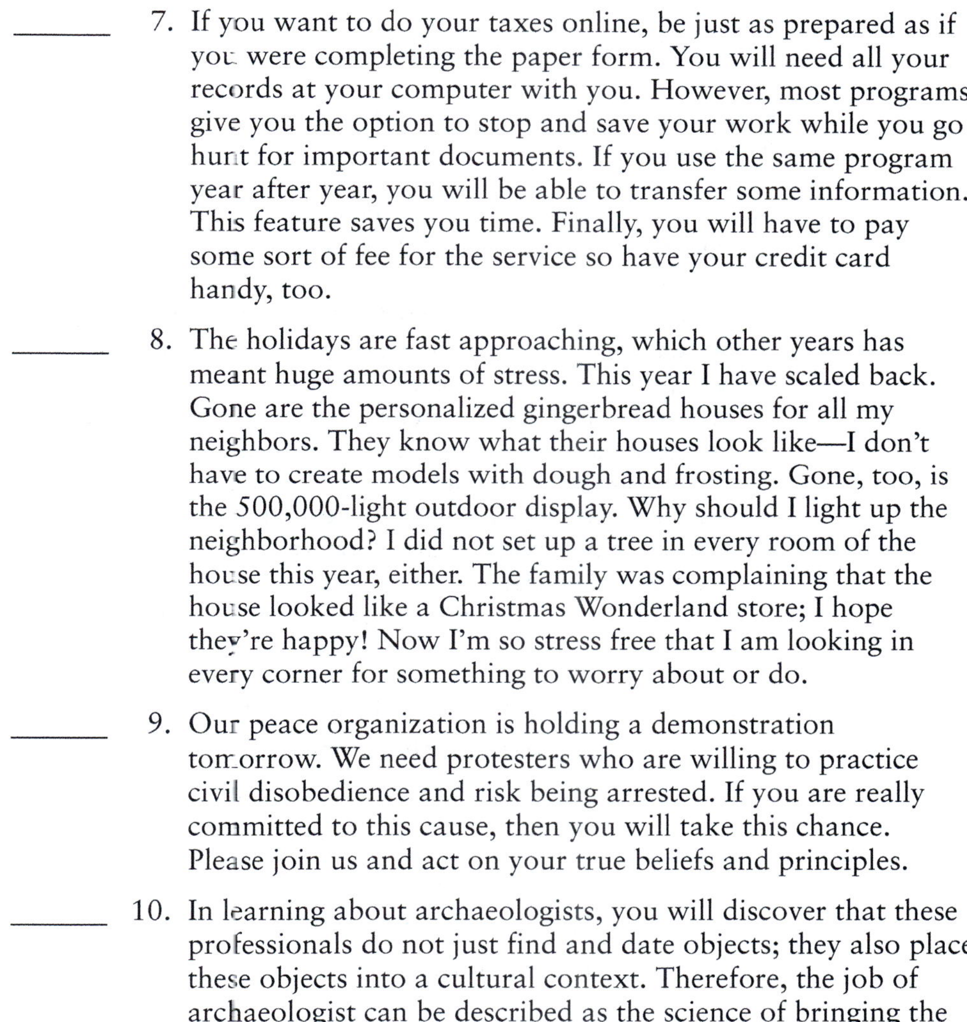

______ 7. If you want to do your taxes online, be just as prepared as if you were completing the paper form. You will need all your records at your computer with you. However, most programs give you the option to stop and save your work while you go hunt for important documents. If you use the same program year after year, you will be able to transfer some information. This feature saves you time. Finally, you will have to pay some sort of fee for the service so have your credit card handy, too.

______ 8. The holidays are fast approaching, which other years has meant huge amounts of stress. This year I have scaled back. Gone are the personalized gingerbread houses for all my neighbors. They know what their houses look like—I don't have to create models with dough and frosting. Gone, too, is the 500,000-light outdoor display. Why should I light up the neighborhood? I did not set up a tree in every room of the house this year, either. The family was complaining that the house looked like a Christmas Wonderland store; I hope they're happy! Now I'm so stress free that I am looking in every corner for something to worry about or do.

______ 9. Our peace organization is holding a demonstration tomorrow. We need protesters who are willing to practice civil disobedience and risk being arrested. If you are really committed to this cause, then you will take this chance. Please join us and act on your true beliefs and principles.

______ 10. In learning about archaeologists, you will discover that these professionals do not just find and date objects; they also place these objects into a cultural context. Therefore, the job of archaeologist can be described as the science of bringing the past to life.

Copyright © 2012 by Pearson Education

PRACTICE TEST 11-2

NAME ______________ SECTION ______________

DATE ______________ SCORE ______________

Evaluating Tone and Bias

Directions: *After reading each of the following passages, select the choice that best completes each of the statements that follow.*

A. In America, bilingualism, biculturalism, and bilingual education have historically been suspect. The legislative advances addressing issues of equity in the 1960s and 1970s have not helped to alleviate the current state of affairs for either bilingual or monolingual children. Our nation is implicitly and explicitly encouraging the loss of home languages. From the bilingual child's point of view, it is clear that you are expected to shed your family language and culture in order to be acceptable to the mainstream society. Yet losing your language and your culture does not guarantee entry into the world of the mythic America. Bilingual/bicultural families have tried to play by the rules in an effort to attain the American dream. Families have worked hard and contributed to the welfare of the nation, yet the data show high poverty rates and low levels of educational attainment.

—Soto, "Is the American Dream for Monolinguals Only?" *The Hispanic Outlook in Higher Education,* January 4, 2010, p. 44

_______ 1. The author reveals bias against
   a. programs that encourage loss of one's native language.
   b. people who speak two languages.
   c. people who experience poverty.
   d. immigrants.

_______ 2. The tone of the passage is
   a. righteous.
   b. mocking.
   c. sarcastic.
   d. concerned.

_______ 3. Which one of the following phrases reveals the author's bias?
   a. "implicitly and explicitly encouraging the loss of home languages"
   b. "play by the rules"
   c. "American dream"
   d. "contributed to the welfare of the nation"

B. Cell phone use has not just increased in recent years, but has become commonplace, normal, and expected. Even children as young as 11 are toting their own phones under the pretense of keeping in touch with their parents.

Our new method of communication has led us down a frightening path of familiarity, and as we all know, familiarity breeds contempt. Sitting in a library, a final bastion of civility and quietude, you can hear one-sided cell phone conversations about pet ailments, baby diaper contents, and last night's alcohol-fueled escapades. People have no qualms about discussing the details of their plane reservations, résumés, and potential purchases. All this unintentional openness at such high volumes pushes us further from loving our neighbors and closer to abandoning them. After all, they have someone on the other end of the "line" that cares about them, right?

_______ 4. The author's tone is

a. worried.
b. condescending.
c. alarmist.
d. irritated.

_______ 5. The passage reveals the author's bias against

a. parents.
b. cell phone users.
c. libraries.
d. children.

_______ 6. Which of the following groups of words best reveals the author's bias?

a. "commonplace, normal, and expected"
b. "toting their own phones"
c. "new method of communication"
d. "frightening path of familiarity"

C. There have been two serious accidents at the intersection of 155th Avenue and Broad Street within the past six days—ten in the past year. Angry residents have been demanding that our city council make traffic safety improvements at this very dangerous corner. However, our leaders are obviously waiting for a couple hundred people to be killed before they act. More important matters are at hand, such as a skateboard park and pay raises for the mayor and his staff. In this year's election, five council members (half of the total) are up for re-election. My guess is that the intersection will be made safer just before Election Day . . . after about six more accidents.

_______ 7. The author reveals a bias against

a. the city council.
b. city residents.
c. drivers.
d. traffic engineers.

Copyright © 2012 by Pearson Education

_______ 8. The author's overall tone is

a. grim.

b. outraged.

c. irreverent.

d. mocking.

_______ 9. When the author writes that the council is "waiting for a couple hundred people to be killed," she is being

a. pessimistic.

b. sarcastic.

c. disapproving.

d. approving.

_______ 10. What important fact might the author be purposely leaving out?

a. The mayor's raise goes into effect next year.

b. Last year's election brought two incumbents back.

c. Three pedestrians were injured over the past year.

d. The city council has met with the residents and several plans of action were discussed.

NAME ______________________ SECTION ______________________

DATE ______________________ SCORE ______________________

MASTERY TEST 11-1

Evaluating Tone and Bias

A. Directions: *Select the word from the box below that best describes the tone of each of the following statements. Use each choice only once.*

instructive	indignant	persuasive	impassioned	insulting

1. Even though our country has made great advances in race equality over the past 50 years, we still have a long, hard road ahead of us. Shamefully, all people are still not presented with the same level of respect and opportunity in the United States. ______________________

2. In order to master a musical instrument, students must practice, practice, practice. Visit the college library's music collection, and just start selecting pieces to learn. Also, try to find a practice space away from the distractions of your dorm. ______________________

3. With mortgage rates so low right now, buying a house has become a better deal than renting. You will have your very own home and be building equity for your future. You cannot afford to miss out. Call your realtor today and start house shopping! ______________________

4. I cannot believe how many parents allow their children to misbehave in restaurants! I am still shocked each time I see children throwing food, crawling under tables, and shouting and screaming.

   ____

5. Our totally incompetent and cowardly town council voted secretly last night to put a sewage treatment plant right near a public beach. These idiots have ruined the only waterfront access our children have without consulting their constituents. ______________________

Copyright © 2012 by Pearson Education

***B. Directions:** Briefly identify the bias in each of the following passages.*

6. Modern farmers are harming our children with their new, stronger pesticides. Young kids all over the country are developing health problems from the chemicals in their foods. I am only going to buy certified organically grown products from now on. They may cost more, but their purity is worth it.

   ____

7. So many of my neighbors have peace symbols and slogans in their windows and on their lawns. Do they really think that these signs make a difference? Some people are so naïve.

   ____

8. Health insurance companies have no right to dictate treatment plans. They should stay out of the personal lives of their patients and go back to the old ways of doing business. Leave the treatment to the doctors—doctors that we choose!

   ____

9. Millions of unwanted animals are euthanized each year. If it weren't for all the uncaring pet owners out there who don't have their animals spayed or neutered, animal shelters wouldn't even have to exist. When is everyone going to get on board with pet birth control?

   ____

10. People who drive gas-guzzling vehicles should be ashamed of themselves. Our country needs to limit its dependence on foreign oil, not create a hot new demand for it.

    ____

NAME ______________________ SECTION ______________________

DATE ______________________ SCORE ______________________

MASTERY TEST 11-2

Analyzing Tone and Bias

Directions: *After reading each passage, select the choice that best completes each of the statements that follow.*

A. My daughter stared at her reflection as she brushed her teeth. Our eyes met in the mirror as she said, "Mama, I'm sad that you're different from us." My heart sank. "We all have brown eyes and yours are blue. Don't you wish you had brown eyes too?" My heart lightened. I had thought Claire was going to ask me about my being the only Catholic in our interfaith household.

Before my wedding, Mother worried about how I would feel if I married a Jewish man and raised Jewish children, and asked if I'd considered converting. I assured my mother that having a different religion or a different last name (I was keeping my maiden name, another source of concern for her) did not mean I had to feel like an outsider in my own family. At 31 I had a strong sense of who I was and what I wanted. My fiancé and I had attended an interfaith couples group and discussed likely scenarios for birth rituals, raising children, and celebrating holidays, and we agreed that the interfaith aspects of our household would be open to reinterpretation as our lives changed. I had tried to think through all the challenges.

It was my idea to raise any future children Jewish. Even though I was no longer attending Mass regularly, I knew I wanted to raise a family that participated together in a religious community. In addition, I was comfortable in synagogues, while Barry was decidedly uncomfortable in churches. So, if I wanted Barry to participate in our children's religious upbringing, the only thing that made sense was to raise them Jewish. If I felt like an outsider at services, I could handle that. I would experience what it feels like to be the minority. Wasn't that what Jews experience all too often?

—McMahon, "The Outsider: Being a Catholic in Temple," *Lilith*, p. 48

______ 1. The author's tone is

a. earnest. c. gentle.

b. joyful. d. worried.

______ 2. At first the author thought her daughter

a. was angry at her.

b. had a condemning tone.

c. might reveal bias against her mother's being Catholic.

d. did not understand why her mother had a different religion.

Copyright © 2012 by Pearson Education

_______ 3. The author's mother's tone was probably
   a. disapproving.
   b. sarcastic.
   c. pessimistic.
   d. concerned.

_______ 4. The author suggests her husband may have had a bias against Catholicism by writing that he
   a. was uncomfortable in churches.
   b. attended an interfaith couples group.
   c. has a different last name.
   d. had a strong attachment to the Jewish faith.

_______ 5. The author felt that she might
   a. develop bias against Jewish people.
   b. experience bias at temple for not being Jewish.
   c. miss the Catholic Church.
   d. pass on her biases to her children.

B. 1 It's a great day for minority kids, for children in the inner cities, and for parents who desperately want to give their children a better education in a safer environment. It's a great day for parents who want the same benefits for their children enjoyed by the offspring of Jesse Jackson, Bill Clinton, our representatives and senators, the wealthy and many public school principals and teachers. It's the opportunity to choose the school where they want their children to go.

2 The U.S. Supreme Court ruled that it is legal for Americans to choose vouchers as an alternative to traditional government-sponsored public education. Essentially, the High Court ruled that government programs permitting vouchers are constitutional, even if the vouchers are used toward tuition at religious schools. "The Court endorsed a six-year-old pilot program in inner-city Cleveland that provides parents a tax-supported education stipend. Parents may use the money to opt out of one of the worst-rated public school systems in the nation," wrote Anne Gearan of the Associated Press.

3 When it comes to educating our children, choice is good. This ruling is good. For too long now, liberal politicians and their supporters in the education establishment have created a climate that tells parents who can't afford private schools—most of us—that choice in education is a bad ideal. "Let's save our public schools. Let's improve them. Don't throw the baby out with the bathwater," are common responses. Well, now we can take the baby out of the bath water and put him in a different tub. Now parents have choice.

4 An inner city single mom can send her kid to a private school, a school that might indeed teach the values that she wants her children to learn, in a safe environment, away from the gangs, the drugs and discipline problems. Isn't this good for all of us?

5 But the liberal education establishment says choice in education is bad. Want to know a dirty little secret? Check out the percentage of public school principals and teachers who send their own children to private schools. They fight feverishly to keep that very same options they enjoy from others—especially from parents in the inner city who need that choice most of all.

—Gibbs, "It's a Great Day for Choice," *New York Voice Inc.*

_______ 6. The author's overall tone is
- a. critical of the Court's decision.
- b. solemn.
- c. indirect and evasive.
- d. approving of the Court decision.

_______ 7. The "different tub" referred to in paragraph 3 is
- a. a new building with modern conveniences.
- b. an improved public school.
- c. a school of the parent's choice.
- d. a school where racial problems do not exist.

_______ 8. The author reveals bias against
- a. private schools.
- b. politicians.
- c. public schools.
- d. parents.

_______ 9. The author thinks that
- a. the Supreme Court is biased against liberals.
- b. inner city parents should not give up on their neighborhood schools.
- c. private schools will welcome students from the inner city.
- d. liberal politicians are biased against lower- and middle-class families.

_______ 10. The tone of Anne Gearan's quote is
- a. critical of the Court decision.
- b. factual and supportive of parents.
- c. intended to be entertaining.
- d. grim and angry.

Copyright © 2012 by Pearson Education

NAME ______________________ SECTION ______________________

DATE ______________________ SCORE ______________________

READING SELECTION

Explaining Away the Hate

Terry Hong

Why do people hate other people? In this reading, which first appeared in *Asian Week*, the author considers this difficult question. Read it to find out how seeing protesters on the street led the author to explore the meaning of hate.

Vocabulary Preview

These are some of the difficult words in this essay. The definitions here will help you if you can't figure out the meanings from the sentence context or word parts.

rhetorical (par. 1) not expecting an answer; just for effect

vehemence (par. 1) intensity, power, passion

factors (par. 1) elements contributing to a particular result or situation

arbitrary (par. 1) randomly chosen based on personal whim

permutations (par. 3) arrangements, sets

determined (par. 2) settled upon, resolved

unconditional (par. 5) absolute, limitless

dogma (par. 6) doctrine, code of beliefs

1 I want to understand hate. This is not a rhetorical statement. I want someone to explain to me, patiently and logically, how people learn to hate with such blindness, vehemence and violence. I want to know how a child can be taught to hate based on such arbitrary factors as what a person looks like, what a person might believe in or who a person might love. I want to know how that child grows up to be a hateful adult. And I want to know how it becomes possible that it is God who supposedly teaches this hate.

2 Last weekend, as I was driving my two young children to a birthday party in the pouring rain, I saw a group of approximately a dozen men carrying large, fluorescent placards. They were posted at the entrance of the very church where I had spent most Sunday mornings growing up. So determined were the demonstrators to make sure their message was loud and clear that these hideous signs were untouched by the downpour—the demonstrators had the foresight to seemingly waterproof them.

3 “God Hates Fags!” the signs screamed in various permutations.

4 “Oh my God!” I shouted in response. My shocked 5-year-old, who is discouraged from using that phrase, asked with great concern, “What’s wrong, Mommy?” And somehow I had to explain that the people with the signs had written “not nice” and “mean” messages on their posters, that they thought that God didn’t like a certain group of people. Ironically, back at home visiting for the weekend was one of our closest friends, who just happened to be homosexual. I cringed, thinking our friend might drive this way.

5 “But Mommy,” my daughter said, “God loves everybody. That’s why he’s God.” And I thought to myself how grateful I am for the innocence of my children. And I silently prayed that my children would never lose that sense of God’s unconditional love.

6 I’m not a religious person. Disappointed with dogma, I left the Catholic Church years ago. My husband and children attend a non-denominational Christian church on a fairly regular basis. When our children get older, we plan to expose them to other religious choices, as my husband was so exposed. The son of a United Church of Christ/Congregational minister who marched with Martin Luther King Jr. and Gloria Steinem, my husband and his siblings were taken to synagogues, Muslim temples, Buddhist services, as well as various Christian houses of worship. My father-in-law wanted his children to have a choice about other religions. In so doing, he taught them so much about tolerance.

7 How do we teach tolerance today in a world so filled with hate—hate that happens in the name of God?

Directions: *Select the choice that best completes each of the following statements.*

CHECKING YOUR COMPREHENSION

_______ 1. The central thought of the reading is that the author is struggling to understand

a. why people believe in God.
b. how children learn to hate adults.
c. how God has become associated with hate.
d. why God hates some people.

_______ 2. The author is disturbed about the demonstrators’ message because it

a. used God to justify their hate.
b. was written on fluorescent placards.
c. seemed insensitive and rude.
d. was being delivered at her childhood church.

Copyright © 2012 by Pearson Education

_______ 3. From the information presented in the reading, it is apparent that the author believes in the freedom to

a. carry weapons.

b. choose a religion.

c. select marriage partners.

d. hold unpopular political views.

_______ 4. How did the author's husband learn about tolerance?

a. by marching with Martin Luther King Jr.

b. by being exposed to a variety of religious experiences

c. from having a minister for a father

d. from the Catholic Church

_______ 5. The author mentions her husband's religious upbringing in order to

a. educate the reader about religion.

b. explain how her father-in-law taught religious tolerance.

c. illustrate that widespread conflict in the name of God exists.

d. comment on the problem of intolerance in organized religions across the globe.

USING WHAT YOU KNOW ABOUT TONE AND BIAS

_______ 6. The author's overall tone is

a. angry.

b. distressed.

c. flippant.

d. pessimistic.

_______ 7. The demonstrators are biased against

a. people of different faiths.

b. atheists.

c. homosexuals.

d. anyone not like themselves.

_______ 8. The daughter's comments reveal

a. bias against the demonstrators.

b. a trusting, innocent tone.

c. an uncaring tone.

d. bias against mean people.

_______ 9. What word best describes the tone expressed on the demonstrators' placards?

a. hateful
b. reluctant
c. fearful
d. hurtful

_______ 10. What is at the root of the hatred described by the author?

a. disputes from ancient times
b. bias taught in churches
c. the tone of the Bible
d. the perceived biases of God

USING CONTEXT CLUES AND WORD PARTS

_______ 11. In paragraph 1, the word **blindness** means

a. lack of rational thought.
b. lack of sight.
c. hiding.
d. darkness.

_______ 12. In paragraph 2, the word **placards** means

a. lights.
b. megaphones.
c. cameras.
d. signs.

_______ 13. In paragraph 2, the word **hideous** means

a. laughable.
b. impolite.
c. indifferent.
d. horrible and disgusting.

_______ 14. In paragraph 2, the word **foresight** means an act of

a. displaying aggression.
b. admitting error.
c. looking forward.
d. showing sympathy.

_______ 15. In paragraph 4, the word **cringed** means

a. cowered in fear.
b. revealed an attitude.
c. explained a difference.
d. displayed anger.

Directions: *Complete each of the following sentences by inserting a word from the Vocabulary Preview on page 440 in the space provided. Use each word only once.*

REVIEWING DIFFICULT VOCABULARY

16. With so many difficult relationships in my life, I need the _______________ affection of my dog.

Copyright © 2012 by Pearson Education

17. Numerous ______________ contribute to a child's readiness to begin kindergarten.

18. The team was ______________to win the game at all costs.

19. The professor's choice of student assistants from among those who applied seemed ______________.

20. My daughter protested with such ______________ against going to visit my sister that I just couldn't take her along.

THNKING CRITICALLY

1. Do you think Hong exhibits bias? If so, explain your position with evidence.
2. What was Hong's purpose in writing the essay?
3. This essay explores the meaning of hate. What other terms does this essay explore or illustrate?
4. A photograph did not accompany this essay when originally published. What photograph or other graphic could Hong have used to strengthen her message?

QUESTIONS FOR DISCUSSION

1. Bring a newspaper to class. Find reports of events that reveal bias. Then categorize them according to the type of bias they demonstrate, for example, religious, racial, ethnic, or gender bias. What do these news reports reveal about our world?
2. Brainstorm ideas for reducing hate and violence in your community. Consider acting on at least some of these as a group.
3. Discuss how the tone of our political leaders affects our attitudes toward government. What types of speeches motivate us?

WRITING ACTIVITIES

1. Describe your day in three different tones. What does this exercise reveal about your daily life?
2. Explore the FBI's site on hate crime at http://www.fbi.gov/hq/cid/civilrights/hate.htm. Write a paragraph that explains how the FBI defines hate crimes and what is done about them.

CHAPTER 11

Analyzing Tone and Bias

RECORDING YOUR PROGRESS

Test	Number Right		Score
Practice Test 11-1	________	× 10 =	________%
Practice Test 11-2	________	× 10 =	________%
Mastery Test 11-1	________	× 10 =	________%
Mastery Test 11-2	________	× 10 =	________%
Mastery Test 11-3	________	× 5 =	________%

GETTING MORE PRACTICE myreadinglab

To get more practice with Analyzing Tone and Bias, go to http://www.myreadinglab.com and click on

> Study Plan

> Reading Skills

> Critical Thinking

EVALUATING YOUR PROGRESS myreadinglab

To measure your progress after reading and viewing the information in the Review Materials section, complete the Practices and Tests in the Activities section. You can check your scores by clicking on the Gradebook tab.

Then, based on your performance in this chapter and/or on the MyReadingLab Practices and Tests, write your own evaluation.

YOUR EVALUATION: ____

____

____

____

____

Copyright © 2012 by Pearson Education

THINKING ABOUT

Reading Arguments

Study the photograph on this page. What issues do the bumper stickers address? Choose one issue. Write a short paragraph that answers the following questions: What position (pro or con) does the bumper sticker take on the issue? What are the possible reasons for agreeing with this position?

The paragraph you have just written is a brief argument. It presents logical reasons to support a point of view on an issue. In this chapter you will learn how to read and evaluate an argument.

CHAPTER 12

Reading Arguments

What Is an Argument?

GOAL 1
Understand what an argument is

myreadinglab
To practice reading arguments, go to
> Study Plan
> Reading Skills
> Critical Thinking

An argument between people can be an angry onslaught of ideas and feelings. Family members might argue over household chores or use of the family car. Workers may argue over work assignments or days off from the job. To be effective, however, an argument should be logical and should present well-thought-out ideas. It may involve emotion, but a sound argument is never simply a sudden, unplanned release of emotions and feelings.

An argument, then, always presents logical reasons and evidence to support a viewpoint. In a government course, you might read arguments for or against free speech; in a literature class, you may read a piece of literary criticism that argues for or against the value of a particular poem, debates its significance, or rejects a particular interpretation.

LEARNING GOALS

GOAL 1 Understand what an argument is

GOAL 2 Identify the parts of an argument

GOAL 3 Evaluate arguments

GOAL 4 Identify errors in logical reasoning

GOAL 5 Read arguments in academic writing carefully

Parts of an Argument

GOAL 2
Identify the parts of an argument

An argument has three essential parts—issue, claim, and support. It may also include a fourth part, refutation.

The Issue

An argument must address an **issue**—a problem or controversy about which people disagree. Abortion, gun control, animal rights, capital punishment, and drug legalization are all examples of issues.

Copyright © 2012 by Pearson Education

The Claim

An argument must take a position on an issue. This position is called a **claim.** An argument may claim that capital punishment should be outlawed or that medical use of marijuana should be legalized. Here are a few more claims:

- Animals should have the same rights that humans do.
- Within ten years, destruction of the rain forest should be halted because it will make hundreds of plant and animal species extinct.
- Requiring community service is a good idea because it will create more community-minded graduates.

EXERCISE 12-1 Understanding Issues

Directions: *For each of the following issues, place a check mark in front of the statement that takes a position on the issue.*

1. Issue: Community service

_______ a. Twenty hours of community service is required at Dodgeville High School.

_______ b. Community service should be required of all high school students.

_______ c. Some students voluntarily perform many hours of community service yearly.

2. Issue: State-required vaccinations

_______ a. Parents who wish to opt out of vaccine requirements for their children should be given that right.

_______ b. Vaccinations prevent deaths in children due to many communicable diseases.

_______ c. States issue lists of vaccines that are required in order for children to attend public school.

3. Issue: Public libraries and the Internet

_______ a. People should be able to view whatever sites they choose at the public library.

_______ b. Filtering software cannot block all offensive Web sites.

_______ c. Many public libraries filter their Internet access.

4. Issue: The Equal Rights Amendment (ERA)
   _______ a. All citizens should be in favor of the principles outlined in the ERA.
   _______ b. Women made gains in the struggle for equality in the first half of the twentieth century.
   _______ c. Feminists did not agree about the value of pushing for the ERA.

5. Issue: Sports fan behavior
   _______ a. Many football stadiums now have alcohol-free seating areas.
   _______ b. Tickets to athletic events are expensive, so fans should be free to act however they choose.
   _______ c. Sports arena security forces eject unruly fans.

EXERCISE 12-2 Understanding Claims

Directions: *For each of the following issues, write a statement that takes a position on the issue. Write your claim in the space provided.*

1. Issue: Minimum wage

   Claim: ____

   ____

2. Issue: Global climate changes

   Claim: ____

   ____

3. Issue: Air travel safety

   Claim: ____

4. Issue: Alternative medicine

   Claim: ____

5. Issue: Pop music

   Claim: ____

Copyright © 2012 by Pearson Education

Support

A writer supports a claim by offering reasons and evidence that the claim should be accepted. A **reason** is a general statement that backs up a claim. Here are a few reasons that support an argument in favor of parental Internet controls:

1. The Internet contains millions of sites that are not appropriate for children, so parents must accept responsibility for controlling what their children see.
2. Parental controls are needed because the Internet can be a place for sexual predators to find victims.
3. Parental controls are needed because the Internet is not controlled by any other entity.

However, for any of these reasons to be believable and convincing, they need to be supported with evidence. **Evidence** consists of facts, personal experience, examples, statistics, and comparisons that demonstrate why the claim is valid.

- **Facts.** Facts are true statements. Writers may use facts to lead readers to a conclusion. However, the conclusion does not always follow from the facts presented. For example, a writer may state that you will not get a cold if you eat a lot of oranges because oranges have vitamin C. It is true that oranges have vitamin C, but that does not necessarily mean that eating them will keep you cold free.
- **Personal experience.** A writer may use his or her own personal account or observation of a situation. For example, in supporting the claim that Internet controls are useful, a writer may report that she has put a filter on her child's computer and her child has never come across a pornographic Web site. Although a writer's personal experience may provide an interesting perspective on an issue, personal experience should not be accepted as proof.
- **Examples.** Examples are descriptions of particular situations that are used to illustrate or explain a principle, concept, or idea. In supporting the statement that people would rather drive their own cars than use public transportation, a writer may give the example that almost no one in his office takes the bus to work. Examples should not be used by themselves to prove the concept or idea they illustrate. The writer's experience may be atypical, or not representative, of what is common.
- **Statistics.** Statistics—the reporting of figures, percentages, averages, and so forth—is a common method of support. For example, in an argument about the overuse of elective surgery in hospitals, a writer may present statistics showing the increase in Caesarean sections over the past few years.

However, this increase could be due to other factors such as physicians' assessment of risk during childbirth or patients' physical conditions. Statistics can be misused, misinterpreted, or used selectively to give other than the most objective, accurate picture of a situation.

- **Comparisons and analogies.** Comparisons or analogies (extended comparisons) serve as illustrations. Their reliability depends on how closely the comparison corresponds or how similar it is to the situation to which it is being compared. For example, Martin Luther King Jr., in his famous letter from the Birmingham jail, compared nonviolent protesters to a robbed man. To evaluate this comparison, you would need to consider how the two are similar and how they are different.

EXERCISE 12-3 Recognizing Support for Claims

Directions: *Read each of the following sets of statements. Identify the statement that is a claim and label it C. Label the one statement that supports the claim as S.*

1. _______ Year-round school is advantageous for both parents and children.

   _______ Continuous, year-round application of skills will prevent forgetting and strengthen students' academic preparation.

   _______ Year-round school may be costly to school districts.

2. _______ Many celebrities have been in trouble with the law lately because of their involvement with theft, drunk driving, violence, and even murder.

   _______ Celebrities do not act as positive role models for the people who admire them.

   _______ Acquiring fame and fortune does not automatically relieve a person of stress and suffering.

3. _______ Millions of students cannot afford to attend college because tuition costs and fees are so high.

   _______ States should find ways to control tuition costs at public colleges and universities.

   _______ Officials at private institutions of higher learning do not have to worry about budget issues since they have huge endowments.

Copyright © 2012 by Pearson Education

4. _______ Drug companies should not be allowed to advertise on television.

_______ My grandparents are easily persuaded to buy expensive medications they do not need.

_______ Physicians do not provide all the necessary information patients need.

5. _______ Today's artists receive more media attention than in previous decades.

_______ Modern art is confusing.

_______ I am never sure what an abstract painting represents.

EXERCISE 12-4 Understanding Types of Evidence

Directions: *Each item below begins with a claim, followed by supporting statements. Identify the type(s) of evidence used to support each claim. Choose from among the following types: personal experience (PE), examples (E), statistics (S), and comparisons (C).*

_______ 1. Library hours should be extended to weekends to make the library more accessible. My sisters have part-time jobs that require them to work late afternoons and evenings during the week. They are unable to use the library during the week.

_______ 2. Because parents have the right to determine their children's sexual attitudes, sex education should take place in the home, not at school. Teaching children about sex in school is like teaching them to sit in assigned seats and walk around quietly in single file at home.

_______ 3. It is more expensive to own a dog than a cat. According to the American Veterinary Medical Association, a dog visits the vet twice as many times as a cat.

_______ 4. Many married couples find that they need to set aside special times to be together. Some married couples find that planning a weekend retreat helps them focus on their special relationship.

_______ 5. American policy on capital punishment is not consistent. In Illinois, an out-going governor granted all death row inmates stays of execution while Texas officials continue their trend of killing the most prisoners of any state.

Questions for Evaluating Arguments

Evaluate arguments

Not all arguments are reasonable and not all arguments are sound and logical. Use the following questions to help you evaluate arguments.

Is the Evidence Relevant?

Evidence that is offered in support of a claim must directly relate to that claim. That is, to be relevant, evidence must apply specifically to the issue at hand. For example, a friend may offer as a reason for his tardiness that he had a flat tire, but this fact is not relevant because he would have had to walk only one block to see you. Writers may intentionally or unintentionally include information that may seem convincing but when analyzed more closely does not directly apply to the issue. Here is an example. Can you identify the irrelevant information the paragraph contains?

> Business students, especially those in MBA programs, need to take more classes in ethics. Stricter requirements in this area will ensure that tomorrow's corporate executives will be more responsible and honest than they have been in the past. More women should be admitted to the top business schools. The trust and confidence that employees and investors have lost can be built back if today's professors commit to teaching right and wrong. Future businesspeople will then move the economy forward without the setbacks created by corporate scandal and bankruptcy.

In this paragraph, the sentence about women being admitted to business school is not relevant because the argument is not about whether women are more honest than men or whether higher numbers of women would make a difference in the ethical business climate.

To decide whether a statement is relevant, reread the claim and then immediately afterward reread the statement in question. Ask yourself, "Are the two logically connected?"

EXERCISE 12-5 Identifying Relevant Evidence

Directions: *For each claim listed below, place a check mark in front of those statements that provide relevant supporting evidence. The number of relevant statements varies, but there are always at least two.*

1. Claim: Alcohol abuse is common among teenagers and needs to be curtailed.

   _______ a. Thousands of young people die each year in alcohol-related crashes.

Copyright © 2012 by Pearson Education

_______ b. According to the National Institute on Alcohol Abuse and Alcoholism, young people who drink have an increased chance of developing problems with alcohol later in life.

_______ c. People who take medication need to limit or cease their alcohol intake.

_______ d. Many teens who drink have a parent who is an alcoholic.

2. Claim: Fish populations are decreasing because of overfishing.

_______ a. The UN Food and Agriculture Organization reports that because of overharvesting, four of the fifteen main fishing areas in the world are depleted and another nine are declining.

_______ b. Regulations to save fish populations will hurt fishermen.

_______ c. The fish cannot reproduce fast enough to keep up with the rate they are harvested.

_______ d. These days people are eating less red meat for health reasons.

3. Claim: Recycling helps the environment.

_______ a. Products made from recycled materials are expensive.

_______ b. Buying items in bulk reduces the need for extra packaging.

_______ c. Recycling keeps reusable materials out of landfills.

_______ d. It takes less energy to make a new product from recycled material.

4. Claim: Controversial art should not be exhibited in public places.

_______ a. Children might see disturbing images, causing them behavioral problems.

_______ b. Taxpayers do not want their money going to fund obscene art.

_______ c. Public funds have to be used for security if there are protesters.

_______ d. Art is covered under the "Freedom of Speech" amendment.

5. Claim: Any stock or bond investment is risky and must be researched before money exchanges hands.

_______ a. The Securities and Exchange Commission collects financial data on public companies.

_______ b. Day traders sometimes use borrowed money for their activities.

_______ c. Stocks and bonds may lose their value.

_______ d. Not all brokers are responsible with their clients' money.

EXERCISE 12-6 Evaluating Claims

Directions: *Each of the following paragraphs contains one sentence that does not support the claim. Identify the sentence and write its number in the space provided.*

_______ 1. [1] Modern architecture makes our cities look and feel sterile and unfriendly. [2] Today's building materials—glass and steel—reflect the world they face instead of inviting the world inside. [3] The lack of ornamental details has rendered our downtowns void of beauty and emotion. [4] Commuters flood the city centers with cars and pollution. [5] Architecture should welcome workers with the same warm and comfortable styles, colors, and materials of our homes to reduce stress in the workplace.

_______ 2. [1] Being an environmentalist does not mean being against economic growth. [2] There are many ways to keep jobs and even create new ones while making responsible choices with regard to the environment. [3] For example, when states such as California require the use of low-emissions vehicles, they are opening up new markets to car manufacturers. [4] Some celebrities even own these special vehicles. [5] Also, oil companies can create new businesses by developing alternative fuels. [6] Meanwhile, employees can be retrained to work with the new technologies.

_______ 3. [1] Despite years of education, antismoking advertising, and skyrocketing prices, cigarettes remain popular among Americans. [2] According to the National Institute on Drug Abuse, 60 million Americans aged 12 and over are smokers. [3] Most people who smoke start smoking when they are teenagers. [4] Since nicotine is extremely addictive, once people start smoking, they find it very difficult to stop even if they have learned about the health hazards. [5] Also, smoking is still perceived as cool and glamorous by millions of young people who see movie and rock stars take part in this proven unhealthy behavior.

Copyright © 2012 by Pearson Education

_______ 4. [1] Digital photography has brought families and friends closer together. [2] These days, most of us have relatives and friends living more than a day's drive or even a day's flight away, and we cannot see them as often as we would like. [3] New York City to Hong Kong is over 20 hours in the air. [4] By using digital cameras and the Internet, we can provide regular updates with pictures on everything from our garden to Junior's soccer season. [5] Using technology for highly enjoyable purposes like this not only keeps us in touch, but also balances out all the more routine computer work we do in our work and school environments.

Is the Evidence Sufficient?

There must be a sufficient number of reasons or pieces of evidence to support a claim. The amount and degree of detail of supporting evidence will vary with the issue, its complexity, and its importance. For any serious issue, it is not usually sufficient to offer a single reason or piece of evidence. For example, to say that our oceans are dying due to coastal development is not convincing because only a portion of the world's oceans are affected by coastal development. Other evidence to support this claim could include industrial waste dumping, oil drilling, ecosystem imbalance, and rising water temperatures.

The evidence a writer offers must also be sufficiently detailed to be convincing and believable. For instance, the statement, "A parrot is an ideal pet because it can be taught to mimic language" does not provide sufficient information to persuade anyone to choose a parrot as a pet. To be convincing, more details would be needed about the habits, personality, longevity, and beauty of parrots.

EXERCISE 12-7 Understanding Types of Evidence

Directions: *For each of the claims listed, find three pieces of evidence in the box on the next page that support it. Write the letters of the evidence in the space provided. Not all pieces of evidence will be used.*

Claims

_______ 1. People are becoming ruder in our country.

_______ 2. Many children who receive special education services do not really need them.

_______ 3. Parents and teachers should fight to keep art and music in the schools.

_______ 4. Standardized tests do not accurately represent what American students know.

Evidence

A. Research shows that children need a variety of ways to express themselves.

B. The media bombard our children with images of violence.

C. Telemarketers just will not take no for an answer.

D. Celebrities live public lives of immorality, making promiscuity, drugs, reckless behavior, and divorce seem normal and even glamorous.

E. Incidents of road rage are increasing every year.

F. Not all teachers realize that every child has a different learning style.

G. Teachers are quick to label any child who needs extra help with a learning disorder.

H. Our society puts pressure on children to be consumers at a young age.

I. Learning to play an instrument helps with math skills.

J. Many students experience test anxiety, which can have a negative impact on their scores.

K. Many people have been storming out of stores because of insulting customer service.

L. In some schools there is tremendous pressure on teachers to boost test scores, forcing teachers to "teach to the test."

M. Studies have shown that learning to read music helps students with their regular reading skills.

N. Special education teachers are too aggressive in identifying students who need their services just so they can keep their jobs.

O. Test writers understand education only in theory and do not write questions that are relevant to today's students.

Does the Author Recognize and Refute Opposing Viewpoints?

Many arguments recognize opposing viewpoints. For example, an author may argue that gays should be allowed to marry. However, the author may recognize or admit that opponents believe marriage should only be allowed between a man and a woman.

Many arguments also attempt to refute the opposing viewpoint (explain why it is wrong, flawed, or unacceptable). For example, a writer may refute the notion that gays will compromise cohesiveness by stating that soldiers are unified against the enemy, not each other. Basically, then, refutation is a process of finding weaknesses in the opponent's argument.

Copyright © 2012 by Pearson Education

When reading arguments that address opposing viewpoints, ask yourself the following questions.

- Does the author address opposing viewpoints clearly and fairly?
- Does the author refute the opposing viewpoint with logic and relevant evidence?

Does the Author Use Emotional Appeals and Are They Used Unfairly?

Emotional appeals are ideas that are targeted toward needs or values that readers are likely to care about. Needs include physiological needs (food, drink, shelter) and psychological needs (sense of belonging, sense of accomplishment, sense of self-worth). An argument on gun control, for example, may appeal to a reader's need for safety, while an argument favoring restrictions on banks sharing personal or financial information may appeal to a reader's need for privacy and financial security.

Unfair emotional appeals attempt to involve or excite readers by appealing to their emotions, thereby controlling the reader's attitude toward the subject. Several types of emotional appeals are described below.

1. **Emotionally Charged or Biased Language.** By using words that create an emotional response, writers establish positive or negative feelings. For example, an advertisement for a new line of fragrances promises to "indulge," "refresh," "nourish," and "pamper" the user. An ad for an automobile uses phrases such as "limousine comfort," "European styling," and "animal sleekness" to interest and excite readers.
2. **False Authority.** False authority involves using the opinion or action of a well-known or famous person. We have all seen athletes endorsing underwear or movie stars selling shampoo. This type of appeal works on the notion that people admire celebrities and strive to be like them, respect their opinion, and are willing to accept their viewpoint.
3. **Association.** An emotional appeal also is made by associating a product, idea, or position with others that are already accepted or highly regarded. Patriotism is already valued, so to call a product All-American in an advertisement is an appeal to the emotions. A car being named a Cougar to remind you of a fast, sleek animal, a cigarette ad picturing a scenic waterfall, or a speaker standing in front of an American flag are other examples.
4. **Appeal to "common folk."** Some people distrust those who are well educated, wealthy, highly artistic, or in other ways distinctly different from the average person. An emotional appeal to this group is made by indicating that a product or idea originated from, is held by, or is bought by ordinary citizens. A commercial may advertise a product by showing its use in an average household. A politician may describe her background and education to suggest that she is like everyone else; a salesperson may dress in styles similar to his clients.

5. ***Ad hominem.*** An argument that attacks the holder of an opposing viewpoint rather than his or her viewpoint is known as *ad hominem,* or an attack on the man. For example, the statement, "How could a woman who does not even hold a college degree criticize a judicial decision?" attacks the woman's level of education, not her viewpoint.
6. **"Join the crowd" appeal.** The appeal to do, believe, or buy what everyone else is doing, believing, or buying is known as crowd appeal or the bandwagon appeal. Commercials that proclaim their product the "#1 best-selling car in America" are appealing to this motive. Essays in support of a position that cite opinion polls on a controversial issue—"68 percent of Americans favor capital punishment"—are also using this appeal.

EXERCISE 12-8 Understanding Emotional Appeals

Directions: *Indicate the type of emotional appeal each of the following statements represents.*

a. emotionally charged or biased language
b. false authority
c. association
d. appeal to common folk
e. *ad hominem*
f. join the crowd

_______ 1. Laura Bush, wife of President George Bush, recommends the book *Beloved*, by Toni Morrison; it must be very good.

_______ 2. We must preserve our historic neighborhoods in order to save the memories of the hardworking men and women who built our cities with their sweat and blood.

_______ 3. Don't go to that restaurant; the owner can't even keep her garden growing.

_______ 4. Everyone who cares about education is voting for Proposition E.

_______ 5. The mayor eats Mrs. Baker's pecan sandies; they must be the best.

_______ 6. Mandatory DNA collection of criminals will stop all brutal sexual assaults on our helpless women and innocent children.

_______ 7. We provide quality service just like in the good old days.

_______ 8. Join together with your brothers and sisters in the union; don't let rich managers and executives oppress you any longer.

_______ 9. No one dresses like that anymore.

_______ 10. My dentist is awful; he drives an old car.

Copyright © 2012 by Pearson Education

Errors in Logical Reasoning

Identify errors in logical reasoning

Errors in reasoning, often called logical fallacies, are common in arguments. These errors invalidate the argument or render it flawed. Several common errors in logic are described next.

Circular Reasoning

Also known as begging the question, this error involves using part of the conclusion as evidence to support it. Here are two examples.

> Cruel medical experimentation on defenseless animals is inhumane.
>
> Female police officers should not be sent to crime scenes because apprehending criminals is a man's job.

In circular reasoning, because no evidence is given to support the claim, there is no reason to accept the conclusion.

Hasty Generalization

This fallacy means that the conclusion has been derived from insufficient evidence. Here is one example: You taste three tangerines and each is sour, so you conclude that all tangerines are sour. Here is another: By observing one performance of a musical group, you conclude the group is unfit to perform.

Non Sequitur ("It Does Not Follow")

The false establishment of cause/effect is known as a *non sequitur.* To say, for example, that "Because my doctor is young, I'm sure she'll be a good doctor" is a non sequitur because youth does not cause good medical practice. Here is another example: "Arturio Alvarez is the best choice for state senator because he is an ordinary citizen." Being an ordinary citizen will not necessarily make someone an effective state senator.

False Cause

The false cause fallacy is the incorrect assumption that two events that follow each other in time are causally related. Suppose you walked under a ladder and then lost your wallet. If you said you lost your wallet because you walked under a ladder, you would be assuming false cause.

Either-Or Fallacy

This fallacy assumes that an issue is only two sided, or that there are only two choices or alternatives for a particular situation. In other words, there is no middle ground. Consider the issue of censorship of violence on television. An either-or fallacy is to assume that violence on TV must be either allowed or banned. This fallacy does not recognize other alternatives such as limiting access through viewing hours, restricting certain types of violence, and so forth.

EXERCISE 12-9 Identifying Fallacies

Directions: *Identify the logical fallacy in each of the following statements.*

a. circular reasoning
b. hasty generalization
c. *non sequitur*
d. false cause
e. either-or fallacy

_______ 1. All African-American students in my biology class earned A grades, so African-Americans must excel in life sciences.

_______ 2. If you are not for nuclear arms control, then you're against protecting our future.

_______ 3. My sister gets nervous when asked to do mathematical computations or balance her checkbook because she has math anxiety.

_______ 4. A well-known mayor, noting a decline in the crime rate in the four largest cities in his state, quickly announced that his new "get-tough on criminals" publicity campaign was successful and took credit for the decline.

_______ 5. I always order a fruit pastry for dessert because I am allergic to chocolate.

Arguments in Academic Writing

Read arguments in academic writing carefully

While textbooks do not usually address popular controversial issues, you will still encounter arguments in your assigned textbook readings. Textbook authors often take a position on pertinent topics within their discipline. A health and fitness textbook author may make a claim that cardiovascular exercise is essential to long-term health. Or a psychology textbook author may argue that compulsive shopping should be officially declared a mental illness.

As when reading any other source of argument, pay attention to the reasons and evidence offered to support the claim. Textbook authors are careful to provide relevant and sufficient evidence. Close attention to evidence is important, though, since it is the evidence that you will need to understand and recall the material for upcoming quizzes and exams.

Copyright © 2012 by Pearson Education

EXERCISE 12-10 Understanding Arguments

Directions: *After reading each of the following paragraphs from college textbooks, select the choice that best answers each of the questions that follow.*

A. As technology continues to develop and change, so must businesses change and adapt to keep pace. The Internet, telecommunications, computers, robotics—all have an impact on business. For example, growing numbers of businesses have Web sites; increasing numbers of employees are telecommuting (working at home); and small robots are used increasingly in manufacturing. Awareness of technology will keep you on the cutting edge of business growth and change.

—McWhorter, *Academic Reading*, p. 385

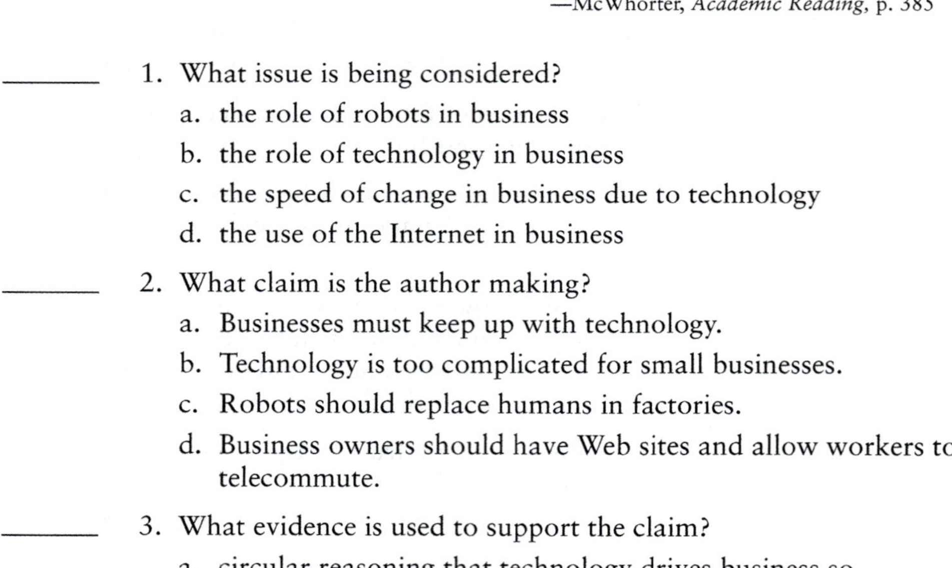

______ 1. What issue is being considered?

a. the role of robots in business
b. the role of technology in business
c. the speed of change in business due to technology
d. the use of the Internet in business

______ 2. What claim is the author making?

a. Businesses must keep up with technology.
b. Technology is too complicated for small businesses.
c. Robots should replace humans in factories.
d. Business owners should have Web sites and allow workers to telecommute.

______ 3. What evidence is used to support the claim?

a. circular reasoning that technology drives business so businesses must adopt technology
b. comparison of old and new business technologies
c. emotional language meant to frighten those who are behind in technology
d. examples of ways in which businesses have adapted technology

B. Literature describes human experience. It is a creative record of the thoughts, feelings, emotions, or experiences of other people. By reading literature, you can learn about yourself and understand both painful and joyful experiences without actually going though them yourself. For example, you can read a poem about the birth of a child and come to understand the range of feelings parents share, even though you may not be a parent. In other words, literature allows you to live vicariously, sharing the lives of others without physical participation.

_______ 4. What issue is being considered?
   a. the role of literature in the lives of children
   b. the value of literature
   c. literature as therapy
   d. why people write books

_______ 5. What claim is the author making?
   a. Novels teach you just as much as nonfiction books.
   b. Reading literature expands your range of emotional experiences.
   c. People who read a lot are in better touch with their emotions.
   d. Books can help you solve problems.

_______ 6. Which of the following is used as evidence to support the claim?
   a. an example of a way in which literature can affect your feelings
   b. an explanation of how to read with emotion
   c. hasty generalization about the value of literature
   d. a comparison between the experience of reading and the pain of childbirth

Copyright © 2012 by Pearson Education

CRITICAL THINKING CHALLENGE

In this section is an excerpt from an editorial on which to practice your critical thinking skills. Review the "Tips for Reading Editorials" and use the steps below to guide your reading and your response.

TIPS for Reading Editorials

When reading editorials, pieces addressing controversial or pro/con issues, be sure to

- **Separate fact from opinion.** Authors usually mix these in an attempt to make their points.
- **Evaluate the evidence.** Look closely at facts, statistics, and reasons.
- **Form your own opinion.** Based on the soundness of the argument, make your own decision about whether you agree with the position the author is taking.

Thinking Critically as You Read

1. **Reading, Highlighting, and Annotating.** As you read, highlight the key ideas. Write marginal notes to record your thinking as you read. Include comments, reactions, questions, opposing ideas, and so forth.
2. **Summarizing.** (Refer to Chapter 6, page 216.) Write a one-paragraph summary of the reading.
3. **Thinking Critically.**
   a. Identify at least three words that have strong connotative meanings. (See Chapter 2, page 69 and Chapter 9, page 344.)
   b. Evaluate the writer's main ideas. Identify at least three facts and three opinions. (See Chapter 3, page 105.)
   c. Study the writer's choice of supporting details. Does his or her choice suggest an emphasis, bias, or a particular viewpoint toward the topic? (See Chapter 4, page 139.) If so, please explain.
   d. What is the author's purpose for writing? (See Chapter 9, page 341.)
   e. Does the author offer relevant evidence to support his or her position?
   f. Is the evidence sufficient?
   g. Does the author include opposing viewpoints?
   h. Identify a hasty generalization in the article.
4. **Responding to Ideas**
   Write a paragraph sharing your reactions and response to one or more of the ideas presented in the reading. Refer to your marginal notes.

OUR VIEW ON **YOUR HEALTH**

What Can Be Done to Shake America's Salt Habit?

We all need some salt in our diet. But there can be too much of a good thing. And right now, Americans are consuming a lot more sodium than they need—an average of 3,400 milligrams daily when the recommended maximum is 2,300 milligrams.

That excessive sodium can lead to high blood pressure, which is associated with strokes, kidney damage and congestive heart failure. In fact, a report released last week by the Institute of Medicine, the independent health arm of the National Academy of Sciences, estimated that reducing sodium intake could prevent 100,000 deaths a year and save $18 billion in medical costs.

Less noticed but just as important is the fact that salt is also a major contributor to the obesity crisis. That's because food makers recognize that combining salt with sugar and fat creates a multilayered cocktail, both tangy and sweet, that leaves taste buds craving more.

These intense flavor combinations can trigger a response in the brain so pleasurable that many people, seeking to recreate the experience, become trapped in a cycle of craving and overeating. Not to mention that salt makes people thirstier for calorie-laden soft drinks and alcoholic beverages, which is why bars put out all those free snacks.

The extra sodium in our diets isn't coming from sprinkling the salt shaker too generously. Instead, 77% of our intake is from prepared and processed foods. Food makers use it as both a preservative and a taste enhancer—and apply it abundantly.

Consider the amount of sodium per serving in these products: Kraft's Catalina dressing (380 milligrams), Progresso's New England Clam Chowder (890 milligrams) and DiGiorno's Supreme pizza (990 milligrams). The result is a climate where even an informed consumer has trouble eating a diet that isn't loaded with salt.

So what's the answer?

For some foods, there isn't a good one. In cheese and bread, for instance, it's hard to reduce sodium content without severely compromising taste and texture. But even in those cases, better disclosure could help consumers keep track of their sodium intake. The Food and Drug Administration is working on front-of-package nutritional labeling that would both be clearer and more prominent than current back labels. In restaurants, meanwhile, fast food is notoriously salty, and the new federal health care law helps by requiring chains to post their menus' nutritional content.

The FDA is also working with food manufacturers to achieve voluntary sodium reductions. In recent years, some companies, including Campbell's Soup and Hormel Foods, have reduced sodium in some of their products. Others have announced plans to do so.

But as long as salt promotes excessive eating, and consumers' tastes are conditioned to prefer products with high sodium content, food sellers have an incentive to pack food with it. That's why the IOM is recommending that the FDA set legal limits for sodium content in foods, implemented gradually so taste buds can adjust.

Given the nation's obesity epidemic, such a move might eventually be needed, but a collaborative approach is preferable. If that effort falls short, however, blatant warning labels on foods with unneeded salt content are an option.

The trick is to give people the means to protect themselves without dictating their choices. The USA would be a healthier nation, however, if fewer people said "pass the salt" and more said "pass up the salt."

Too much salt?

Since the early 1970s, daily sodium intake from foods has increased 55% for men and 69% for women.

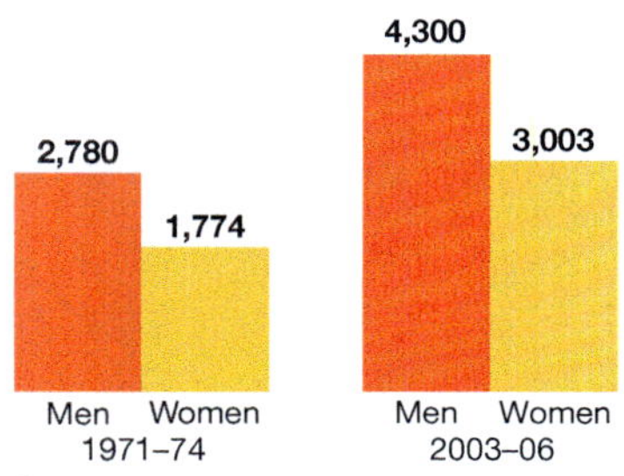

Source: National Health and Nutrition Examination Survey

—Web Bryant, *USA Today*

Copyright © 2012 by Pearson Education

SELF-TEST SUMMARY

To test yourself, cover up the Answer column with a sheet of paper and answer each question listed in the left column. Evaluate each of your answers as you work by sliding the paper down and comparing your answer with what is printed in the Answer column.

	Question	Answer
GOAL 1	What is an argument?	An argument uses evidence and logical reasons to support a point of view.
GOAL 2	How do the three parts of an argument function?	The issue is the topic being discussed, about which there is disagreement. The claim is the position a writer takes about the issue. Support is the evidence and reasons offered for the writer's position.
GOAL 3	When is evidence relevant and sufficient?	Evidence is relevant when it directly relates to the claim, or writer's position. It is sufficient when there is enough of it to support the claim.
GOAL 4	What are common errors in logic that you might come across?	Common logical fallacies include circular reasoning, hasty generalization, *non sequitur*, false cause, and either-or fallacy.
GOAL 5	When reading arguments in academic reading, what should you pay careful attention to and why?	When reading academic arguments, pay attention to evidence, since this will likely be what your instructor will test you on.

NAME ______________________ SECTION ______________________

DATE ______________________ SCORE ______________________

PRACTICE TEST 12-1

Analyzing Supporting Evidence and Errors in Reasoning

A. *Directions:* *Read each claim and determine which three statements provide relevant support for it. Write their letters in the space provided.*

_______ 1. Claim: DNA technology is critical to our criminal justice system and law enforcement agencies.

a. Innocent prisoners can be released when new DNA evidence is presented.

b. Suspects are linked to victims by the presence of their DNA at the crime scene.

c. Most Americans have a basic understanding of the properties of DNA.

d. Researchers are using DNA to find cures for diseases.

e. DNA evidence is more reliable than fingerprints and eyewitness testimony.

_______ 2. Claim: Watching motion pictures lifts our spirits during hard economic times.

a. Some movie theaters now have espresso stands.

b. Movies help us imagine, remember, or hope for better times.

c. Many video rental stores guarantee the availability of all the latest releases.

d. By renting or borrowing DVDs, families can enjoy happy times together without spending a great deal of money.

e. Theater attendance increased dramatically during the Great Depression.

_______ 3. Claim: The United States fills a large humanitarian and peacekeeping role in the world.

a. According to White House statistics, America gave away over $3 billion in 2000 to help other countries.

b. The United States stayed out of WWII until 1941.

c. U.S. troops take part in peacekeeping missions in several countries in Africa.

d. Protestors marched in Washington against the war in Vietnam in the sixties.

e. Millions of refugees have found asylum on American shores.

Copyright © 2012 by Pearson Education

_______ 4. Claim: The government should subsidize the high cost of quality child care so that single mothers can work.

a. Some single moms have relatives who take care of their children.

b. Many of the children in Head Start live with only one parent.

c. Many single mothers prefer to work than to receive welfare, but are unable to do so.

d. Quality child care is expensive; the workers are well educated and command higher rates of pay.

e. Millions of single mothers go without financial support from their ex-husbands or the fathers of their children.

_______ 5. Claim: Children should not be raised in an urban environment.

a. Families that live in the suburbs spend more time in the car than families that live in the city.

b. Asthma rates for children living in cities are rising.

c. Crime rates are rising in urban centers.

d. Cities generally offer many cultural opportunities.

e. Children need lots of wide open spaces for running and playing.

B. Directions: *Choose the type of emotional appeal or logical fallacy used in each set of statements.*

_______ 6. Today's young people are out of control. The only alternative is to impose strict discipline. Otherwise, there will be total chaos in our society.

a. biased language　　c. either-or fallacy

b. join the crowd　　d. circular reasoning

_______ 7. Tall people have an advantage in the workplace. My boss and supervisor are taller than average and no one in a managerial position is short. You must be tall to get a promotion where I work.

a. appeal to common folk　　c. false authority

b. hasty generalizations　　d. *non sequitur*

_______ 8. Your tax dollars are being wasted on overly expensive campaigns. Don't let your hard-earned money pay for extravagant parties and leisure travel for candidates you don't support.

a. *ad hominem*

b. association

c. either-or fallacy

d. emotionally charged language

_______ 9. Every city has at least one charter school. We must encourage our city to keep up with other communities across the country by funding at least one charter school.

a. join the crowd

b. circular reasoning

c. *non sequitur*

d. false authority

_______ 10. Try the musical theater instead of opera. The stories reflect the problems of daily life; the songs are familiar; the lyrics are in a language we understand.

a. false authority

b. join the crowd

c. appeal to common folk

d. circular reasoning

Copyright © 2012 by Pearson Education

PRACTICE TEST 12-2

NAME ________________ SECTION ________________

DATE ________________ SCORE ________________

Analyzing Arguments

***Directions:** After reading each of the paragraphs below, select the choice that best completes each of the statements that follow.*

A. [1] A majority of Americans follow at least one professional sport. [2] Unfortunately, rising costs are making it impossible for the average fan to watch his or her favorite athlete or team in person. [3] According to *Team Marketing Report,* the average ticket price in the NFL is $50.02, and in the NBA it's $43.65. For professional baseball, the average ticket price is $18.30, while in hockey, it's $41.56. [4] Soccer is the most popular professional sport in the world. [5] Some argue that the high prices are justified. [6] After all, they say, in order to please fans, teams must win more games than they lose. [7] The best way to win is to have the top players, but teams must spend large amounts of money to get these players. [8] These costs are passed on to the fans through ticket prices and merchandising. [9] However, instead of raising ticket prices, team owners should raise the fees paid by corporations who sponsor stadiums and put their logo on the TV next to the score or advertise in the arena, making use of the real money in the hands of big business. [10] The love of sports cuts across socioeconomic lines; the ability to enjoy a game in person should too.

_______ 1. The issue being addressed is

a. corporate greed.

b. the cost of professional sports tickets.

c. economic disparity.

d. the entertainment value of professional sports.

_______ 2. The author makes the claim that

a. athletes and team owners are greedy.

b. teams should give away tickets for free.

c. only extremely wealthy people can afford to attend sports events.

d. ticket prices are too high for most fans of professional sports.

_______ 3. The author uses which type of evidence in this argument?

a. analogy

b. direct quote

c. statistics

d. personal experience

_______ 4. The author includes

a. an opposing viewpoint.

b. a "join the crowd" emotional appeal.

c. figurative language.

d. circular reasoning.

_______ 5. Which sentence provides irrelevant evidence?

a. 2

b. 4

c. 6

d. 8

B. Our View on Energy: Good News? Cape Wind OK'd. Bad News? It Took a Decade.

1 Several European countries long ago managed to build many offshore wind farms. But approval of the USA's first such power plant has been stalled for nearly a decade, testament to the nation's lack of seriousness about energy choices.

2 The Obama administration finally acted to stop the bickering, the excuse-making and the somewhere-else demands that have held up the coastal Massachusetts project known as Cape Wind.

3 After weighing the objections—which ranged from oceanfront property owners' worries about their views to more serious concerns about fishing, tourism and ancient tribal burial grounds—Interior Secretary Ken Salazar said

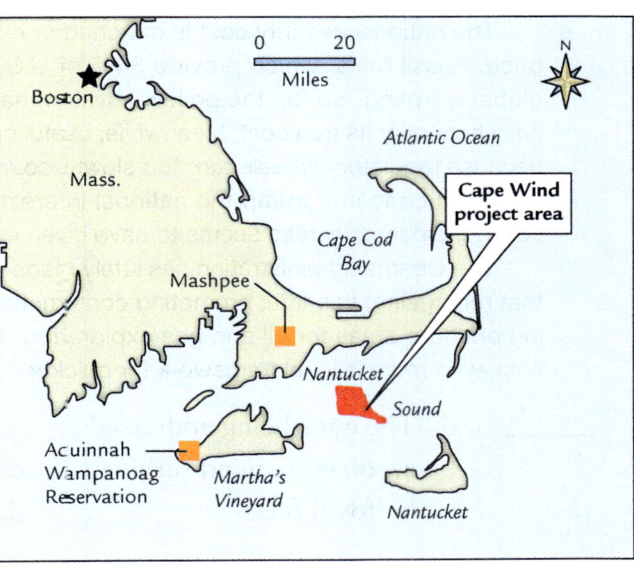

Copyright © 2012 by Pearson Education

he found "the public benefits weigh in favor of approving" the project. Once up and running, the 130 wind turbines in a stretch of ocean near Cape Cod and the islands of Martha's Vineyard and Nantucket could supply an estimated 75% of the area's electricity needs.

4 Salazar got it right. Energy production is about trade-offs. That has been painfully clear lately from the coal mine disaster in West Virginia, which killed 29, and the drilling rig accident in the Gulf of Mexico, which left 11 workers dead and an oil slick spreading toward the coastline. Every form of energy exacts a price, and extracting fossil fuels from the ground is particularly dangerous and dirty. Relative to the risks of coal mining and oil exploration, the downsides of offshore wind turbines seem minor.

5 That's likely to be just as true at other locations where coastal waters are shallow enough to make building wind turbines economical, and where short distances to heavily populated coastal communities make building transmission lines feasible. Projects have been proposed for ocean sites off Delaware, Maryland, New York, New Jersey and Rhode Island, plus Great Lakes sites near Chicago and Cleveland.

6 But finding a way to get those and other energy projects moving is a daunting problem. It's still much easier to stop or slow an energy project—whether it's a wind farm, an oil refinery or a nuclear power plant—than it is to build one. Even Cape Wind isn't home free. Lawsuits and regulatory hurdles could delay the project for several more years.

7 Whatever legitimacy such stalling tactics might have should be outweighed by the frighteningly steep cost of continuing the status quo. The USA gets more than half its oil from the world market, transferring hundreds of billions of dollars every year to unfriendly regimes.

8 The national security cost is matched or exceeded by the environmental price. Fossil fuels, which provide 84% of U.S. energy needs, contribute to global warming. So far, the political system has balked at pricing carbon at anywhere near its true cost. Meanwhile, useful options like Cape Wind stall out because regulatory wheels turn too slowly, court battles drag on too long and parochial concerns trump the national interest. In trying to give everyone a voice, the nation instead seems to have given everyone a veto.

9 The Obama administration has lately made controversial energy decisions that run against this tide, promoting construction of nuclear plants and opening offshore areas for oil and gas exploration. That's promising. What would help even more is legal framework for quicker decisions.

_______ 6. The issue being addressed is

a. offshore wind turbines.
b. fossil fuels.
c. coal mining.
d. energy efficiency.

_______ 7. The author makes the claim that

a. wind turbine energy increases our need for national security spending.

b. wind energy is safer and more environmentally friendly than other energy options.

c. fossil fuel use is more economical in areas that are not located on the coast.

d. if carbon were priced at its true cost, more people would be in favor of wind energy.

_______ 8. In paragraph 1, which of the following emotional appeals is used?

a. *ad hominem* statement

b. association

c. circular reasoning

d. join the crowd appeal

_______ 9. One opposing viewpoint recognized in the argument is

a. the dangers of coal mining.

b. costs of turbines.

c. concerns about fishing.

d. delays by regulatory agencies.

_______ 10. The author uses all of the following types of supporting evidence except

a. facts.

b. analogies.

c. statistics.

d. examples.

Copyright © 2012 by Pearson Education

MASTERY TEST 12-1

NAME ______________________ SECTION ______________________

DATE ______________________ SCORE ______________________

Analyzing Arguments

Directions: *After reading the following paragraphs, select the choice that best completes each of the statements that follow.*

A. [1] As the Internet becomes more and more central to the search for information, students and scholars are demanding that more items in library collections be digitized and made available on the Web. [2] Library directors also see this method of preservation as a perfect way to provide more service for less money. [3] Many library directors are out of touch with the librarians who work for them. [4] However, librarians caution that digital preservation is not without its faults. [5] Many small libraries do not have the budgets to provide equipment and personnel needed to undertake such a project. [6] More important, however, technologies are changing so quickly that files preserved today in one format will not be usable with future formats. [7] If paper documents are scanned and discarded, our heritage will be lost forever somewhere down the road on the digital bandwagon.

______ 1. The issue the argument focuses on is
   a. meeting the needs of scholars and researchers.
   b. treating small libraries unfairly.
   c. reducing library costs.
   d. converting library collections from paper to digital format.

______ 2. To best strengthen this argument, the author could add the following evidence:
   a. actual dollar amounts for the cost of digital preservation to small libraries.
   b. interviews with professors who use digital collections in their research.
   c. comparisons of currently available scanning software.
   d. examples of online collections at small libraries.

______ 3. Which sentence contains information irrelevant to the article?
   a. 2
   b. 3
   c. 5
   d. 7

B. Mandatory retirement rules hurt businesses and families. When my grandfather was required to give up his job of thirty years at age 65, he was forced into economic hardship. His boss was a cold-hearted bachelor with no family. He received a pension and other benefits, but they were not enough to sustain him and his ill wife in their comfortable existence for the rest of their earthly days. Had his employer kept him on for ten or fifteen more years, my grandparents' elderly years would have been much happier. Furthermore, his company would have continued to benefit from his many years of accumulated knowledge and experience in the industry. Employers should treat all employees on a case-by-case basis instead of laying down policies that hurt some and help others.

_______ 4. The author uses which type of evidence in the argument?

a. statistics
b. analogy
c. comparison
d. personal experience

_______ 5. Which statement best expresses the author's claim?

a. Pension benefits should be increased for retirees.
b. The author's grandfather was treated unfairly.
c. Mandatory retirement is unfair and detrimental.
d. Employers need to be more considerate of the needs of their employees.

_______ 6. To best strengthen the argument, the author could add

a. quotations from the boss and grandfather.
b. a sample retirement plan.
c. statistics about the average pension income retirees receive.
d. the opinion of a member of Congress.

_______ 7. In describing the father's boss, the author uses which of the following emotional appeals?

a. *ad hominem*
b. "join the crowd" emotional appeal
c. association
d. false authority

C. Costly medical research requires foundations and universities to spend a great deal of money. In addition American taxpayers contribute to federal research grants that sometimes go to fund controversial projects. Meanwhile, many practicing physicians and their patients feel removed from the entire research process and think the studies being conducted do not directly apply to them. All in all, the entire medical research structure needs a complete overhaul to reduce expenses, educate the public, and demonstrate real progress for real people.

Copyright © 2012 by Pearson Education

_______ 8. The author's claim is that

a. doctors must become more aware of late-breaking research.

b. the medical community spends too much money on research.

c. the medical research system needs to be changed.

d. medical research should be controlled by the government.

_______ 9. To best strengthen this argument, the author could add the following evidence:

a. personal statements from researchers about their studies.

b. a breakdown of medical research funding costs and sources.

c. the names of the major research foundations.

d. a comparison of funding practices in several states.

_______ 10. The first sentence is an example of

a. the false cause fallacy.

b. a *non sequitur*.

c. circular reasoning.

d. the either-or fallacy.

NAME ______________________ SECTION ______________________

DATE ______________________ SCORE ______________________

MASTERY TEST 12-2

Analyzing Arguments

Directions: *After reading the following argument, select the choice that best completes each of the statements that follow.*

Misstep on Video Violence

1 In the booming world of video games, there are more than a few dark corners: Murder and mayhem. Blood and gore. Explicit sex and abuse of women. In one of the best-selling series, Grand Theft Auto, car stealing is accompanied by drug use, shootouts that kill police and bystanders, and simulated sex with comely prostitutes who are beaten with baseball bats afterward.

2 Small wonder some parents are concerned over what game-crazed teens may be up to. And small wonder, too, that legislators in several states are playing to these concerns by trying to outlaw the sale of violent and sexually explicit games to minors. A bill banning the sale of such games to anyone younger than 18 is awaiting the governor's signature in Illinois. A similar proposal is moving in the Michigan Legislature. The issue has been raised this year in at least nine other states and the District of Columbia. But to what useful end?

3 This is the latest chapter in a very old story. When teenage entertainment offends adult sensibilities—think Elvis Presley's pulsating hips or the arrival on newsstands of Hugh Hefner's Playboy—the first response is to see the new phenomenon as a threat to social order. The second is to attempt to ban it. Parents—former teenagers all—seem to forget history's lesson: The bans never work. And they're probably not constitutional, anyway. Courts have ruled that today's sophisticated video games are protected as creative expression. If communities want to limit access, they must show overriding evidence that the games pose a public threat. That evidence does not exist.

4 Lawmakers and activist groups assert that the thrill of engaging in virtual criminal activity will spur teens to try the real thing. But the violent crime rate has gone down nearly 30% since the first bloody shoot-'em-up games debuted in the early 1990s. Youth crime rates have dropped even more. And a Federal Trade Commission survey found parents already involved in 83% of video-game purchases and rentals for minors.

5 Judges have repeatedly rejected as flawed the studies that advocates say show a link between fantasy violence and anti-social behavior. To the extent there is a threat, it is mainly to the individual, vulnerable teenager, and it can be addressed only by parents.

6 Unknown to many parents, they're getting some help. The game industry's rating system classifies games in six categories from "early childhood" to "adults only" and requires detailed content descriptions. Also, newer models

Copyright © 2012 by Pearson Education

of popular games include parental controls that can block their use for age-inappropriate games. Manufacturers have announced an expanded ratings-education program, and major retailers are tightening their restrictions on sales to minors.

7 There will always be a market for the dark, tasteless, even the outrageous, and parents ought to keep kids away from it. But even with the best intentions of legislators, the problem is beyond their reach. New laws are likely to give parents only the false impression that someone else is solving that problem for them.

—*USA Today,* June 6, 2005

_______ 1. The author addresses which of the following issues?

a. the proven effectiveness of legislation in controlling behavior

b. parents' inability to monitor their children's video game usage

c. the reluctance of game companies to rate their games

d. the impact of violent video games on teen behavior

_______ 2. The author's claim is that

a. violent video games do not result in violent behavior.

b. Grand Theft Auto is appropriate for teens.

c. more laws need to be passed regulating video games.

d. parents are already too involved in video game choices.

_______ 3. Which type of evidence does the author use to support the argument?

a. personal experience

b. statistics

c. comparison

d. analogy

_______ 4. This argument could best be strengthened by adding

a. information about studies that show no link between violent video games and violent behavior.

b. evidence that laws banning violent video games reduce violent behavior.

c. examples of teens who play video games and have no history of violence.

d. details about the type of violence portrayed in other violent video games.

_______ 5. The purpose of this argument is to

a. urge readers to support legislation banning violent video games.

b. convince readers that violent video games have actually contributed to a reduction in violent crime.

c. cast doubt upon the belief that violent video games lead to violent behavior.

d. describe ways parents can limit video game usage.

_______ 6. The use of "false authority" can be found where the author argues that

a. judges have found no link between fantasy violence and behavior.

b. new legislation in Illinois is unnecessary.

c. manufacturers are taking steps to limit access to violent games.

d. parents need to have more control over their children's game activities.

_______ 7. Legislators who think that all violent video games must either be banned for anyone under 18 or be available to all teens have made what error in reasoning?

a. circular reasoning

b. *non sequitur*

c. either-or fallacy

d. *ad hominem* attack

_______ 8. The author's mention of Elvis and *Playboy* is a type of supporting evidence known as

a. personal experience.

b. example.

c. statistics.

d. appeal to the common folk.

_______ 9. Which of the following would further support the author's argument?

a. statistics about the growth of the market for violent games

b. the author's describing a personal experience of how easy it is to buy violent games

c. statistics demonstrating the relationship between gender and level of violent behavior

d. the results of a study that tracks teenage behavior after playing violent video games

Copyright © 2012 by Pearson Education

_______ 10. The author fails to offer sufficient supporting evidence when he or she writes

a. "A bill banning the sale of such games to anyone younger than 18 is awaiting the governor's signature in Illinois" (par. 2).

b. "The bans never work" (par. 3).

c. "But the violent crime rate has gone down nearly 30% since the first bloody shoot-'em up games debuted" (par. 4).

d. "Unknown to many parents, they're getting some help." (par. 6).

NAME ______________________ SECTION ______________________

DATE ______________________ SCORE ______________________

MASTERY TEST 12-3

READING SELECTION

Don't Panic: How Our Frenzied Response to Terrorism Only Feeds It

Fareed Zakaria

In this article from *Newsweek*, the author examines our country's response to terrorism and argues for a more sensible reaction. Read the selection to discover how and why he believes we should react differently to acts of terrorism.

Vocabulary Preview

These are some of the difficult words in this essay. The definitions here will help you if you can't figure out the meanings from the sentence context or word parts.

affiliate (par. 3) partner or associate

makeshift (par. 3) improvised using whatever is available

passivity (par. 4) inactivity

convenes (par. 4) calls together

rogue (par. 7) operating outside normal controls

1 In responding to the attempted bombing of an airliner on Christmas Day, Sen. Dianne Feinstein voiced the feelings of many when she said that to prevent such situations, "I'd rather . . . overreact than underreact." This now appears to be the consensus view in Washington, but it is quite wrong. In fact, precisely the opposite is true. The purpose of terrorism is to provoke an over-

Copyright © 2012 by Pearson Education

reaction. Its real aim is not to kill the hundreds of people directly targeted, but to sow fear in the rest of the population. Terrorism is an unusual military tactic in that it depends on the response of the onlookers. If we are not terrorized, then the attack didn't work. Alas, this one worked very well.

2 The attempted bombing says more about Al Qaeda's weakened state than its strength. In the eight years before, 9/11, Al Qaeda was able to launch large-scale terrorist attacks on several continents. It targeted important symbols of American powers—embassies in Africa; a naval destroyer, the USS *Cole*; and, of course, the World Trade Center. The operations were complex—a simultaneous bombing of two embassies in different countries—and involved dozens of people of different nationalities who trained around the world, moved significant sums of money around, and coordinated their efforts over months, sometimes years. And every attack succeeded.

3 On Christmas a Qaeda affiliate launched an operation using one person, with no special target, and a failed technique tried eight years ago by "shoe bomber" Richard Reid. The plot seems to have been an opportunity that the group seized rather than the result of a well-considered strategic plan. A Nigerian fanatic with (what appeared to be) a clean background volunteered for service; he was wired up with a makeshift explosive and put on a plane. His mission failed entirely, killing not a single person. The suicide bomber was not even able to commit suicide. But Al Qaeda succeeded in its real aim, which was to throw the American system into turmoil. That's why the terror group proudly boasted about the success of its mission.

4 Is there some sensible reaction between panic and passivity? Philip Zelikow, the executive director of the 9/11 Commission and later a senior State Department official in the Bush administration, suggests that we should try to analyze failures in homeland security the way we do airplane catastrophes. When an airliner suffers an accident, major or minor, the National Transportation Safety Board convenes a group of nonpartisan experts who calmly and methodically examine what went wrong and then issue a set of recommendations to improve the situation. "We approach airline security with the understanding that it's a complex problem, that we have a pretty good system, but that there will be failures—caused by human beings, technology, or other factors. The point is to constantly fix what's broken and keep improving the design and execution," says Zelikow.

5 Imagine if that were the process after a lapse in homeland security. The public would know that any attack, successful or not, would trigger an automatic, serious process to analyze the problem and fix it. Politicians might find it harder to use every such event for political advantage. The people on the front lines of homeland security would not get demoralized as they watched politicians and the media bash them and grandstand with little knowledge.

6 Overreacting to terrorist attacks plays into Al Qaeda's hands. It also provokes responses that are likely to be large scale, expensive, ineffective, and perhaps even counterproductive, More screening for every passenger makes no sense. When searching for needles in haystacks, adding hay doesn't help. What's needed is a larger, more robust watch list that is instantly available to all relevant agencies in the government. Almost 2 million people travel on planes in the United States every day. We need to isolate the tiny percentage of suspicious characters and search them, not cause needless fear in everyone else.

7 As for the calls to treat the would-be Christmas bomber as an enemy combatant, torture him, and toss him into Guantánamo, God knows he deserves it. But keep in mind the crucial intelligence we received was from the boy's father. If that father had believed that the United States was a rogue superpower that would torture and abuse his child without any sense of decency, would he have turned him in? To keep this country safe we need many more fathers and uncles and friends and colleagues to have enough trust in America that they too would turn in the terrorist next door.

Directions: *Select the choice that best completes each of the following statements.*

CHECKING YOUR COMPREHENSION

_______ 1. The focus of this selection is on
a. who is responsible for homeland security.
b. where terrorists recruit and train.
c. why people join terrorist groups.
d. how we respond to terrorism.

_______ 2. According to the author, the real purpose of terrorism is to
a. provoke an overreaction.
b. cause widespread destruction.
c. set a war in motion.
d. target symbols of power.

_______ 3. The topic sentence of paragraph 2 begins with the words
a. "The attempted bombing."
b. "In the eight years."
c. "It targeted."
d. "The operations."

Copyright © 2012 by Pearson Education

_______ 4. The point of paragraph 3 is that the failed bombing attempt on Christmas

a. was carried out by someone who appeared to have a clean background.

b. relied on the same technique that the "shoe bomber" tried eight years ago.

c. was launched by an Al Qaida affiliate using one person.

d. succeeded in throwing the American system into turmoil.

_______ 5. The author believes that we should improve security by

a. adding more screening for every airline passenger.

b. launching large-scale, expensive responses to terrorist attacks.

c. treating the would-be Christmas bomber as an enemy combatant.

d. making a better watch list instantly available to relevant government agencies.

USING WHAT YOU KNOW ABOUT ARGUMENT

_______ 6. The main issue being considered in this selection is

a. our treatment of enemy combatants.

b. our response to terrorism.

c. failures in airline security.

d. terrorist military tactics.

_______ 7. The author makes the claim that we should respond to failures in homeland security by

a. penalizing politicians who use such events for political gain.

b. disrupting terrorist networks before they can organize an attack.

c. developing technology that will isolate and search suspicious characters.

d. using a calm, methodical process like the one used to address airline accidents.

_______ 8. In paragraph 5, the author reveals a bias against
a. the public.
b. people who work in homeland security.
c. politicians and the media.
d. nonpartisan experts.

_______ 9. The author supports his argument primarily with
a. facts and examples.
b. statistics.
c. analogies.
d. personal experience.

_______ 10. An example of emotionally charged language in this selection is
a. "Terrorism is an unusual military tactic in that it depends on the response of the onlookers."
b. "The plot seems to have been an opportunity that the group seized rather than the result of a well-considered strategic plan."
c. "Almost two million people travel on planes in the United States every day."
d. "To keep this country safe we need many more fathers and uncles and friends and colleagues to have enough trust in America that they too would turn in the terrorist next door."

USING CONTEXT CLUES AND WORD PARTS

_______ 11. In paragraph 2, the word **launch** means
a. find.
b. set in motion.
c. transport.
d. make smooth.

_______ 12. In paragraph 2, the word **simultaneous** means
a. simple.
b. unrelated.
c. at the same time.
d. accidental.

Copyright © 2012 by Pearson Education

______ 13. In paragraph 4, the word **nonpartisan** means
a. independent.
b. amateur.
c. critical.
d. uninformed.

______ 14. In paragraph 5, the word **demoralized** means
a. optimistic.
b. qualified.
c. supported.
d. discouraged.

______ 15. In paragraph 6, the word **robust** means
a. small.
b. strong.
c. harmless.
d. rich.

Directions: *Complete each of the following sentences by inserting a word from the Vocabulary Preview on page 481 in the space provided. Use each word only once.*

REVIEWING DIFFICULT VOCABULARY

16. The companion dog was trained to respond with ______________ when approached by strangers.
17. Before Carole transferred to the main office in Atlanta, she worked for the company's ______________ in Savannah.
18. Each year, the school ______________ its student leaders and alumni to kick off the fund-raising drive.
19. The United Nations considered imposing sanctions on the ______________ nation for its efforts to develop long-range missiles.
20. Emilio used a stick as a ______________ crutch when he sprained his ankle on the hike.

THINKING CRITICALLY

1. What is the purpose of the photograph that accompanies this selection? Which aspects of the article does the photograph illustrate or correspond to?
2. How does the author try to influence your opinions in this selection? Is he successful?
3. Evaluate the author's argument. Does the author use emotional appeals or recognize opposing viewpoints?

QUESTIONS FOR DISCUSSION

1. Discuss your own response to terrorism. Where would you say it falls in the range between "panic and passivity"?
2. Do you agree with the author's assessment of the purpose of terrorism? What other purposes might you attribute to terrorism?
3. What types of facts has the author omitted from this article? How would these facts change your reaction or opinion?

WRITING ACTIVITIES

1. Write a paragraph either agreeing or disagreeing with the author's recommendations about airline passenger screenings. Support your position with personal experience, examples, or other convincing evidence.
2. Consider the meaning of the term *terrorism*. What would you add to the author's definition in this selection? What do you consider to be the most sensible response to terrorism? Write your answers in a paragraph.
3. Take an opposing viewpoint to one of the issues in this article (responses to failures in homeland security or treatment of enemy combatants, for example). Make a list of reasons that support this opposing position.
4. Read over FEMA's information on terrorism: http://www.fema.gov/hazard/terrorism/index.shtm. Write a paragraph that identifies the type of terrorism that worries you the most. What are some ways to fight against this type of terrorism?

Copyright © 2012 by Pearson Education

CHAPTER 12

Reading Arguments

RECORDING YOUR PROGRESS

Test	Number Right		Score
Practice Test 12-1	________	× 10 =	________%
Practice Test 12-2	________	× 10 =	________%
Mastery Test 12-1	________	× 10 =	________%
Mastery Test 12-2	________	× 10 =	________%
Mastery Test 12-3	________	× 5 =	________%

GETTING MORE PRACTICE myreadinglab

To get more practice with Reading Arguments, go to http://www.myreadinglab.com and click on

- Study Plan
- Reading Skills
- Critical Thinking

EVALUATING YOUR PROGRESS myreadinglab

To measure your progress after reading and viewing the information in the Review Materials section, complete the Practices and Tests in the Activities section. You can check your scores by clicking on the Gradebook tab.

Then, based on your performance in this chapter and/or on the MyReadingLab Practices and Tests, write your own evaluation.

YOUR EVALUATION: ____

____

____

____

____

PART

Student Resource Guide

Copyright © 2012 by Pearson Education

STUDENT RESOURCE GUIDE 

Test-Taking, Exit Exams, and Competency Tests

Test-Taking Strategies

Taking exams demands sharp thinking and reasoning skills. This guide is intended to show you how to approach all types of exams with an advantage and how to apply thinking and reasoning skills to objective exams.

Starting with an Advantage

One key to success on any type of examination is to approach it in a confident, organized, and systematic manner.

- **Bring the necessary materials.** When going to any examination, take along any materials you might be asked or allowed to use. Be sure you have a watch and an extra pen, and take several number 2 pencils in case you must make a drawing or diagram or fill in an electronically scored answer sheet. Take paper—you may need it for computing figures or writing essay answers. Take along anything you have been allowed to use throughout the semester, such as a pocket calculator, conversion chart, or dictionary. If you are not sure whether you may use them, ask the instructor.
- **Time your arrival carefully.** Arrive at the examination room a few minutes early, in time to get a seat and get organized before the instructor arrives. If you are late, you may miss instructions and feel rushed as you begin the exam. If you arrive too early (more than 15 minutes ahead of time), you risk anxiety induced by panic-stricken students who are questioning each other, trading last-minute memory tricks, and worrying about how difficult the exam will be.
- **Sit in the front of the room.** The most practical place to sit in an exam is in the front. There, you often receive the test first and get a head start. Also, it is easier to concentrate and avoid distractions.

- **Listen carefully to your instructor's directions.** Your instructor may give specific instructions that are not included in the exam's written directions. If these are detailed instructions, jot them down on your exam paper or on scrap paper.
- **Preview the exam.** Before you start to answer any of the questions, quickly page through the exam, noticing the directions, the length, the type of questions, the general topics covered, the number of points the questions are worth, and where to put your answers. Previewing provides an overview of the whole exam and helps to reduce anxiety.
- **Plan your time.** After previewing, you will know the number and types of questions included. The next step is to estimate how much time you should spend on each part of the exam.
- **Avoid reading too much into questions.** Most instructors word their questions so that what is expected is clear. Do not anticipate hidden meanings or trick questions.

General Suggestions for Objective Exams

Before we examine particular types of objective exams, here are a few general suggestions to follow in approaching all types of objective exams.

- **Read the directions.** Before answering any questions, read the directions. Often, an instructor will want the correct answer marked in a particular way (for example, underlined rather than circled). The directions may contain crucial information that you must be aware of in order to answer the questions correctly.
- **Leave nothing blank.** Before turning in your exam, check through it to be sure you have answered every question. If you have no idea about the correct answer to a question, guess. You might be right!
- **Look for clues.** If you encounter a difficult question, choose what seems to be the best answer, mark the question with an X or check mark so that you can return to it, and keep the item in mind as you go through the rest of the exam. Sometimes you will see some piece of information later in the exam that reminds you of a fact or idea.
- **Write your answers clearly.** If your instructor cannot be sure of the answer you wrote, he or she will mark it wrong. Answer with block letters on multiple-choice and matching tests to avoid confusion. Write or print responses to fill-in-the-blank tests legibly. Be sure that your answers to short-answer questions not only are written neatly but are to the point and express complete thoughts. Fill in electronically scored answer sheets carefully and completely; be sure not to mark outside of the answer bubble or bar.

Copyright © 2012 by Pearson Education

- **Check over your answers before you turn in the exam.** As mentioned earlier, reserve some time at the end of the exam for reviewing your answers. Check to be sure you didn't use the same matching-test answer twice. Be sure your multiple-choice answers are written in the correct blanks or marked in the correct place on the answer grid. One answer marked out of sequence could lead to a series of answers being in error. If there is a separate answer sheet, verify that your fill-in-the-blanks and short answers correspond to the correct question numbers.
- **Don't change answers without a good reason.** When reviewing your answers during an exam, don't make a change unless you have a reason for doing so. Very often your first impressions are correct. If clues from a later test item prompt your recall of information for a previous item, change your answer.

Techniques for Taking Multiple-Choice Tests

Multiple choice is the most frequently used type of exam and is often the most difficult to answer. The following suggestions should improve your success in taking this type of exam.

- **Read all choices first, considering each.** Do not stop reading after the second or third choice, even if you are certain that you have found the correct answer. Remember, on most multiple-choice tests your job is to pick the *best* answer, and the last choice may be a better answer than any of the first three.
- **Read combination choices.** Some multiple-choice tests include choices that are combinations of previously listed choices, as in the following item:

  The mesodermal tissue layer contains cells that will become

  a. skin, sensory organs, and nervous systems.
  b. skin, sensory organs, and blood vessels.
  c. bones and muscle.
  d. stomach, liver, and pancreas.
  e. a and c
  f. b, c, and d
  g. a, c, and d

  The addition of choices that are combinations of the preceding choices tends to make items even more confusing. Treat each choice, when combined with the stem, as a true or false statement. As you consider each choice, mark it true or false. If you find more than one true statement, then select the choice that contains the letters of all the true statements you identified.
- **Use logic and common sense.** Even if you are unfamiliar with the subject matter, you can sometimes reason out the correct answer. The following test

item is taken from a history exam on Japanese-American relations after World War II:

Prejudice and discrimination are

a. harmful to our society because they waste our economic, political, and social resources.

b. helpful because they ensure us against attack from within.

c. harmful because they create negative images of the United States in foreign countries.

d. helpful because they keep the majority pure and united against minorities.

Through logic and common sense, it is possible to eliminate choices *b* and *d*. Prejudice and discrimination are seldom, if ever, regarded as positive, desirable, or helpful since they are inconsistent with democratic ideals. Having narrowed your answer to two choices, *a* or *c*, you can see that choice *a* offers a stronger, more substantial reason why prejudice and discrimination are harmful. The attitude of other countries toward the United States is not as serious as a waste of economic, political, and social resources.

- **Closely examine items that are very similar.** Often, when two similar choices are presented, one is likely to be correct. Carefully compare the two choices. First, try to express each in your own words, and then analyze how they differ. Often, this process will enable you to recognize the right answer.
- **Pay special attention to the level of qualifying words.** Qualifying words are important. Since many statements, ideas, principles, and rules have exceptions, be careful in selecting items that contain such extreme qualifying words as *best, always, all, no, never, none, entirely,* and *completely,* all of which suggest that a condition exists without exception. Items containing words that provide for some level of exception, or qualification, are more likely to be correct. Here are a few examples of such words: *often, usually, less, seldom, few, more,* and *most.* Likewise, numerical answers that are about in the middle of a range of choices are probably correct. In the following example, notice the use of the italicized qualifying words:

In most societies

a. values are *highly* consistent.

b. people *often* believe and act on values that are contradictory.

c. *all* legitimate organizations support values of the majority.

d. values of equality *never* exist alongside prejudice and discrimination.

In this question, items *c* and *d* contain the words *all* and *never,* suggesting that those statements are true without exception. Thus, if you did not know the answer to this question based on content, you could eliminate items *c* and *d* on the basis of the level of qualifiers.

Copyright © 2012 by Pearson Education

- **Avoid the unfamiliar.** Avoid choosing answers that are unfamiliar or that you do not understand. A choice that looks complicated or uses difficult words is not necessarily correct. If you have studied carefully, a choice that is unfamiliar to you or contains unfamiliar terminology is probably incorrect.
- **Eliminate choices that are obviously false.** Treat each choice in a troublesome question like you would a statement on a true/false test.
- **Choose the longest or most inclusive answers.** As a last resort, when you do not know the answer and are unable to eliminate any of the choices as wrong, guess by picking the one that seems most complete and contains the most information. This is a good choice because instructors are usually careful to make the correct answer complete. Thus, the answer often becomes long or detailed.
- **Make educated guesses.** In most instances, you can eliminate one or more of the choices as obviously wrong. Even if you can eliminate only one choice, you have increased your odds on a four-choice item from one in four to one in three. If you can eliminate two choices, you have increased your odds to one in two, or 50 percent. Don't hesitate to play the odds and make a guess—you may gain points.

EXERCISE A-1 Analyzing Test Items

Directions: *The following multiple-choice items appeared on a psychology exam. Study each item and use your reasoning skills to eliminate choices that seem incorrect. Then, making an educated guess, choose the choice that best completes the statement.*

_____ 1. Modern psychological researchers maintain that the mind as well as behavior can be scientifically examined primarily by

a. observing behavior and making inferences about mental functioning.

b. observing mental activity and making inferences about behavior.

c. making inferences about behavior.

d. direct observation of behavior.

_____ 2. Jane Goodall has studied the behavior of chimpanzees in their own habitat. She exemplifies a school of psychology that is concerned with

a. theories.

b. mental processes.

c. the individual's potential for growth.
d. naturalistic behavior.

_______ 3. If a psychologist were personally to witness the effects of a tornado upon the residents of a small town, what technique would he or she be using?

a. experimentation
b. correlational research
c. observation
d. none of the above

_______ 4. A case study is a(n)

a. observation of an event.
b. comparison of similar events.
c. study of changes and their effects.
d. intense investigation of a particular occurrence.

_______ 5. Events that we are aware of at a given time make up the

a. unconscious.
b. subconscious.
c. consciousness.
d. triconscious.

Taking Exit Exams and Competency Tests

Many college reading courses require students to pass an exam at the end of the course in order to progress to the next course in the sequence or to enroll in courses for which the reading course is a prerequisite. Called exit exams or competency tests, these exams measure your ability to apply the skills taught in your reading course. Some exams are prepared and required by the state (such as those required in Texas and California); others are prepared by the college you are attending; still others may be prepared by individual instructors. Use the suggestions in the following section to do well on these exams.

Preparing for the Exam

Use the following suggestions for preparing for standardized tests:

- **Find out as much as possible about the test.** Meet with your advisor or check the career center to obtain brochures and application forms. Find out about its general content, length, and timing. Determine its format and the scoring procedures used. Know when and where the test is given.

Copyright © 2012 by Pearson Education

- **Check Web sites.** For statewide and some college-wide exams, check the Web site to learn more about the exam and obtain practice tests.
- **Obtain a review book.** Review books may be available to help you prepare for statewide exams. Purchase a review book at your college bookstore, at a large off-campus bookstore, or online.
- **Begin your review early.** Start to study well ahead of the exam so that you can fit the necessary review time into your already hectic schedule.
- **Take practice tests.** To become as comfortable as possible with the test, take numerous timed practice tests and score them. Make your practice tests as much like the actual test as possible. Work at a well-lighted desk or table in a quiet setting and time yourself carefully.
- **Review your answers.** Thoroughly review the questions you answered incorrectly. Read through the explanations given and try to see why the keyed answer is best.
- **Keep track of your scores.** Keep a record of both your total score and subtest scores on practice tests. This will help you judge your progress and can give you insights into areas of weakness that require extra review.

General Suggestions for Taking the Exam

Use the following suggestions to get as many points as possible on a standardized test:

- **Arrive in the exam room prepared.** Get to the testing site early so you can choose a good seat and become comfortable with the surroundings. Wear a watch, and bring two sharpened pencils with erasers (in case one breaks) and two pens (in case one runs out).
- **Get organized before the timing begins.** Line up your answer sheet and test booklet so you can move between them rapidly without losing your place. Carefully fill out your answer sheet.
- **Work quickly and steadily.** Most exit tests are timed, so the pace you work at is a critical factor. You need to work at a fairly rapid rate, but not so fast as to make careless errors.
- **Check your answer sheet periodically.** If you have skipped a question, make sure that later answers match their questions. If the test has several parts, check to see that you are marking answers in the correct answer grid.
- **Don't just stop if you finish early.** If you have time left over, use it. Review as many answers as you can. Check over your answer sheet for stray marks and darken your answer marks.

Taking an Exam on a Computer

Use the following tips for taking computerized exams:

- **Don't wait until the due date to schedule the exam.** Last minute computer problems or connection issues may force you to miss the deadline.
- **Avoid technical problems and glitches by taking the exam on a computer you are familiar with.** Close all other programs so nothing interferes with the exam's operation or interrupts your thought.
- **Wait until the exam is fully loaded on your computer before you start working on it.**
- **Read the instructions closely to be sure you move forward and backward correctly, use the right format for entering responses, and submit your final answers properly.**
- **If you are uncomfortable with computerized exams, ask if a print exam is available.**

Suggestions for Taking Specific Parts of the Exam

Vocabulary Sections of the Test Many vocabulary test items are multiple choice and consist of a word and four or five choices for its meaning. On some tests the words appear alone; on other tests they appear in the context of a word or passage.

Words Without Context Use the following suggestions for approaching test items without context.

- **Try pronouncing the word to yourself.** "Hearing" the word may make it more familiar.
- **Read all the choices before you select and mark an answer.** Usually the directions tell you to choose the *best* answer. So while choice *b* may be somewhat close to the meaning or seem right at first, choice *d* may be a more exact and precise answer, as in the following example:

Example

1. seriority

   a. degrees held   c. importance

   b. age   d. length of service

While you may see the word *senior* in the word *seniority* and think of age (choice *b*), as in *senior citizen*, and think that those who have seniority are usually older, the correct answer is choice *d*.

Copyright © 2012 by Pearson Education

Words in Context When answering questions about the meaning of a word when it appears in a sentence or paragraph, use the following suggestions:

- **Test writers do not ask questions that students are unable to answer.** So, if you are being asked the meaning of a particular word, there is probably a way to figure it out.
- **Read beyond the word in question.** Look beyond the word to find a clue to its meaning. Sometimes the context clue appears after the unknown word, either in the same sentence in a later sentence.

Example

The economy was in a constant state of *flux*. One month inflation increased; the next month it decreased.

In this example, the clue to the meaning of *flux* appears in the sentence following the one in which the word is used.

- **Be sure to choose the meaning of the word as it is used in the passage.** Some test item choices may include other definitions of the word that appear in the dictionary but do not fit the context of the passage.
- **When you are unsure about your answer, first try to eliminate one or more choices.** Then substitute the choice(s) you are considering for the unknown word in the sentence in which it appears. Select the choice that makes the most sense and seems to fit.

Example

After the shopper *succumbed* to the temptation of buying an expensive new dress, she was filled with regret.

a. gave in c. alerted
b. resisted d. ridiculed

Choice *a* is correct. Choice *b*, *resisted,* does not fit because the shopper would not be filled with regret if she had resisted. Choice *c*, *alerted,* does not make sense—temptation is not usually alerted. Choice *d* does not make sense because temptation is usually not ridiculed.

Using Word Parts Use your knowledge of word parts to help you figure out the meaning of vocabulary test items. Here are some specific suggestions:

- **Pronounce the word in question to yourself.** By saying the word, you may hear a part (prefix, root, or suffix) that is familiar.

Example

Configuration means

a. detail. c. shape.
b. distance. d. reason.

If you hear the word *figure* in the word *configuration,* then you may be able to reason that *configuration* means shape (choice *c*) or outline.

- **If you do not recognize the root of a word, concentrate on the prefix, if there is one.** Often, knowing the meaning of the prefix can help you figure out the right answer, or at least help you identify one or more choices as wrong.

Example

A *monologue* is

a. a debate among politicians. c. an intimate conversation.
b. secrets shared by friends. d. a long, uninterrupted speech.

If you know that *mono-* means "one," then you can figure out that the right answer is choice *d*, because choices *a, b,* and *c* each involve two or more people.

- **Pay attention to suffixes.** Like prefixes, they can help you figure out a word, even if you do not know the root.

Example

Someone who believes in positive outcomes is a(n)

a. isogenic. c. feticide.
b. micelle. d. optimist.

If you know that *–ist* means "a person involved in an activity" then you can figure out the right answer is choice *d.*

Comprehension Sections of the Test Reading comprehension tests consist of passages to read and questions to answer based on each passage. Use the following suggestions for reading passages:

- **Since many tests are timed, you cannot afford to take time to preview the passage, but you should assess the passage by quickly glancing through it.** What is it about and where might it have come from? Is it factual and textbooklike, or does it express a point of view on an issue? Having some idea of what you are about to read will help focus your attention, give you an idea of how to approach it, and improve your comprehension.
- **The thinking process you use on reading comprehension tests is slightly different from what you use to read textbooks.** Do *not* approach the passage as something you have to learn, as you would textbooks. Instead, approach it as something you need to simply understand. Almost all tests allow you to

Copyright © 2012 by Pearson Education

look back to the passage to answer the questions. The tests do not measure your recall; they measure your ability to understand, locate, and interpret information in the passage.

- **As you read, do not try to remember all the facts and details.** Instead, just try to remember what information is given. For example, if a passage gives the population of India, do not try to remember the exact number; instead, just note that the figure is given. If you need to answer a question about it, you can always look back and find the number.
- **Since many tests are timed, it is important to work efficiently.** Do not spend too much time on any one troublesome item.

Questions About Topic and Main Idea. Reading comprehension tests often include questions that ask you to identify the topic and main idea of a paragraph. Test writers do not always use the terms *topic* and *main idea.* Once you understand what a test item is asking you to identify, you'll probably be able to answer it.

Topic—Here are a few ways reading tests may ask you to identify the topic of a paragraph:

- This paragraph is primarily about . . .
- This paragraph concerns . . .
- This paragraph focuses on . . .
- The best title for the paragraph would be . . .

Main Idea—Here are a few words reading tests may use to mean main idea of a paragraph:

- Thesis
- Central point
- Central idea
- Controlling idea
- Most important idea
- Primary idea

So a question that asks, "Which of the following statements expresses the central point of the paragraph?" is really asking you to identify the main idea.

Questions About Supporting Details. Reading comprehension tests often include questions about supporting details in the paragraph or passage. Test writers do not usually use the term *supporting details.* Instead, they just ask questions that test your ability to understand the supporting details in a paragraph or passage. These may begin with the phrase "According to this passage . . ."

or "According to the author . . . ." Use the following suggestions to answer questions about supporting details:

- **Don't try to memorize factual information as you read the passage the first time.** Plan on looking back to the passage in order to answer questions based on it.
- **As you read, pay attention to how the writer supports the main idea.** You may discover the writer is giving a definition, or is making a comparison, or is offering an example.
- **Don't trust your memory.** If a question asks you a factual question, look back to the passage and find the answer. For example, if a question asks you to identify the date on which something happened or to identify the name of a person who performed an action, look back to the passage to find the date or name.
- **It may be necessary to consider several details together in order to answer a question.** For example, a passage may give the date of one event and state that a second event occurred 10 years later (BuildingBlocks, Inc. was founded in 1991. . . . Ten years later the company began its first national advertising campaign.). The question may ask you to identify the date on which the second event occurred (On what date did BuildingBlocks, Inc. begin its national advertising campaign?).
- **Be alert for questions containing the words *except* or *not*.** These questions are asking you to choose the one answer that is *not* correct.

Questions About Thought Patterns. Reading comprehension tests often contain questions about thought patterns and their transitions. Use the following suggestions to answer these questions correctly:

- **If you are uncertain about the pattern of a particular paragraph, study the transitions.** These may suggest the pattern.
- **If you are having trouble identifying a pattern, ask yourself the following question: "How does the author explain his or her main idea?"** You will hear yourself saying things such as "by giving examples" (the example pattern), "by explaining how it is done" (the process pattern), or "by telling what it is" (the definition pattern).
- **A question may not use the term *pattern of organization*, but it may be asking you to identify the pattern, as this example shows.**

Example

In the above paragraph, the writer supports her ideas by

a. giving examples. c. offering definitions.

b. listing information. d. explaining a process.

Copyright © 2012 by Pearson Education

- **The topic sentence of a paragraph often reveals or suggests the pattern to be used.**

  Examples of Topic Sentences:

  - The majority of Americans will be better off in the year 2050 than they are today. (contrast)
  - Both Werner (2002) and Waible (2000) focus on genetic traces as a means of pinpointing cancer. (comparison)
  - Computer users suffer in numerous ways when spam clogs their e-mail systems. (example)
  - Acute stress may lead to the inability to think clearly and to make sensible decisions. (cause/effect)

Critical Thinking and Reading Questions. Reading comprehension tests usually ask questions that require you to read and think critically. Answers to these questions, unlike questions about details, are not directly stated in the passage. Instead, you have to reason out the answer. Use the following suggestions to answer these questions correctly:

- **Remember, all questions are answerable if you use the information contained in the passage.**
- **To answer an inferential question, you need to add up the facts contained in the passage and come to your own conclusion.** Unless you can point to some evidence in the passage to support a particular answer, do not choose it.
- **To answer a question about an author's purpose, ask yourself: "What does the writer intend to accomplish by writing this?"** Then match your answer with the available choices.
- **You may also be asked questions about tone.** To find the tone of a passage, ask yourself the following question: "How does the author feel toward his or her subject?" Also pay particular attention to connotative language. Words that carry emotional meanings often reveal tone, especially verbs, adjectives, and adverbs.
- **Questions about intended audience are often worded as follows: "This passage is written for . . ." or "This passage is intended to appeal to . . . ."** To answer this type of question, consider each choice and look for evidence in the passage that supports one of the choices.
- **Questions about relationships within a sentence or between sentences focus on patterns of organization with the sentence or sentences.** To answer these questions, look for transitional words and phrases that suggest the pattern. It may also be helpful to express the sentence(s) in your own words. Understand that the relationship expressed within or between sentences may or may not be the same pattern used in the passage as a whole.

- **Questions about biased language ask you to examine the author's attitude toward the subject.** To answer these questions, begin by identifying the topic and main idea; these may offer clues. Look for opinions, words that suggest positive or negative relationships, and emotionally charged language.
- **Questions may ask you to distinguish fact and opinion.** To answer these, identify those statements that are verifiable (facts) and those that express a belief or judgment.
- **When answering questions about arguments, be sure to identify the issue and claim.** Examine and evaluate the statements that support the claim. Also examine the argument's logic.

Sample Exit Exam Questions

The following sets of passages and questions are designed to give you practice taking exit exams. For additional practice be sure to refer to the test's Web site and your College Testing Center.

EXERCISE A-2 Vocabulary Without Context

Directions: *Each of the following words contains a root with a prefix and/or a suffix. Using your knowledge of word parts, choose the best definition for each word.*

_______ 1. Semicentennial

a. 10th anniversary
b. 50th anniversary
c. 100th anniversary
d. 200th anniversary

_______ 2. Bipolar

a. without poles
b. having one pole
c. having two poles
d. having equal poles

_______ 3. Milligram

a. one tenth of a gram
b. one hundredth of a gram
c. one thousandth of a gram
d. one millionth of a gram

_______ 4. Equiangular

a. without angles
b. having one angle
c. having equal angles
d. having too many angles

Copyright © 2012 by Pearson Education

_______ 5. Multilingual
- a. using one language
- b. using two languages
- c. using several languages
- d. without language

_______ 6. Unifoliate
- a. without leaves
- b. having one leaf
- c. having two leaves
- d. having equal numbers of leaves

_______ 7. Asymptomatic
- a. without symptoms
- b. many symptoms
- c. before symptoms
- d. after symptoms

_______ 8. Antipathy
- a. sympathy
- b. dislike
- c. affection
- d. respect

_______ 9. Contravene
- a. prefer
- b. work toward
- c. act against
- d. support

_______ 10. Dissuade
- a. advise against
- b. win over
- c. select
- d. force

EXERCISE A-3 Vocabulary in Context

Directions: *Read each of the following passages. Then, using your knowledge of context clues, select the choice that best completes each of the statements that follow.*

In classrooms across the United States we continue to find marginalized children. The rewards go to the popular, athletic, wealthy, and compliant students who conform to dominant social and cultural patterns. Intimidation, bullying, and abuse of students who do not conform are far too pervasive. We continue to see program reduction, scheduling conflicts, and underfunding in the arts and humanities while the popular athletic programs and the administration enjoy favorable treatment and ample funding. Of course, we do recognize that there are also inequities in funding for some athletics—particularly in so-called "minor" sports and women's sports—and important administrative programs as well.

—Kincheloe et al., *Contextualizing Teaching*, p. 43

_______ 1. The word **compliant** means
   a. obedient.
   b. complete.
   c. stubborn.
   d. individual.

_______ 2. The word **conform** means
   a. ignore.
   b. discover.
   c. follow.
   d. oppose.

_______ 3. The word **pervasive** means
   a. controversial.
   b. widespread.
   c. unheard of.
   d. comfortable.

_______ 4. The word **ample** means
   a. unsatisfactory.
   b. unnecessary.
   c. amount.
   d. abundant.

_______ 5. The word **inequities** means
   a. fairness.
   b. incompetence.
   c. lacking equality.
   d. oversupplies.

EXERCISE A-4 Main Ideas and Details

Directions: *After reading each of the following passages, select the choice that best completes each of the statements that follow.*

Removing a discredited president before the end of a term is not easy. The Constitution prescribes the process through impeachment, which is roughly the political equivalent of an indictment in criminal law. The House of Representatives may, by majority vote, impeach the president for "Treason, Bribery, or other High Crimes and Misdemeanors." Once the House votes for impeachment, the case goes to the Senate, which tries the accused president, with the chief justice of the Supreme Court presiding. By a two-thirds vote, the Senate may convict and remove the president from office.

Only two presidents have been impeached. The House impeached Andrew Johnson, Lincoln's successor, in 1868 on charges stemming from his disagreement with radical Republicans. He narrowly escaped conviction. On July 31, 1974, the House Judiciary Committee voted to recommend Richard Nixon's impeachment to the full House as a result of the Watergate scandal. Nixon escaped a certain vote for impeachment by resigning. In 1998, the House voted two articles of impeachment against President Clinton on party-line votes. The public clearly opposed the idea, however, and the Senate voted to acquit the president on both counts in 1999.

—Edwards et al., *Government in America,* 12e, p. 396

Copyright © 2012 by Pearson Education

_______ 1. The topic of the first paragraph is
a. impeachment.
b. criminal indictment.
c. term limits.
d. treason.

_______ 2. In the first paragraph, the topic sentence begins with the words
a. "Removing a discredited president . . ."
b. "The Constitution prescribes . . ."
c. "The House of Representatives . . ."
d. "Once the House . . ."

_______ 3. The topic of the second paragraph is
a. presidents who have been impeached.
b. Andrew Johnson.
c. Watergate and Richard Nixon.
d. President Clinton's acquittal.

_______ 4. In the second paragraph, the topic sentence begins with the words
a. "Only two . . ."
b. "The House . . ."
c. "Nixon escaped . . ."
d. "The public . . ."

_______ 5. The author compares impeachment to
a. high crimes and misdemeanors.
b. conviction.
c. removal from office.
d. an indictment in criminal law.

EXERCISE A-5 Thought Patterns

Directions: *Read each of the following passages. Then, using your knowledge of thought patterns, answer the questions that follow each passage.*

We have found many similarities between the Earth and other terrestrial worlds, and also some important differences. For example, the Earth's surface is shaped by the same four geological processes (impact cratering, volcanism, tectonics, and erosion) that shape other worlds, but Earth is the only planet on which the lithosphere is clearly broken into plates that move around in what we call plate tectonics. The Earth's atmosphere shows even more substantial differences from the atmospheres of its neighbors: It is the only planet with significant atmospheric oxygen and the only terrestrial world with an ultraviolet-absorbing stratosphere.

But the greatest differences between Earth and other worlds lie in two features totally unique to Earth. First, the surface of the Earth is covered by huge amounts of water. Oceans cover nearly three-fourths of the Earth's surface. Water is also significant on land, where it flows through streams and rivers, fills lakes and underground water tables, and sometimes lies frozen in glaciers. Frozen water covers nearly the entire continent of Antarctica in the form of the southern ice cap. The northern ice cap sits atop the Arctic Ocean and covers the large island of Greenland. Water plays such an important role that some scientists treat it as a distinct planetary layer, called the **hydrosphere**, between the lithosphere and the atmosphere.

The second totally unique feature of Earth is its diversity of life. We find life nearly everywhere on Earth's surface, throughout the oceans, and even underground. The layer of life on Earth is sometimes called the **biosphere**. The biosphere helps shape many of the Earth's physical characteristics. For example, the biosphere explains the presence of oxygen in Earth's atmosphere. Without life, Earth's atmosphere would be very different.

—adapted from Bennett et al., *The Cosmic Perspective,* 2e, p. 352

_______ 6. The primary thought pattern in the first paragraph is
- a. comparison and contrast.
- b. cause and effect.
- c. classification.
- d. chronological order.

_______ 7. The primary thought pattern in the second paragraph is
- a. statement and clarification.
- b. comparison and contrast.
- c. definition.
- d. classification.

_______ 8. One way that Earth is similar to other terrestrial planets is that
- a. significant atmospheric oxygen is present on Earth and on other planets.
- b. the lithosphere on Earth and on other planets is broken into movable plates.
- c. its surface was shaped by the same processes that shaped other worlds.
- d. an ultraviolet-absorbing stratosphere is common to Earth and other planets.

Copyright © 2012 by Pearson Education

_______ 9. Throughout the passage, the authors are comparing and contrasting
   a. North and South America.
   b. water and diversity of life.
   c. Antarctica and Greenland.
   d. Earth and other planets.

_______ 10. The term *biosphere* refers to the
   a. sections of frozen water covering Earth.
   b. layer of life on Earth.
   c. geological process that formed Earth's surface.
   d. presence of water under the Earth's surface.

EXERCISE A-6 Critical Thinking and Reading

Directions: *After reading the passage, select the choice that best completes each of the statements that follow.*

PERSPECTIVES IN SOCIAL SERVICES

In January 1964, fresh out of college with a B.A. in English, I began my social work career as a social investigator with the New York Department of Welfare. At that time, we were implementing the 1962 Defined Service Amendments to the Social Security Act. The plan was to "casework" everybody out of poverty—or at least those who were "willing to help themselves." We were to emphasize the social rather than the investigative part of our roles. Having just completed my mandatory training week, I made an appointment with Matilda Jones for her quarterly recertification visit.

Matilda had four children. Two were literally lost in the foster care system. Following agency advice, Matilda had voluntarily placed her children during a time of family crisis. Also at our urging, she had not visited them for a long time; the practice wisdom of the time suggested that Matilda should not visit in order to give everyone "time to adjust." Now we were unable to locate the children in the labyrinthine maze of contract agencies to which we had entrusted their care. Matilda's third child had already been labeled "high risk" at his school—a school he attended when Matilda was able to get him there, which was not very often. Matilda had just brought her newborn home from the hospital; he had several congenital conditions that reflected poor prenatal care and marginal obstetrical services.

These were the days before the programmatic separation of income maintenance and services, so I went prepared by my training to recertify the family's eligibility for AFDC as well as to proffer social services. I could see Matilda in the window of her tenement as I turned off Broadway and walked cautiously through the rubble of the West Side Urban Renewal District. From her observation post at the front end of her railroad apartment, she signaled to the men hanging out on the street below to give me safe passage. It was 10:00 a.m. and she was having her breakfast: a piece of toast and a can of beer.

Matilda had learned the system when I was still in grade school. She was ready for me. She had her rent receipt, her electric bill, her clothing inventory, her list of clothing and furniture needs for the baby, and the baby's health department card. She was prepared to discuss the baby's paternity. I made the requisite notes in my little caseworker's book, then closed it and invoked my training. I said, "Mrs. Jones, you know all of this paperwork is very important, but there are other important things we could do together. I really want to work with you on problems and issues and concerns that are important to you. Now I'm going to leave my book closed, and I'd really like to talk with you, just talk about stuff together, and about things we could do together that'll result in better things happening in your life."

Matilda studied me for a very long moment before she leaned into the space between us and said, "Look, white girl, I wanna tell you something. I got to document my life to you—because I'm poor. I got to show you all my papers, prove I paid my bills, take my baby to your pig doctor, and show you this card that says I take care of my baby—all because I'm poor. I even have to talk about my sex life with you—because I'm poor. I gotta do all that—but I don't have to take your social workin'.

Now I'm gonna tell you three things about your social workin'," she continued. "Number one, it ain't got nothin' to do with my life. Number two, I can't eat it. And number three, it don't dull the pain like my Pabst Blue Ribbon. Now you get along, white girl—and you think about that."

I have thought about that for 30 years. One of the results has been my participation in efforts to build a strengths-oriented practice in the public social services. Two components of that effort in which I have been involved included designing a statewide competency-based training program and conducting field research on the characteristics and activities of effective workers in that state. This chapter will describe the ways our strengths orientation expanded our conceptual framework for the former, and how it was validated by the results of the latter.

—Bricker-Jenkins, *The Strengths Perspective in Social Work Practice*, 2e, pp. 133–34

Copyright © 2012 by Pearson Education

_______ 1. The article was written by

a. a welfare recipient.
b. a caseworker.
c. a novelist.
d. a researcher.

_______ 2. The author's tone in this passage can best be described as
a. concerned.
b. positive.
c. angry.
d. hopeful.

_______ 3. The author's primary purpose for writing about Matilda is to
a. analyze the causes of poverty.
b. critique the system's earlier assumptions about social work.
c. demonstrate the correct methods of casework she used in 1964.
d. report on a current client's recertification visit.

_______ 4. The author's main idea is that
a. social workers know more than their clients.
b. as a social worker in 1964, she had nothing to offer her client.
c. the standard approach to social work must be changed.
d. social work is primarily useful for those "willing to help themselves."

_______ 5. The author supports her ideas primarily with
a. personal experience.
b. statistical research.
c. inferences.
d. generalizations.

_______ 6. A word from the selection that has a strong connotative meaning is
a. components.
b. effective.
c. social.
d. poverty.

_______ 7. One inference the reader can make based on this selection is that
a. Matilda did not want to improve her life.
b. the author was nervous when she arrived in Matilda's neighborhood.
c. Matilda did not want to visit her children in foster care.
d. the author was angry and offended by Matilda's comments.

_______ 8. An example of figurative language in this selection is
a. "the labyrinthine maze."
b. "she signaled to the men."
c. "it don't dull the pain."
d. "the characteristics and activities of effective workers."

_______ 9. Of the following statements made by Matilda, the one that is an opinion is:

a. "It ain't got nothin' to do with my life."

b. "Now I'm gonna tell you three things."

c. "I got to show you all my papers."

d. "Number two, I can't eat it."

_______ 10. The statement from the selection that best reveals Matilda's attitude toward the social worker is:

a. "She was prepared to discuss the baby's paternity."

b. "I gotta do all that—but I don't have to take any of your social workin'."

c. "She signaled to the men hanging out on the street below to give me safe passage."

d. "She was having her breakfast: a piece of toast and a can of beer."

Copyright © 2012 by Pearson Education

STUDENT RESOURCE GUIDE 

Evaluating Internet Sources

How to Evaluate an Internet Source

Although the Internet contains a great deal of valuable information and resources, it also contains rumor, gossip, hoaxes, and misinformation. In other words, not all Internet sources are trustworthy. You must evaluate a source before accepting it. Here are some guidelines to follow when evaluating Internet sources.

Discover the Purpose of the Web Site

There are many thousands of Web sites and they vary widely in purpose. Five primary types of Web sites are summarized in Table B-1.

Evaluate the Content of the Web Site

When evaluating the content of a Web site, evaluate its appropriateness, its source, its level of technical detail, its presentation, its completeness, and its links.

Evaluate Appropriateness To be worthwhile, a Web site should contain the information you need. It should answer one or more of your search questions. If the site only touches upon answers to your questions and does not address them in detail, check the links on the site to see if they will lead you to more detailed information. If they do not, search for another more useful site.

Evaluate Source Another important step in evaluating a Web site is to determine its source. Ask yourself, "Who is the sponsor?" and "Why was this site put up on the Web?" The sponsor of a Web site is the person or organization who paid for it to be created and placed on the Web. The sponsor will often suggest the purpose of a Web site. For example, a Web site sponsored by Nike is designed to promote its products, while a site sponsored by a university library is designed to help students learn to use its resources more effectively.

TABLE B-1 Types of Web Sites

Type	Purpose and Description	Domain	Sample Sites
Informational	To present facts, information, and research data. May contain reports, statistical data, results of research studies, and reference materials.	.edu or .gov	http://www.haskins.yale.edu/ http://www.census.gov/
News	To provide current information on local, national, and international news. Often supplements print newspapers, periodicals, and television news programs.	.com or .org	http://news.yahoo.com/ http://www.theheart.org/index.cfm
Advocacy	To promote a particular cause or point of view. Usually concerned with a controversial issue; often sponsored by nonprofit groups.	.com or .org	http://www.goveg.com/ http://www.bradycampaign.org/
Personal	To provide information about an individual and his or her interests and accomplishments. May list publications or include the individual's résumé.	Varies . . . may contain .com, .org, .biz, .edu, .info. May contain a tilde (~).	http://www.jessamyn.com/ http://www.maryrusell.info/
Commercial	To promote goods or services. May provide news and information related to their products.	.com, .biz, .info	http://www.nmgroup.biz/ http://www.alhemer.com/ http://vintageradio.info/

If you are uncertain of who sponsors a Web site, check its URL, its copyright, and the links it offers. The ending of the URL often suggests the type of sponsorship, as you saw in Table B-1. The copyright indicates the owner of the site. Links may also reveal the sponsor. Some links may lead to commercial advertising; others may lead to sites sponsored by nonprofit groups, for example. Another way to check the ownership of a Web site is to try to locate the site's home page. You can do this by using only the first part of its URL—up to the first slash (/) mark. For example, suppose you found some information on Medicare on the Internet and you wanted to track its source. Its URL is http://www.mbf.com.au/Healthinsurance/Commonquestions/Governmentcharges/AvoidingMedicarelevy. This page does deal with health insurance, but closer examination reveals it is about Australian health coverage. If you go back in the

Copyright © 2012 by Pearson Education

URL to http://www.mbf.com.au, you will discover that the sponsoring organization is the MBF Group, a private health insurer in Australia.

Evaluate Level of Technical Detail A Web site should contain the level of detail that is suited to your purpose. Some sites may provide information that is too sketchy for your search purposes; others assume a level of background knowledge or technical sophistication that you lack. For example, if you are writing a short, introductory-level paper on global warming, information on the University of New Hampshire's NASA Earth Observing System site (http://www.eos-ids.sr.unh.edu/) may be too technical and contain more information than you need unless you have some previous knowledge in that field.

Evaluate Presentation Information on a Web site should be presented clearly; it should be well written. If you find a site that is not clear and well written, you should be suspicious of it. If the author did not take time to present ideas clearly and correctly, he or she may not have taken time to collect accurate information, either.

Evaluate Completeness Determine whether the site provides complete information on its topic. Does it address all aspects of the topic that you feel it should? For example, if a Web site on important twentieth-century American poets does not mention Robert Frost, then the site is incomplete. If you discover that a site is incomplete, search for sites that provide a more thorough treatment of the topic.

Evaluate Links Many reputable sites supply links to other related sites. Make sure that the links work and are current. Also check to see if the sites to which you were sent are reliable sources of information. If the links do not work or the sources appear unreliable, you should question the reliability of the site itself. Also determine whether the links provided are comprehensive or present only a representative sample. Either is acceptable, but the site should make clear the nature of the links it is providing.

Evaluate the Accuracy of the Web Site

When using information on a Web site for an academic paper, it is important to be sure that you have found accurate information. One way to determine the accuracy of a Web site is to compare it with print sources (periodicals and books) on the same topic. If you find a wide discrepancy between the Web site and the print sources, do not trust the Web site. Another way to determine accuracy of information on a site is to compare it with other Web sites that address the same topic. If discrepancies exist, further research is needed to determine which site is more accurate.

The site itself will also provide clues about the accuracy of its information. Ask yourself the following questions:

- **Are the author's name and credentials provided?** A well-known writer with established credentials is likely to author only reliable, accurate information. If no author is given, you should question whether the information is accurate.
- **Is contact information for the author included on the site?** Often, sites provide an e-mail address where the author can be contacted.
- **Is the information complete or in summary form?** If it is a summary, use the site to find the original source. Original information has less chance of error and is usually preferred in academic papers.
- **If opinions are offered, are they presented clearly as opinions?** Authors who disguise their opinions as facts are not trustworthy. (See Chapter 10, "Distinguishing Fact from Opinion," p. 372.)
- **Does the writer make unsubstantiated assumptions or base his or her ideas on misconceptions?** If so, the information presented may not be accurate.
- **Does the site provide a list of works cited?** As with any form of research, sources used to put information up on a Web site must be documented. If sources are not credited, you should question the accuracy of the Web site.

It may be helpful to determine whether the information is available in print form. If it is, try to obtain the print version. Errors may occur when the article or essay is put up on the Web. Web sites move, change, and delete information, so it may be difficult for a reader of an academic paper to locate the Web site that you used in writing it. Also, page numbers are easier to cite in print sources than in electronic ones.

Evaluate the Timeliness of the Web Site

Although the Web is well known for providing up-to-the-minute information, not all Web sites are current. Evaluate a site's timeliness by checking

- the date on which the Web site was mounted (put on the Web).
- the date when the document you are using was added.
- the date when the site was last revised.
- the date when the links were last checked.

This information is usually provided at the end of the site's home page or at the end of the document you are using.

Copyright © 2012 by Pearson Education

EXERCISE B-1 Evaluating Internet Sources

Directions: *Evaluate each of the sites listed below. Assign each a rating of 1–5 (1 = low reliability; 5 = high reliability). Be prepared to discuss your ratings.*

1. A Virtual Visit to Expo '74
   http://expo74.brandx.net/
2. Ten Commandments of How to Work Effectively with Lawyers
   http://enterpriseforum.mit.edu/mindshare/startingup/ten-commandments.html
3. World War II
   http://blogs.ksbe.edu/anchung/2007/11/29/world-war-ii-a-world-on-fire/
4. U.S. Economy at a Glance
   http://www.bls.gov/eag/eag.us.htm
5. How to Communicate with Journalists
   http://www.fair.org/index.php?page=122

CREDITS

Photo Credits

p. 2: Photo and Co/Getty Images; **p. 18:** 3D5guru/Shutterstock; **p. 23:** Tina Tedaldi/culturea/Corbis; **p. 39:** Exactostock/SuperStock; **p. 48:** Tim Tadder/Corbis; **p. 72:** Nick Garbutt/Steve Bloom Images/Alamy; **p. 84:** Stanislaw Tokarski/Shutterstock; **p. 90:** Richard Cartwriting/CBS/ Everett Collection; **p. 124:** Zia Soleil/Getty Images; **p. 130:** PictureNet/Corbis; **p. 142:** William West/AFP/Getty Images; **p. 157:** Keith Brofsky/Getty Images; **p. 164:** Cathy Wilcox; **p. 168:** Billy E. Barnes/PhotoEdit Inc.; **p. 170:** Spencer Grant/PhotoEdit Inc.; **p. 177 (top):** Exactostock/SuperStock; **(bottom):** Jim West/ PhotoEdit Inc.; **p. 179:** dst dst/Photolibrary; **p. 180 (left):** hjschneider/Shutterstock; **(right)** detewo/Shutterstock; **p. 181:** Frank Morgan/Photo Researchers, Inc.; **p. 202:** age fotostock/SuperStock; **p. 237:** radius/SuperStock; **p. 244:** Foodcollection RF/Getty Images; **p. 280:** Justin Sullivan/Getty Images; **p. 330:** Emmanuel Dunand/AFP/Getty Images; **p. 340 (clockwise from top left):** Kurhan/Shutterstock; Jaimie Duplass/Shutterstock; Tatjana Strelkova/Shutterstock; Galina Barskaya/Shutterstock; StockLite/Shutterstock; Monkey Business Images/Shutterstock; Monkey Business Images/Shutterstock; **p. 347:** Rick Gomez/Corbis; **p. 356:** Bob Daemmrich/Getty Images; **p. 372:** Clara/Shutterstock; **p. 410 (top):** Frank Micelotta/Getty Images; **(bottom):** Lucky Mat/Getty Images; **p. 427:** Courtesy Infected and Affected, photo: Joan L. Brown; **p. 446:** LHB Photo/Alamy; **p. 481:** Ivan Cholakov/Shutterstock.

Text Credits

Chapter 1

p. 8: Michael R. Solomon et al., from *Better Business*, 1/e, pp. 264–265. © 2010. Reproduced by permission of Pearson Education, Inc., Upper Saddle River, NJ.

p. 20: Rebecca Donatelle, from *Health: The Basics,* Green Edition, 9/e, p. 255. © 2011. Reproduced by permission of Pearson Education, Inc., Upper Saddle River, NJ.

p. 22: Shelley D. Lane, from *Interpersonal Communication: Competence and Contexts,* 2/e, pp. 154–156. © 2010, 2008 by Pearson Education, Inc. Reproduced by permission of Pearson Education, Inc.

p. 28: From "How Stressed Are You?" in *Health,* 1994.

p. 32: James M. Henslin, from *Sociology: A Down-to-Earth Approach*, 6/e, pp. 623–624. © 2003 James M. Henslin. Reproduced by permission of Pearson Education, Inc.

p. 34: James Henslin, from *Social Problems,* 7/e, pp. 293, 295, 296. © 2006. Reproduced by permission of Pearson Education, Inc.

p. 38: James M. Henslin, from *Sociology: A Down-to-Earth Approach*, 10/e, pp. 474–478, including Fig 10.6. © 2011 by James M. Henslin. Reproduced by permission of Pearson Education, Inc.

Chapter 2

p. 70: James M. Henslin, from *Sociology: A Down-to-Earth Approach*, 10/e, p. 399. © 2011 by James M. Henslin. Reproduced by permission of Pearson Education, Inc.

p. 72: Teresa Audesirk et al., from *Life on Earth,* 5/e, pp. 249–251. © 2009. Reproduced by permission of Pearson Education, Inc., Upper Saddle River, NJ.

p. 77: William J. Germann and Cindy Stanfield, from *Principles of Human Physiology,* p. 9. © 2002. Reproduced by permission of Pearson Education, Inc.

p. 79: Janice Thompson and Melinda Manore, from *Nutrition for Life,* 2/e, p. 54. © 2010. Reproduced by permission of Pearson Education, Inc.

p. 81: Mark Carnes and John Garraty, *The American Nation: A History of the United States,* 11/e, pp. 175–176. New York: Longman, 2003.

p. 82: Teresea Audesirk et al, *Life on Earth,* 3/e, pp. 95, 104. Upper Saddle River, NJ: Pearson Education, 2003.

Chapter 3

p. 91: J. Snow, "Are Super-Sized Meals Super-Sizing Americans?" *Akron Beacon Journal,* May 24, 2000.

p. 94: Joseph A. DeVito, *Human Communication: The Basic Course,* 9/e, p. 178. Boston: Allyn and bacon, 2003.

p. 94: John D. Carl, *Think Sociology,* p. 211. Upper Saddle River, NJ: Pearson Education, Inc., 2010.

p. 95: Jenifer Kunz, from *Think Marriages & Families,* p. 8. © 2011 Pearson Education, Inc. Reproduced by permission of Pearson Education, Inc.

p. 95: Jenifer Kunz, from *Think Marriages & Families,* p. 82. © 2011 Pearson Education, Inc. Reproduced by permission of Pearson Education, Inc.

p. 96: George C. Edwards et al., from *Government in America: People, Politics, and Policy,* 14/e, p. 313. © 2009. Reproduced by permission of Pearson Education, Inc.

p. 96: X.J. Kennedy and Dana Gioia, *Literature: An Introduction to Fiction, Poetry, Drama, and Writing,* 11/e, p. 1243. New York: Pearson Education, Inc., 2010.

p. 98: Jenifer Kunz, from *Think Marriages & Families,* p. 36. © 2011 Pearson Education, Inc. Reproduced by permission of Pearson Education, Inc.

p. 98: Richard T. Wright and Dorothy Boorse, from *Environmental Science: Toward a Sustainable Future,* 11/e, p. 247. © 2011. Reproduced by permission of Pearson Education, Inc., Upper Saddle River, NJ.

p. 99: Richard T. Wright and Dorothy Boorse, from *Environmental Science: Toward a Sustainable Future,* 11/e, p. 150. © 2011. Reproduced by permission of Pearson Education, Inc., Upper Saddle River, NJ.

p. 99: Colleen Belk and Virginia Borden Maier, *Biology: Science for Life*, 3/e, p. 334. San Francisco: Pearson Education, Inc., 2010.

p. 100: James N. Gilbert, from *Criminal Investigation,* 8/e, p. 33. © 2010. Reproduced by permission of Pearson Education, Inc., Upper Saddle River, NJ.

p. 100: Shirley Badasch and Doreen Chesebro, *Health Science Fundamentals: Exploring Career Pathways,* p. 138. Upper Saddle River, NJ: Pearson Education, Inc., 2009.

p. 100: Jason B. Loyd and James Richardson, *Fundamentals of Fire and Emergency Services,* p. 12. Upper Saddle River, NJ: Pearson Education, Inc., 2010.

p. 101: Mike Johnston et al., *The Pharmacy Technician: Foundations and Practices,* p. 455. Upper Saddle River, NJ: Pearson Education, Inc., 2009.

p. 101: Louis Giannetti, *Understanding Movies,* 12/e, p. 251. Boston: Pearson Education, Inc., 2011.

p. 101: Rebecca Donatelle, from *Health: The Basics,* Green Edition, 9/e, p. 6. © 2011. Reproduced by permission of Pearson Education, Inc., Upper Saddle River, NJ.

Copyright © 2012 by Pearson Education

p. 102: Robert C. Nickerson, *Business and Information Systems*, p. 249. Reading, MA: Addison-Wesley, 1998.

p. 102: Rebecca Donatelle, from *Health: The Basics,* Green Edition, 9/e, p. 66. © 2011. Reproduced by permission of Pearson Education, Inc., Upper Saddle River, NJ.

p. 102: Thomas F. Goldman and Henry R. Cheeseman, *The Paralegal Professional,* 3/e, p. 459. Upper Saddle River, NJ: Pearson Education, Inc., 2011.

p. 102: S.A. Beebe et al., *Interpersonal Communication: Relating to Others*, 3/e, pp. 243, 248. Boston" Allyn & Bacon, 2001

p. 103: James M. Henslin, from *Sociology: A Down-to-Earth Approach,* 10/e, p. 664. © 2011 by James M. Henslin. Reproduced by permission of Pearson Education, Inc.

p. 105: John Vivian, *The Media of Mass Communication,* 10/e, pp. 278–279. Boston: Pearson Education, Inc., 2011.

p. 108: Kenneth Clow and Donald Baack, from *Integrated Advertising, Promotion, and Marketing Communications,* 4/e, pp. 274–276. © 2010. Reproduced by permission of Pearson Education, Inc., Upper Saddle River, NJ.

p. 112: James M. Henslin, from *Sociology: A Down-to-Earth Approach,* 6/e, p. 246. © 2003 James M. Henslin. Reproduced by permission of Pearson Education, Inc.

p. 112: Ronald Ebert and Ricky Griffin, from *Business Essentials,* 4/e, p. 208. © 2003 Prentice-Hall, Inc. Reproduced by permission of Pearson Education, Inc.

p. 112: Daniel M. Dunn and Lisa J. Goodnight, from *Communication: Embracing Difference,* 1/e, p. 92. © 2003 by Pearson Education, Inc. Reproduced by permission of Pearson Education, Inc.

p. 113: Michael E. Moore and Jennifer Sward, *Introduction to the Game Industry,* p. 681. Upper; Saddle River, NJ: Pearson Education, Inc., 2007.

p. 114: Jason B. Loyd and James Richardson, *Fundamentals of Fire and Emergency Services,* p. 12. Upper Saddle River, NJ: Pearson Education, Inc., 2010.

p. 115: Janice Thompson and Melinda Manore, from *Nutrition for Life,* 2/e, p. 242 © 2010. Reproduced by permission of Pearson Education, Inc.

p. 118: Daniel M. Dunn and Lisa J. Goodnight, from *Communication: Embracing Difference,* 1/e, p. 103. © 2003 by Pearson Education, Inc. Reproduced by permission of Pearson Education, Inc.

p. 120: Rebecca Donatelle, from *Health: The Basics,* 5/e, p. 105. © 2003. Reproduced by permission of Pearson Education, Inc.

p. 122: Scott Keyes, "Stop Asking Me My Major," *The Chronicle of Education,* January 10, 2010. Reprinted by permission of the author.

Chapter 4

p. 121: James M. Henslin, from *Sociology: A Down-to-Earth Approach,* 6/e, pp. 380–381. © 2003 James M. Henslin. Reproduced by permission of Pearson Education, Inc.

p. 139: Jenifer Kunz, from *Think Marriages & Families,* p. 83. © 2011 Pearson Education, Inc. Reproduced by permission of Pearson Education, Inc.

p. 140: Janice Thompson and Melinda Manore, from *Nutrition for Life,* 2/e, p. 302. © 2010. Reproduced by permission of Pearson Education, Inc.

p. 140: Richard T. Wright and Dorothy Boorse, from *Environmental Science: Toward a Sustainable Future,* 11/e, p. 604. © 2011. Reproduced by permission of Pearson Education, Inc., Upper Saddle River, NJ.

p. 142: John Randolph Fuller, from *Criminal Justice: Mainstream and Crosscurrents,* 2/e, pp. 65–67. © 2010. Reproduced by permission of Pearson Education, Inc., Upper Saddle River, NJ.

p. 146: Stephen M. Kosslyn and Robin S. Rosenberg, from *Fundamentals of Psychology: The Brain, The Person, The World,* 1/e, pp. 368–369. © 2003. Reproduced by permission of Pearson Education, Inc. Upper Saddle River, NJ.

p. 147: Joseph A. DeVito, from *Messages: Building Interpersonal Skills,* 5/e, p. 121. © 2002. Reproduced by permission of Pearson Education, Inc.

p. 148: Joseph A. DeVito, from *Messages: Building Interpersonal Skills,* 5/e, pp. 197, 199. © 2002. Reproduced by permission of Pearson Education, Inc.

p. 150: Daniel M. Dunn and Lisa J. Goodnight, from *Communication: Embracing Difference,* 1/e, pp. 100–101. © 2003 by Pearson Education, Inc. Reproduced by permission of Pearson Education, Inc.

p. 153: Ronald Ebert and Ricky Griffin, from *Business Essentials,* 4/e, pp. 210–211. © 2003 Prentice-Hall, Inc. Reproduced by permission of Pearson Education, Inc.

p. 156: Sherry Amatanstein, "Talking a Stranger through the Night." From *Newsweek,* November 18, 2002. © 2002 Newsweek Inc. All rights reserved. Used by permission and protected by the Copyright Laws of the United States. The printing, copying, redistribution, or retransmission of the Material without express written permission is prohibited. www.newsweek.com.

Chapter 5

p. 171: Joseph A. DeVito, from *Messages: Building Interpersonal Skills,* 5/e, p. 290. © 2002. Reproduced by permission of Pearson Education, Inc.

p. 172: Michael R. Solomon, *Consumer Behavior: Buying, Having, and Being,* 4/e, p. 184. Upper Saddle River, NJ: Prentice-Hall, 1999.

p. 173: Philip Kotler and Gary Armstrong, *Principles of Marketing,* 13/e, p. 44. Upper Saddle River, NJ: Pearson Education, Inc., 2010.

p. 174: Josh Gerow, *Psychology: An Introduction,* 3/e, p. 700. New York: HarperCollins College Publishers, 1996.

p. 174: Nora Newcombe, *Child Development: Change Over Time,* 8/e, p. 354. New York: HarperCollins College Publishers, 1996.

p. 175: Thomas F. Goldman and Henry R. Cheeseman, *The Paralegal Professional,* 3/e, p. 372. Upper Saddle River, NJ: Pearson Education, Inc., 2011.

p. 176: Maxine Baca Zinn and D. Stanley Eitzen, from *Diversity in Families,* 4/e. © 1996 HarperCollins College Publishers. Reproduced by permission of Pearson Education, Inc.

p. 178: James M. Henslin, from *Essentials of Sociology: A Down-to-Earth Approach,* 7/e, Fig. 11-3, p. 308. © 2007. Reproduced by permission of Pearson Education, Inc.

p. 179: James M. Henslin, from *Sociology: A Down-to-Earth Approach,* 10/e, pp. 580–581. © 2011 by James M. Henslin. Reproduced by permission of Pearson Education, Inc.

p. 179: Colleen Belk and Virginia Borden Maier, *Biology: Science for Life*, 3/e, pp. 22-23. San Francisco: Pearson Education, Inc., 2010.

p. 181: James M. Henslin, from *Sociology: A Down-to-Earth Approach*, 10/e, p. 577. © 2011 by James M. Henslin. Reproduced by permission of Pearson Education, Inc.

p. 184: Jeffrey Bennett et al., *The Solar System,* 2/e, p. 40. San Francisco: Addison-Wesley, 2002.

p. 185: Rebecca Donatelle, from *Health: The Basics,* Green Edition, 9/e, p. 300. © 2011. Reproduced by permission of Pearson Education, Inc., Upper Saddle River, NJ.

p. 186: George C. Edwards et al., from *Government in America: People, Politics, and Policy,* 10/e, p. 422. © 2002. Reproduced by permission of Pearson Education, Inc.

p. 186: Roy A. Cook, *Tourism: The Business of Travel,* 2/e, p. 370. Upper Saddle River, NJ: Prentice-Hall, 2001.

p. 187: Elaine N. Marieb, *Human Anatomy & Physiology,* 5/e, p. 9. San Francisco: Benjamin Cummings, 2001.

p. 188: Joseph A. DeVito, from *Messages: Building Interpersonal Skills,* 5/e, p. 161. © 2002. Reproduced by permission of Pearson Education, Inc.

p. 189: Gini Stephens Frings, *Fashion: From Concept to Consumer,* 9/e, pp. 281–282. Upper Saddle River, NJ: Pearson Education, Inc., 2008.

p. 190: Michael R. Solomon, *Consumer Behavior: Buying, Having, and Being,* 5/e, p. 19. Upper Saddle River, NJ: Prentice-Hall, 2002.

p. 192: George C. Edwards et al., from *Government in America: People, Politics, and Policy,* 14/e, p. 31. © 2009. Reproduced by permission of Pearson Education, Inc.

p. 194: Jeffrey Zaslow, "Friendship for Guys (No Tears!)." Reprinted by permission of *The Wall Street Journal,* Copyright © 2010 Dow Jones and Company, Inc. All Rights Reserved Worldwide. License number 2526790449255/2526790813555.

Chapter 6

p. 204: Rebecca Donatelle, from *Health: The Basics,* 5/e, p. 286. © 2003. Reproduced by permission of Pearson Education, Inc.

p. 205: Steve Russo and Mike Silver, *Introductory Chemistry Essentials,* 2/e, pp. 3–4. San Francisco: Benjamin Cummings, 2001.

p. 206: Michael R. Solomon, *Consumer Behavior: Buying, Having, and Being,* 4/e, p. 301. Upper Saddle River, NJ: Prentice-Hall, 1999.

p. 207: Shirley Badasch and Doreen Chesebro, *Health Science Fundamentals: Exploring Career Pathways,* p. 425. Upper Saddle River, NJ: Pearson Education, Inc., 2009.

p. 209: Jenifer Kunz, from *Think Marriages & Families,* p. 207. © 2011 Pearson Education, Inc. Reproduced by permission of Pearson Education, Inc.

p. 210: James N. Gilbert, from *Criminal Investigation,* 8/e, 64–65, including Figure 3.5. © 2010. Reproduced by permission of Pearson Education, Inc., Upper Saddle River, NJ.

p. 215: Joseph A. DeVito, from *Messages: Building Interpersonal Communication,* 5/e, p. 317. © 2002. Reproduced by permission of Pearson Education, Inc.

p. 215: Teresa Audesirk et al., from *Life on Earth,* 5/e. © 2009. Reproduced by permission of Pearson Education, Inc., Upper Saddle River, NJ.

p. 217: Edward Bergman and William Renwick, from *Introduction to Geography: People, Places, and Environment,* Updated 2/e, pp. 504–505. © 2003. Reproduced by permission of Pearson Education, Inc., Upper Saddle River, NJ.

p. 218: Rebecca Donatelle, from *Health: The Basics,* 5/e, p. 350. © 2003. Reproduced by permission of Pearson Education, Inc.

p. 222: Rebecca Donatelle, from *Access to Health,* Green Edition, 11/e, p. 14. ©2010. Reproduced by permission of Pearson Education, Inc.

p. 225: Duane Preble et al., *Artforms: An Introduction to the Visual Arts,* 7/e, p. 110. © 2002. Reproduced by permission of Pearson Education, Inc., Upper Saddle River, NJ.

p. 227: William Thompson and Joseph Hickey, *Society in Focus,* 4/e, p. 147. Boston: Allyn and Bacon, 2002.

p. 229: Michael R. Solomon and Elnora Stuart, from *Marketing: Real People, Real Choices,* 2/e, pp. 266–269. © 2000. Reproduced by permission of Pearson Education, Inc., Upper Saddle River, NJ.

p. 232: Ronald Ebert and Ricky Griffin, from *Business Essentials,* 4/e, p. 266–267. © 2003 Prentice-Hall, Inc. Reproduced by permission of Pearson Education, Inc.

p. 235: Dennis Wilcox and Glen Cameron, from *Public Relations: Strategies and Tactics,* 9/e, Study Edition, pp. 326–328. © 2010 Pearson Education, Inc. Reproduced by permission of Pearson Education, Inc.

Chapter 7

p. 247: Edward Bergman and William Renwick, *Introduction to Geography,* 2/e, p. 356. Upper Saddle River, NJ: Pearson Prentice Hall, 2002, and Mark Carnes and John Garraty, *The American Nation: A History of the United States,* 10/e, p. 916. New York: Longman, 2000.

p. 248: Richard T. Wright and Dorothy Boorse, from *Environmental Science: Toward a Sustainable Future,* 11/e, pp. 56–57. © 2011. Reproduced by permission of Pearson Education, Inc., Upper Saddle River, NJ.

p. 249: Richard T. Wright and Dorothy Boorse, from *Environmental Science: Toward a Sustainable Future,* 11/e, p. 57. © 2011. Reproduced by permission of Pearson Education, Inc., Upper Saddle River, NJ.

p. 250: Edward Bergman and William Renwick, from *Introduction to Geography: People, Places and Environment,* Updated 2/e, p. 280. © 2003. Reproduced by permission of Pearson Education, Inc., Upper Saddle River, NJ.

p. 251: Rebecca Donatelle and Lorraine G. Davis, from *Access to Health,* 7/e, p. 65. ©2002. Reproduced by permission of Pearson Education, Inc.

p. 252: Jenifer Kunz, from *Think Marriages & Families,* p. 119. © 2011 Pearson Education, Inc. Reproduced by permission of Pearson Education, Inc.

p. 252: William Bennett et al., *The Cosmic Perspective,* Brief Edition, p. 28. San Francisco: Addison Wesley Longman, 2000.

p. 253: X.J. Kennedy and Dana Gioia, *Literature: An Introduction to Fiction, Poetry, and Drama,* 3rd Compact Edition, p. 7. New York: Longman, 2003.

p. 253: Elaine N. Marieb, *Human Anatomy & Physiology,* 5/e, p. 387. San Francisco: Benjamin Cummings, 2001.

p. 255: Mark Carnes and John Garraty, *The American Nation: A History of the United States,* 11/e, p. 518. New York: Longman, 2003.

p. 256: Roy A. Cook, *Tourism: The Business of Travel,* 2/e, p. 102. Upper Saddle River, NJ: Prentice-Hall, 2001.

p. 256: Elaine N. Marieb, *Human Anatomy & Physiology,* 5/e, p. 13. San Francisco: Benjamin Cummings, 2001.

p. 256: Mark Carnes and John Garraty, *The American Nation: A History of the United States,* 11/e, p. 455. New York: Longman, 2003.

p. 257: Rebecca Donatelle and Lorraine G. Davis, from *Access to Health,* 7/e, p. 533. ©2002. Reproduced by permission of Pearson Education, Inc.

p. 258: Stephen M. Kosslyn and Robin S. Rosenberg, from *Fundamentals of Psychology: The Brain, The Person, The World,* 1/e, p. 102. © 2003. Reproduced by permission of Pearson Education, Inc. Upper saddle River, NJ.

p. 259: George C. Edwards et al., from *Government in America: People, Politics, and Policy,* 11/e, pp. 478–479. © 2002. Reproduced by permission of Pearson Education, Inc.

p. 260: Roy A. Cook, *Tourism: The Business of Travel,* 4/e, pp. 211–212. Upper Saddle River, NJ: Prentice-Hall, 2010.

p. 261: Michael E. Moore and Jennifer Sward, *Introduction to the Game Industry,* p. 61. Upper Saddle River, NJ: Pearson Education, Inc., 2007.

p. 262: Rebecca Donatelle, from *Health: The Basics,* Green Edition, 9/e, p. 511. © 2011. Reproduced by permission of Pearson Education, Inc., Upper Saddle River, NJ.

p. 264: David Pike and Ana Acosta, "What Is Fiction?" from *Literature: A World of Writing,* pp. 131–132. © 2011. Reprinted by permission of Pearson Education, Inc.

p. 265: Padgett Powell, "A Gentleman's C" from *Typical.* © 1991. Reprinted by permission of the author.

p. 270: Rebecca Donatelle and Lorraine G. Davis, from *Access to Health,* 7/e, p. 17. ©2002. Reproduced by permission of Pearson Education, Inc.

p. 271: William J. Germann and Cindy Stanfield, from *Principles of Human Physiology,* pp. 606–607. © 2002. Reproduced by permission of Pearson Education, Inc.

p. 272: Jeffrey Bennett et al., *The Solar System,* 2/e, pp. 58–59. San Francisco, Addison-Wesley, 2002.

Copyright © 2012 by Pearson Education

p. 272: Stephen M. Kosslyn and Robin S. Rosenberg, from *Fundamentals of Psychology: The Brain, The Person, The World,* 1/e, p. 331. © 2003. Reproduced by permission of Pearson Education, Inc. Upper Saddle River, NJ.
p. 275: Wendy Lehnert, *Light on the Web: Essentials to Make the Net Work,* pp. 32–33. Boston: Addison-Wesley, 2002.
p. 278: Richard T. Wright and Dorothy Boorse, from *Environmental Science: Toward a Sustainable Future,* 11/e, pp. 611–612. © 2011. Reproduced by permission of Pearson Education, Inc., Upper Saddle River, NJ.
p. 280: Kofi Annan, "Beyond the Horizon" in *Time,* August 26, 2002.
p. 281: Quote from Edmund Burke (1729–1797).

Chapter 8

p. 286: Gerald Audesirk, Teresa Audesirk, and Bruce E. Byers, from *Biology: Life on Earth with Physiology,* 8/e, Fig 28-11, p. 570. © 2008. Reproduced by permission of Pearson Education, Inc., Upper Saddle River, NJ.
p. 289: Jeffrey Bennett et al., *The Cosmic Perspective,* 2/e, p. 249. © 2002. Reproduced by permission of Pearson Education, Inc., Upper Saddle River, NJ.
p. 290: Rebecca Donatelle, from *Health: The Basics,* 5/e, p. 324. © 2003. Reproduced by permission of Pearson Education, Inc.
p. 295: William J. Germann and Cindy Stanfield, from *Principles of Human Physiology,* p. 622. © 2002. Reproduced by permission of Pearson Education, Inc.
p. 297: Ronald Ebert and Ricky Griffin, from *Business Essentials,* 4/e, p. 117. © 2003 Prentice-Hall, Inc. Reproduced by permission of Pearson Education, Inc.
p. 298: Nanda Bandyo-padhyay, *Computing for Non-Specialists,* p. 260. New York: Addison-Wesley, 2000.
p. 299: James M. Henslin, from *Sociology: A Down-to-Earth Approach,* 6/e, p. 637. © 2003 James M. Henslin. Reproduced by permission of Pearson Education, Inc.
p. 299: Samuel Certo and S. Trevis Certo, *Modern Management: Concepts and Skills,* 11/e, p. 127. Upper Saddle River, NJ: Pearson Education, Inc., 2009.
p. 300: William J. Germann and Cindy Stanfield, from *Principles of Human Physiology,* pp. 303–304. © 2002. Reproduced by permission of Pearson Education, Inc.
p. 301: Stephen M. Kosslyn and Robin S. Rosenberg, from *Fundamentals of Psychology: The Brain, The Person, The World,* 1/e, p. 197. © 2003. Reproduced by permission of Pearson Education, Inc. Upper Saddle River, NJ.
p. 301: Elaine N. Marieb, *Anatomy and Physiology,* pp. 402–403. San Francisco: Benjamin Cummings, 2002.
p. 301: Joseph A. DeVito, *The Essential Elements of Public Speaking,* p. 46. Boston: Allyn and Bacon, 2003.
p. 302: Ronald Ebert and Ricky Griffin, from *Business Essentials,* 4/e, p. 117. © 2003 Prentice-Hall, Inc. Reproduced by permission of Pearson Education, Inc.
p. 302: Michael R. Solomon, *Consumer Behavior: Buying, Having, and Being,* 5/e, p. 89. Upper Saddle River, NJ: Prentice-Hall, 2002.
p. 305: George C. Edwards et al., from *Government in America: People, Politics, and Policy,* 14/e, pp. 312–314. © 2009. Reproduced by permission of Pearson Education, Inc.
p. 310: X.J. Kennedy and Dana Gioia, *Literature: An Introduction to Fiction, Poetry, and Drama,* 3rd Compact Edition, pp. 885–886. New York: Longman, 2003.
p. 311: David Krough, *Biology: Guide to the Natural World,* 4/e, p. 172. San Francisco: Pearson Education, Inc., 2009.
p. 312: Ronald Ebert and Ricky Griffin, from *Business Essentials,* 4/e, pp. 212–213. © 2003 Prentice-Hall, Inc. Reproduced by permission of Pearson Education, Inc.
p. 313: Jeffrey Bennett et al., *The Cosmic Perspective,* 2/e, p. 326. © 2002. Reproduced by permission of Pearson Education, Inc., Upper Saddle River, NJ.
p. 315: Edward Bergman and William Renwick, from *Introduction to Geography: People, Places, and Environment,* Updated 2/e, pp. 215–217. © 2003. Reproduced by permission of Pearson Education, Inc., Upper Saddle River, NJ.
p. 317: Louis Giannetti, *Understanding Movies,* 12/e, p. 260. Boston: Pearson Education, Inc., 2011.
p. 319: Edward Bergman and William Renwick, from *Introduction to Geography: People, Places, and Environment,* 4/e, pp. 89–90, including Fig 2-57. © 2008. Reproduced by permission of Pearson Education, Inc., Upper Saddle River, NJ.

Chapter 9

p. 333: John Robbins, "Greed, Cancer, and Pink KFC Buckets," *Huffington Post,* May 18, 2010. Reprinted by permission of the author.
p. 335: Gary Armstrong and Philip Kotler, *Marketing: An Introduction,* 10/e, p. 192. Upper Saddle River, NJ: Pearson Education, Inc., 2011.
p. 336: Philip Zimbardo and Richard Gerrig, *Psychology and Life,* 14/e, p. 501. New York: HarperCollins College Publishers, 1996.
p. 337: James M. Henslin, from *Sociology: A Down-to-Earth Approach,* 10/e, p. 152. © 2011 by James M. Henslin. Reproduced by permission of Pearson Education, Inc.
p. 340: Courtland L. Bovée and John V. Thill, *Business Communication Today,* Ninth Edition, © 2008, Figure 12.8d (p. 376). Reproduced in print and electronic formats by permission of Pearson Education, Ins. Upper Saddle River, New Jersey.
p. 340: Abigail Baird, from *Think Psychology,* 1/e, p. 280. © 2010. Reproduced by permission of Pearson Education, Inc. Upper Saddle River, NJ.
p. 343: Steven Brown, "The Musilanguage Model of Music Evolution," *The Origins of Music,* Wallin, Merker, Brown, eds., p. 271. Cambridge, MA: Massachusetts Institute of Technology, 2000.
p. 344: Martin Luther King, Jr., from "Letter from Birmingham Jail," *Why We Can't Wait.* New York: Harper & Row, 1964.
p. 347: Keith Goetzman, "'Green Exercise' Better Than Just Plain Exercise." Reprinted with permission from *Utne Reader,* May 7, 2010. www.utne.com.
p. 350: Cynthia Audet, "Scar" from *The Sun,* Issue 325, January 2003, p. 96. By permission of the author.
p. 353: Darra Goldstein, "Remembrance of Food Past," *Gastronomica,* Vol. 9, No. 4: iii-iv. © 2009 The Regents of the University of California. All rights reserved. By permission of the University of California press and the author. http://www.ucpress.edu/journals.
p. 357: Karen Olson, from "Eat It Raw." Reprinted by permission from *Utne Reader,* March/April 2002.
p. 359: Toddi Gutner, "Working Moms: Don't Feel So Guilty." Reprinted from the September 23, 2002 issue of *Bloomberg Businessweek* by special permission. Copyright © 2002 by Bloomberg L.P.
p. 363: Melissa del Bosque, "Boots on the Ground: A Day in the Life of a Border Sheriff" from *The Texas Observer,* October 27, 2009. Reprinted by permission of The Texas Observer.

Chapter 10

p. 382: George C. Edwards et al., from *Government in America: People, Politics, and Policy,* 14/e, p. 34. © 2009. Reproduced by permission of Pearson Education, Inc.
p. 382: Autism Fact Sheet, excerpted from "Gluten and Casein-free Diet for Autism." www.autism-org.
p. 385: Janine Zuniga, "College Apologizes after Instructor Says English Can't Be Spoken in Class," *San Diego Union-Tribune,* May 25, 2010. Reprinted by permission.
p. 388: James Crawford, from "English Learners in American Classrooms" from report "Bilingual Education vs. English Immersion," Kenneth Jost, ed., *CQ Researcher* 19, December 2009, p. 1045. By permission of CQ Press.

p. 389: Richard Piechowicz, "Let Students Pay Their Own Way," *The Buffalo News*, February 8, 2003, B5. Reprinted by permission of the author.

p. 391: LaDonna Redmond, "Food Is Freedom." Reprinted with permission from the September 21, 2009 issue of *The Nation*. For subscription information, call 1-800333-8536. Portions of each week's *Nation* magazine can be accessed at http://www.thenation.com.

p. 393: Ed Hiserodt, from "Is This Really Our Choice" Review of *Our Choice: A Plan to Solve the Climate Crisis*. From *The New American*, January 18, 2010, p. 30. Reprinted by permission of the John Birch Society.

p. 395: Farley, Smith, and Boyle, *Introduction to Social Work*, 9/e, p. 13. Boston: Allyn and Bacon, 2003.

p. 398: Barrett Brenton and Kevin McIntyre from "Organic Foods" in *The Oxford Encyclopedia of Food and Drink in America, Volume 2*, edited by A.F. Smith (2004), p. 219. By permission of Oxford University Press, Inc.

p. 400: June Payne Palaceo and Monica Theis, eds., *West and Wood's Introduction to Foodservice*, p. 403. Upper Saddle River, NJ: Prentice-Hall, 2001.

p. 402: Michelle Park, "Profanity Becoming Hard to Avoid," *Reading Eagle*, March 2009. Reprinted by permission of Reading Eagle Company.

Chapter 11

p. 417: David Krough, *Biology: Guide to the Natural World*, 4/e, p. 366. San Francisco: Pearson Education, Inc., 2009.

p. 418: X.J. Kennedy and Dana Gioia, *Literature: An Introduction to Fiction, Poetry, and Drama*, 3rd Compact Edition, p. 789. New York: Longman, 2003.

p. 420: President Herbert Hoover, www.hooverassoc.org.

p. 422: Excerpt from Editorial "Car Seizure Law Invites Abuses" from *Sacramento Bee*, February 20, 2010, p. A10. © The Sacramento Bee, 2010. Reprinted by permission.

p. 424: Rebecca Terrell, from "Are the Polar Ice Caps Melting?" From *The New American*, February 15, 2010, p. 23. Reprinted by permission of the John Birch Society.

p. 424: Betty P. Morrow, excerpt from Letter to the Editor: "Life after Prison," *Tulsa World*, April 8, 2010. Reprinted by permission of World Publishing Company.

p. 425: Carol Masters, from "Playing at War" from *WAMM Newsletter* Vol. 28, No. 2, March 2010. Reprinted by permission of Carol Masters.

p. 427: Regan Hofmann, "Fear Itself: AIDS Stigma Destroys Careers and Friendships" adapted from *POZ*, December 2009. Excerpted and reprinted with permission. Copyright © 2010 CDM Publishing, LLC.

p. 432: Lourdes Soto, from "Is the American Dream for Monolinguals Only?" in *The Hispanic Outlook in Education*, January 4, 2010. Reprinted by permission of *Hispanic Outlook* Magazine, www.HispanicOutlook.com.

p. 437: Teresa McMahon, from "The Outsider: Being a Catholic in Temple," *Lilith*, January 31, 2003, Vol. 27, No. 4. Reprinted by permission.

p. 438: Murdock Gibbs, from "It's a Great Day for Choice" from *New York Voice/Harlem USA*, October 2, 2002, V. 44, No. 25, p. 4. Reprinted by permission of the author.

p. 440: Terry Hong, from "Voices from the Community: Explaining Away the Hate," *Asianweek*, July 31, 2002. Reprinted by permission of the author.

Chapter 12

p. 462: Kathleen McWhorter, *Academic Reading*, 6/e, p. 385. New York: Longman, 2007.

p. 465: "Our View on Health: What Can Be Done to Shake Americans' Salt Habit?" from *USA Today*, April 27, 2010, including figure labeled "Too Much Salt?" by Web Bryant, *USA Today*. Text and figure reprinted with permission.

p. 471: "Our View on Energy: Good News? Cape Wind OK'd. Bad News? It Took a Decade" from *USA Today*, April 29, 2010. Text and figure reprinted with permission.

p. 477: "Misstep on Video Violence" from *USA Today*, (Today's Debate/Our View), June 6, 2005, 12A. Reprinted with permission.

p. 481: Fareed Zakaria, "Don't Panic: How Our Frenzied Response to Terrorism Only Feeds It" From *Newsweek*, January 9, 2010. © 2010 Newsweek Inc. All rights reserved. Used by permission and protected by the Copyright Laws of the United States. The printing, copying, redistribution, or retransmission of the Material without express written permission is prohibited. www.newsweek.com.

Part 3

p. 504: Joe L. Kincheloe, et al., *Contextualizing Teaching*, p. 43. New York: Addison Wesley Longman, 2000.

p. 505: X.J. Kennedy and Dana Gioia, *Literature: An Introduction to Fiction, Poetry, and Drama*, 3rd Compact Edition, p. 7. New York: Longman, 2003.

p. 506: George C. Edwards et al., *Government in America: People, Politics, and Policy*, 12/e, p. 396. © 2006. Reprinted by permission of Pearson Education, Inc.

p. 507: Paul R. Gregory, *Essentials of Economics*, 4/e, p. 39. Reading, MA: Addison Wesley Longman, 1999.

p. 509: Duane Preble et al., *Artforms: An Introduction to the Visual Arts*, 7/e, p. 213. © 2002. Reproduced by permission of Pearson Education, Inc., Upper Saddle River, NJ.

p. 510: Jeffrey Bennett et al., *The Cosmic Perspective*, 2/e, p. 352. © 2002. Reproduced by permission of Pearson Education, Inc., Upper Saddle River, NJ.

p. 511: Mary Bricker-Jenkins, "Perspectives in Social Services" adapted from *The Strengths Perspective in Social Work Practice*, 2/e, pp. 133–134, Dennis Saleebey, ed. © 1997 Allyn & Bacon. Reproduced by permission of Pearson Education, Inc.

Copyright © 2012 by Pearson Education

INDEX

D

E

F

G

Copyright © 2012 by Pearson Education

P

Q

R

S

Copyright © 2012 by Pearson Education

T

U

V

W

Z